Praise for *The New Cider Maker's Handbook*

"Claude Jolicoeur's *The New Cider Maker's Handbook* is an invaluable resource for the serious home cider maker. However, serious professionals will also find a lot of great reference material, especially the sections devoted to apple varieties."

—**Mike Beck**, president, US Association of Cider Makers

"This is the book so many craft cider makers have been waiting for: at once comprehensive, detailed, and authoritative. Planting an orchard? There are guidelines and suggestions. Need a mill or a press? There are plans and instructions. Trying to grasp the process, or to know how to measure? It's there—sugar, acidity, pH, tannin, balance. Troubleshooting a problem? All the common shortcomings are covered. It really is 'orchard to bottle,' with both guidance and technical background all along the way."

—**Dick Dunn**, president, Rocky Mountain Cider Association

"J. M. Trowbridge wrote the first *Cider Makers' Hand Book in 1890*. This modern take on the apple fermenter's art picks up the trail anew. Claude Jolicoeur makes exceptional cider doable for even a guy like me. Balancing the acids and sugars of righteous juice lies at the heart of the method. Pour your friends the 'nectar of the gods' from here on in when next you pop a cork."

—**Michael Phillips**, author of *The Apple Grower* and *The Holistic Orchard*

"Based on Claude Jolicoeur's twenty-five years' experience in craft cider making, *The New Cider Maker's Handbook* combines the author's personal perspectives with solidly researched information from cider makers worldwide to create a manual that is both practical and inspirational. Some of the detail, for instance on press design, alcohol measurement, and naturally sweet and ice ciders, is simply unavailable elsewhere. The focus on North American apple varieties and conditions will be welcomed by many, but this book is invaluable to hobbyists and small commercial cider makers no matter where they live. A worthy addition to the modern cider literature."

—**Andrew Lea**, food scientist and author of *Craft Cider Making*

"We wish we'd had this book when we were starting out. Cider making is an art, of course, but it's also very much a science, and Claude shows he is among the leading experts in both aspects. *The New Cider Maker's Handbook* is a practical, approachable, well-organized, extensively researched guide to cider making, from apple selection to pressing to fermentation and beyond. As experienced cider makers, we find it essential, but it's excellent for beginners as well. As craft cider grows in popularity and stature throughout the United States and Canada, we expect Claude's book to become North America's preeminent cider reference."

—**Scott Heath** and **Ellen Cavalli**, co-owners,
Tilted Shed Ciderworks, Sonoma County, CA

"Have you ever tasted a true farmhouse cider, full-bodied and richly flavored, or finished a meal with a sweet ice cider? Then you know the astonishing range of this once nearly forgotten drink. Whether you're a hobbyist interested in learning about fruit selection, or a commercial producer looking for better quality and consistency, this is your book. Claude Jolicoeur informs every page of his hands-on, comprehensive guide with twenty-five years of research and experience. For anyone who aspires to make the finest quality fermented cider, *The New Cider Maker's Handbook* is as indispensable as an apple press."

—**David Buchanan**, author of *Taste, Memory*

"Claude Jolicoeur is a true student of the art and science of cider. From clear, concise discussions of the technical aspects of cider making to the selection of proper cider apples, this is a treatise for all time. The text is straightforward, and can be an excellent guide to novice cider makers, but it is endowed with a wealth of information that will benefit ciderists at all levels of the craft. I only wish this book had been available when I first began making cider."

—**Chuck Shelton**, ciderist, Albemarle CiderWorks, North Garden, VA

"Over the years Claude has been inspiring—and challenging—his friends and acquaintances, including me, to make better cider. He approaches cider making and life with an analytical mind, a keen intellect, and a wry sense of humor. That all comes through in *The New Cider Maker's Handbook*. Designed for experienced cider makers as well as for serious beginners, it's a gold mine for everyone who'd like to make good cider. It's packed with excellent, detailed explanations and information. It is well organized and clearly written. What an excellent contribution to the cider library."

—**John Bunker**, apple historian and author of *Not Far from the Tree*

THE NEW
CIDER MAKER'S
HANDBOOK

THE NEW CIDER MAKER'S HANDBOOK

IIII *A Comprehensive Guide for Craft Producers* IIII

CLAUDE JOLICOEUR

Chelsea Green Publishing
White River Junction, Vermont

PUBLISHER'S NOTE
Although the advice and information in this book are believed
to be accurate and true at the time of going to press, neither the
authors nor the publisher can accept any legal responsability or
liability for any errors or omissions that may have been made
nor for any inaccuracies nor for any loss, harm, or injury that
comes about from following instructions or advice in this book.

Project Manager: Hillary Gregory
Project Editor: Benjamin Watson
Proofreader: Helen Walden
Indexer: Linda Hallinger
Designer: Melissa Jacobson

Printed in the United States of America.
First printing September, 2013.
10 9 8 7 6 5   17 18 19 20

Chelsea Green Publishing is committed to preserving
ancient forests and natural resources. We elected to print
this title on paper containing at least 10% postconsumer
recycled paper, processed chlorine-free. As a result, for this
printing, we have saved:

16 Trees (40' tall and 6-8" diameter)
7,129 Gallons of Wastewater
7 million BTUs Total Energy
478 Pounds of Solid Waste
1,315 Pounds of Greenhouse Gases

Chelsea Green Publishing made this paper choice because
we are a member of the Green Press Initiative, a nonprofit
program dedicated to supporting authors, publishers, and
suppliers in their efforts to reduce their use of fiber obtained
from endangered forests. For more information, visit
www.greenpressinitiative.org.

Environmental impact estimates were made using the
Environmental Defense Paper Calculator. For more information visit: www.papercalculator.org.

Our Commitment to Green Publishing
Chelsea Green sees publishing as a tool for cultural change and
ecological stewardship. We strive to align our book manufactur-
ing practices with our editorial mission and to reduce the impact of our business enterprise in the environment. We print our books and
catalogs on chlorine-free recycled paper, using vegetable-based inks whenever possible. This book may cost slightly more because it was
printed on paper that contains recycled fiber, and we hope you'll agree that it's worth it. Chelsea Green is a member of the Green Press
Initiative (www.greenpressinitiative.org), a nonprofit coalition of publishers, manufacturers, and authors working to protect the world's
endangered forests and conserve natural resources. *The New Cider Maker's Handbook* was printed on paper supplied by QuadGraphics
that contains at least 10% postconsumer recycled fiber.

Library of Congress Cataloging-in-Publication Data
Jolicoeur, Claude, 1954–
  The new cider maker's handbook : a comprehensive guide for craft producers / Claude Jolicoeur.
      p. cm.
  Includes bibliographical references and index.
  ISBN 978-1-60358-473-9 (hardback)—ISBN 978-1-60358-474-6 (ebook)
1. Cider—Handbooks, manuals, etc. I. Title.

TP563.J65 2013
663'.63—dc23
                          2013018621

Chelsea Green Publishing
85 North Main Street, Suite 120
White River Junction, VT 05001
(802) 295-6300
www.chelseagreen.com

CONTENTS

PREFACE

I am pleased to present to the cider community this modest contribution to the art and science of cider making. You will find in this book a number of texts and discussions, or articles, dealing with different aspects of the preparation of cider. The first part is on basic cider-making practices. Before going on to more in-depth discussions, I thought it was important to present a simple, proven, and sound method to prepare a good cider without any distraction. Once the cider maker has mastered the basic practices, it is time to start experimenting with new or more complex things. Each of the subsequent parts, then, concentrates on a single facet of cider making. Part II is on obtaining the best possible apples for preparing the cider through adequate cultural practices and varietal selection. As you will see by reading further, I believe the quality of the apples to be a most important factor in obtaining a superior cider. Part III covers the extraction of the juice from the apples. Making use of my mechanical engineering background, I present a design guide for mills and presses based on sound engineering. Part IV is on the apple juice and how its properties may be influential in the cider that will be obtained from it. And Part V is on cider making itself, the process of fermentation and transformation of the

juice into cider. You will notice that I have used the word *cider* in its true international sense: an alcoholic beverage made from the fermentation of apple juice—what is usually called *hard cider* in the United States. (What is often called *sweet cider* or simply *cider* in the United States is really the fresh apple juice, or the must, from which we make true cider.)

What you will not find in this book is a history of cider. Quite a few authors have already done that work, and most of them did it better than I could have. In particular, Ben Watson, in his book *Cider, Hard and Sweet* (2009) covers the history of cider from the beginning of civilization through the Roman era and its evolution in Europe and America. And Joan Morgan, with Alison Richards, in *The New Book of Apples* (2002), also gives an excellent historical account, with more emphasis on the story of cider in England. Some excellent books written in French do the same for France and Quebec. For similar reasons, you will not find elaborate tasting sheets and procedures, nor recipes of good food you could prepare with cider and apples, or methods to make such drinks as fruit flavored ciders, apple flavored wines or enhanced ciders. Right from the start, I wanted this book to focus on the preparation of pure juice,

unadulterated cider and understanding the phenomena that occur during the transformation
from an apple flower bud in the orchard to an
apple, then to the must or fresh juice, which finally becomes cider—all of this with a view toward
obtaining a final product of the highest quality
possible. In retrospect, this was enough to keep
an author busy for a while.

There are many reasons you might come to
cider making. It could be that you have some
apples available that would be lost if not processed
into cider. Or it may be for health reasons: cider
certainly is one of the healthiest drinks; you may
have an intolerance to some chemical product and
want a drink whose ingredients you can control,
or you may want to make it from entirely organic
fruit. It may even be for economic reasons or to
avoid paying taxes on your tipple. All reasons are
good! For my part, a long and winding road has
brought me to this point. It all started in 1982:
I was a young mechanical engineer pursuing a
master's degree in solar energy. I enjoyed alpine
skiing and fell in love with a piece of land about
an hour's drive from the city of Quebec, close to
a beautiful but still undeveloped ski center. The
land was on a gentle slope facing south with a
beautiful view on the Saint Lawrence River. It was
an ideal spot to build the concept passive solar
energy house I had been thinking about. Nothing
there predestined me toward becoming a cider
maker, except that there were a few rows of old
abandoned apple trees on the land. At the time I
had no particular liking for apples or apple trees,
but I thought this was no reason not to buy this
land, which was, in all other aspects, ideal for my
projects. But then I started cutting the bushes
growing on the orchard floor and providing some
care to the old trees, which rewarded my efforts by

giving me loads of apples that I didn't know what
to do with—that is, until some friends convinced
me to make cider with them. I was reluctant at
first, as cider had a very bad reputation at the time,
a consequence of low-quality ciders made indus-
trially during the 1970s in Quebec. But my first
trials convinced me it was worthwhile to continue,
and the following year I had a brand-new press to
extract the juice from my apples. A few rows of old
apple trees changed my life—the life of a young
engineer who became a cider maker and author.

The book you now hold is really the book I
wish I had had when I started to gain interest
in cider making and wanted to know more. Yes,
there were some books, and some good ones, but
they were never as complete as I would have liked
them to be. There are also some very specialized
books on oenology, but there was a large gap between these two classes of books, which I have
tried to fill, at least in part. If a book such as this
one had existed back then, it would have saved me
quite a bit of work, and I could have progressed
faster in my cider-making abilities. But then I
wouldn't have had the challenge of writing it. An
important point about this book is that it is based
mostly on my notes and tests, my personal experience and research, and borrows relatively little
from other publications. In a certain sense, this is
influenced by the style of the books that were written 100 to 120 years ago by some true pioneers.
In those days, cider making was essentially an art
based on intuition and tradition. These men, who
were true scientists, spent literally years in their
laboratories analyzing samples of apple juices
and ciders with rudimentary instruments. They
built the foundations of the scientific knowledge
we now have on cider, and the books they wrote
are extremely inspiring.

There are many people to whom I am indebted and who have contributed more or less directly to this book. It started in 1988, when I went with a couple of carloads of apples to the orchard of Pierre Lafond, the owner of Cidrerie Saint-Nicolas, who lent me his press so I could produce my first juice. He encouraged me, gave me good advice—in particular to read the book by Georges Warcollier that was at the university library—and I became a cider maker. He and his wife, Patricia Daigneault, were also helpful when it came time to write about ice cider (see chapter 15).

The next important step was when I started to participate in the Cider Digest discussion group on the Internet. For this I thank Dick Dunn, the self-styled "janitor" of the digest, for the exceptional work he has done over the years, and still does. With the digest, I started to communicate with other cider makers, exchange ideas, discuss methods of preparing the cider, and sort out technical details. Many of the discussions on the digest have evolved into one article or another of this book. Through the digest I was also able to meet some other extraordinary cider makers, in particular, Andrew Lea, the "official cider scientist" of our community. Andrew has helped me settle numerous technical details, giving this book a sounder scientific base. Gary Awdey, the president of the Great Lakes Cider and Perry Association, allowed my first trials of keeved ciders, as he generously made available the PME enzyme to the community of cider makers. Gary is also responsible for having me participate in cider competitions. At first I was hesitant, but since my ciders have won their share of medals, I started to like that! I discussed details of cider making with many other participants in the Cider Digest and the Cider Workshop discussion forums; I thank them all.

Two other very important persons in my cider life have been Terry Maloney, who unfortunately left us prematurely while working on his cider, and his wife, Judith. With the annual Cider Days event that they initiated, I was able to meet in person most of the people mentioned here. Some cider makers have participated more directly in this book: Steve Wood showed great patience when I went to meet him for an interview, and he and Derek Bisset, John Brett, Chuck Shelton, Dick Dunn, and Gary Awdey helped by making recommendations on the most appropriate varietal selection for different regions of North America. Michael Phillips, the maker of an infamous "battery-acid cider," is a great inspiration to us, always searching for better ways to grow apples; he kindly reviewed some of my writing on apple growing. Ben Watson, my editor, as well as a cider lover and promoter, believed I could make a good book on cider and managed to convince Chelsea Green of this, after having seen only about twenty pages of text, mostly written in French. And for the third time, I thank Dick Dunn, who reviewed the first draft of the manuscript and made many good suggestions. Finally, I would like to mention my wife, Banou Khamzina, who first said innocently, "Claude, I think you should write a book." She didn't know what she was getting into.

I close this preface with a warning: cider making is highly addictive. Once you start, it may be very difficult to stop! It might change your life completely (and the life of the people that surround you also).

CLAUDE JOLICOEUR
QUÉBEC, JANUARY 2013

III PART I III

The Basics of Cider Making

The art of making a good cider is of a great simplicity.
Harvest clean fruits during dry weather;
  split the varieties;
Use only well-ripened fruits; discard rotten fruits
  and do not use those that have frozen;
Do not add water to the pomace;
From the freshly pressed juice, fill well-prepared
  barrels that have no bad taste nor bad smell;
Let the must ferment in a sheltered area, at a
  temperature of 50 to 60 degrees Fahrenheit;
Rack when fermentation slows;
Collect the liquid in very clean barrels,
  purged from air;
Then a few months later, you will have a clear cider,
  of a nice orange color, and with a fruity taste,
  well appreciated by the gourmets.

L. de Boutteville and **A. Hauchecorne**,
Le Cidre, 1875

One couldn't present a better summary of the art of making a good cider. However, we may note that Messieurs de Boutteville and Hauchecorne wrote a 400-page monograph to develop what appears in this short summary...

The first part of this book is intended for the novice cider maker. I will start with the materials needed, tips on how to procure good apple juice for cider, and a basic method that will, I hope, help you make a cider good enough on your first trials so that you will want to continue experimenting and improving your cider-making abilities.

First, however, I would like to introduce my mantras, short guidelines or principles that I will repeat often and that guided me as I learned cider making.

1. Seek Quality Cider.

In my opinion, there is no real point in making our own cider (or any other drink, for that matter) if we don't create a product of great quality. To make cider, we need to invest time and energy. And the cider needs to be really good to justify this activity. If you prefer a ten-dollar bottle of cider, wine, or beer bought at the store to the cider that you produce, you probably won't be making cider for a long time. On the other hand, if you put a bottle of your own cider on a table beside a bottle of real French Champagne and discover that your cider is being drunk faster than the Champagne because people think it tastes better, then that is a really rewarding experience.

2. *Good Cider Needs Great Apples.*

To produce this excellent cider, well, you need great apples. The quality of the cider will never exceed that of the apples used to make it. So let's never forget this statement of utmost importance: It is at the orchard that the quality of the cider makes itself. This, because it is at the orchard that the apples fill up with sugar and flavor, with the help of sunshine, soil, and everything else that surrounds the tree—in other words, the terroir.

3. *The Cider Makes Itself.*

As cider makers, we need to be modest. We don't really "make" the cider. The cider makes itself, and as such the term *cider maker* is not really appropriate. We will see later that the apple juice naturally contains all the required ingredients to transform itself into cider. And to be precise, cider making is in fact a complex biochemical transformation that is performed by microorganisms called yeast. The cider maker is merely a guide. What we do is to provide favorable conditions that will permit the cider

to evolve in the best possible environment to yield a high-quality product. And we should not forget that we can't control everything: cider is alive, and sometimes it doesn't go the way that we anticipated. Sometimes this variability will be for the better, sometimes for the worse. When this happens, though, it is important to try to understand and learn why.

4. *Good Cider Needs Time; Cider Makers Need Patience.*

On the Internet discussion forums, beginners often ask why their cider is not ready a few weeks after starting the fermentation process. Beginners are generally impatient. We need to repeat that *Patience is the mother of all virtues for a cider maker*—at least for those who seek quality. Good cider needs time to make itself. It should not be rushed. So if you prepare your cider in October and follow the guidelines set forth in this book, please don't expect to be drinking it by New Year's Day (though you may safely plan to enjoy it by the following year's holiday season).

5. *The KISS Principle.*

KISS stands for "Keep it simple, stupid." In addition to being a cider maker, I am also a mechanical engineer, and KISS is an important concept in machine design: one should always seek the simplest solution that will do the required job. (Note that not all machines are designed with this concept in mind, but that's another story.) I have found with time that KISS also applies to cider making. It often happens that inexperienced cider makers want to do too much on their first trials: chaptalize the juice (adding sugar, molasses, or honey); use other fruits to modify the flavor; make acidity corrections; add some tannins; or even make a naturally sweet (keeved) cider or provoke a malolactic fermentation. (Don't worry about these technical terms; they will be explained later on.) And then they come to the discussion forums on the Internet and ask what they should do next because things don't seem to go that well. In my opinion, it is far better just to keep things simple, to ferment good-quality, pure juice without additives and use well-proven techniques—at least in the beginning. Once you have mastered the basic cider-making practices, then it is time to try new things and experiment.

6. Clean Before Storing; Sanitize Before Using.

No piece of equipment, bottle, or anything else should be put into storage until the next usage without having first been well washed. This is particularly important for bottles and carboys, as they are very easy to clean when just emptied but not so easy to clean once a deposit has dried in them. All pieces of equipment need to be sanitized or disinfected just before use. One should not assume that because something has been stored well cleaned, it may be used as is whenever it's required. Although not very glamorous, hygiene and cleanliness are of the utmost importance in all cider-making operations. The cider room or cider house, as well as all the material, should always be perfectly clean. A great deal of the time we spend in cider making is in fact spent cleaning, the price we pay to avoid cider troubles.

7. Remember What You Did.

Good note-taking and rigor are the keys to both good quality and improvement over time.

By documenting what you do, you can closely monitor how things are going with your cider and make interventions, if necessary, at the best moment. Good notes also permit you to compare results from year to year, from one blend to another. That way, when you make a cider that is particularly successful, you can repeat the same process, just as a scientist strives to achieve "reproducible results." Conversely, when things don't go that well, good notes are useful to avoid repeating the same mistakes.

A Note on Units

A final point I would like to make before beginning with chapter 1 is on the units that will be used throughout this book. I expect that most of the readers will be from the United States, and the US customary units will be used first. But then, I also expect this book will have readers in Canada, England, and other English-speaking countries where apples are grown, and where the International system of units (SI) is used; so the SI equivalent unit will be added in parentheses, as in the following examples: 50°F (10°C), 55 gallons (208 liters). In some occasions, the order will be inverted, as for example, a reference temperature that is defined in Celsius would be given in that scale first: 20°C (68°F).

When discussing small measured quantities, I will use grams (g) and milliliters (mL) since even in the United States, most precision scales and graduated cylinders are in these units, and they are much easier to use than ounces.

There are also a few standard units that I will use often without giving the equivalent in the other system. One of them is the 5-gallon carboy, which permits making a 5-gallon cider batch. This really describes a big bottle that is commonly used as fermenting vessel by hobbyist wine, beer, and cider makers. In SI this volume is 18.9 liters, which is usually rounded to 19 liters. Similarly, a standard quantity of apples that I use often is the bushel, which contains between 33 to 40 lb. (15 to 18 kg) depending on whether it is level or well filled. For more on units and their conversion from one system to another, please see Appendix 1.

CHAPTER 1

MATERIAL
AND SUPPLIES

Before starting your cider-making adventure, you will want to make a visit to the wine- or beer-making supply store. Below are the main items that the future cider maker's shopping list should include.

The Essentials

The basic materials consist of fermentation vessels, an airlock, a racking tube, a hydrometer, some sulfite, yeast, and bottles. Most of these items are the same as for beer or wine making, so if you have a friend or relative who used to make wine or beer at home and doesn't use their equipment anymore, that would certainly be the easiest way to procure all of the basic kit.

CARBOY FOR SECONDARY FERMENTATION

Carboys can be made of glass or plastic. Personally, I prefer glass carboys, even though they are fragile. I have never broken one in over twenty years of cider making, but they do need to be handled with care. Glass carboys are sold in 3-, 5-, and 6-gallon (11-, 19-, and 23-liter) size often used for water coolers, as shown in figure 1.2. For larger batches, you can find glass carboys with capacities of 9 and 14 gallons (34 and 54 liters). These are called demijohns (from French, *dame-jeanne*) and are usually enclosed in a plastic or straw basket that includes handles. There are also plastic fermentation vessels of various sizes as well as stainless steel tanks for serious hobbyists or commercial cider makers. I discuss those later.

A brush for cleaning the carboy is also very useful. Although figure 1.2 shows a straight brush, bent models are available to clean the inside shoulder with more ease.

The size of the carboy will determine the quantity of cider you make, as it needs to be filled to capacity: you don't want any air coming into contact with the fermenting cider. For your first batch, I recommend using a 5-gallon carboy. This is the most common and economical size, and a good size to start with. It is also relatively easy to lift and move, which is not the case for larger fermenters.

Primary fermentation vessel

For the primary fermentation, a large, food-grade plastic bucket with a lid works well. It should have at least 20 percent more capacity than the carboy, because during the vigorous primary fermentation some foam is produced, and this will spill over if the fermentation vessel is too small. If the carboy you're using for secondary fermentation is 5 gallons in volume, you could use a 6- or 6.5-gallon (23-liter) bucket as your primary fermenter. But if you can find a 7.5- or 8-gallon (30-liter) pail, go for it. This size is also large enough for use with the 6-gallon carboys. A useful trick is to mark this pail at different levels corresponding to the quantity of liquid contained.

A hermetically sealing lid is not absolutely necessary, but I recommend it. A hole may then be drilled into the top of the lid, which will be fitted with an airlock.

Racking tube

A siphon is used for racking the cider from one fermentation vessel to another and for bottling. It consists of a rigid plastic tube with a tip at the end that prevents the lees from being sucked up by the siphon. It is often bent at its other end and fitted with a flexible tube with a clamp that regulates or stops the flow. Make sure the flexible tube is long enough—approximately 6 feet is good.

With larger fermentation vessels, once they become too heavy to elevate higher than the receiving vessel, a pump will be required, as the siphon works with gravity and requires a difference in height.

Airlock

The airlock is a small gadget that lets carbon dioxide gas (produced by the fermentation) escape while preventing air from coming in. Thus, it is a one-way valve. This is an essential accessory, for if the fermentation vessel were hermetically sealed, the carbon dioxide produced would cause a pressure increase that would eventually cause the stopper to be ejected or the vessel to break. The airlock is also important to keep air from coming

Figure 1.1. Two types of fermentation airlocks.

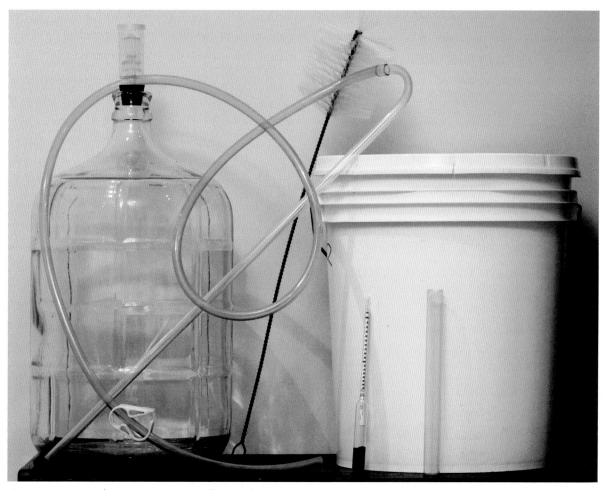

Figure 1.2. Essential equipment: a 5-gallon carboy with airlock and brush; a racking tube; a hydrometer; and a 7.5-gallon food-grade bucket with cover.

into contact with the cider, as this could cause some cider sicknesses.

Figure 1.1 shows a so-called three-piece airlock. It fits on a rubber stopper of the right size for the neck of the carboy and holds a small reservoir that is filled with an antiseptic liquid such as a neutral alcohol or a 0.5 percent sulfite solution. There is generally a mark indicating the fill level required. There are also S-shaped airlocks, shown on the right side of figure 1.1, that are more difficult to clean but may be preferred during the later phases of fermentation, as they make it easier to see the fermentation rate.

HYDROMETER

A hydrometer is an instrument that measures the density of a liquid. It is lowered into the liquid, and a graduated scale in its stem indicates the density of the liquid according to the height at which it floats. For cider makers, this density gives an indication of the sugar concentration of the juice or cider. The fresh juice has maximum density just after pressing; as the fermentation progresses, this density decreases because the sugar is being transformed into alcohol.

For your first trials in making cider, you will probably buy a low-cost triple-scale hydrometer, as these are sold in all wine-making supply stores. They are not very precise, but they are good enough for a start. As you gain experience in cider making, you will probably want to buy a better-quality hydrometer; these are sold in laboratory supply stores. Also, make sure you have a test cylinder that fits the size of the hydrometer.

SULFITE, YEAST, SUGAR, PECTINASE, AND CLEANING AND SANITIZING SOLUTIONS

What we generally call "sulfite" is in fact potassium or sodium metabisulfite. This is an antiseptic and an antioxidant chemical compound used to sanitize equipment and protect the cider from some sicknesses. It is a powder similar in appearance to very fine table salt. You should purchase about 4 to 6 ounces for a start.

For your first cider batch, I would suggest that you use a good champagne-type yeast that will ensure a strong fermentation. I often use Lalvin EC-1118 or Red Star Pasteur Champagne dried yeasts, but there are other equivalent products distributed under different trademarks. These yeasts are sold in small foil packages containing the amount required to make a 5-gallon batch of cider.

If you want to prime the cider to give some carbonation, you will need sugar. While you are at the beer and wine supply store, buy a few pounds of dextrose (corn sugar). The normal white granulated sugar in your kitchen cupboard will also work for priming, but dextrose is more recommended as it produces finer bubbles and a lighter foam.

Pectinase is an enzyme that degrades pectins, and this will help the cider to clear at the end of fermentation. Its use is not always required but generally recommended. It, too, is available from most beer- and wine-making supply stores.

You will also need products for cleaning and sanitizing your equipment. It is important to make the distinction between a *cleaner* such as soap or washing soda and a *sanitizer* that kills microorganisms. For your first trials, you may use liquid dish soap for a cleaner and prepare your own sulfite-base antiseptic solution for sanitizing as follows: dilute 2 teaspoons of potassium or sodium metabisulfite and 2 teaspoons of malic, citric, or tartaric acid in 1 quart (1 liter) of water. Advanced hobbyists and commercial cider makers generally use dedicated cleaners and sanitizers available from a wine-making supply store.

ACIDITY MEASUREMENT KIT

It is important to be able to measure the acidity of the juice in order to make a well-balanced blend. You may skip this for your first cider, but as you continue, such a kit will become essential. Your kit should contain some pH indicator strips covering the range from about 2.8 to 4.2 and a total acidity titration set.

BOTTLES

As you begin making your first cider, you should start hunting for bottles. For each 5-gallon batch, you will need twenty-four wine-size bottles (more if smaller beer-size bottles are used). Here are a few possibilities:

- The *champenoise*, or champagne bottle, is the best bottle, as it can hold the high pressure of a fully sparkling cider. You will also need

Figure 1.3. Bottle variety.

mushroom-shaped corks or plastic stoppers and wire caps. The stoppers may be reused many times. These bottles may also be closed by metal crown caps.

- The mineral water glass bottle is very good but not as resistant as the *champenoise*. Recommended for *pétillant*, or lightly sparkling, cider. Closures are screw caps—very practical and reusable.
- A regular wine bottle may be used with a still, or *perlant*, cider. These bottles should not be pressurized. You may have such bottles with screw caps (second from the right in figure 1.3)

or ones that take a traditional wine cork. In the latter case, you will also need to procure the corks and a corking tool (see below).

- Beer bottles come in many sizes, and most take metal crown caps. Many cider makers have a strong bias in favor of these bottles, as the caps are inexpensive and reliable and the capping quickly done. However, be advised that the caps come in two sizes: 26 and 29 mm. Try to avoid having to deal with many different bottle shapes and also try to have all bottles of the same cap size. Some European and North American craft beers are sold in bottles equipped with ceramic closures on metal hinges, which are extremely practical. Beer bottles, though, are not as robust as *champenoise* and should be used only for lightly sparkling ciders, not fully sparkling ciders.

Many new cider makers develop the habit of looking in recycling bins for bottles. An excellent time for this activity is at the beginning of January, after the New Year celebrations, when *champenoise* bottles abound. Another possibility is to ask restaurants for used bottles. Once you have collected used bottles, you will face the inevitable task of label removal. Some labels come off easily after a soak in hot water, especially with the addition of household ammonia. But other labels use a glue that is not soluble in water, and these have to be

scraped off. On some types, you will even need paint solvent to remove the last remnants of the glue and label.

CORKING AND CAPPING TOOLS

Depending on the type of bottles you have, you might need to cork or cap them. For this, you need special tools. Let's first look at cappers. When we buy crown caps, they are open. A capper is a crimping head (also called a bell), which, when driven downward over the cap, forces the sides together and crimps them around the lip of the bottle. One important thing to note again is that there are two sizes of crown caps. Beer and champagne-type bottles in the United States generally use the 26-mm size, but you may also cap French

Figure 1.4. A hand-held push corker and twin-handle capper.

champagne bottles or Belgian beer bottles, and for those 29-mm caps are the norm. Most cappers will fit only one of the sizes, although some models have interchangeable crimping heads, with one for each size. Hobbyists may buy one of two types of cappers: the tabletop model with a lever, or the twin-handle model. For my part, I use the twin-handled model shown in figure 1.4: it is fine when there aren't too many bottles to cap. A tabletop model is definitely better for larger batches.

A corker must compress the cork to a smaller diameter than the bottle neck and push it into place. There are three types available for hobbyists: a handheld push model as shown in figure 1.4 is adequate to cork only a dozen or so bottles at a time. Twin-handled models are slightly better, and tabletop or floor models are much preferable for larger batches, as they have a long lever that makes the operation much easier. If you consider corking champagne bottles with a mushroom cork, then only a few tabletop or floor models will do the job, and these are more expensive, as they need to have a larger opening for the head of the cork. The Ferrari floor corker will do champagne and regular cylindrical corks and can be equipped with a capping head to be used as a capper as well. The total cost with the capper attachment is around $150, and this may be a good option if you do a lot of capping and corking.

KITCHEN UTENSILS

Many kitchen utensils find a use in cider making. (See figure 1.5.) In particular, you will use a funnel,

Figure 1.5. Kitchen utensils.

measuring cups and spoons, a strainer, a turkey baster to take cider samples, and a thermometer covering a range from 32°F to approximately 120°F (0°C to 50°C) for correcting the hydrometer readings and when preparing yeast culture.

For your first experiences, you may borrow these from your kitchen. If you continue as a cider maker, however, you will find it preferable to reserve sets only for cider making.

Optional Recommended Equipment

The area where you prepare the cider will become like a small laboratory. There, you will run tests and other manipulations. Some basic laboratory equipment is always useful. In particular, the following items have become indispensable to me. (See figure 1.6.)

GRADUATED CYLINDERS

These cylinders allow you to measure quantities of liquids with much better precision than a measuring cup. The most useful sizes are 100 mL and 250 mL. The 250-mL cylinder is also a good size for use with a hydrometer. Graduated cylinders may be made of plastic or glass. Both are good, but I tend to prefer the glass, even if they are more expensive.

BEAKER SET

Beakers are the ideal recipient for many types of manipulations. I use them all the time. The ideal is the borosilicate glass type, which can be used to heat a liquid on the stove as long as the heat is not

at the maximum. The sizes I use most are 1,500 mL and 600 mL, but most companies offer a starter set of five beakers of different sizes, which is a good deal.

FILTER COFFEE SET

You can find an old Melitta coffeepot with a filter funnel and #6 filters for almost nothing at any flea market. I also have a Melior coffeemaker with a piston. Either type will do to filter small quantities of cider. They are simple and efficient.

A few other items that I like to have are test tubes, in particular to make the total acidity tests; syringes, for the precise measurement of very small quantities of liquid; and a precision digital scale with a resolution of 0.1 gram. Note that this optional material is not required for your first cider-making trials, and some of it would be useful only for the more advanced testing described later in the book, but eventually you may want to put in an order at a specialized laboratory equipment supplier.

The Cider Room

The room where you will establish your cidery is not really part of your grocery list, but it's important to plan in advance where you will let your cider ferment. The ideal would be an unheated place—maybe in the garage or basement—where the temperature could fall to around 45°F to 55°F (8°C to 12°C) during winter and would keep cool during summer. There can be some temperature variations, but the most important is that on average the place stays rather cool. If you don't have such a place, you can always let the cider ferment at room temperature, but then the fermentation

Figure 1.6. Glassware useful for cider making.

will proceed faster, and you may not get the full complexity and bouquet of a cider that has gone through a long, slow fermentation (although it could still be very good). Eventually, you could look at other possibilities, like adapting an old refrigerator or chest freezer and adjusting the controls for it to be at the ideal temperature (with a freezer you would use an external control) or installing an air-conditioning unit in a small room.

In England and France, many cider makers let their cider ferment outside almost without protection, and some years the cider may even freeze.

Once the temperature gets warmer, the cider thaws, and the fermentation restarts slowly. This doesn't really have any negative consequences other than slowing down the whole process. However, in areas where the winter is much colder this would not be possible, and the cider should be in a place that's protected from the severe cold.

You will also need a work area, ideally with a small counter and a sink and a closet nearby to store all the material. And finally you will want a washing area with a bath or a large laundry sink to clean items such as fermenting vessels.

CHAPTER 2

THE RAW MATERIAL: APPLE JUICE

The apple juice is the raw material from which the cider is prepared. The quality of the cider depends on the quality of the juice. Remember, it is impossible to prepare a great cider from a low-quality juice.

A quality apple juice will have certain characteristics that we will discuss in greater depth in part IV. But generally speaking, it should have a high sugar concentration and be low in acidity. When you taste it, the first impression should be one of sweetness and richness, with only a slight acidity. For comparison, a juice that is good for drinking gives a sensation of freshness, indicating a more preeminent acidity, and generally does not contain as much sugar. Although when you taste such a juice it is well balanced, it will likely yield a very sharp cider, because, when it is transformed into cider, the sugar ferments into alcohol and will no longer balance the acidity, making the finished cider much more acidic to the taste buds.

The question then becomes how to procure a good-quality juice for cider making. Here are a few possible situations:

- *You have access to apples and a press.* This is the ideal situation, since you can press your own juice, control its quality, and work on your blend.
- *You have apples but no press.* You could try to make an arrangement with an apple grower who has a press to do the pressing for you. If you live in an area where there are commercial orchards, such a person should not be too difficult to find. Another possible solution is to rent a press from a wine-making supply store.

If the quantities involved are not too important, you could get away with the milling by using some rudimentary methods or by freezing the apples. (For more details, see the article "Main Characteristics of Mills," section 6.1.)

- *You have neither apples nor a press.* In this case you will have to buy the juice. Apple juice sold in stores is not recommended, as it usually contains additives such as sodium benzoate that will prevent fermentation. It would be preferable to seek freshly pressed juice, unpasteurized and without additives, from an apple grower. You can also ask the grower for the varieties that contain the most sugar and the least acidity. It would be a good idea to bring your hydrometer and acidity testing kit to evaluate the juice before buying it. The articles on sugar and acidity in chapters 8 and 9 will give you some indications of the properties to look for in the juice. You should plan to buy about a half gallon (2 liters) of extra juice for each carboy to compensate for losses that will occur upon racking.

Gathering the Apples

If you pick or buy your apples, count on approximately three bushels to get enough juice for a 5-gallon cider batch, more or less depending on the efficiency of your press and the juiciness of the apples. Do play safe on this as there is nothing worse than being just a bit short when time comes to fill your carboy up to the neck.

Here are some tips that will help you get the best-quality juice:

- If possible, try to avoid apples from large commercial operations, as such apples are often low in sugar and rich in nitrogenous substances (see chapters 4 and 11). Apples gathered in traditional or old style orchards are far better for cider. Even wild seedling trees may sometimes give apples of amazing quality, but I would suggest testing the acidity and density before using such apples to make sure they have the required qualities.

- If you grow your own apples, choose preferentially the apples from your older trees, as these will contain more sugar and flavor. And remember that fertilizing the trees lowers the quality of the fruit, as fertilization increases the amount of water (thus diluting the juice) and nitrogenous substances.

- Do not overlook scabby apples. In effect, apple scab causes a decrease of the water content in the apple, thus increasing the concentration of sugar and flavor. On the other hand, scabby apples will yield less juice.

- Apples that have been attacked by insects may also be used. But avoid apples that are so badly damaged that they have started to rot.

- Choose apples from late midseason or later-maturing varieties. Summer and early midseason varieties generally do not possess the qualities required for good cider.

- Harvest the apples when they are well matured. Often in commercial orchards the apples are harvested before maturity, as they keep better this way. From the point of view of a cider maker, however, this is not the best way to go.

- Leave your apples to ripen in cool temperatures, ideally under cover, for some time before pressing. This is called *sweating* the apples. The ideal moment for pressing is when the apples have started to soften and yield a bit under pressure from the thumb.

Pressing the Apples to Extract the Juice

Before starting the operation, you should gather all your pressing equipment and also plenty of buckets. Then prepare about a quart of antiseptic cleaning solution. This may be a sulfite solution, as described above, or some other commercial sanitizer for surfaces that come in contact with food. Make sure all the equipment that will come in contact with the juice is perfectly clean, rinse it with the antiseptic solution, and make a final rinse with clear water.

If the apples have been picked from off the ground, they should be washed and scanned carefully to remove any that are rotten. With tree-picked apples, washing may be skipped, although many cider makers prefer to wash them anyway. If the orchard is in a dusty area or if sprays have been applied, washing would definitely be advisable even for tree-picked apples. Washing may be done in a tub or large pail with a garden hose. A nice feature of apples is that the healthy ones float, while the rotten ones and the dirt sink, making the separation easier.

The next step is the *milling,* or *grinding,* of the apples. Apples should be used whole: there is no point in coring or peeling them. The most rudimentary technique would be to crush the apples with a piece of timber in a bucket, or you may use a nice motorized mill. In any case, by grinding the apples you will obtain what is called the *pomace*. It should be fine enough so the juice escapes easily from it but not so fine as to make a slush, since some blockage may then occur in the press. The chunky bits of apples should ideally have a size of ⅛ inch (3 mm). Some mills produce much coarser bits, and this reduces the yield.

Figure 2.1. A new press!

An alternative to milling is freezing the apples. Once thawed, the apples may be pressed whole. See chapter 6 for more information on these subjects, and also on how to build your own grinder.

The pomace is then pressed to extract the juice from it. Note that the pressing doesn't have to be done immediately after milling. A delay of a few hours will not harm the juice, and some cider makers actually delay on purpose. I discuss *maceration,* as it is called, in the more advanced parts of this book. Different pressing techniques are used depending on the type of press. The easiest is the cylindrical basket press, with a screw like the one seen in figure 2.1. We use a nylon net inside the basket to retain the pomace. This net has a mesh aperture of about 1/16 inch (1 mm) and is pulled up over the pomace. The pressing plate is then placed on top and pressure is applied with the screw. The load should be applied gradually, as too much pressure too fast may cause instability: the pressing plate may swivel for example, requiring that you remove it, replace the pomace, and start again. If you are not familiar with the press, it's better not to load it to its full capacity and thus avoid instability.

With such a press, a run may take between half an hour and an hour. The longer you press, the better the extraction. But there comes a point where the quantity of juice that escapes becomes insignificant, and it is not worth the time anymore.

Another important type of press is the rack-and-cloth press. Such presses are normally more efficient than basket presses because the juice doesn't have to travel as far to escape the pomace. However the preparation takes more time: thin layers of pomace are spread out on a press cloth, which is then folded over the pomace. Racks are laid between each layer to improve the drainage of the juice. A full load (traditionally called a "cheese") may contain from four to fifteen such layers, depending on the size of the press. A pressing plate is finally placed on top of the cheese and the load is applied. On rack-and-cloth presses, hydraulic cylinders are more often used than screws. Rack-and-cloth presses are the most common type of homemade presses, and complete instructions on how to build and use your own are given in chapter 7.

Once the pressing is complete, you will need to unload the dry pomace and dispose of it. It makes a nice compost material or a supplemental feed for livestock.

Finally, don't forget to clean everything thoroughly when you are finished. In particular, the press cloths and/or net often retain small particles of apple flesh that have to be dislodged. A garden hose or a high-pressure spray is handy.

Pressing is hard work, but it may also be an occasion for festivities. Figure 2.1 dates back to 1989. I had just set up my first cider press, and this pressing party was an event!

Expression of the Measurable Juice Properties

Throughout this book, I refer to the measurable properties of the apple juice, and in particular its sugar, acid, and tannin content. I discuss these in detail later in chapters 8, 9, and 10, respectively, but for the moment, let's just say that the sugar will be transformed into alcohol, the acid will give a sensation of freshness, and the tannin will give body or structure to the cider. I will here simply introduce the units used for those properties:

- **Sugar.** Strictly speaking, the sugar content should be expressed in grams per liter of juice (g/L). However, in cider making we most often use the density or *specific gravity* (SG) as a more or less precise indication of the sugar content, because it is much easier to measure with a hydrometer (see chapter 8 for more on this). Typical juices for cider making will have an SG in the range of 1.045 to 1.065.
- **Acidity.** This property, as measured by titration, is expressed as grams of equivalent malic acid per liter of juice (g/L). Other books express this property in different units. See section 9.2 on acidity titration for a further discussion. A juice blend for cider making should have an acidity in the range of approximately 4.5 to 7.5 g/L.
- **Tannins.** This property is more complicated to measure, and I rely on analyses done in laboratories and reported by different authors. For units I use grams of equivalent tannic acid per liter of juice (g/L). Typical blends for cider contain anywhere from 0.5 to 3 g/L of tannins.

CHAPTER 3

CIDER PREPARATION

We could say that the preparation of the cider starts in the spring, because all the interactions between the trees, the environment, and the humans tending the trees influence the cider and its quality. The maturity of the apples at harvest and the degree of sweating will likewise have some effect. But for the present discussion, we will assume that everything mentioned above has been well done and that the apple juice (which we will now call the *must*) is already in its primary fermentation vessel and ready to be transformed into cider.

We may divide the cider-making operations into a few main stages:

1. Preparation for fermentation
   - Sanitation
   - Density and acidity measurements
   - Additives: sulfite and pectinase
   - Yeast culture and inoculation

2. Fermentation
   - Primary phase
   - First racking
   - Secondary phase

3. Final racking, bottling, and in-bottle maturation

In the following description, I limit my discussion to a basic and well-proven method of making cider. I try to keep it as simple as possible and obtain a dry, natural cider, with perhaps some effervescence. My objective is that you, the novice cider maker, will successfully make a good enough cider on your first trial that you will have the desire to persist and strive to produce even better ciders in the future. Note that later in this book you will find more detailed discussions on most of the subjects touched upon here.

Preparation for Fermentation

I recap here what is done to the must (juice) in preparation for the fermentation.

SANITATION

If you haven't already done so, prepare your sulfite stock solution and your antiseptic solution. (See above on materials and supplies, and section 14.1 on sulfite.) All the materials—utensils, vessels, measuring instruments, siphon tubes, anything that will come into contact with the cider—should be perfectly clean. Before use, sanitize all equipment by either soaking it in the antiseptic solution or by wiping or pouring some solution onto it. For containers, pour some solution inside and agitate so all interior surfaces get wetted. For a racking tube, pour some solution so it goes through the tube and wets all of the interior. Rinse with clear water and let drain a few minutes. Note that some sanitizers don't require rinsing.

DENSITY AND ACIDITY MEASUREMENTS

These measurements are not absolutely necessary and will not make the cider any better; however, I strongly recommend you make them to learn about their influence on the final product. The hydrometer is used to measure the density of the must, usually expressed as specific gravity (SG). This allows you to estimate the quantity of sugar and the final alcoholic strength that the cider will have when fully fermented. The measurement of the pH is necessary only for the dosage of sulfite to the must (see the following section "Sulfite treatment"). And the total acidity (TA) will give you some clue in relation to the acidity sensation you experience when you taste the cider. For example, if you measure 7.5 grams of malic acid per liter, and you think the finished cider is too sharp, then you will know for next time to start with a blend that has a lower total acidity.

SULFITE TREATMENT

Sulfite addition to the must is strongly recommended for your first trials at cider making in order to kill or inhibit wild and spoiling yeasts and bacteria. It should be done as soon as possible after pressing. If you have measured the pH of the must, you can add the recommended amount of sulfite as a function of the acidity. (See the article on sulfite, section 14.1, for this amount.) If you don't know the pH and use mainly North American eating apples that are fairly sharp, a dosage of 40 to 50 ppm of sulfur dioxide (SO_2) is usually adequate. For a 5-gallon batch, this level is achieved by adding 1.8 grams (a bit less than ½ teaspoon) of potassium metabisulfite, first dissolved in a little water or juice, then mixed with the must. If you use apples that are sweeter and haven't much sharpness, you may double this dosage. Alternatively, you may use Campden tablets: four tablets dissolved in a 5-gallon batch will give 50 ppm of SO_2. However, be warned that these tablets don't dissolve easily and need to be broken up into powder before trying to dissolve them in water or juice.

If you have an intolerance to sulfites or wish for some reason not to add any to the must, please read the article on sulfite, section 14.1.

Caution: Do not drink the freshly sulfited juice. Also, avoid smelling the fumes coming from the sulfite solution.

PECTINASE ADDITION

Pectic enzyme, or *pectinase*, breaks the pectin chains in the juice, and this will help the cider to clear once the fermentation is completed. Most of the time, the cider will clear (or "fall bright") naturally when it's done, even if a pectic enzyme hasn't been used. However, if the must contains a lot of pectin, then this treatment acts a bit like an insurance policy, improving the odds that you will obtain a perfectly clear cider. There are many such products on the market, and they don't all have the same activity, so you will need to follow the dosage instructions that came with the particular product you have bought. Simply add the required quantity of pectinase to the must, making sure you dilute it first in a small quantity of juice, and stir. This addition may be done just after the sulfite treatment. Other types of treatments that may be done on pectin are covered in the article "The Pectic Substances," chapter 12.

Yeast culture and inoculation

The objective when adding yeast is to introduce a strong population of a selected pure yeast strain whose main characteristics are well known. For cider, there are many yeast strains that will give excellent results, most being wine yeasts, and this is a vast area for experimentation. The use of cultured yeast often goes along with a sulfite treatment. The principle is as follows: with the sulfite, we kill off (or greatly suppress) bacteria and wild yeasts, and then we introduce the selected yeast that will take over the fermentation and give the character we want for the cider. Without a sulfite treatment, the wild yeasts may give unpredictable flavors to the cider. This can sometimes be for the better, but not always. (See the article on yeasts, section 14.2, for a more complete discussion on this.)

Caution: After a sulfite treatment, it is necessary to wait a minimum of twenty-four hours before adding a yeast culture to the juice, as a freshly sulfited must is toxic for the yeasts.

For your first trials at making cider, I would recommend a champagne strain of dried yeast. This is one of the most common types and is considered an all-purpose yeast. It is inexpensive, gives excellent results in cider, and is sold in small packages sized for a 5-gallon batch in all wine-making supply stores.

Dried yeast needs to be rehydrated before inoculation to the must. Instructions are on the package and essentially consist of emptying the contents of the package into a small quantity of warm water (105°F, or 40°C) and letting the yeast hydrate itself for about fifteen minutes. The mixture may then be stirred and poured into the must.

Once you have inoculated the must with the yeast, you need to cover the fermentation vessel. A hermetically sealed cover is not really necessary, because during the first phase of fermentation a lot of carbon dioxide gas is produced, which acts like a blanket and gives protection to the cider by preventing oxygen from coming into contact with the fermenting must. This said, I nonetheless prefer to use a cover that closes hermetically, and I install an airlock on it.

It might appear paradoxical that I recommend a relatively complex procedure for the novice cider maker to follow in preparation for the fermentation, while the accomplished cider maker may simply let the must ferment naturally without any cultured yeasts or other and obtain an exquisite cider. However, you have to consider that this experienced cider maker acts with full knowledge of the facts (at least we hope so) and knows about the risks of getting a lower-quality cider. With experience, he or she will be able to evaluate if a must is a good candidate for natural fermentation.

Fermentation

We generally consider the start of the fermentation to be the moment at which the yeast is introduced into the must. The fermentation phases are described in the article on monitoring and control of the fermentation, section 14.3, so I will give just a very short summary here.

PRIMARY, OR TURBULENT, PHASE

After the inoculation of yeast, there is a lag phase that may last a few hours to over a week, during which the yeast population establishes itself. Then the turbulent fermentation begins. A foam will form on top that may reach a couple of inches in thickness, white in the beginning, and later turning a brownish color. This foam will vanish after a week or two, leaving some brown deposits on the surface.

During this phase, you should visually check the cider about once a week. When the foam has gone and you can actually see the surface of the liquid, it is good practice to check the density again with a hydrometer and get a feeling for the fermentation speed of this particular batch of cider. If you have a fast fermentation, the specific gravity reading at this moment may be at 1.020 or lower, and you may then proceed with the first racking. If you have a slow fermentation, then the SG may be at 1.030 or higher. In this case you could delay the first racking until the SG reaches about 1.015.

FIRST RACKING

The first racking consists in moving the cider from the primary fermentation vessel to a secondary fermenter or carboy, while leaving the lees (the bottom sediment) undisturbed in the first vessel. The actual moving of the cider is usually done with a siphon (the racking tube) except in larger operations, where pumps are used. The vessel from which you rack needs to be higher than the carboy that will receive the cider for the siphon to work. If this vessel is on the floor, you will need to put it on something higher, such as a table, at least a day before racking because you will disturb the lees while displacing the tank and they will need a bit of time to settle back to the bottom.

Before racking, you will need to sanitize with the antiseptic solution—as you would before any operation on the cider. You may then start the racking process: insert the racking cane (the rigid part of the racking tube with a tip to prevent it from picking the lees) in the primary fermentation vessel, making sure you don't disturb the lees. The best way to do this is to lower the cane so the tip is a couple of inches higher than the bottom and hold it there (an extra pair of hands or a rubber band may come in handy here). Then prime the siphon by sucking the air from the end of the flexible tubing to create a vacuum: the cider will start to flow into the empty carboy. Some cider makers object to sucking air for priming the siphon, preferring either to use a small priming pump or to fill the flexible tube with clean water. However, there is no evidence that the microorganisms present in our mouths can survive in the cider, and most cider makers don't bother with pumps. In any case, after a bit of practice, you will develop a racking procedure that works well for you.

Let the end of the flexible tube go all the way to the bottom of the receiving carboy. When about three-quarters of the cider has been transferred, you may slowly lower the cane, always making sure the siphon doesn't collect lees. Fill up the carboy completely and install the airlock. Don't forget to fill the airlock with some sulfite solution or alcohol. The carboy should be filled to the neck, with the minimum possible headspace between the cider surface and the bottom of the rubber stopper holding the airlock. Note that this headspace will increase with time because there is a slight reduction in the volume of cider as fermentation proceeds.

Once the carboy is filled, if there is still some cider left over the lees in the primary fermenter, you may put some aside and freeze it or fill a small jug, also with an airlock, to continue fermenting. This extra cider could be useful if you need to fill up the carboy later. And there is absolutely no harm in having a taste of the cider at this point! Actually, this is part of the fun.

SECONDARY PHASE

After the first racking, the cider will enter a mode where the fermentation is much less vigorous. During this period of secondary fermentation, the cider will develop its flavor, aromas, and bouquet. The cider maker really doesn't have much to do except be patient. The cider shouldn't be rushed, and in order to obtain a high-quality cider, it is desirable to have a slow fermentation at this stage. A low temperature will help, and ideally it should be around 50°F (10°C). Some monitoring is useful, and recording the density about once a month is good practice. You may plot these density readings on a graph and see how fast your cider is reaching dryness.

As the cider approaches dryness, the fermentation slows and eventually stops completely; at this point you shouldn't see any more bubbles rising in the carboy or the airlock. Or at least there will be far

fewer bubbles, because some phenomena may still cause a bit of carbon dioxide to escape. The cider will probably still be opaque at this moment, and some time is required before it clears itself. This is a period of maturation, and again patience is required. Some ciders will take their time to clear, sometimes as long as four months, and others will be clear after just a couple of weeks. If you have made the pectinase addition at the beginning of the process, it should help you to get a clear cider in less time. During that period, you need to check the airlock regularly and change the antiseptic liquid in the reservoir about once a month. All in all, this phase of fermentation may last anywhere from three months to a full year, depending on the type of apples, the amount of nitrogenous nutrients present in the juice, and the temperature.

During the secondary phase of the fermentation and maturation of the cider, there are a few problems that may arise. The most common are:

- **A "stuck" fermentation.** The density stops dropping while still at a level substantially higher than dryness. You then have the choice of either making a sweet cider or restarting the fermentation. (See the articles on sweetness and fermentation monitoring and control in chapter 14.) Before settling on this diagnosis, however, you need two SG readings at the same value that have been taken at least one month apart. Keep in mind also that if the temperature in the cider room is very low (below 45°F, or 7°C), the fermentation will be very slow, to the point you may think it is stuck. Slightly raise the temperature before you diagnose a stuck fermentation.

- **A cider that doesn't clear.** If the cider hasn't cleared four months after the fermentation has stopped and it has reached dryness, you might have some sort of haze. Fining might be required. See the article on cider troubles, chapter 16.

- **A film yeast.** If you see a thin, whitish film on the surface of the cider, it is probably a film yeast, which was caused by some air coming into contact with the cider. Check the airlock, as this is probably the culprit in letting air in. This is a quite minor problem. See the article on cider troubles, chapter 16, for a cure.

When you notice that the cider is becoming more translucent, this is a sign it has started to clear. I generally put my hand in the back of the carboy, and if I can see the movement of my hand through the carboy, it means it is ready for bottling. Another test is to use a flashlight: if the ray of light goes through, the cider is ready. The color may be more or less dark depending on the varieties of apples you've used.

Final Racking and Bottling

Now that the cider has cleared, you need to have your bottles ready and decide if you want a sparkling, *pétillant*, or still cider. This decision will obviously depend on the type of bottles you have. You will need twenty-four wine-size bottles per 5-gallon carboy batch.

In order to have carbonation in the cider, you will need to prime it with sugar at bottling. The different levels of carbonation are:

- **Still.** No priming necessary.
- *Perlant*. This is a very slight effervescence for which 2 g/L of priming sugar is required. Any type of bottle may be used.

- *Pétillant* (aka crackling). Priming sugar required is approximately 6 g/L. Use bottles that can handle some pressure, like beer or mineral water bottles.
- **Sparkling.** A fully sparkling cider is like a champagne and will produce a good foam when served. Full-weight champagne bottles are required, as the internal pressure may exceed 100 psi. Use approximately 12 g/L of priming sugar.

It is essential that at this point you measure the density again. If the SG is more than 1.000, it means there is still some residual sugar in the cider, and the amount of priming sugar should be reduced accordingly. More details are given in section 15.2.

As an example, here are the calculations for a 5-gallon carboy of dry cider to be primed for a *pétillant* cider with 6 g/L of sugar. Since 5 gallons is 19 liters, this makes 114 grams of sugar. You may use ordinary white granulated sugar or dextrose if you bought some while you were at the wine-making supply store. The ideal is to weigh the sugar, but if you prefer to measure the volume, one cup of white sugar weighs approximately 180 g, and one cup of dextrose weighs approximately 140 g. To get your 114 g of sugar you will thus need a little less than a cup of dextrose or 2/3 cup white granulated sugar. Note that these volume measures are approximations and will vary if the sugar is more or less compacted.

For bottling, there is a specific sequence of operations:

- **Preparation of the bottles.** Preferably this should be done the day before bottling. If you have an automatic dishwasher, that is ideal. Simply remove the top tray and stack the bottles on the bottom tray. A normal-sized dishwasher holds up to thirty bottles. Set the control to maximum heat, as it is the high temperature that will actually sterilize the bottles (well, it is not as hot as a true sterilization, but almost, and hot enough for our needs). I usually put a bit of bleach in, but this is probably not absolutely necessary. If you don't have a dishwasher, you will have to wash the bottles manually, sulfite them, and let them drain. You could also buy a bottle rinser, sold in wine-making supply stores, that will spray a disinfectant into the bottles, and a bottle tree, which is handy for draining.

- **Preparation of the bottle closures.** These may be corks if you are using wine bottles, crown caps for beer bottles, mushroom-shaped plastic stoppers for champagne bottles, or screw caps. The stoppers should be sanitized prior to installing. You may boil them a few minutes or soak them in a sulfite solution. Some types of screw caps and crown caps have sealing material that will not sustain heat, so those should not be boiled. Corks should be soaked for a few hours in warm water so they become more easily deformable and therefore easier to drive into the bottle.

- **Preparation of the priming sugar solution.** Skip this step if you are making a still cider. I have noted the required quantity of sugar above. You now need to make a solution with this sugar so it dilutes easily in the cider. To prepare the sugar solution, put the sugar with some water in a heat-resistant container that can go on the stovetop, such as a beaker, then slowly heat the mixture and stir occasionally until all the sugar is dissolved. The quantity of water required to dissolve the sugar is about the same as the weight of the sugar. In the case of the example given above, we needed 114 grams of sugar. The same quantity of water will be 114 mL, or ½ cup.

Figure 3.1. A home setup for bottle filling.

- **Preparation of the yeast.** While the sugar heats, you will need to get the yeast ready. Again, skip this step if you are making a still cider. This yeast is for insuring the sugar you add will ferment in the bottles to produce the carbon dioxide gas and the effervescence. A third to a half of the normal quantity of yeast is sufficient at bottling, so part of a package is all you need. Keep the rest in the refrigerator until next usage. Simply rehydrate the yeast as per normal instructions. Champagne yeast is recommended for in-bottle fermentation, as it forms nice and compact lees in the bottom of the bottle.

- **Racking the cider.** You may use your primary fermentation vessel as a receiving container. While the cider is flowing, add the sugar solution and the yeast: the flow of cider will thoroughly mix everything. As for all racking, be careful not to disturb the lees. Once you have finished racking the cider, you may put the lees aside for use in the kitchen: they are excellent in many recipes!

- **Filling the bottles.** Figure 3.1 shows a simple home setup. The cider is in the pail on top of the counter and flows into the siphon to fill the bottles. You need good light to see the level of cider and stop the flow as the bottles become full. When bottling, you should remove the tip of the siphon, as it isn't required anymore, the lees having already been separated by the previous racking. There has to be at least half an inch (12 mm) of airspace in the bottle under the stopper, otherwise the pressure might become excessive if the bottle were left at a higher storage temperature. For my part, I prefer to keep this airspace to the minimum, as this limits the quantity of oxygen in the bottle. However, some cider makers leave larger airspaces, apparently without any ill effect.
- **Closing the bottles.** Once the bottles are filled, the closures or stoppers should be installed as soon as possible. If you use corks or caps, the appropriate corking or capping tool should be close at hand.

Once the bottles are filled and the stoppers properly installed, if you have added priming sugar you may leave the bottles for two weeks at room temperature to let the in-bottle fermentation establish itself. After that, leave your cases in your cooler cider room for maturation. Store the bottles upright, so that any lees will deposit on the bottom. Ideally, you should forget about them for at least six months before trying the cider, but I know such restraint is very difficult for a new cider maker. You may, however, consider keeping a few bottles for tasting later when the cider has had a longer maturation.

Tasting and Appreciation

This is the fun part. If you have made a sparkling cider, there will be lees in the bottom of the bottle; hence you should pour the cider with caution to avoid mixing them. You may also decant the cider into another container. And, no, I will not tell you how you should taste your cider. Some people have designed very nice tasting cards on which the taster notes different impressions, but I have never used these. It is nonetheless important to record some comments on each of your batches, for example, the acidity balance, sweetness perception, effervescence, and the overall impression. The most important questions really are:

- Do you find this cider good enough so you will want to keep on making cider and improving your skills?
- Do you see something you could try to improve next time—maybe make it sweeter, drier, more or less acid, more or less bitter?

I truly hope the answer to the first question is yes, as then the rest of this book is for you. And I hope the answer to the second question is yes, too, because your first cider can't be perfect and there is always room for improvement!

III PART II III

Growing Apples for Cider

This part of the book is for the cider makers who also grow (or wish to grow) the apples they will use for cider. I have said previously that the quality of the cider depends in great part on the apples used to make it. And as you can see from the quote above, I share this belief with the author of an older cider makers' handbook. Hence the cultural practices used in the orchard are of great importance. In the following chapters I present two very different approaches for growing quality apples. The first is my own, which I either call the "lazy apple grower's" or "minimum intervention" approach. It is excellent for producing very high quality apples for cider on a small scale, but unfortunately it may not be economically viable for larger-scale operations. The second approach is from a successful commercial apple grower who also produces excellent cider.

I will not try to cover the vast and complex subject of apple growing, as there are already many excellent books on this, some of which I list in the bibliography. I intend instead to emphasize the difference between apple growing and cider-apple growing. On first thought we might consider these the same: after all, an apple tree is an apple tree, and it produces apples, whether for eating or for cider. But if you think about it a little more, the

Figure II.1.

objectives are quite different. Apple growing for wholesale and retail markets is first and foremost about producing visually attractive fruits—large, a nice color, and without blemishes. The flavor is frankly a secondary consideration, because what will make a person choose one fruit over another is its visual appearance. Cider-apple growing is fundamentally different in that the person who will drink the product will not actually see the fruit. Hence the cider-apple grower may put all his efforts into the flavor of the fruit, as he doesn't have to worry about its appearance. And this should have a great influence on the cultural practices.

Another fundamental difference between apple growing and cider-apple growing is in the varieties. True, some eating-apple varieties are also good for cider. But they most often will need to be blended with some special cider apples to smooth out the acidity and increase the tannins in the blend. A typical cider-apple orchard should also contain many different varieties in order to obtain nicely balanced blends in the face of year-to-year variations. So chapter 5 focuses on varieties of apples (and some pears) that we can use for cider (and perry). I describe

many of these varieties from my personal experience in growing them and using them in cider.

And finally, harvesting and storage are done differently for cider apples than for eating apples. When intended for eating, the apples are picked in the trees before they are fully mature and are put in cold storage as soon as possible after picking. There are two reasons for this. First, if the grower waited until the apples were fully mature before harvesting, there would be great losses because a large proportion of the apples would have fallen from the trees, and those fallen apples don't have the same value on the market. Second, the apples will keep longer in storage if harvested before being fully mature (or "tree-ripe"). For cider apples, the apples are harvested when they are fully mature and a good number have fallen. Often trees are shaken so that the rest of the apples fall. The apples are then picked from the ground, sometimes mechanically in larger orchards. A few blemishes on the fruit from this drop won't hurt the cider. Then the apples are left to further ripen in a cool area: the cider maker wants to prepare cider during fall and has no need for apples that will keep for months in cold storage.

CHAPTER 4

THE CIDER ORCHARD

I present here my personal views on how to manage an orchard to produce high-quality apples for cider. These views correspond to the way I manage my own small orchard. In particular, you will see that I believe the best apples for cider come from low-productivity orchards.

As mentioned above, the first principle to always bear in mind is that cider-apple growing is different. If you permit me an analogy with wine: could you imagine that a wine maker would make his wine from table grapes? Worse, could you imagine that a law would *require* a wine maker to be a commercial producer of table grapes in order to sell his wine? Table grapes and wine grapes are two different things; they are not grown in the same way or by the same people. Why should it be different for apples and cider? Well, even if the answer seems obvious, the reality isn't always so simple.

For example, in Quebec in the 1970s, a law was voted to rule the commercial production of cider. This new legislation stipulated that only commercial apple producers could become cider makers and obtain the right to sell their products. The underlying intent was to find a market for surplus apples. Naturally, what had to happen did happen: the law provoked a boom in industrial cider production. But the quality wasn't there because the cider wasn't being produced from appropriate apples, and soon production decreased, as no one wanted to drink the cider, even if was very inexpensive.

Also, many commercially produced ciders come from cideries that are first and foremost commercial orchards that grow apples to eat. For them, cider production is often a way to increase the value of the lower-grade apples they can't sell at a good price. So the apples they use for their cider are the same varieties as their mainstream table apples: they are grown on a large scale using techniques aimed at increasing the productivity and maximizing the attractiveness of the fruit. This is far from ideal for cider making, as I show below; if you seek quality—and I am talking here about the quality of a *grand cru* cider, which may be compared with a great wine or a Champagne—then you must find other ways to obtain the fruit quality required for such great ciders.

We may now look at some more specific issues relative to cider orchards. In particular, there are two fundamental aspects that we need to consider: the cultural practices, which I discuss just below, and the varietal selection, which will be the object of the following chapter.

◀ 4.1 ▶
The Cultural Practices

The cultural practices you employ will have a great influence on the quality of the cider produced. We may classify the different options into a few groups:

- **The extensive, or traditional, old-style orchard.** This type of orchard corresponds to the way apples were grown in the past. Among its main features are large-size trees grafted on standard (nondwarfing) rootstocks, with ample spacing between trees. Typical planting density varies between fifty to eighty trees per acre. The orchard floor is grass with other diverse flora (wild herbs and flowers), the soil is generally not fertilized, and there is minimal pest and disease control. The productivity of an extensive orchard such as this is relatively low: when well maintained, it may yield an annual production of 2 to 5 tons of apples per acre (5 to 12 per hectare), depending on the climatic conditions; the health, age, and alternating fruiting habit of the trees; and the fertility of the soil. On the other hand, it needs only minimal maintenance and input from the grower. Traditional cider-apple growers of the Old World often let livestock graze in such orchards, and these are a common sight in the countryside of Normandy, northern Spain, or the southwest of England.

- **The intensive orchard.** Intensive orcharding was developed during the twentieth century to increase productivity. To achieve this goal, intensive orchards rely on dwarf rootstocks planted at a high density, which may be from four hundred to over one thousand trees per acre. With these small trees, different training, floor management, fertilization, thinning, and pest control strategies are used, making this cultural system a fairly complex one. The production costs are high, but the productivity may be four to six times higher than that of a traditional orchard. In addition, the fruit produced is generally larger, more uniform, and more marketable. Intensive orcharding may be done organically or conventionally. This will change the strategies and products applied, but the end result as far as cider production is concerned isn't changed much. Large-scale commercial apple production is nowadays always done in such intensive orchards.

- **The cider-bush orchard.** The intensive orcharding techniques are often judged as too costly for cider-apple production because such perfect and handsome fruit isn't needed. Thus research was done during the twentieth century to develop higher-productivity orchards but at a lower production cost. A good part of this work was conducted at the Long Ashton Research Station (LARS) in Bristol, England, and is best described in the small book by Ray Williams and coauthors: *Cider and Juice Apples: Growing and Processing* (1988). Essentially, the techniques are inspired by the intensive cultural techniques for commercial apples but adapted for the special crop of cider apples. In particular, the pest control is reduced, and the trees are slightly larger (i.e., semidwarf or semistandard) and more robust to permit mechanical harvesting by shaking the tree. In England, where this model is mostly used, the tree densities vary between two hundred to four hundred trees per acre. For an example of a North American adaptation of this model, see section 4.4 on Steve Wood's orchard.

In addition to these, there are a number of intermediate models that we may call semi-intensive orchards, where trees are planted at intermediate densities between the traditional model and the intensive orchard, with varying management strategies. In particular I would like to mention here the holistic orcharding approach led by my friend Michael Phillips and described in his two books, *The Apple Grower* and *The Holistic Orchard*. This approach is much softer than the intensive methods mentioned above in the sense that the apple grower does not systematically use poisons (either conventional chemical or organic) to protect the crop but instead works on the health of the tree, from the premise that a healthy tree will defend itself against the pest that may attack it. Holistic orchardists make use of diverse flora on the orchard floor, and improve the soil with the use of compost and ramial wood chips (a mulch made from small-diameter hardwood branches, sometimes including clippings from apple tree pruning). Foliar sprays and compost teas are used to create a microorganism-rich environment that will provide balanced nutrition and enhance the tree's natural defenses. It is, however, an approach that is fairly demanding of the grower hoping to produce commercial-quality fruit for sale. It becomes much easier and less intensive if cider-quality fruit is being grown. Michael has told me that a good orchard, planted at a density of 120 trees per acre on semistandard rootstocks such as the MM-111 variety, and maintained following the holistic approach, will yield two to three times that of a traditional model—so about 7 to 10 tons per acre.

INFLUENCE OF CULTURAL PRACTICES ON APPLE AND CIDER QUALITY

Intensive apple growing requires the use of dwarfing rootstocks, as these are far more productive than standard trees and start production sooner. These small trees also produce larger and more handsome fruit, but essentially such beautiful fruits contain more water, which dilutes the sugar and flavor.

Nitrogenous fertilization is required with the use of dwarfing rootstocks and contributes to producing a large quantity of beautiful fruit. Unfortunately, such fertilization also increases the amount of nitrogenous substances in the apples. Nitrogen is an important component in fertilizers, whether they are synthetic or natural, like compost. So this nitrogen migrates into the fruit, where it forms compounds, which act as yeast nutrients, with the consequence that a nitrogen-rich juice ferments much more rapidly than a juice low in nitrogen.

During the 1970s, British cider expert Andrew Lea did some experiments with pot-cultivated Dabinett apple trees. He fed some of the trees with a fertilizer and left other trees unfed. He then analyzed the fruit, juice, and cider from the two groups of trees, and he obtained the following interesting results:

- Fertilized trees yielded a 50 percent greater weight of crop.
- The content of nitrogenous substances was double in apples from fertilized trees.
- The fermentation time was reduced by half with the juice from fertilized trees.
- Fertilization caused a 15 percent reduction of tannins.

Such observations are not recent: already in 1890, Georges Power was writing, "Un sol très riche en azote produit des fruits volumineux, mais relativement pauvres en sucre et en tanin" (which I may translate as, "A soil very rich in nitrogen produces voluminous fruits, but they are relatively poor in sugar and tannins.")

Orchard floor management is a fairly similar issue. In intensive orchards this is an important element in the overall orchard management strategy. Often herbicides or some other method to control grass and weeds are employed. The important point is to reduce the competition that could come from other plants growing near the apple tree. This is because dwarf apple trees have a superficial root system, and thus the competition from other plants growing nearby reduces their productivity. In contrast, with full-sized trees the root system goes much deeper in the soil, and it then becomes useful to let a diverse flora grow in the orchard to attract beneficial insects and improve the soil health.

To summarize, most large, attractive commercially grown apples taste somewhat bland. Their substance is reduced or, rather, diluted: from tests I have done with the same variety grown in my orchard and bought at the market, the commercially grown apples had from 20 to 40 percent less sugar and acids. It is a bit as if I were to extract some great juice, high in sugar and flavor, and then dilute it with a third of the volume of water before fermenting it to make cider. And this is just as true for organically grown commercial apples: I have done tests on juice produced from certified organic apples and found it also very low in sugar. Furthermore, commercially grown apples will contain more nitrogen, which, as I have noted, encourages a fast fermentation, whereas a quality cider should be obtained by a slow fermentation. So modern intensive orcharding practices used for commercial apple production are detrimental to the quality of the apples for cider making. A much better quality of apples will be obtained from a more traditional but less productive orcharding approach or simply from wild or untended trees.

As for the cider-bush orchards, I have not yet seen a research paper that compared the quality of the apples produced in these orchards with that of traditional, old-style orchards, nor have I done such tests myself, but I would suspect the sugar level and overall quality of the apples from these orchards to be somewhat intermediate between the traditional and the intensive orchards.

A last point of interest on this topic on cultural practices concerns apple scab, a fungus (*Venturia inaequalis*) that does cosmetic damage to the fruit. Scab has to be fully controlled for the apples to have any commercial value, but scab damage is of no concern if the apples are to be pressed for cider. And I have noticed that scabby apples yield less juice, but this juice is richer in flavor and sugar. So actually, some scab may improve the quality of the cider, though decreasing the yield. But scab control will nonetheless be required when the health of the trees is threatened.

Figure 4.1 illustrates my point. On the top are two commercially grown Cortland apples that I bought at the market. They are big, nice-looking, and without any visible blemishes. On the other hand, they contain a lot of water, relatively little sugar and flavor, and a lot of nitrogenous compounds.

Figure 4.1. Cultural practice effects on apple quality

The three smaller apples below are also Cortland apples, but from my orchard, which is described below. They come from old, unfertilized trees, and we can see some scab lesions and insect damage. Their sugar concentration is much higher, producing a juice with an SG of approximately 1.060 (i.e., 15 percent sugar by weight) while the big ones are at about 1.045 (11 percent sugar by weight). They also contain much less nitrogen, will ferment slowly, and will produce a cider of much higher quality.

◀ 4.2 ▶
An Extensive Cider Orchard Example

As an example of a cider orchard that produces high-quality apples for cider, let's have a look at my own orchard, which is managed according to the traditional or extensive orcharding approach.

This orchard is quite old. From my estimates, the trees were planted during the 1940s. The rootstocks are without a doubt seedlings, and tree spacing is 25 feet (7.5 m). The original orchard was approximately 5 acres in area and included many of the traditional varieties grown in eastern Canada at the time: Cortland, McIntosh, Lobo, Wealthy, Fameuse, Yellow Transparent, and Duchess. When I bought this piece of land in 1982, I acquired the first four rows of the old orchard, with twenty-one trees, and these were

mainly of the Cortland variety. The orchard had been abandoned for about ten years, and there was a lot of rejuvenation work to do on the trees. You can see in figure 4.2 a row of these old Cortland trees in bloom.

I made my first cider in 1988, almost exclusively from Cortland apples. It was quite sharp tasting but very well flavored and certainly good enough to give me the desire to continue. I soon started to introduce some true cider-apple varieties, mostly by top-grafting the existing trees to different varieties but also by planting new trees. Today this has become a mixed orchard for varietal selection, where true cider apples account for about 25 percent of the total production. (See chapter 5 for an

Figure 4.2. Old Standard trees in an extensive orchard.

explanation of mixed orchard.) Not all the production is used for cider, though; a part is used for fresh consumption and cooking/preserving.

As far as cultural practices are concerned, I like to call this the minimum intervention approach. In effect, since the orchard is located an hour's drive from my residence, I go there only on weekends, and it is impossible to maintain an intensive or even a semi-intensive management approach. I do some pruning during winter and spring and then practically no spraying, with the exception of occasional local interventions when really required. I mow the grass twice a year, spread around some ramial wood chips from the clippings of the pruning, and that is about it—no fertilization and no scab control sprays. The productivity has been quite close to what might be expected from a traditional orchard, but it has been decreasing these last few years because the old Cortland trees are getting close to the end of their

life. I have planted many young trees that are starting to take the baton as the old trees get older.

I must say it took quite a few years before I understood that the mostly small and unappealing apples produced by those trees (although there is a portion of the crop that is very nice, but this is not used for cider) were of very special quality for cider. I first noticed that the sugar concentration of these apples was much greater than that of other apples. Then, by talking with other cider makers, I became known as "the guy who makes the slowest cider": my fermentations, I discovered, were always slower than the others. And when I started regularly to attend the Cider Days in Massachusetts, I brought along some of my cider, which was always considered one of the best. It took some time, but I was finally able to link all of these qualities with the slowness of the fermentation, the cultural practices, the fertilization (or, rather, the absence of it), the age and size of the trees, and the terroir of my orchard.

◀ 4.3 ▶
Planning the Cider Orchard

When planning a cider orchard, of whatever size, you have two possible situations. The first involves the transformation of an existing orchard plot by *top-working* some of the trees—grafting cider varieties onto the limbs of existing trees, usually of a less desirable variety. Depending on the varietal selection that existed in the orchard before the transformation, a number of the existing trees may be left untouched if their variety could be useful in a cider blend. In general, if the apple tree produces a high-flavored, late-maturing variety, it could make a positive contribution to the cider. You would then end up with a mixed orchard for the varietal selection. Naturally, you will have to live with and make the best of the existing trees, whether they are large standard trees or smaller semidwarf or dwarf trees. But the great advantage of using an existing orchard is the relatively short period of time required for a graft to start producing fruit versus planting a new young tree. And in the meantime, the cider maker will gain some experience by making cider with the existing varieties in the orchard.

The second situation is to plant a new orchard. This is a longer-term project, as a newly planted tree takes more time to start producing fruit than a top-grafted tree. However, it gives you more latitude for the varietal selection and the tree size and spacing, as you don't have to work with an existing orchard, which may not be ideal. If you are patient enough, I would recommend planting full-sized trees or at least midsized trees, as they

are much more robust and securely rooted than smaller trees. I have tried planting some small trees in my orchard and have lost a good fraction of them by the trees' simply breaking at ground level because of wind, snow, or too heavy a load of apples—or even in one case because a bear decided he wanted the apples. Yes, it was partly my fault because they were not well enough attached to stakes, but this never happens with large and sturdy trees. There are situations, mostly in warmer climates, on fertile soils and in protected situations, where small trees will be appropriate, but they will always need more care. As for midsized trees, such as those grafted on MM-106, M-7, or EMLA-7 rootstock varieties, they may be an excellent choice in many situations, as they will permit you to obtain the same production with a smaller piece of land and will start producing fruit a bit faster than standard trees. Midsized trees may be managed according to the extensive model and give high-quality apples for cider. They will not, though, have the same resistance to extreme conditions as full-sized trees.

Whichever of the two above situations is yours, you will need to make your varietal selection with care. You may use the true cider-apple model or the mixed model, and the varieties should be chosen according to the recommendations given in the next chapter. It is, however, not always easy to find all the varieties we would like: nurseries that offer a good selection of cider-apple varieties are few, and they are often

Figure 4.3. Top-grafting in an existing tree.

sold out, so you have to plan and order well in advance. You may find that you will need to learn the art of grafting (R. J. Garner's *The Grafter's Handbook* may be useful for this). The Internet and the discussion forums on cider are excellent ways to procure grafting wood of lesser-known cider-apple varieties.

ORCHARD SIZE FOR A HOBBYIST CIDER MAKER

Another important question is the size of the orchard. The following assumptions may give you an idea of what to expect in terms of cider production, using the traditional, low-yield orchard model:

- A standard-sized, healthy tree may yield 10 bushels of apples in a good year and even more in an exceptional year. However, most apple trees are not regular croppers by nature, hence an average of 3 bushels per tree annually is a conservative number that takes into account that some trees have an off year after a heavy fruit set, and others may not be so healthy. This is also the average production I get from my old Cortland trees. Note that the productivity per tree will increase as the climate is milder and the soil richer.

- On a per acre basis, with tree and row spacing of 25 feet (7.5 m), we can have eight rows of eight trees, so sixty-four trees in an acre of land, with 192 bushels annually on average. At 40 pounds (18 kg) per bushel, this is more or less 3.8 tons per acre (8.5 per hectare)—a fairly typical yield from a traditional-type orchard that is relatively well maintained.

- With midsized trees on an extensive management model, you could use a spacing of 20 × 12 feet (6 × 3.5 m) for 165 trees per acre and count on an average annual production of approximately 1.5 bushels per tree. This would give approximately 5 tons per acre (12 per hectare). And as mentioned earlier, intensive orcharding practices will yield more tonnage per area of land, but possibly at the expense of cider quality.

- From one full bushel of apples, you may obtain 3 gallons (11.5 L) of juice with juicy apples and efficient pressing equipment. But if you have small and possibly scabby apples from a traditional, unfertilized orchard and domestic pressing equipment of relative efficiency, a little over 2 gallons (8 L) per bushel would be a more realistic although slightly conservative number for the juice yield.

- You will lose at least 10 percent of this juice during the cider-making process, mostly in the form of lees. If you make a sweet cider with the keeving process (see the article on sweetness in cider, section 15.1), this number will increase to about a 25 percent loss.

Putting all this information together, one standard-sized tree from an orchard that is traditionally managed will annually produce on average 3 bushels of apples, 6.3 gallons of juice, 5.7 gallons of cider, or twenty-eight wine-size bottles of cider. On a per acre basis, and with a more efficient press, this would give approximately 2,000 to 2,500 bottles annually (the higher number is more likely with with mid-sized trees), or 5,000 to 6,000 bottles per hectare.

For a home or kitchen orchard, which is ideal for a serious hobbyist cider maker, a small mixed orchard of fifteen standard trees (or twice that many midsized trees) is a nice number. Half of the trees could be true cider varieties and the other half good table varieties that would also be used for cider, plus maybe a crabapple for processing and a summer apple that wouldn't be used for cider but is always pleasant to have. So let's say we use the production of twelve standard trees for cider making: this would give a production in the range of 325 to 350 bottles annually, which should be enough for family and friends' consumption. But be forewarned: if you have a few grownup children and a couple of annual gatherings of family and friends, this number of bottles, even if it sounds like a lot, vanishes quite quickly (if the cider is as good as it should be).

The orchard described above would require an area of 10,000 square feet (1,000 m²) (which comes to 7,500 ft² or 750 m² for midsized trees), and not everyone has this amount of land available for planting apple trees. There is an alternative, which is to have only one or two trees in the backyard, the varieties chosen for low acidity, high tannins, and as high a sugar concentration as possible. Then for the bulk of the juice you could buy apples of standard varieties from an apple grower. This way, with just one tree that would produce 3 bushels of apples and 3 to 5 bushels bought from the grower, you could produce 12 to 15 gallons (50 to 60 L) of cider annually.

Orchard size for a commercial cider maker

When considering commercial cider making of whatever size, we need to look at some economic and legislative considerations. The law in particular is extremely different from one part of the world to another. In general, European laws allow and even promote very small cider (and wine) making for commercial purposes. For example, in England there is tax exemption for cider producers who make less than 7,000 liters (1,850 gallons) annually. On the other hand, in Quebec, only those commercial apple growers who exploit at least 1 hectare (2.5 acres) of apple trees may apply for a permit that will allow them to sell cider, thus excluding potential very small cider makers, whatever the quality of their cider and the seriousness of their project. Also this legislation makes it practically impossible to plant a true cider orchard, as the varietal selection won't match. From this we can see that the first step in planning a commercial cider orchard is to check the local laws.

As far as the orchard size is concerned, we saw above that 1 acre of orchard could yield approximately 2,000 to 2,500 bottles of cider annually in the case of a low-yield, extensive orchard. We may then ask, Could such a small orchard permit a successful commercial cider-making venture? Personally, I think the answer to this is yes, in certain circumstances. For instance, for a retired person, managing a small cider-making business might provide both a nice additional income to the retirement pension and a rewarding activity. It could also be an addition to a regular job, providing supplementary revenue. We have to consider that the maintenance of a traditional orchard requires very little input from the grower, and one person may easily care for a 1-acre orchard in his or her spare time. Fall would, however, be a period of more work, and help from family and friends would probably be welcome in that season for harvesting the apples and pressing to obtain the juice. After that, the transformation into cider and the production of 2,500 bottles of cider could be done by that one person during his or her spare time with a minimum of equipment (note that this "minimum equipment" is still considerable compared to what a hobbyist needs and will require a small cider house, tanks, etc.). Such a small production could nevertheless provide a substantial secondary income, considering that the production costs would be minimal. This type of "microcidery" is quite common in Europe but much less so in America.

If cider making is to become the main income of a family, then obviously a much larger orchard will be required, and probably also the semi-intensive or intensive orcharding management approach should be considered, as the traditional low-yield orchard described above might not be economically viable on a larger scale. It then becomes a true business, and each project will be different and require its specific orchard size. In the following section we will have a closer look at a large commercial cider orchard model.

◄ 4.4 ►
A Commercial Orchard Example: Poverty Lane Orchards

For a few reasons, I have chosen to present here a profile of Steve Wood, owner of Poverty Lane Orchards and Farnum Hill Ciders. Steve owns and manages a large commercial orchard, and an important part of the production of this orchard is of true cider apples. Steve also makes some of the best commercial cider in America. His views on growing cider apples could bring a different perspective from my own experience, which I've discussed above.

Historical Background

The history of Poverty Lane Orchards starts in 1960, when a dairy farm was transformed into an apple production farm. The land was planted with mostly McIntosh and Cortland apple trees, which were then the two leading commercial apple varieties. These were standard-sized trees, planted with large spacing between trees, a layout typical of that period. The farm is located in Lebanon, in western New Hampshire, close to Vermont. This is in USDA zone 5, which is fairly representative of a good part of the New England climate. In 1965 the farm was acquired by Steve's father in coownership with other partners. Steve was then just a boy, and this was his first experience with apple trees. In 1979, after years of intermittent contact with the farm, Steve started to really manage it himself, and he finally bought it a few years

later. At the time the farm consisted of 90 acres of orchards growing standard commercial varieties, with some storage and packing facilities.

In the beginning of the 1980s, Steve started experimenting with true European cider apples: grafting some varieties, evaluating them, and making cider. At the time he also had members of his family living in England, and during a trip to visit them he was introduced to some leading cider specialists in that country, most notably Bertram Bulmer and Ray Williams. All this led him to plant in 1989 what is regarded as one of the first true cider orchards of modern times in America: 5 acres with one thousand trees of mainly English cider varieties, including Dabinett, Somerset Redstreak, Bulmer's Norman, Medaille d'or, Stoke Red, Kingston Black, plus some Yarlington Mill and Tremlett's Bitter (though this last variety turned out to be untrue to its name). This was clearly a visionary undertaking, as very few Americans were drinking or making cider at the time, and the small quantity of cider that did exist was being made with standard American varieties.

At the beginning of the 1990s, Steve decided to diversify the production of the farm, and he planted some orchards with uncommon heirloom apples of great flavor, such as Esopus Spitzenburg, Calville blanc d'hiver, Pomme grise, Ribston Pippin, and Hudson's Golden Gem. Hence the 1990s were a decade of profound transition for Poverty

Lane Orchards: old standard trees were cut down and replaced with new plantings of cider apples, heirloom varieties, and commercial varieties. From then up to the present time, the acreage of the farm has been divided in three production acreages of approximately the same size:

- one-third regular eating/dessert varieties, which are sold as retail and pick-your-own;
- one-third "uncommon" (heirloom) varieties of great flavor sold to specialty and niche markets; and
- one-third true cider apples.

In 1995 Steve also started to make cider commercially and founded Farnum Hill Ciders a little while later. Nowadays Farnum Hill produces nearly 100,000 bottles of cider annually, which uses on average two-thirds of the cider apples produced by the farm. The surplus is sold to other cider makers. When I asked him if this wasn't a bit strange, to sell his surplus fruit to competitors, he said no, as he feels this can only improve the quality of the cider produced in the country, which will bring more people to appreciate good cider, and which in turn will have a positive impact on his operations. I had to admit it made sense.

Figure 4.4. Steve Wood surrounded by Dabinett trees.

Management of the Cider Orchard at Poverty Lane

This brings us to the main question here: how does Steve Wood manage his cider-apple orchard, and how different is this management compared to the management of eating-apple varieties? Generally speaking, his strategy for cider apples is mostly inspired by the English bush-orchard model.

ESTABLISHMENT OF THE ORCHARD

The planting density has been around 200 to 220 trees per acre, with distance between rows 20 feet (6 m) and distance between trees 10 feet (3 m), and in some cases a bit less. Steve uses mostly the MM-111 rootstock, which makes a fairly robust tree and is considered a semistandard size (see figure 4.4). With his accumulated experience, he feels he could improve the productivity in future plantings by reducing the distance between trees to about 7 feet (2 m) in the row, which would make a density of nearly 300 trees per acre. His planting strategy is to maintain a grass-free strip for the first two or three years of the life of the tree, as this helps them become established; after that he sows grass in this strip, so that the whole floor of the orchard is covered with grass when the trees start production.

For eating apples, the technique is essentially the same for the grass-free strip during the first years of the life of the tree and the resowing of this strip in grass after. The main difference is that he uses smaller rootstocks, mainly Bud-9 and M-9,

and the planting density is higher, around 450 to 500 trees per acre.

PRODUCTION ORCHARD MANAGEMENT

Steve Wood is a leader in the application of integrated pest management (IPM; see sidebar "Integrated Pest Management" on page 42) techniques. And although he uses conventional pesticides, IPM allows him to reduce drastically the amount of pesticides required to control any given situation.

Let's now look at his strategies in a little more detail. For apple scab, Steve insists on having complete control of the disease, even in the cider-apple orchard. He reckons that some scab would not necessarily adversely affect the cider, but his reasoning is that if he permits even just a little bit of uncontrolled scab, there is just too much risk that in a large orchard this scab could simply go wild and become uncontrollable after some time. And scab is detrimental to the health and productivity of the tree.

For the early-season insect pests, essentially the plum curculio and apple sawfly, he also insists on maintaining a good control, and he uses the same strategy in the cider-apple orchards as in the eating-apple orchards. This is because both these insects can cause the fruitlets to drop, and if left uncontrolled can cause an unacceptable decrease of production.

Thinning is another area where the strategies are the same in all orchard blocks. Steve uses chemical spraying to thin fruit set. He wants good thinning for his cider-apple trees because many of the varieties have a strong biennial tendency, even more so than commercial eating varieties. Thinning permits some modification of this biennial habit,

Integrated Pest Management

Integrated pest management (IPM) is an evolution of conventional orcharding techniques to decrease the use of pesticides for two main reasons: pesticides are very expensive, and pesticides are not really good for our health or the environment (although they are definitely not as bad as they used to be).

Good IPM practices require a lot of knowledge on the part of the grower and are a great improvement over conventional chemical practices, where pesticides were systematically applied whether they were necessary or not. With IPM the effect of each application of a pesticide is maximized because it is used with discernment, and only after monitoring indicates that an action is really required. The timing of the sprays is also of prime importance. Pest insects and mites are trapped and counted, and a pesticide will be applied only if the count has exceeded a certain threshold and only in the area where this threshold has been exceeded. For fungal diseases such as scab, climatic and weather conditions are closely monitored to predict the exact moment at which a spray is required to annihilate the first infection and thus permit control with a minimum of intervention.

Many other actions are also involved in IPM, such as promoting natural predators and sexual confusion of some insect pests. For more information on IPM, there are many good guides on the Internet, which are usually adapted for regional situations.

as the tree is not permitted to overcrop one year, which causes it to have almost no crop the following year. However, some of the cider varieties are so strongly biennial that even a good thinning program isn't enough to insure a regular production.

As for fertilization, Steve applies some mineral fertilizer to his trees rather than high-nitrogen fertilizers. This increases the health of the tree and the amount of minerals in the apples, which is a good thing, without increasing the amount of nitrogenous substances, which would not be so good for cider, as I have previously discussed.

The management strategies of the cider-apple trees versus the eating-apple trees really start to differ by the middle or end of June. Late-season insects and fungal diseases do not have to be controlled as strictly in the cider-apple orchards because most of these will cause only cosmetic damage without greatly affecting the yield.

Harvest

Harvest of the cider apples is done by shaking the trees by hand, usually with a pole for the higher branches. The apples are then collected by hand on the ground, sometimes a few days after the shaking. There is no mechanical harvester at Poverty Lane as there are in some large cider orchards in Europe. Two harvests are usually performed in order to obtain maximum ripeness in all apples: in the first, only the fully mature apples will fall, and in the second all the remaining apples are shaken until they fall. We can see here the usefulness of a thick grass carpet under the trees!

As for the productivity of his orchards, Steve claims he gets approximately 8 to 10 tons of cider apples per acre (18 to 23 per hectare), while for eating apples he obtains a little more, around 12 tons per acre (27 per hectare). He thinks this difference is largely due to the biennial habit of many cider-apple varieties rather than any difference in cultural practices. The difference in planting densities may also have an influence on this. The productivity of Steve's orchards is lower than what is obtained in high-yield intensive orchards, which may reach 15 to 20 tons per acre (35 to 45 per hectare). But as Steve pointed out, these higher productivities are generally attained in regions with a warmer climate and more fertile soils than his, as in the Hudson Valley of New York.

All in all, it appears from my discussions with Steve Wood that when done on a large commercial scale, cider-apple growing may not be as different from eating-apple growing as I had anticipated. Yes, there are significant differences in the size of trees and spacing, late-season pest control and harvest, but these don't have that much influence on the production costs. However, this is also in large part due to the fact that Steve is so good at using IPM techniques that he is able to successfully grow high-quality eating apples with a minimum of interventions.

CHAPTER 5

THE VARIETAL SELECTION

If we observe cider orchards in different producing regions of the world, we will find three important models for the varietal selection:

- **The true cider-apple orchard**. This type of orchard is found mostly in Europe, in particular in France, England, and Spain, where there is a rich tradition of cider-apple varieties. In fact, many orchards are exclusively composed of such varieties. Usually a large number of varieties are grown, chosen among different categories of apples. For example, in England these categories are *sweet, bittersweet, sharp,* and *bittersharp,* and a typical orchard will contain a certain percentage of trees in each of these categories to make sure that a well-balanced blend can be obtained every year. We will see more of this in section 5.1 a little further on.
- **The dessert-apple orchard**. This is mainly a North American type of orchard, where table (or dessert) apples are used for making cider. In Canada and the United States, dedicated cider varieties were not known before the 1970s, when they started to be imported from Europe. Many classic American cider varieties had for all practical purposes been lost and have been rediscovered only recently. Hence, cider was traditionally produced from the same varieties used for general consumption. Many cideries still use this type of varietal selection. In general, the ciders thus obtained are fairly sharp and don't have the body and mouthfeel that may be obtained with cider apples that contain more tannins.
- **The mixed orchard**. This is a compromise between the two preceding types. Here some dessert apple varieties are grown to form the bulk of the juice, and a selection of special cider varieties are used to balance the blend and add some tannins. Mixed orchards may also contain cooking apples and crabs. They are a net improvement

over the pure dessert-apple orchard. An interesting feature of the mixed orchard is that the nice specimens of fruit may be selected for consumption, while those with insect damage or other blemishes are used for the cider. A mixed varietal selection may yield a cider of as good quality as a true cider-apple selection. This is the preferred model for a home or kitchen orchard.

Usually the varietal selection will depend a lot on the region where the orchard is located. All the main cider regions have their traditional varieties, which will give a local character to the cider. The varieties from England and France are better known in North America because many of them are now available, but other countries like Spain and Germany also have their traditional cider varieties and cider styles.

Finally, when planning the varietal selection for a cider orchard, it is important to take into account the following points:

- The adaptability of the varieties in relation to the climate at the location of the orchard: this may be winter hardiness in cold regions or chill requirement in warm locations. Additionally, the required length of the growing season should be considered in areas where the summers are short.
- The traditional cider varieties of the region, if any.

- Whether some varieties are required for uses other than cider—for example, dessert apples, cooking apples, or crabs—which would call for the mixed-orchard model.
- A sufficient number of varieties to obtain enough apples every year that are rich in sugar, low in acidity, and will give tannins to the cider, keeping in mind that many of these varieties will tend to have an alternating (biennial) bearing habit.
- Pollination requirements: all varieties must have pollinators that bloom at the same period. This point is most important in areas where bloom time is spread over a long period and if there are relatively few varieties in the orchard. Note also that *triploid* varieties do not have viable pollen and thus will not pollinate other varieties.
- The sensitivity (or resistance) of different varieties to major apple diseases, particularly scab, if you don't intend to follow a complete spraying schedule, and fireblight, if the pressure is high at the proposed location.

In the following sections, we will look more in depth at the classification of cider apples, an important issue in the planning of a varietal selection. I then make some recommendations for the best apple varieties and describe the main varieties that are likely to be grown for cider in North America.

◀ 5.1 ▶
Cider-Apple Classification

Throughout history, cider has been made by blending apples of different types, so it has always been useful to classify the numerous varieties according to their main characteristics. Moreover, the ripening and pressing dates differ from one variety to another, and we also class them according to their season of use. Let us begin with the classifications used in England, France, and Spain, as these countries have a long tradition of cider-apple culture.

ENGLAND

In England the classification that is generally used was developed by Professor B. T. P. Barker of the Long Ashton Research Station at the beginning of the twentieth century (Lea, 2008). It is shown in table 5.1.

We can see that *sharp* indicates a relatively higher content in acidity, while *sweet* indicates lower acidity. Hence, in this context *sweet* has no relation whatsoever to the sugar content, and thus this classification gives no indication of the sugar concentration of the apples. We also have the term *bitter,* which is associated with a higher content in tannins, and its omission indicates a lower tannin level.

In addition to these main classes, a qualifier is sometimes used for the type of tannin:

- **Hard** indicates that the tannin is rather bitter.
- **Soft** indicates that the tannin is rather astringent.

For the bittersweet and bittersharp apples, an additional qualifier is often used to quantify the intensity of the tannins (Copas, 2001; Williams, 1988):

- **Full** for an apple that has pronounced tannins, producing a cider that is very bitter or astringent;
- **Mild** for a light tannin, yielding a cider that is slightly bitter or astringent; or
- **Medium** for an in-between situation.

TABLE 5.1:
Cider-apple classification used in England

CLASS	ACIDITY (g/L as malic acid)	TANNINS (g/L as tannic acid)
Sharp	over 4.5	less than 2
Bittersharp	over 4.5	over 2
Bittersweet	less than 4.5	over 2
Sweet	less than 4.5	less than 2

Furthermore, some apples are called **vintage**, which indicates that the variety in question is of superior quality for cider making. This qualifier has been historically used in England for a number of varieties, although it is not perfectly defined and doesn't represent anything we can easily measure from the juice of those apples. Ray Williams, who was an authority on English cider, wrote in the book *Cider and Juice Apples: Growing and Processing* (1988), "Despite such wide differences [in measurable chemical composition] the varieties in question may possess the other characters detected by the palate and requisite for vintage qualification. Therefore, to obtain a well balanced cider it is usually necessary to blend appropriate varieties. However, there are a few varieties with acid and tannin sufficiently evenly balanced to produce the desired flavour without blending." He then goes on to list the varieties that are widely considered *vintage* and that include some apples in all the classes defined in table 5.1. Note that some authors have implied that vintage-quality apples were suitable for making single-variety ciders (i.e., used on their own, without the need for blending with other varieties). And while this may be true for some, this certainly contradicts Williams's writing. According to Lea (2008), trees of

TABLE 5.2:

Cider-apple classification used in France

CLASS	ACIDITY (g/L as malic acid)	TANNINS (g/L as tannic acid)
Douce (Sweet)	less than 4	less than 2
Douce amère (Sweet and bitter)	less than 4	2 to 3
Amère (Bitter)	less than 4	over 3
Acidulée (Mildly acid)	4 to 6	less than 2
Aigre (Acid)	over 6	less than 2
Aigre amère (Acid and bitter)	over 6	over 3

vintage-quality varieties would have the particular attribute of taking up less nitrogen from the soil into the fruit, thus promoting a slower fermentation and the development of bouquet and flavor. In any case, a variety qualified as vintage in England may not perform as well in America, and, conversely, an ordinary English variety could become of superior quality when grown in an American terroir. Hence we should not put too much importance on this qualifier in North America.

As to the season of use of English cider apples, they are classified as early, midseason, or late, indicating respectively that the fruit matures by the end of September, in October, or in November.

A typical cider from the traditional cidermaking counties of the southwest of England could contain approximately 40 percent apples from the bittersweet class, 30 percent sharps, 20 percent bittersharps, and 10 percent sweets. Naturally, these proportions would vary from one cider

maker to another and also from year to year, but ideally most cider makers would like to see about equal amounts of low- and high-acidity apples and slightly more than half of tannin-rich apples.

FRANCE

The French classification for cider apples is relatively similar to the English but contains a larger number of classes. Michel Gautier (*Les espèces fruitières*, Paris: Hachette, 1978) presents it as shown in table 5.2.

Note that here again there are no indications of the sugar concentration in these classes. However, it is generally taken for granted (Boré et Fleckinger, 1997) that apples in the *douce* class have a higher concentration of sugar than others. Apples in the *amère* and *douce amère* classes bring the tannins, and those in the *acidulée* and *aigre* classes provide the acids necessary to obtain a well-balanced cider.

There are three seasons of maturity in France:

- Apples of the first season ripen in September and should be milled and pressed soon after harvest, as they don't keep long.
- Apples of the second season are harvested in October or beginning of November. These apples normally need to be kept in storage for two to three weeks before processing.
- Apples of the third season are hard apples that are harvested in late November but still need a long ripening period before being used. They will usually be pressed in December or January.

The third-season apples are generally considered those that make the best cider. Bauduin (2006) proposes the following proportions to give to each of the classes for a standard French cider:

10 percent of apples from the *aigre* or *acidulée* class, 40 percent *douce,* 40 percent *douce amère,* and 10 percent *amère.* These proportions may vary depending on whether a more bitter or more acid cider is wanted. If we compare these proportions with those seen for England, we see that it includes proportionately fewer apples that have a high acidity (only 10 percent), while the ideal proportion of tannin-rich apples is at 50 percent.

SPAIN

Spain is a major cider-producing country of Europe, but we often forget this because Spanish cider is not well known outside of its country of origin. This may be changing, however, because there are now importers of Spanish ciders in the United States. The cider is produced mainly in the northern part of the country, where there is a protected designation of origin for Asturian cider (*DOP Sidra de Asturias*).

The classification of cider apples in Spain is quite similar to that of England and France, but it is more complete, as the acidity and the tannins are quantified as low, medium, or high. The demarcation points between the classes are different, though. Most of the Spanish cider apples fall into one of the classes defined in table 5.3.

Other classes are defined but not used much, as there are very few apples that would fall into these. For example, *Amarga-semiacida* would be a class for medium acidity and high tannin. According to Pereda Rodriguez (2011), a typical *sidra de Asturias* would contain approximately 40 percent *acida* apples, 25 percent *semiacida,* 15 percent *dulce,* 15 percent *dulce amarga,* and 5 percent *amarga.* By comparing these proportions with those of typical English and French ciders shown above, we can easily see that the Spanish ciders are much more acidic and less tannic.

TABLE 5.3:

Cider-apple classification used in Spain

CLASS	ACIDITY (g/L as malic acid)	TANNINS (g/L as tannic acid)
Acida (High acid, low tannin)	over 6.6	less than 1.45
Semiacida (Medium acid, low tannin)	4.9 to 6.6	less than 1.45
Dulce (Low acid, low tannin)	less than 4.9	less than 1.45
Dulce amarga (Low acid, medium tannin)	less than 4.9	1.45 to 2.0
Amarga (Low acid, high tannin)	less than 4.9	over 2

NORTH AMERICA

Except for a few rare exceptions, in North America and in particular in eastern Canada, New England, and the Mid-Atlantic coastal states, where we find the richest and most ancient cider traditions, true cider apples are not grown especially for the purpose of making cider. The classes of cider apples seen above have never been defined or used on this continent. American cider has typically been made from apples obtained from seedling trees and/or heirloom varieties or downgraded commercial apple varieties. As I've mentioned, only since the 1970s have European cider apples been imported and propagated here, mainly in research stations and governmental gene banks.

We need to understand that in France and England the sugar is provided for the most part

TABLE 5.4:
Classification according to the concentration of properties

CONCENTRATION	SUGAR Specific Gravity (SG)	ACIDITY (g/L as malic acid)	TANNINS (g/L as tannic acid)
Low	less than 1.045	less than 4.5	less than 1.5
Medium	1.045 to 1.060	4.5 to 7.5	1.5 to 2.5
High	1.060 to 1.070	7.5 to 11	over 2.5
Very high	over 1.070	over 11	

by the low-acidity varieties, which make up the bulk of the blend. Higher-acidity varieties are used to raise the acidity of the blend when it is too low. French and English cider makers, then, don't put much emphasis on the sugar content of the high-acidity varieties, as this is not their purpose, and they are not used in large quantities. In America the situation is the opposite: it is the high-acidity apples that are grown in abundance, and we rely on these to provide the better part of the sugar. The low-acidity apples are used mainly to reduce the acidity of the blend to a balanced value. So a high-acid variety that is also rich in sugar will have more value for a cider maker than another variety that has the same acidity but a lower sugar concentration. And for a low-acidity apple, we won't insist as much on its having a high sugar content.

Hence, in the North American context I find it more useful simply to qualify the three main properties by their relative concentration, stated as *low*, *medium*, or *high* (and sometimes *very high* is also useful). For example, saying that an apple is "medium sugar, high acid, and low tannin" is in fact clearer than any formal classification. We may put numbers on these qualifiers as in table 5.4.

Note that these numbers are those that best suit my own cider making, but they could be different in other locations. For example, in Spain and England specific gravities are often lower, and an apple that normally has an SG higher than 1.055 might be considered a high-sugar variety. Similarly, English and French ciders are traditionally less acidic, and thus a total acidity of 6.5 or 7 g/L might be considered to be high acid in this context. It should also be noted that an apple may have very different properties depending on how and where it is grown. In general, apples of a certain variety will have a lower acidity when grown in a location where the season is longer and warmer. For example, some English cider apples that I grow in my orchard have much higher acidity than when grown in the UK.

We might still find it useful to group the varieties according to certain criteria for blending purposes. We will see more of this in chapter 13. The following groups may be defined when discussing the sugar-acid balance:

1. **The perfect apples**
   (high sugar, medium acidity, medium tannin).
   Such apples could be used to make a single-variety cider without need for blending.

Unfortunately, there are very few apples that have this perfect combination of properties. The famous English variety Kingston Black is one of the few considered a perfect apple for cider.

2. The sugar-rich apples
(high sugar and high acidity).

These apples bring most of the sugar needed to attain a good alcoholic level, but they have too much acidity to make a balanced cider and need to be blended. This group includes many russet apples that have a high SG and other late-ripening, sugar-rich apples balanced by a sprightly acidity (often referred to as having a "high flavor"). Some bittersharps of the English and some *aigre* of the French would also be in this class when their SG is high enough.

3. The low-acidity apples
(low acidity with low to high sugar).

These apples are necessary for blending with the sugar-rich apples in order to bring down the acidity of the blend. Their sugar content is not of prime importance and may vary between low to high. This class will include the sweets and bittersweets of the English and the *douce, douce amère,* and *amère* of the French, as well as the few American apples that have similar properties. Often these apples will additionally be rich in tannins. Many varieties of pears could also be included in this group.

4. The medium-sugar apples
(medium sugar, medium to high acidity).

This group will include many apples that do not contain as much sugar as those of the sugar-rich group but can nevertheless be used for making a good-quality cider. Some English and French cider apples with moderate to high acidity may be in this class, as well as a large number of American dessert apples of midseason or late maturation.

5. The low-sugar apples
(low sugar, medium to high acidity).

These apples would generally not be recommended for cider unless they have a very special quality. On the other hand, such apples may give good juice for fresh consumption, or a cider made with them may make a good cooking cider or may be used for making vinegar or for distillation. Many of the apples in this group ripen early in the season.

I like to illustrate these groups in graph form as in figure 5.1, which makes it clearer. Note that we will see this graph again in the article on blending (chapter 13).

Apple varieties from the first three groups are the ones to be chosen first for the best-quality cider and should be given priority when planting a new orchard. Many apples from the medium-sugar group are also excellent choices for a mixed-orchard planting, as they are often very good for eating fresh or for fresh juice, as well as for cider.

As for classifying apples by their season of maturation, in the warmer regions of North America, where the growing season is longer, the three seasons of classification similar to those used in England and France may be appropriate. But in colder zones like eastern Canada, New England, or the Great Lakes region, the third season is too late for reliable maturation and harvest, and we would have to limit the classification to two seasons:

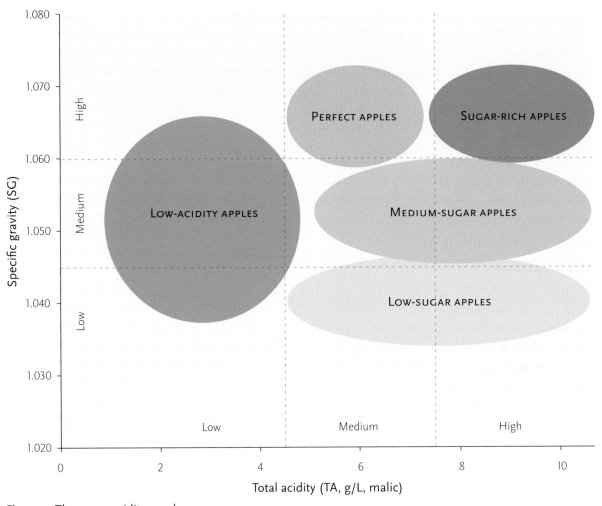

Figure 5.1. The sugar-acidity graph

- First season, for those apples that ripen by mid-September and will be pressed in late September or early October.
- Late season, for the apples that are harvested in October and may be kept some time in storage to be pressed from late October until December. As a matter of fact, we often wait until the primary fermentation of the first-season cider is complete before pressing for the late-season cider. This way the same fermentation vessels may be used twice in the same year.

The first-season ciders are a bit lighter than those of late season, in part because earlier-ripening apples normally contain less sugar, and thus the alcoholic strength isn't as high. We note also that first-season ciders ferment more rapidly and more easily to dryness; thus, first-season ciders will tend to be drier. It is nevertheless possible to produce first-season ciders of excellent quality, as we have European cider apples that ripen earlier in a colder location than they do in Europe. These apples have a good richness in tannins that permits us to make ciders with a lot of character.

◀ 5.2 ▶
Recommended Varieties by Region

It happens fairly often that people ask me which variety I would recommend for the planting of a small orchard of ten to fifteen trees, mostly for cider but including also some good eating varieties. This is always a bit difficult to answer, as any varietal selection implies compromises. Also, a varietal recommendation would naturally be different depending on the location of the prospective orchard. Hence, in addition to my own recommendations (which would apply to a cold zone 4 area), I have asked this same question of some of my cider-making friends in diverse locations of Canada and the United States, thus permitting us to draw a wider perspective.

QUEBEC
(COLD CLIMATE, HARDINESS ZONE 4)

I have tested apple and pear varieties since the mid-1980s in my orchard—located in an area of short and cool summers and cold winters with a thick snow cover. And although I found that many excellent varieties are not hardy enough to survive the winters and others don't find the necessary conditions to ripen their fruits properly in this climate, I also found a good number that are well adapted to these conditions and that permit the making of some excellent cider.

For a small mixed orchard where eating and cider varieties are needed, the following selection would be good in such a cold-climate location:

- For the first-season cider: Bilodeau (sugar rich), Douce de Charlevoix and Bulmer's Norman (low acidity and providers of tannins), to which I would add Lobo, which is good for eating and also useful in a first-season blend. However, Lobo is quite sensitive to scab, and if this is not acceptable, I would recommend Wealthy instead.

- For the late-season cider, I would select Banane amère and two trees of Yarlington Mill as low-acidity varieties and for the tannins they contain. Then as sugar-rich varieties with high acidity, I would recommend three trees from the following, which are some of my favorites: Belle de Boskoop, Golden Russet, Golden Nugget, Reine des reinettes, Rubinette. And I would complete the selection with Cortland, Liberty, and Honeygold, which are excellent varieties in a cider blend as well as for fresh eating.

- If this were my orchard, I would certainly want one tree for early-season eating and cooking. There are many interesting varieties in that category, and I would graft a selection of some of the best in one multivariety tree. The surplus fruit from these could be used to make a summer cider for cooking or making vinegar.

- Finally, I would also want a tree of crabapples for making jellies, butters, and other delicious stuff. My favorites are Dolgo, Kerr, and Chestnut. Again, I would graft them all onto one tree. Note that these crabs may also be used in the cider, where they add flavorful notes, but in small quantity because of their high acidity.

This would give a small orchard of fifteen trees hardy in zone 4. And if a few pear trees are desired, I would choose Patten for fresh eating and Golden Spice and Thorn for juice, cider blending, and perry.

On occasion someone may wish to plant a single tree in the backyard. The selection in that case would depend on whether an all-purpose tree is desired or a tree for making cider. For an all-purpose tree, I usually recommend the Liberty apple because I find it is the easiest tree for people who don't wish to apply chemical spray treatments. The fruit is also quite good (although not the best), keeps well, and can be used for many purposes, including cider. Last and not least, trees of this variety are very easily found in any gardening center. If only one tree for cider is wanted, to be eventually blended with some other apples that could be bought from a grower or found in wild or unattended trees, then Yarlington Mill or Dabinett would be the best selections in my opinion. Yarlington Mill could be favored in a colder location where there is no fireblight pressure, while Dabinett may perform better in a warmer zone. Again, it is possible to graft more than one variety onto a single tree.

New England: Steve Wood, Farnum Hill Ciders

When I went to interview Steve Wood (see previous section), I also asked him for his varietal recommendations. His orchard is located in western New Hampshire, in USDA zone 5, an area where the growing season is a good three weeks longer than in my own orchard, and where summer temperatures are also warmer. This makes a large difference, and some varieties that don't ripen their fruits properly up north do so perfectly in Steve's orchard. Here are his most recommended varieties:

- For low-acidity varieties with a hard and bitter tannin, his favorite is Dabinett. He also has Chisel Jersey and Ellis Bitter, which do well, too.
- For low-acidity varieties with soft and rather astringent tannin, his favorite is Yarlington Mill, although he cautions about its susceptibility to fireblight. He also recommends Somerset Redstreak, Harry Master's Jersey, and Major.
- For high-sugar/high-acid varieties, Steve mostly uses some flavorful heirloom varieties; among his favorites are Esopus Spitzenburg, Wickson, Ashmead's Kernel, Ribston Pippin, and Golden Russet. He also uses the two English bittersharp cider apples, Stoke Red and Kingston Black. In the case of the Kingston Black, however, he doesn't think it blends well, and he prefers to use it for making a single-variety cider.
- In a mixed orchard, he would also have some Idared, Golden Delicious, and Elstar. These are commercial eating varieties of good quality when well grown that can also be used in the cider blend.
- Steve has a weak spot for the famous French apple Calville blanc d'hiver, although he doesn't particularly recommend it for cider. This is an apple of outstanding flavor that is mostly used for cooking but is also great for fresh eating. He grows them to perfection! I have tried to grow this apple in my orchard, but it was a complete failure there.

When asked about varieties that didn't do so well in his orchard, Steve mentioned he has been displeased by Michelin, and he also warns about some Tremlett's Bitter and Yarlington Mill that are propagated in America but are not the true variety. There is also the Foxwhelp (whether this is a true Foxwhelp or not) propagated in America that he doesn't recommend.

And for a very small mixed orchard of six trees, Steve would restrain himself and plant Dabinett, Yarlington Mill, Esopus Spitzenburg, Golden Russet, Wickson, and Calville blanc d'hiver. This selection includes different types that can be used for cooking, processing, eating, and cider.

Canadian Maritime Provinces: John Brett, Tideview Cider

John Brett is co-owner of Tideview Cider, one of the leading cideries in the Canadian Maritime provinces. Tideview ciders have earned several awards, and in particular their Heritage Dry won a gold medal and an honorable mention Best of Show in 2011 at the Great Lakes International Cider and Perry Competition (GLINTCAP). Their apples are grown in the Annapolis Valley of Nova Scotia, Canadian hardiness zone 5, where the soils are fertile and the climate ideal for apple growing. John commented on his preferred varieties:

Apple varieties we particularly like to use in our cider blends are: Golden Russet, Ribston Pippin, Bishop Pippin (also known as Yellow Bellflower), Cox's Orange Pippin, Northern Spy, Tompkins King, and Jonagold. As for eating apples, I'd go with that same list plus: Crispin [also known as Mutsu], Golden Delicious, Cortland, and Empire. If it is absolutely fresh and crisp, I am also very fond of McIntosh.

British Columbia and Pacific Northwest Region: Derek Bisset

Derek Bisset is a small-scale amateur apple grower and cider maker in Langley, in the southern part of British Columbia, Canadian hardiness zone 8. This is a typical maritime climate with wet and mild winters and a long growing season. Similar climates are found in Washington and Oregon along the US Pacific coast.

One particularity of this climate is the pressure from anthracnose canker, which causes problems with many apple varieties in such wet climates. All varieties may be affected, but some more than others. For example, Derek doesn't recommend Michelin because it is extremely susceptible. The varieties recommended below generally have moderate resistance to anthracnose, although they may still be affected.

Derek has done extensive varietal testing in his orchard since 1990 and is an active member of the British Columbia Fruit Testing Association (BCFTA). His favorite and most recommended varieties for a small cider orchard would be:

- For low-acidity and high-tannin apples, Yarlington Mill, Dabinett, Chisel Jersey, and Marechal.
- Apples selected as sharper varieties for blending would be Locard vert, Belle de Boskoop, Gravenstein, Golden Russet, and Tompkins King. Locard vert is a well-known French cider apple, not widely available in North America, but it may be procured via the BCFTA.

And additionally, for dessert and cooking varieties, Derek would select Suntan, Egremont Russet, Cox's Orange Pippin, and Northern Spy as eaters and Bramley's Seedling and Bountiful as cookers. As Derek says, this selection is according to his very personal choices, but all these varieties perform well in his orchard, generally have good productivity, and are relatively trouble-free.

COLORADO AND ROCKY MOUNTAIN REGION: DICK DUNN

Dick Dunn is a longtime cider maker who grows apples in Hygiene, Colorado, at an elevation of 5,200 feet (1,680 m), and on the boundary between USDA zones 4 and 5. This region generally has abundant sunshine and a dry climate with cold nights, the combination of which tends to produce fruit with higher than average sugar and acidity levels.

Dick is cofounder and president of the Rocky Mountain Cider Association and was the principal author of the Beer Judge Certification Program (BJCP) cider guidelines that are used for competitions. But he is better known as the man behind the Cider Digest since 1994, and as such he has sparked very useful discussions among both amateur and commercial cider makers in North America. Dick has grown and tested over sixty varieties of apples, and his recommendations for a small cider orchard are given here in order of preference:

- Baldwin: valuable multipurpose, great in all categories—eating, cooking, and cider. Mild sharp, good in blend or as a single-variety cider.
- Cortland: good multipurpose, good addition to a cider blend and as a single-variety cider in this area.
- Golden Russet: sweet to slightly sharp; strong, rich flavor with high sugar.
- White Jersey: vintage English mild bittersweet, precocious but shy cropper, high quality for tannic component.
- Somerset Redstreak: English bittersweet tending to bittersharp in this location, background variety in a blend.

- Sweet Coppin: vintage English pure sweet, precocious; helps balance over-sharp cider blends.
- Redfield: American strong bittersharp, red flesh, should be better known; a keynote in a blend because of the red color of the juice.
- Blenheim Orange: English multipurpose, particularly good for cooking; sharp, aromatic addition to cider.
- Kingston Black: vintage English bittersharp; difficult tree to manage but worth it.
- Bulmer's Norman: English bittersweet, heavy cropper, plain but useful to build tannic background of a cider.

And as a final note, Dick mentions the following good cider varieties that he has excluded because of fireblight problems he has had with them: Yarlington Mill, Brown Snout, and Harry Master's Jersey. Additionally, he has found that some English cider varieties fail to survive the winter in his region, probably because of extreme dry periods during the cold season. He believes this is the reason why Dabinett has not performed well in his orchard.

SOUTH AND MID-ATLANTIC REGIONS: CHUCK SHELTON, VINTAGE VIRGINIA APPLES

Vintage Virginia Apples is a commercial orchard owned and run by the Shelton family. They grow over 230 apple varieties, mainly heirlooms, and including many old southern apples. This orchard is located in the central part of Virginia, in USDA hardiness zone 7, an area that may be fairly representative of the growing conditions from New York to Georgia. The Sheltons also operate Albemarle Ciderworks, where Chuck Shelton is the chief cider maker. Chuck has prepared a list of his fifteen favorite apples that he uses in his ciders and that do well in this region. Most are also excellent culinary or dessert varieties. In alphabetical order they are:

- Albemarle (Newtown) Pippin
- Arkansas Black
- Ashmead's Kernel
- Baldwin
- Black Twig
- GoldRush
- Grimes Golden
- Harrison
- Hyslop Crab
- Pink Lady (Cripp's Pink)
- Stayman
- Virginia (Hewe's) Crab
- Wickson Crab
- Winesap
- York

GREAT LAKES REGION: GARY AWDEY

Gary Awdey is the president of the Great Lakes Cider and Perry Association (GLCPA), which hosts the annual Great Lakes International Cider and Perry Competition (GLINTCAP), which has become a very important and prestigious cider competition under the management of Gary and his partners. He has been a regular contributor to the Cider Digest and has presented many workshops at the Cider Days festival and elsewhere. Gary has also been a judge in national and international competitions, and his ciders have distinguished themselves in well-respected competitions in the United States, England, and Australia.

Gary is currently planting a cider orchard at his new home in Valparaiso, Indiana, in USDA hardiness zone 5. Before that, he had some cider-apple trees in Eden, New York, where he gathered a good part of his experience growing and using cider-apple varieties. The states touching the Great Lakes show an immense range of climate, from zone 2 for Hudson Bay areas of Ontario and 3 in northern Minnesota to 7 in areas of Pennsylvania and New York close to the Atlantic Ocean. The present recommendation is for areas in fairly close proximity to the lakes, which are typically in the range of zones 5 to 6. An important feature of this area is the high disease pressure from fireblight, so resistance to this disease is one of the major selection criteria for varieties grown here. For a colder location, such as Minnesota's Lake Superior lakefront, the recommendation given above for Quebec, in zone 4, may be considered.

Gary's highest-recommended varieties for the Great Lakes region are:

- English bittersweets: Dabinett and White Jersey. These will give the character of an English cider to the blend, add some astringency, and lower the acidity. They are chosen for their resistance to disease and, in the case of Dabinett, for heavy and reliable annual cropping.
- Northern Spy, a classic American late-season apple with notable resistance to fireblight, a good source of acid where needed in blending, and popular as a pie apple.
- Liberty, which blends well with Northern Spy (though it ripens earlier), is highly disease resistant, and has a full, rich flavor.
- Russets: Ashmead's Kernel and Golden Russet may be more susceptible to fireblight, but the

richness they add to the blend makes them well worth the added trouble. The famous English dessert apple Cox's Orange Pippin may also be included here, although it may be difficult to grow well in some drier localities. It blends well with Ashmead's Kernel.

- Historic American cider apples: Harrison, an eighteenth-century New Jersey apple, and Virginia (Hewe's) Crab, a distinctly flavored early-eighteenth-century apple that contains higher tannins than most American varieties. Both Harrison and Virginia Crab yield a dark, sugar-rich, almost viscous juice when pressed.
- GoldRush, a very late harvested, modern apple with great flavor and high disease resistance.
- Winter Banana, a nineteenth-century Indiana apple, is regaining popularity in the region and adds fruity notes in a blend.

In addition to these apples, Gary recommends the Gelbmostler pear for perry makers. This is an astringent pear that blends well with the commonly available dessert pears.

CONCLUDING REMARKS

We have seen above a total of sixty-two apple varieties that have been recommended by seven experienced cider apple growers and cider makers from different regions of North America. For each of those experts, the recommended list represents the best varietal selection that could be planted for making a quality cider in their respective regions. The first thing that strikes me when I look at these lists is the great diversity of the recommendations. Of the sixty-two varieties mentioned, forty are recommended by only one of our experts. This is 65 percent,

almost two-thirds of the total number! This shows more than anything else that no recommendation is universal and that any cider maker considering the planting of an orchard should be ready to experiment in order to find the varieties that will work best for that specific location. Another interesting point is that two of our experts use exclusively North American varieties for their ciders, while the other five like to use European cider apples blended with North American varieties.

I would also like to emphasize that the Golden Russet apple is in the top list of six of our experts, which demonstrates the great quality and adaptability of this apple. It should certainly be among the very first varieties to be considered by any cider-apple grower in any part of North America. We then have six varieties that appear in the top list of three of our experts: Ashmead's Kernel, Cortland, Cox's Orange Pippin, Dabinett, Northern Spy, and Yarlington Mill. These represent two English bittersweet cider apples, two English dessert apples, and two classic American apples. And interestingly, all of these seven top-recommended apples are more than one hundred years old, the youngest of the group being Cortland, which was propagated from an 1898 pip.

As a final note, just because none of our invited experts has suggested a particular variety for a region doesn't mean the variety wouldn't succeed there! It may simply indicate they haven't tried it, or maybe their trees are still too young to warrant a recommendation, or maybe it simply isn't in the top ten favorites because of personal preferences but would be the eleventh. So don't stop yourself from trying a variety because it wasn't on the list. It might still be great for you.

◀ 5·3 ▶
Directory of Apple Varieties

The selection of varieties for a cider orchard is very important. You have to choose varieties that have excellent properties for cider making but will also succeed in the climatic conditions and the soil where the trees will grow. Moreover, you will need many varieties, such that every year there will be enough of the low-acidity apples to blend with the high-sugar ones. And you will need to consider that many varieties have a strong alternating habit and will produce just every other year.

In the following directory, I will not attempt to include all the varieties that are suitable for making a good-quality cider, as there are simply too many to mention. I will, however, try to include:

- Those that I myself use for cider.
- The varieties that I have tested, successfully or not.
- The most important French and English cider apples.
- The most important North American varieties that have a good reputation for cider.
- Those that have been recommended by more than one of our invited experts.

For many apple and pear varieties that I have tested and used for cider, I have done some analysis of the juice, and I will indicate the results obtained as follows:

- Sugar content, indicated by a specific density reading (SG).

- Acidity content, measured by titration (TA) and expressed in grams of malic acid per liter of juice.

I give the average value obtained for all the samples I have analyzed, plus, in parentheses, the minimum and maximum values observed. The following observations are also indicated:

- The tannin level and type, which are evaluated simply by tasting the juice.
- The juice yield, which is evaluated as the quantity of juice obtained in relation to the quantity of apples pressed. I will not give values here, as the extraction is greatly dependent upon the type of equipment used. However, the relative evaluation may be useful.
- Comments on the dates of harvest and pressing, as well as some cultural characteristics.

For an apple variety to make a positive contribution to a cider, it should have **at least one** of the following qualities:

- A high concentration of sugar to produce the alcohol,
- A moderate or low level of acidity to balance the blend,
- Some tannin to give body and mouthfeel.

When an apple is a known *triploid,* which means it contains a third set of chromosomes and its pollen may not pollinate other varieties, I will note this, as it may be an important selection criteria, especially in a small orchard planting.

For some of the apples for which I haven't done juice tests, when available I will give similar information that comes from the following references:

- For English cider apples: Copas, *A Somerset Pomona* (2001).
- For French cider apples: Boré and Fleckinger, *Pommiers à cidre, variétés de France* (1997).

In some cases I have adjusted the numbers for the units used here. For example, in the French reference, the densities are expressed as volumic mass and the acidity as meq/L. I have converted these into SG and g/L of equivalent malic acid. For the tannin, I use g/L of equivalent tannic acid as the base unit.

Apple Varieties

Ashmead's Kernel
Ashmead's Kernel is an English dessert apple that originated in Gloucester by 1720. It is of average size and entirely russeted. It somewhat resembles Golden Russet, which is better known in North America, but the taste is different and much sharper. It is used by many cider makers in England and in the United States, where it is well liked for its high flavor and sugar concentration. Its acidity is also very high, so it will need to be blended with juice from low-acidity varieties. This apple is currently being tested in my orchard in zone 4, where it has shown good winter hardiness.

The tree is just starting to bear and hasn't given enough fruit yet to permit an analysis of the juice. Ashmead's Kernel has been recommended for cider by our experts from New England, Virginia, and the Great Lakes regions. Recent investigation has determined that this variety is triploid (this is not mentioned in older references) and thus requires at least two other trees that bloom around the same time for reliable cross-pollination.

Ashton Bitter
An English early season cider apple, Ashton Bitter was introduced in 1985 by the Long Ashton Research Station from a cross of Dabinett × Stoke Red done in 1947. It is a "full bittersweet" apple, whose complete description may be found in Copas (2001). It was planted in many modern bush orchards in England during the 1990s and is currently being tested in my orchard but hasn't fruited yet.

Baldwin
This apple has been used for more than 200 years for cider making in the United States and is still used by many. In particular, I have had some Baldwin cider from West County Cider in Massachusetts a few years ago. It is also popular in the Great Lakes area and has been highly recommended by our experts for the Rocky Mountains and Virginia. The Baldwin is a triploid, ripens late to very late, and is generally considered hardy to zone 5.

Banane amère
Number of samples tested: 8
Sugar: medium to high, SG 1.059 (1.050–1.067)
Acidity: low, TA 2.4 g/L (1.3–3.6)
Tannin: high, juice very bitter
Juice yield: low

Harvest date: late September to early October; pressing season: late

Cultural notes: good hardiness, medium scab sensitivity

This apple is from a huge multitrunk seedling tree that I discovered growing on my property. It is inedible, but it has excellent qualities for cider making: it is very bitter, with a faint banana aroma, and hence I named it Banane amère, which would translate as "bitter banana" in English. (See figure 5.2.) This tree is about 50 feet high, and its lowest branches are still too high to pick even with a ladder! So I harvest the apples on the ground when they fall, usually by the end of September or beginning of October. The Banane amère apples normally reach 2.5 inches across and are mostly green with a bit of pale red. Some years the fruits gets scab fairly badly, but in most years they are almost clean of it. I started to propagate it in 2005, and it is currently being tested by apple growers and cider makers in a variety of regions to assess its adaptability. One nursery in Ontario has started to sell trees.

This apple would be classified as a full bittersweet with hard tannins. It shows some similarities with Yarlington Mill, but the latter has a milder tannin and doesn't always ripen perfectly in this climate. Banane amère is a first-class cider apple, suitable in late-season blends, mostly with table apples that have a lot of acidity and no bitterness. It adds a lot of body and tannin to the cider and can give the character of an English cider to a blend of juices with no such character. However, in my experience, it should not be used in a ratio exceeding 25 percent of the blend, as the cider may become too harsh because of the tannin.

Figure 5.2. Banane amère

Belle de Boskoop

Number of samples tested: 3

Sugar: very high, SG 1.070 (1.066–1.074)

Acidity: very high, TA 12.8 g/L (11.6–13.4)

Tannin: low

Juice yield: high

Harvest date: late September;
   pressing season: late

Cultural notes: very vigorous, triploid,
   good hardiness, no scab issue

Belle de Boskoop (figure 5.3) is a Dutch apple, discovered in 1856 and generally considered to be a mutation of Reinette Montfort. The original name is Schoener von Boskoop, and it is often called simply Boskoop. It is popular in France, in particular in the northern part of the country. This is an all-purpose apple, good for dessert, cooking, and cider. The fruit is large and beautiful, heavily russeted and with an excellent flavor with a hint of lemon taste. It is one of my favorites, and I consider it a first-choice apple for cider with its very high sugar concentration, though one has to be careful with its acidity, which will need to be blended down with some low-acidity varieties.

Bilodeau

Number of samples tested: 9

Sugar: high, SG 1.065 (1.050–1.076)

Acidity: high, TA 7.5 g/L (6.2–8.9)

Tannin: medium, juice slightly astringent

Juice yield: medium to high

Harvest date: early to mid-September;
   first pressing season

Figure 5.3. Belle de Boskoop

Cultural notes: good vigor, excellent hardiness,
no scab issue

Bilodeau (figure 5.4) is a large crabapple that appeared as a tagging error from a nursery-bought tree—an error that turned out to be very beneficial, as this apple is of an exceptional quality for fresh eating, jelly, and cider. I named it Bilodeau after the name of the person who gave me grafting wood from it and who got this tree by mistake around 1985. It is small, usually 1¾ inches (40–45 mm) across, and very beautiful, bright yellow covered with a nice red, some years with varying amount of russet. It never gets any scab. The tree is hardy and vigorous.

I have never been able to ascertain if it is a named variety and to identify it. It mostly looks like the Robin crab, but it has some notable differences. I showed some of the fruits to a cider maker in Virginia, who thought it could possibly be the Virginia (or Hewe's) Crab, which is a famous cider apple in that region. But I recently had fruit from my own Virginia Crab graft, and they are definitely different, with Bilodeau ripening about two weeks earlier in my orchard.

This small apple is a first-class cider variety for first-season blends. It makes a perfect blend with Douce de Charlevoix, as both apples complement each other very well, Bilodeau bringing the sugar while Douce de Charlevoix mellows the acidity and adds its mild bitterness, resulting in a cider with remarkable depth considering its early season. Some years the acidity content is lower, and Bilodeau can then be used to make a very nice single-variety cider.

Figure 5.4. Bilodeau

The Difficult Birth of a New Cider Apple Variety: Extract from a Letter to my Friend Martin, 1997

I also include some wood of a crab that I call Bilodeau. This one really has a strange story. A small stick was given to me by the friend of a friend whose name is Claude Bilodeau (hence the name I give to the variety). This guy had bought this tree from a nursery and it was supposed to be a Ure pear. At the time, I didn't know pears very well—I thought the wood looked like apple, but maybe it could be a pear. . . . So I grafted it—only one graft, as it was a small piece—on a young apple tree (remember I used to make those intergenous grafts?). Some time later, I went to inspect my graft, and there was a beautiful green caterpillar happily eating the second half of the third and last bud of my Ure pear! A few minutes later and it would have been gone forever. I'm sure you would have done exactly the same thing that I did. Anyway, the remainder of the bud survived and started to grow vigorously. Before the end of the summer, I was already considering this graft as my best success in intergenous grafts. But I still thought the leaves looked a lot like apple leaves, and not very much like the leaves of my Clapp pear tree, which was my only pear at the time. I explained this by the fact that Ure was a *P. ussuriensis* hybrid, and these

hybrids probably look more like apples. I lost my illusions a little while later when I bought my Golden Spice, which looked a lot more like the Clapp than like my pseudo Ure. But the young tree was looking good and I let it go. In the meanwhile, I ordered a true Ure pear. After that, the poor tree had to survive two other misfortunes: the rootstock started to experience collar rot, but I've been able to save it, and in the big bear fall, it was completely put down by the bears, who seemed to enjoy the fruits. I put it back up and it survived that also. Now, what's most interesting of this crab is that it is, by far, the nicest-tasting and best-looking crab I've seen yet. It averages 40–45 mm and is bright yellow, half covered with bright red—no stripes. It has never had a spot of scab yet. It is crisp and better than most apples for eating off the tree. The juice contains more sugar than any other apple juice I've tested yet, but at the same time has a good sharpness that keeps it well balanced. I haven't yet had enough production to have it make a substantial ratio in a cider batch, but I'm convinced it will make excellent cider. It is midseason, being ripe a bit before Lobo and McIntosh in September. So I would be pleased if you tried it.

Bramley's Seedling

This is a very popular cooking apple in England. It has a low sugar content, a high acidity, and little tannin. According to Lea (2008), the following numbers are typical of the variety: SG 1.040, TA > 10 g/L, tannin < 0.5 g/L. As such these properties are not interesting at all for cider making. However, Bramleys are often used by English cider makers to raise the acidity of their blends, which consist mostly of low-acid bittersweet apples. I have tested Bramley in my orchard, but I found it insufficiently hardy for this zone 4 climate. It is a triploid variety.

Bramtôt

A French cider apple from Normandy introduced in 1872, Bramtôt is of the *douce amère* class (similar to bittersweet) and harvested midseason. It is well esteemed in France. I have this apple currently under trial at my orchard, but it is still too early to know if it will succeed in a cold climate. Boré and Fleckinger (1997) give the following properties for its juice: SG 1.069, TA 2.3 g/L, tannin 3.5 g/L. Some North American growers also report very high sugar content with this apple.

Breakwell's Seedling

Breakwell's Seedling is an English cider apple of the medium bittersharp type. It is a seedling of

Foxwhelp introduced in 1890. I have tested it in my orchard, but the variety didn't perform satisfactorily for me: although it appears to be hardy enough, it is not healthy, the fruit ripens too early, and the sugar concentration is quite low.

Britegold

Number of samples tested: 8
Sugar: medium, SG 1.054 (1.046–1.063)
Acidity: low, TA 2.4 g/L (1.8–3.6)
Tannin: low
Juice yield: medium
Harvest date: mid-September;
    first pressing season
Cultural notes: good vigor, good hardiness,
    productive, scab-resistant

Britegold (figure 5.5) is a Canadian variety introduced in 1980, a cross of Sandel × Ottawa 522. This is a scab-free apple that contains the Vf gene

Figure 5.5. Britegold

of resistance. It was introduced as a hardy and scab-resistant substitute for Golden Delicious. It is remarkably beautiful, of a golden yellow ground color with a red blush, and medium size.

This is a sweet apple that contains very little acidity, and thus it is not very interesting for fresh eating: it tastes a bit bland. I would not recommend it for cooking for the same reason. However, I have started using it for cider, and I find it very useful in a blend to reduce the acidity of the must, especially given the numerous high-acidity varieties that we have here in North America.

Brown Snout

An English, late-ripening cider apple of the bittersweet class, Brown Snout originated around the middle of the nineteenth century. It was imported into Quebec during the 1970s and was grown at the Frelighsburg research station. A full description is given in the book *Our Apples* by Khanizadeh and Cousineau (1998). It is currently under trial in my orchard but doesn't seem to feel at home there: it lacks vigor, and the few fruits produced did not develop well. Copas (2001) gives the following analysis of its juice: SG 1.053, TA 2.4 g/L, tannin 2.4 g/L.

Brown's Apple

Number of samples tested: 13
Sugar: medium, SG 1.052 (1.045–1.065)
Acidity: high to very high, TA 9.7 g/L (8.0–12.5)
Tannin: low to medium
Juice yield: medium
Harvest date: late September;
  pressing season: October
Cultural notes: good vigor and hardiness;
  no scab issue

Brown's Apple is a vintage-quality, sharp English cider apple that has been popular in Devon since the 1920s. Copas (2001) gives the following results for its juice: SG 1.048, TA 6.7 g/L, tannin 1.2 g/L. Although the sugar content is similar, the acidity of the fruit grown in my orchard is much higher than that grown in England. This makes the variety much less attractive for cider. This is unfortunate, because the variety is well adapted and grows and produces successfully.

Bulmer's Norman

Number of samples tested: 11
Sugar: medium, SG 1.056 (1.048–1.066)
Acidity: low, TA 3.4 g/L (2.7–4.9)
Tannin: medium
Juice yield: medium to high
Harvest date: mid-September;
  first pressing season
Cultural notes: triploid, very vigorous, good
  hardiness, productive, no scab issue

Bulmer's Norman (figure 5.6) is a medium bittersweet English cider apple that was introduced by the famous cider-making Bulmer family in the early 1900s. As the name indicates, it probably originally came from Normandy, or from seeds imported from Normandy, but it is not known there, at least under this name. In England it is not generally viewed as an apple of great value. However, as grown in my orchard, I consider it a first-choice apple for first-season cider. It blends very well with the Bilodeau and other apples of the same season and is very useful to reduce the acidity of the blend and give some tannin. This variety is one of the most successful of the English cider apples that I have tested.

This apple is far from beautiful. However, it sizes well and is a greenish color with a slight red

Figure 5.6. Bulmer's Norman

bloom. It is not sensitive to scab in my orchard, which is surprising, as the English authors usually mention it as being susceptible.

Chestnut Crab

Obtained from a cross of Malinda × Siberian crab *(Malus baccata)*, the Chestnut Crab was introduced in Minnesota in 1946. This crabapple is beautiful, its skin a bronze color with dark red stripes, and of a fair size for a crab, reaching 2 inches (50 mm) across. Its taste is somewhat peculiar, often described as "nutty," a quality also indicated by its name.

Chestnut is currently under trial in my orchard, but is suffering a bad canker. Some preliminary juicing tests with two samples indicate an excellent sugar richness and an average acidity. These

results are encouraging, but it is still too early to recommend it, considering its susceptibility to canker and the fact it hasn't been very productive to date. It usually ripens by mid-September. There are, however, quite a few growers for which this variety is successful, and it is certainly of great quality.

Chisel Jersey

Chisel Jersey is an important English cider apple of the full bittersweet type, and it is generally recommended for planting in the modern intensive bush orchards in England. It did not thrive in my orchard, probably because of some lack of hardiness in zone 4. Many cider-apple growers in warmer areas such as Massachusetts or southern Vermont and New Hampshire (zones 5 and 6) grow it with success. According to Copas (2001),

Figure 5.7. Coat Jersey

the juice has the following properties: SG 1.059, TA 2.2 g/L, tannin 4 g/L. It is highly recommended by two of our experts for the Pacific Northwest and New England regions.

Coat Jersey
Number of samples tested: 3
Sugar: high, SG 1.067 (1.064–1.068)
Acidity: low, TA 2.7 g/L (1.3–3.6)
Tannin: high, bitter juice
Juice yield: low to medium
Harvest date: late September or early October; pressing season: mid-October to December
Cultural notes: medium vigor, good hardiness, low sensitivity to scab

Coat Jersey (figure 5.7) is a full bittersweet English cider apple whose origin dates from the late nineteenth century. It is well liked in England and is planted in modern orchards. Strangely, Copas (2001) says it is very sensitive to scab, while in my orchard it has been rather resistant to this fungus. Further, Copas gives Coat Jersey a rather low SG of 1.047, while my own tests have shown much higher sugar content. From this we may ask whether the Coat Jersey found in North America is true to its name. But even if it isn't, it is nonetheless an excellent cider apple. The variety has adapted well to my orchard conditions and gives fruits of great quality for cider, though it hasn't been very vigorous or very productive yet.

Cortland

Number of samples tested: 61

Sugar: medium to high, SG 1.059 (1.053–1.072)

Acidity: medium to high, TA 7.3 g/L (3.6–11.1)

Tannin: low to average, sometimes
    slightly astringent

Juice yield: medium

Harvest date: early October; pressing season:
    mid-October to December

Cultural notes: good vigor and hardiness,
    prone to scab

Cortland is the first commercially successful apple to have been deliberately crossed by introduction of the pollen of one selected variety into the pistil of another. Spencer A. Beach, the author of the well-known *The Apples of New York* (1905), made this cross in 1898 between Ben Davis and McIntosh in Geneva, New York. The Cortland apple was introduced in 1915, and it is still an important commercial variety in many parts of the United States and Canada.

When I bought my property in 1982, the old orchard included eighteen large Cortland trees plus a few McIntosh and a Fameuse. Hence, Cortland has always made up the largest part of my harvest, and I have used it a lot in cider making. It is excellent as a blending base to which some high-sugar apples and some low-acid and tannic apples may be added. Some years, when the acidity is not too high, I can make a very good single-variety cider with it. As grown in my orchard, Cortland is definitely a first-choice apple for cider. However, commercially grown Cortland apples don't always have the same quality. Also, from discussions I've had with cider makers in warmer regions who don't appreciate it as much as I do, it would appear that the quality of this apple is much better when it is grown in northern and colder climates. In addition to the cold Quebec region, it has been recommended by our experts for the Canadian Maritimes and the Rocky Mountains.

Cox's Orange Pippin

This venerable dessert apple is one of the most highly acclaimed of all English apples. Its flavor is considered as the most complex, aromatic, and rich of all apples. It is said to be a seedling of Ribston Pippin, possibly crossed by Blenheim Orange in 1832. The tree will not grow well and be productive everywhere, however. It prefers a humid and oceanic climate and will not tolerate colder winter temperatures than those seen in zone 5. Its culture is considered to be difficult. For cider, the fruit is often considered as too expensive to grow in large enough quantities, but in the regions where it thrives it is excellent. It is used in England for the eastern style of cider and has been recommended by three of our experts for the Canadian Maritimes, Pacific Northwest, and Great Lakes regions.

Dabinett

Dabinett is an English cider apple of the full bittersweet category and of vintage quality. It is possibly a seedling of Chisel Jersey, discovered in Somerset around 1850. It is presently one of the most popular varieties in modern orchards in England, where it is particularly productive. Its juice properties according to Copas (2001) are: SG 1.057, TA 1.8 g/L, tannin 2.9 g/L. Dabinett is also grown by many cider-apple growers in America, where it is one of the best performing among the English bittersweet group. It does well in areas of high fireblight pressure and is hardy to zone 5 but appears to lack hardiness in colder zones. It has been recommended by three of our experts for New England, the Pacific Northwest, and the Great Lakes regions.

Douce de Charlevoix

Number of samples tested: 22

Sugar: medium, SG 1.052 (1.045–1.060)

Acidity: low, TA 2.9 g/L (2.2–4.0)

Tannin: medium, astringent juice, slightly bitter

Juice yield: high

Harvest date: early to mid September;
    first pressing season

Cultural notes: vigorous, excellent hardiness,
    no sensitivity to scab

I discovered the Douce de Charlevoix apple in the village of Baie-Saint-Paul, Charlevoix county, Quebec. It appears to be from a seedling rootstock that overgrew the grafted variety. In fact, I thought I was taking grafting wood from the grafted variety, but I didn't have much experience at the time (it was in 1984), and by mistake I took the wood from the rootstock sucker. This error was fortunate, as this apple turned out to be an excellent cider apple with low acidity and a slight bitterness.

Douce de Charlevoix (figure 5.8) is a very handsome apple that reaches about 2.5 inches (65 mm) across; it is rather conical in shape and striped orange-red on a greenish background. It is productive annually, vigorous, and perfectly hardy in zone 4, though its hardiness in colder locations is still unknown. In my orchard it gets very little scab even if I don't spray. The juice has a nice flavor with a mild bitterness. Some cider-apple growers are currently testing it in different locations, which should eventually permit us to assess its qualities in various growing conditions. One nursery has recently started to sell trees. This is a first-class apple for early-season cider. It blends nicely with the Bilodeau in particular and gives a touch of bitterness and a mouthfeel that are quite remarkable for such an early-season cider.

Figure 5.8. Douce de Charlevoix

Empire

This apple, developed at the Geneva Agricultural Experiment Station in western New York from a McIntosh × Delicious cross, was introduced in 1966. It doesn't perform well in my orchard: it lacks vigor, and the fruit doesn't ripen well most years. Its properties for cider appear to be similar to that of the Cortland apple. The Empire apple is used a lot by commercial cider makers in the warmer areas of Quebec.

Fameuse

Number of samples tested: 6

Sugar: medium to high, SG 1.058 (1.050–1.066)

Acidity: medium to high, TA 6.8 g/L (4.0–9.8)

Tannin: low to medium

Juice yield: medium

Harvest date: early October; pressing season:
mid-October to November

Cultural notes: medium vigor, good hardiness,
prone to scab

Fameuse (sometimes called Snow or Snow Apple) is one of the oldest apples to have been grown in North America, dating back to the French regime in Canada. In the beginning of the twentieth century, growers ceased to plant it, and it was replaced by the McIntosh variety, which was more profitable in commercial culture. In fact, Fameuse is widely considered to be the parent of McIntosh.

I have an old tree of Fameuse. The tree broke in 1992 but has survived and keeps on producing fruit despite being laid on the ground. The juice obtained from these apples is very similar to that of Cortland and may be used in the same manner. However, if I had to choose between the two varieties, I would choose the Cortland, as it is more productive and somewhat less prone to scab.

Foxwhelp

The true Foxwhelp is an English bittersharp cider apple that dates back to the seventeenth century. This original strain might not exist anymore—we aren't sure—but it has many descendants that are still grown. The better known of them are Broxwood Foxwhelp and Bulmer's Foxwhelp, both of which are considered vintage-quality medium bittersharp apples. In the *Herefordshire Pomona* (Hogg & Bull, 1878), we find the descriptions of many other apples that are related to the Foxwhelp but are nowadays forgotten: Rejuvenated Foxwhelp, Bastard Foxwhelp, Red Foxwhelp, Black Foxwhelp, and others. The true Foxwhelp was renowned for its extremely high acidity (in the range of 20 g/L of malic acid).

Unfortunately, the Foxwhelp available in North America doesn't correspond to the description of any of the Foxwhelps from England, and it is believed some error was made when the scion wood was collected. In fact, this variety is often called "Fauxwhelp" within the cider community of North America. I have grown this Fauxwhelp and didn't see any value in it for cider making. Other cider makers, however, appreciate it and think it is a decent apple with mild to moderate bitterness.

Fréquin rouge

A French cider apple from Normandy, Fréquin rouge is of the category *amère* and ripens in the second season of maturation in France. Its origin is ancient; it was a very popular variety in most cider areas of France by the end of the nineteenth century, and many authors of that time considered it as an important variety. Nowadays there are many variants with distinct names, such as Fréquin rouge petit or Fréquin rouge de la Guerche, and it is not certain whether all those named simply

Fréquin rouge belong to the same variety. I have recently grafted the Fréquin rouge that is available in North America, but I still haven't seen the fruit and can't yet be sure if it corresponds to the description of one of the French types.

Geneva

Number of samples tested: 3
Sugar: low, SG 1.044 (1.040–1.047)
Acidity: very high, TA 11.3 g/L (10.7–11.6)
Tannin: medium
Juice yield: high
Harvest date: mid-September;
   first pressing season

Cultural notes: good vigor and hardiness,
   no scab issue

During the 1920s there was a program at the Ottawa Experimental Farm in Canada for the development of decorative crabapple varieties with pink or red blossoms. As a parent, they used *Malus niedzwetzkyana,* which originated in central Asia and which carries a gene for colored flowers and red fruit flesh. The varieties issued from this program were called the Rosybloom series. The Geneva (figure 5.9) is one of these Rosybloom crabs, and it is sometimes used for cider making because of the dark ruby flesh of the fruit, which gives a brilliant

Figure 5.9. Geneva

red juice. If it weren't for this red juice, however, we wouldn't think of using the Geneva for cider, as its other properties are not very good, in particular its low sugar content and the very high acidity of the juice.

I often wish we could produce a rosé cider of good quality, but it is very difficult to achieve this with the Geneva: if we use it in a blend, we need to combine it with an apple that has a very high sugar concentration and a very low acidity, which is quite rare. Further, the blending will fade the color. The Cidrerie Michel Jodoin in Quebec does produce a rosé cider with this apple, but Mr. Jodoin will not reveal his recipe.

Figure 5.10. Golden Nugget

Golden Nugget

Number of samples tested: 3

Sugar: high to very high, SG 1.068 (1.064–1.074)

Acidity: medium to high, TA 7.3 g/L (5.3–8.5)

Tannin: low

Juice yield: low to medium

Harvest date: mid- to late September;
   pressing season: October

Cultural notes: good vigor and hardiness,
   no scab issue

Golden Nugget (figure 5.10) is a cross of Golden Russet × Cox's Orange Pippin introduced by the Kentville Station in Nova Scotia in 1964. It is a small apple that just reaches 2½ inches (60 mm) across in my orchard in a good year. Its taste is exceptionally rich, very sugary and delicious. Some

years the skin may crack, but this is only cosmetic and will not affect the quality of the cider. Golden Nugget is a first-class and very commendable apple for eating and for cider. Unfortunately, it is not well known and is difficult to find.

Golden Russet

Number of samples tested: 7

Sugar: very high, SG 1.074 (1.064–1.096)

Acidity: high to very high, TA 9.2 g/L (7.1–13.4)

Tannin: low

Juice yield: medium

Harvest date: October; pressing season: late

Cultural notes: medium vigor, good hardiness,
   no scab issue

This apple has one of the longest traditions in cider making in North America. It first appeared in the United States around 1850, but it could be of English or French origin, perhaps dating back to the 1700s. Beach, in his *The Apples of New York* (1905), mentions it as being excellent for cider. And in fact its great richness in sugar combined with a good flavor and aroma makes it a high-quality addition to a late-season cider. Many authors have mentioned that it can make a good single-variety cider. However, as grown in my orchard, the Golden Russet's acidity is quite high, and it is preferable to blend it with a low-acidity apple. When grown in warmer locations, it seems the acidity is lower.

Besides being a first-class apple for cider, Golden Russet is also an exceptional eating apple that keeps well until spring. This apple is on the recommended lists of six of our experts, which demonstrates its great quality and adaptability. It is one of the first varieties to choose when planting a cider orchard.

Harrison

Harrison is one of the few American apples to have been specially grown for cider. It was quite popular in New Jersey during the nineteenth century, and its qualities for cider were described by Coxe in 1817. It is known for giving a rich, syrupy, and very dark juice, this darkness indicating a good tannin content. It was long thought that the variety was lost, but it was rediscovered in 1976 near an old cider mill in New Jersey. In recent years it has been propagated and is now grown by cider makers all around North America. It has been recommended by two of our experts, for Virginia and the Great Lakes regions. Its hardiness in locations colder than zone 5 is still unknown.

Harry Master's Jersey

This is an English cider apple, from Somerset, whose origin dates back to the end of the nineteenth century. It is a medium-full bittersweet of vintage quality and ripens rather late in the season.

Harry Master's Jersey is used a lot in modern English bush orchards. Copas (2001) gives the following properties for its juice: SG 1.056, TA 2 g/L, tannin 3.2 g/L. Its susceptibility to fireblight has been noted, which limits its use in North America.

Honeygold

Number of samples tested: 14
Sugar: medium to high, SG 1.060 (1.052–1.069)
Acidity: medium to high, TA 6.1 g/L (3.6–9.8)
Tannin: low
Juice yield: medium
Harvest date: late September; pressing season: October and November
Cultural notes: medium vigor, good hardiness, scab-sensitive

The Honeygold was introduced by the University of Minnesota in 1969. It was obtained from a cross of Golden Delicious × Haralson and is often considered a substitute for the Golden Delicious in colder climates.

I very much like the Honeygold for cider and consider it a first-choice apple. It is one of the few to give a juice rich in sugar, while the acidity in most years is close to the ideal for a blend. Its flavor is excellent, and I use it a lot in my late-season blends.

Jonagold

Jonagold is a 1968 introduction from the Geneva Agricultural Experiment Station in western New York, from a cross of Golden Delicious × Jonathan. It is a triploid apple, grown mostly in northern continental Europe as a commercial apple of great quality. It is also a popular variety in the Pacific Northwest and in the Canadian Maritimes. For cider, this apple has an interesting history, as it has only recently been tested for this purpose, in

England and in Washington State, and the testers were quite surprised by the quality of the cider they obtained. Our invited expert for the Canadian Maritimes region recommends it.

Kermerrien

Kermerrien is a French cider apple of the *douce-amère* category that ripens in the second season. It originated from the Quimperlé region in Brittany, where its name is written "Kêrmerien." This apple is one of the most commonly used for the traditional Breton cider. It is available in North America and is currently being tested in my orchard, where it has shown good vigor and hardiness. It is, however, still too early to evaluate it. Boré and Fleckinger (1997) give the following average properties for its juice based on seven samples: SG 1.064, TA 1.5 g/L, tannin 4.3 g/L.

King of the Pippins

See Reine des reinettes.

Kingston Black

This is an English cider apple from Somerset that first appeared at the beginning of the nineteenth century. The Kingston Black is often regarded as the perfect cider apple, one that may yield an excellent and perfectly balanced cider without blending. It is classified as a bittersharp type of vintage quality, and it ripens rather late. Copas (2001) gives the following properties for its juice: SG 1.061, TA 5.8 g/L, tannin 1.9 g/L. From these numbers we can see a high sugar content combined with an ideal acidity and moderate tannin. On the other hand, this apple has the reputation of being capricious: it doesn't succeed well in all locations and may be difficult to grow and unproductive if the conditions aren't suitable.

During Cider Days 2009 in Massachusetts, we had the privilege of tasting some excellent ciders made with Kingston Black by three US cideries: West County Cider (Massachusetts), Farnum Hill Ciders (New Hampshire), and Slyboro Cider House (New York). All of the fruit was grown at Steve Wood's Poverty Lane Orchards in New Hampshire, so this was a rare opportunity to see how three different cider makers used the same raw material and achieved somewhat different products. It also demonstrated that this exceptional apple may be grown to perfection in New England (zone 5). Its hardiness is still unknown in colder locations.

Liberty

Number of samples tested: 17
Sugar: medium to high, SG 1.058 (1.052–1.074)
Acidity: medium to high, TA 6.9 g/L (4.0–10.7)
Tannin: low
Juice yield: high
Harvest date: late September; pressing season: October and November
Cultural notes: good vigor and hardiness, genetically resistant to scab

This is a variety that was developed by Cornell University in New York State in a program aimed at breeding apple varieties genetically resistant to scab. It was introduced in 1978 and arose from a cross between Macoun and a selected variety that carries the Vf scab resistance gene. Liberty is one of the first scab-resistant apples from such a program to have some commercial success. Although most traditional apple growers didn't adopt it, it is quite popular among a good number of organic growers.

In my orchard the Liberty apple tree is my favorite tree. Note that I say *tree* and not *apple*: this tree is vigorous, naturally takes a good shape, and is easy to prune. It is also hardy and productive every year and isn't bothered by any disease—in short, the perfect tree. As for the fruit, in my opinion there are better ones, but this one is nonetheless excellent for cider as well as for eating. Thus I consider Liberty a first-choice variety, in part because the tree is so easy but also because its juice has very good properties for cider. It is in fact rather similar to the Cortland and may be used in the same manner. Liberty is the variety I recommend most often to people who want to plant just one apple tree in their backyard.

Lobo

Number of samples tested: 14
Sugar: medium, SG 1.056 (1.050–1.065)
Acidity: high, TA 8.3 g/L (6.2–10.7)
Tannin: low
Juice yield: high
Harvest date: mid-September; first pressing season
Cultural notes: good vigor and hardiness,
    prone to scab

This classic Quebec apple is a seedling of McIntosh, whose pollen parent most probably is Alexander. It was introduced in 1930 by the Ottawa Experimental Farm in Canada and selected by W. T. Macoun, who was at the time the head horticulturist of that farm. (It is, by the way, very interesting to read Macoun's own reports, as he had great influence on the development of Canadian apple growing. Some of these reports are referenced in the Bibliography.)

As grown in my orchard, Lobo is an excellent apple for first-season cider, its main drawback being its sensitivity to scab. However, I have done a few juice tests from commercially grown Lobo apples, and the results were not as good as those mentioned above: out of three samples, I got an average SG of only 1.045.

Major

Major is a typical Jersey-type variety from Somerset. It is a full bittersweet of vintage quality and ripens relatively early in the season. Copas (2001) gives the following analysis results for its juice: SG 1.054, TA 1.8 g/L, tannin 4.1 g/L. It is used in modern cider orchards in England and is appreciated for its early ripening, which permits cider makers to start the pressing season earlier. It is currently under trial in my orchard, but it hasn't fruited yet.

McIntosh

Number of samples tested: 29
Sugar: medium to very high,
    SG 1.067 (1.056–1.080)
Acidity: medium to very high, TA 9.8 g/L (4.5–16)
Tannin: low
Juice yield: low to medium
Harvest date: late September; pressing season:
    October and November
Cultural notes: good vigor and hardiness,
    prone to scab

The McIntosh really doesn't need any introduction, as it is one of the most widely grown apples in Canada and the United States. It is mostly a commercial apple, but it is also used for cider in eastern Canada and New England. Many cideries in Quebec use it as their main variety. The properties of its juice vary a lot based on the cultural practices used. In particular its susceptibility to scab in a natural (unsprayed) orchard will cause the fruit to stay small. I have sometimes seen McIntosh trees covered with apples the size of Ping-Pong balls and almost completely black from the scab. Such apples, however, yield a juice of an exceptional richness and extremely high specific gravity. It seems the scab fungus removes water from the fruit, thus concentrating the sugar and flavor. Naturally, the yield is then greatly reduced. In the years where there is less scab, the sugar and acidity content of the juice will have medium values.

Médaille d'or

The Médaille d'or apple was obtained in 1865 from a seed planted by Mr. Godard near Rouen in Normandy. It is a French cider apple classified as an *amère* variety of second-season maturation. Also grown in England, it is often described by English authors. Strangely, some authors at the end of the nineteenth century (for example Baltet, 1884) report an incredible SG of over 1.100 for this apple, while modern authors like Boré and Fleckinger (1997) give a more reasonable SG value of 1.058, with TA 2.1 g/L and tannin 4.4 g/L. I wonder if this large difference could be caused by the difference in cultural practices between the nineteenth century and now. Médaille d'or didn't survive in my orchard, obviously lacking the necessary cold resistance for my

zone 4 location. Some reports from more southern and warmer locations (i.e., zone 5 or better) indicate it performs very well and produces high-quality fruit. In New England it ripens by early October.

Michelin

A cider apple of French origin but nowadays grown primarily in England, where the Michelin was introduced in 1884. It is classified as medium bittersweet and ripens mid-season. Copas (2001) gives the following analysis results for its juice: SG 1.050, TA 2.5 g/L, tannin 2.3 g/L. It is currently under trial in my orchard but hasn't been a strong grower and seems to lack hardiness. In England the Michelin is not considered a variety of high quality but useful for its regular and heavy cropping.

Muscadet de Dieppe

Number of samples tested: 4
Sugar: medium, SG 1.058 (1.046–1.063)
Acidity: low, TA 3.1 g/L (1.8–4.5)

Figure 5.11. Muscadet de Dieppe

Tannin: medium to high, bitter juice
Juice yield: medium
Harvest date: mid-September; first pressing
    season and can be kept longer
Cultural notes: good vigor and hardiness,
    no scab issue, low productivity

Muscadet de Dieppe (figure 5.11 on page 77) is a French cider apple classified as a *douce amère* and maturing early in the season. It appeared in Normandy around 1750. It is an excellent apple used mostly for first-season cider. It adapted well and shows excellent hardiness in a cold zone 4 climate. However, it has a few drawbacks: when the summer is dry the apples fall to the ground before being mature, and it hasn't been very productive for me yet. Boré and Fleckinger (1997) give the following results from five samples tested: SG 1.057, TA 2.1 g/L, and tannin 2.5 g/L; these are very similar to my own results.

Northern Spy

This variety has been around for a long time and is one of the most important heirloom American apples. It appeared in New York State in the beginning of the nineteenth century. Beach (1905) gives a complete description with historical notes. Northern Spy is used by cider makers in many parts of the United States, notably New England and the Great Lakes, and is in the top recommended variety list of our experts from the Canadian Maritimes, Pacific Northwest, and Great Lakes regions. It ripens very late in the season, and although it is relatively hardy its fruit will not ripen properly in a colder climate with a short growing season. I have tasted ciders made from Northern Spy on many occasions, and I must confess I have never been too excited about them: I

generally found them too sharp, and they had an unusual (for me) bouquet that I didn't appreciate much. However, I think this is mainly a question of habit, as the people who regularly drink these ciders like them very much. So this is a good example of a traditional variety that gives some local character to cider.

Porter's Perfection

Number of samples tested: 3
Sugar: high, SG 1.060 (1.056–1.066)
Acidity: very high, TA 15 g/L (13–18)
Tannin: medium, juice slightly bitter
Juice yield: medium
Harvest date: October; pressing season: late
    October to December
Cultural notes: good vigor and hardiness, no scab
    issue, low productivity

Porter's Perfection is a late-season English cider apple classified as medium bittersharp. It dates back to the nineteenth century, but it started being known and propagated only around 1907. This variety has the peculiarity of often producing pairs of fused apples (see figure 5.12). As grown in my orchard, Porter's Perfection is not a very useful apple for cider because of the very high acidity of its juice. On the other hand, it seems this might be caused by local climate and growing conditions, as Copas (2001) gives the TA as 8.2 g/L, a much more reasonable value.

Redfield

Redfield is a large, red-fleshed apple obtained from a cross of Wolf River × *Malus niedzwetzkyana* and introduced by the Geneva Agricultural Experiment Station in western New York in 1938. (See the description of Geneva for more on *M.*

Figure 5.12. Porter's Perfection

niedzwetzkyana, which is the parent of most red-fleshed apple varieties.)

Redfield is one of the most beautiful trees in the orchard, with bronze-red leaves, dark reddish bark, and deep pink blossoms in the spring. The apple is absolutely no good for eating but very good for baking, making an especially good pie. West County Cider in Massachusetts makes a very good rosé cider from this apple.

Reine des reinettes

Number of samples tested: 9
Sugar: high, SG 1.061 (1.052–1.072)
Acidity: high, TA 9.8 g/L (7.6 –12.0)
Tannin: low to medium
Juice yield: medium
Harvest date: early October; pressing season:
    mid-October to December

Cultural notes: good vigor and hardiness,
    no scab issue

The origin of this apple is uncertain. It may be from the Netherlands, France, or another country in northern Europe. Many pomologists of the nineteenth century have written about its origin, giving different stories. The likeliest is that the apple appeared in the Netherlands and was named Kroon Renet. From there it would have migrated to France, probably around 1770, which is when it is first mentioned in the French literature. There it was called *Reine des reinettes,* and it became so popular it was eventually declared a French national variety. This is the apple that should be used in the preparation of the *tarte Tatin,* a classic of French pastry. From the Netherlands it would also have migrated to England (probably a little before

Figure 5.13. Reine des reinettes

1790), where it was first named Golden Winter Pearmain. Some time after, someone probably noticed that Golden Winter Pearmain was identical with Reine des reinettes, so it was dubbed King of the Pippins in England. However, someone else in England imported Reine des reinettes from France and named it Queen of the Pippins. Much confusion ensued. There would then have been in England two distinct strains of the same apple, and no one was absolutely sure if they were identical or not. Nowadays most pomologists believe all these names refer to the same apple. However, the great French pomologist of the nineteenth century, André Leroy, thought the English line of Golden Winter Pearmain and King of the Pippins was a distinct variety, although very similar.

Reine des reinettes (figure 5.13) soon became one of my favorites. In my orchard it is an excellent late apple with a strong flavor. It keeps well

and is an excellent eating apple. It is first choice for cider, with its high sugar concentration and good flavor, but it needs to be blended with low-acidity varieties.

Reine des pommes

This is a French cider apple from Brittany, classified as a *douce amère* of the second season. It is possible that there is more than one variety by this name in France because Boré and Fleckinger (1997) show a red apple, but on the Internet there are pictures of Reine des pommes that are green with some russet. It is currently under trial in my orchard, but it is still too early to evaluate it. West County Cider in Massachusetts makes a nice cider from this variety.

Ribston Pippin

Ribston Pippin is a triploid eating apple from England that also has a good reputation for cider.

Figure 5.14. Rubinette

Its origin dates back to around 1700 in Yorkshire, and it has been cultivated in America for a long time. Beach in *The Apples of New York* (1905) gives a complete description of it. It is under trial in my orchard, and preliminary results on two samples indicate an excellent richness of sugar with high acidity. Its productivity, however, is rather low, which Beach also mentions. It appears to be hardy in my cold climate and ripens late September.

Roxbury Russet

Roxbury Russet is thought to be the oldest American apple still under cultivation. It originated near Boston before 1650. It is an excellent eating apple with a rich taste and a lot of sugar and also quite sharp. It ripens a week or two before Golden Russet, around the end of September, and was considered valuable for its good storage quality; fruit can be kept in cold, humid storage until spring,

though the rough, russeted skin sometimes shrivels. It has always been highly regarded for cider. It didn't succeed in my orchard, however: I did obtain a few fruits, but they never developed well, and the tree, never vigorous, finally died. This failure probably is for other reasons than hardiness, though, as this apple is considered widely adapted and quite hardy in zone 4.

Rubinette

Number of samples tested: 4
Sugar: very high, SG 1.073 (1.064–1.086)
Acidity: high, TA 8.9 g/L (7.1–12.0)
Tannin: low
Juice yield: low to medium
Harvest date: late September to early October;
    pressing season: mid-October to December
Cultural notes: good vigor and hardiness,
    medium sensitivity to scab

Rubinette (figure 5.14, page 81), a modern table apple from Switzerland, was introduced in 1966, obtained from a cross of Golden Delicious × Cox's Orange Pippin. It is now starting to be better known and grown commercially in North America. It is a delicious apple with a rich taste. When I grafted it in 1995, I was a bit skeptical about its chances of success because neither of its parents is hardy enough for the climate of my orchard. I was wrong, however, which shows once more that we need to make trials! It is a first-class apple for cider and also very commendable for fresh eating.

Sandow

This is an underrated eating apple that was developed by Agriculture Canada at the Ottawa Experimental Farm. A natural seedling of Northern Spy that was introduced in 1935, Sandow is hardier than its parent and ripens earlier, which makes its cultivation possible in colder locations. It is under trial in my orchard, and preliminary results from two samples tested are encouraging, with a high sugar content and also a high acidity. It hasn't been very productive yet, but this may be due to the youthfulness of the tree.

Somerset Redstreak

An old English cider apple from Somerset, this is a bittersweet type that is rather astringent and of early maturation. Copas (2001) gives the following analysis results for its juice: SG 1.050, TA 1.9 g/L, tannin 3.5 g/L. It is used in modern bush orchards in England, where, however, its biennialism has been noted. Somerset Redstreak has been recommended by our experts for the New England and Rocky Mountain regions. Its winter hardiness in areas colder than zone 5 is not known.

Spartan

Spartan is one of the important commercial apples in Canada. It was introduced in 1936 by the Summerland Station in British Columbia and is from a McIntosh × Newton Pippin cross. Many cideries in Quebec use it in their blends.

Stoke Red

This is an English cider apple classified as bittersharp and of vintage quality. It originated in Somerset around 1920. Stoke Red is generally well appreciated in England, but it is not successful in my orchard: although it is vigorous and hardy, it simply refuses to produce any flower buds. Since planting it in 1993, I have seen only a few fruits, in 2008. This variety leafs out much later in spring than any other apple. According to Copas (2001) the properties of its juice are: SG 1.052, TA 6.4 g/L, tannin 3.1 g/L.

Sweet Coppin

Sweet Coppin, an old variety that originated in Devon, is an English cider apple classified as a full sweet of vintage quality. It has a medium-late maturation, and Copas (2001) gives the following juice data: SG 1.052, TA 2 g/L, tannin 1.4 g/L. This variety is not grown much in North America but is recommended by our expert from the Rocky Mountain region, who mentions its good hardiness (in a zone 5, borderline zone 4, location), high sugar content, and not-so-late ripening.

Tremlett's Bitter

A full bittersweet English cider apple, Tremlett's Bitter (figure 5.15) is known for its hard and bitter tannin. It originated in Devon around the end of the nineteenth century. It is under trial in my orchard but produces very little fruit and is not vigorous. The apples ripen in early October. According

Figure 5.15. Tremlett's Bitter

to Copas (2001), the juice has the following properties: SG 1.052, TA 2.7 g/L, tannin 3.4 g/L. (Note that many of the Tremlett's Bitter trees growing in North America are not of the true variety, as there has been some identification error in the past.)

Virginia (Hewe's) Crab

The Virginia Crab, also called Hewe's Crab, originated in Virginia at the beginning of the eighteenth century. It is possible that in its ancestor there could be the indigenous southern crab *Malus angustifolia*. This small apple has a longtime reputation for producing an exceptional cider, as Coxe in particular noted in 1817, and it is one of the few to be considered a true North American cider apple. Its juice has a very high sugar content, a high acidity, and is quite astringent. Also, according to Macoun (1916), it should be extremely hardy, as it was successfully grown in Manitoba in zone 2 or 3. It is currently under trial in my orchard and gave its first fruits in 2012, but not in enough quantity to make a juice test.

Wealthy

Number of samples tested: 11
Sugar: low to medium, SG 1.048 (1.042–1.055)
Acidity: high, TA 9.2 g/L (6.7–12.0)
Tannin: low
Juice yield: high
Harvest date: early September;
    first pressing season
Cultural notes: good vigor, excellent hardiness,
    low sensitivity to scab

The Wealthy apple originated in Minnesota from a seed of Cherry Crab, which itself is a seedling of the Siberian crab *(Malus baccata)*. The Wealthy was introduced in 1869 and rapidly became very popular in the colder areas because of its great resistance to cold and its good quality as an eating apple. Unfortunately, its relatively low sugar content combined with a high acidity limits its use for cider making, and it is necessary to blend it with low-acidity varieties of the same season, such as Douce de Charlevoix or Bulmer's Norman. Its juice is excellent fresh, and this apple is a good addition in a mixed orchard in cold regions.

White Jersey

This apple is an early-season English bittersweet cider apple of vintage quality popular in the nineteenth century on the farms of Somerset. It has also been planted more recently in intensive bush orchards, where its good productivity has been noted. Copas (2001) gives the following juice data: SG 1.051, TA 2.9 g/L, tannin 2.6 g/L. In America this variety is not as well known as some other English cider apples, but it has nonetheless been recommended by our experts for the Rocky Mountain and Great Lakes regions.

Wickson

This is a crab (or at any rate a diminutive, crablike apple) that was introduced in 1944 by Albert Etter in California. Some say it is a cross of Esopus Spitzenburg × Newton Pippin, others that it is the result of a Spitzenburg Crab × Newton Crab cross. Whichever is true, this small apple is well appreciated by many cider makers in the United States. It produces a juice of a remarkable richness in sugar. The acidity is also high; hence, for cider it would have to be blended with some low-acidity varieties. The tree is known to be annually productive, and although it originated in California, it is hardy in zone 4 and possibly to zone 3. I am currently testing it in my orchard, but it is still too young to give fruit. Wickson is on the list of top recommended varieties for the New England and Virginia regions.

Winter Banana

Number of samples tested: 3
Sugar: medium, SG 1.052 (1.049–1.055)
Acidity: medium, TA 6.7 g/L (6.2–7.1)

Tannin: low, sometimes has a touch of bitterness
Juice yield: medium
Harvest date: late September; pressing season: October
Cultural notes: low to medium vigor, marginal hardiness, low sensitivity to scab

Winter Banana is an heirloom American apple that originated in Indiana around 1875 and is described by Beach in *The Apples of New York* (1905). This is a very handsome apple with a delicate yellow ground color blushed with a pinkish red cheek. For cider, we note its naturally balanced acidity and nice flavor. Some cider makers in the United States use it, notably in the Great Lakes area. In my orchard it hasn't been productive enough to make a positive contribution to the cider.

Yarlington Mill

Number of samples tested: 10
Sugar: high, SG 1.061 (1.053–1.075)
Acidity: low, TA 3.4 g/L (1.3–4.5)
Tannin: high, astringent and bitter juice
Juice yield: medium
Harvest date: late September; pressing season: mid-October to December
Cultural notes: good vigor and hardiness, low sensitivity to scab, prone to fireblight

Yarlington Mill (figure 5.16) is an English cider apple classified as a medium bittersweet of vintage quality that dates back to the end of the nineteenth century. This apple is probably one of the most popular worldwide of all bittersweet cider apples. It is used in modern English orchards and is still planted in more traditional orchards of standard trees. In England this apple ripens very late, at the end of October or even in November. Interestingly, most growers I have been in contact with

Figure 5.16. Yarlington Mill

report it ripens much earlier in North America, which is what I have also noticed in my orchard, where it ripens around the end of September.

Yarlington Mill is definitely a first-choice apple. It is one of the few late-ripening European cider-apple varieties with low acidity to succeed in my orchard. This makes it very valuable. The production is never sufficient, as I could always use more in my blends that contain higher-acidity American apples. It is also interesting to note that this apple has a great adaptability to different climates: in addition to its cold-hardiness, it also succeeds in some very hot climates, such as in Australia. Almost all participants in Internet discussion forums grow it successfully, the only exception being those where fireblight is severe, as some have reported losing trees to this disease. In addition to

my recommendation for the cold climate of Quebec, this variety appears on our experts' lists for New England and the Pacific Northwest regions.

Other Apple Varieties

As I mentioned at the beginning of this directory, I couldn't include even a small fraction of all the apples that are being used for cider making around the world. I haven't included any Spanish or German varieties, for example, even though these countries have longtime cider-making traditions. These apples are practically unknown outside of their region of origin.

In addition there are many American apples, often heirlooms, that I don't know well enough since they are grown in warmer areas of the United States and couldn't succeed in cold zone 4 orchards. Some of those have been used for cider for a long time and have been recommended by some of the experts in the previous section, various authors, or participants in Internet forums. To name just a few: Esopus Spitzenburg, Gravenstein (mostly for the West Coast of Canada and the United States and in the Maritime provinces of Canada), Newtown Pippin (in Virginia), Rhode Island Greening, Sops of Wine, Stayman, Winesap, and York Imperial.

I haven't included any summer apples that ripen in August. Some cider makers do use summer apples, and I have seen some recommended in books. However, I have never been able to make a truly good cider from early-ripening apples because their sugar content is low, their acidity is high, and they usually don't have much flavor. The combination of all these factors produces a thin and sharp cider that is not to my liking. Further, early apples contain a lot more nitrogenous substances, which promote too fast a fermentation. Note, however, that a cider made from summer apples is ideal for the production of vinegar and may also be used for cooking. Hence, I generally do a small batch of summer cider every year for these uses.

Crabapples should not be overlooked. I have included a few in the directory, mainly those that have a reasonable acidity. I sometimes also use small quantities of Dolgo or Kerr crabs in my blends. These have an exceptional flavor but feature a particularly high acidity that may attain 30 g/L of malic acid in the case of Dolgo. This makes it difficult to obtain a balanced blend if too much is used.

Finally, there are wild apples, those that grow on the side of the road and have been sown by animals. Such apples may make a positive contribution to a cider more often than we think. With a little bit of practice, just by tasting the apple, we can roughly estimate its sugar, acidity, and tannin content. Then, for the ones that seem most promising, a juice test will give us more information on its potential for cider.

Pear Varieties

Pears are used to make perry, which is the pear counterpart of cider. I haven't talked much about perry yet, as it is a much more specialized drink. Some producers in England and France make perry from true perry pears, and a few in North America also make perry from either perry or eating pears or a blend of both types. Pears may also make a positive contribution in a cider blend. The diverse types of pears have completely different properties and thus have to be used accordingly in a cider:

- **Eating pears** of the European type are low in acidity and tannin while having a relatively good sugar concentration. Thus they may be useful in a cider blend to reduce the acidity of the must. Most of the known varieties of pears are of this type, including Bartlett, Anjou, Bosc, and so on.
- **Perry pears** contain a high concentration of tannin and are relatively acidic. They are very bitter and astringent, more so than any apple I have tasted. These pears aren't pleasant to eat fresh. In a blend they are used for their tannin.
- **Hybrid pears** are a group of hardy pears obtained by hybridization between the European pear *(Pyrus communis)* and *P. ussuriensis*, which is an extremely hardy pear that originated in

northern China and Siberia. Usually these varieties have a higher acidity than the European pears, and this acidity is often close to the ideal of a perfectly balanced blend. They also have a noticeable amount of tannin but much less than the perry pears have. They can make a very nice addition to a blend.

An important difference between apples and pears is that the latter contain more sorbitol, a sweetener that is not fermentable. Thus a perry or a cider that contains a significant proportion of pears in its blend will retain a bit of sweetness and will be more fruity.

I didn't include any pressing season for pears because the maturation is very different than for apples: while apples soften slowly as the pectins degrade during maturation, pears become soft and brown inside within just a few days (this is called *blet*). Quite a few times I have completely lost a batch of pears because I thought they were hard and not yet ready for pressing, and when I came back a week later they had turned blet. Once the pear has become blet, the flesh is dark and mushy, and it is impossible to press and extract the juice. Hence pears have to be monitored much more closely than apples to determine the right pressing time, and if this time frame is passed by just a few days, the pears may be a complete loss. Most of the time I now press pears within a week of harvest, but some varieties need many weeks of ripening before being ready for pressing.

Below I have written comments on a few of the pears that I grow and for which I have done some juice analyses. Note that in my cold zone 4 climate, better-known varieties are not hardy and only some noncommercial and lesser-known varieties may be grown successfully.

Golden Spice

Number of samples tested: 10
Sugar: high, SG 1.061 (1.056–1.066)
Acidity: low to high, TA 6.4 g/L (3.6–9.8)
Tannin: variable, medium, sometimes high,
    juice has some bitterness and astringency
Juice yield: medium
Harvest date: late September to mid-October
Cultural notes: good vigor and hardiness,
    tree easy to manage, good health,
    irregular production

The Golden Spice pear is from the University of Minnesota, introduced in 1949. It is usually rated for hardiness zone 3. The parentage is unknown but probably contains a good fraction of *P. ussuriensis*. Golden Spice makes good juice, sharp and sweet at the same time. Some years, however, the tannins make the juice a bit too bitter and astringent. The pears press easily and have a yield comparable to apples. This pear is excellent in cider, contributing a high sugar concentration, an acidity that is often well balanced, and some tannin. It also has a very good flavor. Golden Spice is a good representative of the hybrid group of pears. I also grow a few other hybrid varieties, including the Ure pear: its juice has quite similar properties, but the fruit ripens earlier and doesn't keep as long.

Patten

Number of samples tested: 6
Sugar: medium, SG 1.053 (1.045–1.058)
Acidity: low, TA 1.9 g/L (1.3–3.1)
Tannin: low
Juice yield: medium
Harvest date: late September
Cultural notes: very vigorous, good hardiness,
    good productivity, healthy and easy tree

Patten originated in Iowa in the early 1920s from a cross of Orel 15 × Beurré d'Anjou. (Anjou is one of the hardier of the high-quality European pears, but, as I found out, it is still not hardy enough for my zone.) Patten is considered resistant to fireblight and usually rated for hardiness zone 4. The pears are still green and hard when picked at the end of September and keep a good month.

For eating, this pear is comparable to many well-known commercial varieties. It surely is among the best eating pears of the European type for cold climates. The properties of its juice are also quite representative of other pears of this group. As fresh juice, it is very bland because of the lack of acidity, but in cider it may be very useful to reduce the acidity of the blend. Other pears that I grow successfully and that have similar properties are Flemish Beauty, Luscious, and Southworth.

Thorn

Number of samples tested: 5
Sugar: high, SG 1.061 (1.050–1.072)
Acidity: very high, TA 10.3 g/L (8.9–11.6)

Tannin: high, astringent and bitter juice
Juice yield: low to medium
Harvest date: late September
Cultural notes: good vigor and hardiness,
    fairly regular but medium productivity

The Thorn (figure 5.17) is a very old English perry pear, known since the seventeenth century. It is one of the earlier-maturing varieties and is fully described by Luckwill and Pollard (1963) in the beautiful book *Perry Pears*, where they give the following analysis as the mean of seven samples: SG 1.062, TA 5.7 g/L, tannin 1.0 g/L. Although the SG is fairly similar, the TA measured from pears grown in my orchard has twice the value of that from pears grown in England. Additionally, the value quoted for tannin at 1.0 g/L incidates a low tannin content, whereas the fruit harvested in my orchard clearly has a high tannin content.

I have six varieties of true English perry pears under trial in my orchard: Thorn, Hendre Huffcap, Winnal's Longdon, Blakeney Red, Gin, and Yellow Huffcap. Of those, only the first three mentioned produce more or less regular crops, and Thorn is the best-adapted one, mainly because it ripens earlier. In all cases the fruit obtained is much more acidic and astringent than what is reported in Luckwill and Pollard. This makes me believe that although the varieties do survive and crop in a cold climate, the conditions of growth during the season don't seem to permit them to properly ripen their fruits.

Figure 5.17. Thorn

III PART III III

Juice Extraction

Most cider makers will one day or another consider the acquisition of the necessary equipment for extracting the apple juice. Yes, it is possible to make cider without having a press: you may rent a press, have your apples custom-pressed at some facility, or buy juice at an orchard. But it is so much easier when you have your own mill and press. For my part, I got a simple press and mill kit the second year I made cider. This is an important investment, but it is worth it, as the equipment lasts many seasons.

Sweating the Apples

Before you extract the juice from the apples, you must make sure the apples are at their peak of ripeness. Ripeness is different from maturation: we harvest the apples when they are mature, meaning that they have fallen or are just ready to fall from the tree. They are usually still hard at that moment. To obtain the best cider quality, the apples should be left in a cool and dry area (covered if outside),

Figure III.1. Twin-screw cider press on Jersey, Channel Islands, UK. Photo by Man Vyi, Wikimedia Commons.

but not in cold storage, for a varying period of time depending on the variety: a couple of weeks or over a month, until they start to soften. In the cider language, this postharvest ripening period is called *sweating*, and during this time the residual starch transforms into sugar, the pectin starts to degrade (hence the softening of the apples), the nitrogen goes through transformations that will decrease the concentration of its assimilable fraction, and the apples lose some water by evaporation through the skin, thus concentrating their sugar and flavor (hence some shriveling of the skin). An adequate degree of ripeness is usually simply checked with the thumb: when the apples feel a bit soft, it is time for pressing. In some climates sweating may not be possible for more than a few days if autumn air temperatures are too high.

Pressing Sequence

Apple juice is extracted in a sequence of distinct operations with different pieces of equipment:

- **Washing**. We have already discussed washing in chapter 2. This operation is ideally done in a large pail or bath.
- **Milling**. The first operation is to break the rigid structure of the flesh so that the apple may yield its juice easily. We thus obtain the *pulp* or *pomace*. For this, we use a *mill* or a *grinder*, which is the subject of the following sections.
- **Maceration**. After milling, the pomace may be left for *maceration*. This optional step consists in leaving the pomace to rest for a period of time before pressing. See just below for more details.
- **Pressing**. The next operation is done on a *press*. The pomace is placed between two plates, and

under the action of an actuator, which exerts pressure, the juice is expelled. This apple juice may then be called the *must*.
- **Second pressing**. The pressed pomace may be pressed a second time to extract more juice. I discuss this later, where I explain how to use a rack-and-cloth press.

Maceration

According to old traditional French and English methods, the pomace can be left for maceration for as long as a full day. We now understand that this process has real effect on the pomace. First, some natural enzymes present in the apple start working on the pectin, which improves the pressing yield and increases the chances for a successful *keeve* (this term will be discussed later, in the article on sweetness in cider, section 15.1). Another effect is on the tannins: the oxygen in the air comes into contact with the pomace, and some browning occurs. This gives color to the cider and mellows the bitterness and astringency. Most perry makers still practice maceration for this purpose, as perry pears are extremely astringent. Nowadays it is generally agreed that two to four hours of maceration is sufficient and that too long a period of maceration may augment the risks of contamination. In warm temperatures maceration time should be reduced. In fact, maceration is not at all essential in most cases, and with some types of mill-press tandem it is not practical to leave the pomace to macerate, as the pomace falls directly into the press basket. An effective way to do the maceration with a mill that delivers into a bucket is to mill the equivalent of three or four loads of the press and then proceed to press the first load. This way, as the pressing advances, you always manage to have a two-hour queue for the pomace before it gets pressed. The pomace may be left in large buckets during the maceration, but it is more effective if wide pans are used, as this maximizes the contact with air.

Evaluating your Needs

The following two chapters are meant to be a guide for either buying or making your own mill and press. You will have many decisions to make.

First, you need to decide if you would rather buy or make these machines. Making them is not so difficult, but it requires a minimum of skill in wood- or metal-working as well as some tools, and naturally some time.

Second, you will have to figure the capacity needed. The greater the capacity the higher the cost, but the time it takes for pressing will be reduced. The press capacity should be chosen as a function of the projected total annual production. And the mill capacity should also be appropriate for the size of the press. In general, I believe that for a hobbyist the total annual juice production should be obtained from between fifteen and fifty press loads. For a professional, this may be different, and the press could be used for a larger number of loads. The capacity of the mill should be such that it takes less than ten minutes, and ideally less than 5 minutes, to mill enough apples to fill the press.

For example, if you expect to juice approximately a ton of apples annually, this is 50 to 55 bushels. Your press should have a minimum capacity of 1 bushel (40 lb., or 18 kg) of apples, and a press with a capacity of more than 3.5 bushels would be

oversized for such a production. With a press capacity of 1 bushel, the mill should have the capacity of processing this bushel in less than ten minutes, which makes 6 bushels per hour (240 lb./h, or 110 kg/h) at minimum. But if you choose a larger-capacity press, for example a 3-bushel press, you would then make about seventeen pressing loads during the season and would choose a mill that can process a bushel in three minutes or less. This ton of apples would give you about 145 gallons (550 liters) of juice, more or less depending on the juiciness of the apples and the yield efficiency of the equipment. As for the time required to process this amount of apples, on average we should count about 1.5 hours per press load, including setup and cleaning. With a larger press, this could be a bit more, as it takes more time to build the cheese. So to process a ton of apples, if we talk fifty loads with a 1-bushel-capacity press, this would take about seventy-five hours of work; while for seventeen loads on a 3-bushel press, it would take about thirty hours of work.

Finally, you will need to decide which type of equipment you want. For example, there are manual and motorized mills (your choice will depend on the production anticipated), and there are many types of presses.

Fruit and Vegetable Juice Extractor

For a small batch of cider, it is possible to use a kitchen juicer instead of a mill-press tandem. These appliances have a high-speed rotating cage that grinds the apples, and the juice is extracted by centrifugal force. They work just as well with carrots or celery as with apples. Most of these juicers,

The Double-Tub Press

Figure III.2.

Figure III.3.

Double-tub presses have been very popular on farms in North America. This is a classic design that includes two baskets: while one is under the press, the other gets filled by the grinder. This particular unit is in excellent order and is owned by my friend David Maxwell, who grows apples and makes cider in Nova Scotia. And interestingly, it was manufactured by David Maxwell and sons in Ontario, probably a few years before 1900. It features a geared hand crank that permits a great increase in the grinder speed and efficiency.

however, are designed to extract one glass of juice at a time, so it may take a long while before there is enough for a batch of cider. Further, the motor may overheat with such heavy usage. But some models are better suited for juicing large quantities of apples, and some cider makers report using two such heavy-duty juicers side by side to produce enough juice for a sizable quantity of cider. One last point on these juicers: the juice produced contains a lot more particles in suspension than juice from a press, and so it is strongly recommended that you strain the juice.

CHAPTER 6

APPLE MILLS

The mill is a machine used to break the apples up into small particles before you press them. In general, particles of approximately ⅛-inch (3-mm) thickness will permit a better juice extraction. However, the particles shouldn't be so small as to make a purée or a slush, which might make the extraction more difficult. Additionally, we usually don't want the mill to break open the seeds (or at least not too many of them). This is because open apple pips release a small amount of a bitter compound called amygdalin that degrades into cyanide when metabolized in the digestive system of an animal or human. The cyanide itself is toxic and may even be fatal in large doses. But we shouldn't worry too much about this, as the cider drinker is much more likely to be dead drunk way before approaching the fatal dose of cyanide. At most, an excessive amount of broken seeds would increase the bitterness of the cider.

Following you will find a description of the main types of apple mills, and a guide for building your own.

◀ 6.1 ▶
Main Characteristics of Mills

There are three main types of mill designs:
- **Crusher mills** crush the apples between two hard surfaces under a very high pressure.
- **Grater mills** or **grinders** are made of a rotating drum equipped with cutting blades that grind or grate the apples.

- **Centrifugal mills** and **hammer mills** have a high-speed rotating blade or masses that cut and/or shatter the apples.

In the following pages, we will see the main characteristics of these mills and discuss the options for a cider maker.

Crusher Mills

Most of the ancient apple mill designs are of the crusher type. The most ancient of them doubtless involved simply crushing apples between two rocks. A slightly improved design is the pestle and mortar, which can be made large enough to accommodate a dozen apples at a time. This may still be used for a small quantity of apples if nothing else is available, using, for example, a plastic pail and a heavy piece of wood (a baseball bat would do) as the pestle. But the true evolution of crusher mills is the wheel crusher, which had the capacity to process relatively large quantities of apples. It consists of a wheel that rolls over the apples laid in a circular trough (see figure 6.1). This wheel, which is heavy and often made

of stone, turns around a central axis and is usually driven by a horsedrawn wooden sweep. Such crushers were very common in Normandy and other cider regions of Europe dating back to medieval times. They aren't used much anymore, as they have some major inconveniences: they are quite cumbersome, difficult to keep clean and sanitized, and tend to crush open too many seeds—plus they require a horse. Interestingly however, in Spain the horse-drawn wheel crushers weren't used much and, up to the beginning of the twentieth century, the apples were still crushed the traditional way in elongated troughs by men using wooden pestles.

With the industrial revolution and the development of the steel industry in the middle of the nineteenth century, many improved and more compact crushers were made using a variety of designs:

- **Counterrotating wheels.** In these, apples were crushed by being forced to pass between two large wheels (often made of stone) in counterrotation. The free distance between the wheels dictated the size of the pomace. Actually, the principle of the counterrotating-wheels crusher predates the industrial revolution, as it was first described in John Worlidge's *Vinetum Britannicum* of 1676.
- **Gear crushers**, also called **nut mills**. These consist of two wheels with large teeth in counterrotation (figure 6.2). The apples are trapped by the gears and crushed in between the geared wheels. Again, the adjustment of the distance between the axles permitted the mill operator to change the size of the pomace. In addition these crushers were often equipped with a spring system that let the stones go through without breaking the machine.
- **Rotating-drum crushers.** These are of a more complex design. They consist of a drum

Figure 6.1. An old stone wheel crusher being used in Jersey, Channel Islands, UK. Photo by Man Vyi, Wikimedia Commons.

Figure 6.2. Gear crusher mechanism. Illustration from Power (1890–1891).

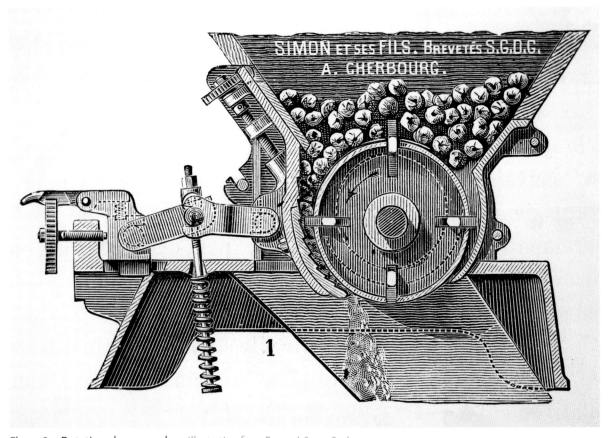

Figure 6.3. Rotating-drum crusher. Illustration from Power (1890–1891).

rotating against a fixed plate, or stator, and the apples are crushed between these two elements. Often, as in the Simon crusher shown in figure 6.3 on page 95, there are retractable slats that force the apples into the mechanism. These Simon crushers were very popular in France at the end of the nineteenth and beginning of the twentieth centuries. They were made in different sizes, with the smaller ones driven by human force and the larger ones by horse. Some later models had steam or petroleum engines. (See the guide by Établissements Simon Frères in the bibliography for more on these.)

In those days stainless steel wasn't known, and the extended contact of the juice with mild steel or cast iron caused some corrosion, with some iron oxide contaminating the juice, which may eventually be the cause of a blackening of the cider. It was thus essential to clean regularly and thoroughly all the components that could be in contact with the juice.

Crushers aren't used much anymore, and modern mills are pretty much all of the grater or centrifugal designs discussed below.

Grater Mills

The *grater mill*, also called a *grinder*, works in a similar fashion as a cheese grater. It consists of a rotating drum equipped with blades that each cut

Figure 6.4. Small, manually cranked grater mill.

a small piece of the apple. Thus the size of the pomace is set mainly by the height of the blades. The general layout of these mills bears some resemblance to the Simon crusher seen above, with a rotor (the drum) and a stator (the back plate), in between which the apples have to pass. The difference is that in one case the apples are crushed and in the other they are cut. The first grater mills appeared in the United States around 1825.

Grater mills are quite popular in America. This is the type of mill that accompanies small traditional farm presses (see the double-tub press shown in figure III.3 on page 92). It is also a common design for do-it-yourself projects, as such mills are relatively easy to make. Grater mills of all sizes are available commercially, from small, manually cranked models all the way up to large-capacity industrial models that can mill 10 tons of fruit per hour. Figure 6.4 shows my first grinder, which came with the Jaffrey press that I acquired in 1989.

For small hobbyist cider production, a hand-cranked mill as shown in figure 6.4 may be sufficient if you are young and have strong arms. Two people are needed to work the machine, one cranking while the other feeds the apples. Many manufacturers produce such models, and they are all quite similar. I wouldn't recommend a hand-cranked mill if you intend to make more than 30 gallons of cider annually, although some models that I have seen with ancient presses were geared to turn faster and were much more efficient. For my part, after a couple of years I replaced this manually cranked mill with a motorized machine. The other great advantage of a motorized mill is that it can be fed by a single operator while the motor takes care of driving the rotor. Note that the grinder provided with the press manufactured by Correll (www

Figure 6.5. The HDPE rotor of the OESCO grater mill.

.correllciderpresses.com) has an electric motor and that some manufacturers offer an electric motor attachment to go with a grinder originally designed to be hand-cranked. See, for example, the HVR grinder (www.happyvalleyranch.com).

One of the important providers of juice extraction equipment of all sizes is OESCO in Massachusetts (www.oescoinc.com), which manufactures and sells efficient motorized grater mills. Their small model is particularly popular with serious hobbyists and small commercial cider makers. Its rotor (figure 6.5) is made of high-density polyethylene (HDPE), and it has the capacity to grind a bushel of apples in approximately ninety seconds. They also have larger models that can handle greater quantities of fruit.

A search on the Internet will yield many examples of home-built grater mills, either motorized or hand-cranked. Some of them appear to be quite efficient, while others are much less so. In one example that looked neat, the rotor was driven by a bicycle-pedal mechanism. In section 6.2, we will see in detail how to build an efficient grater mill.

Centrifugal Mills

Centrifugal mills represent the most recent evolution in milling, as some modern technology is required to make them. These mills use blades that rotate at high speed inside a chamber to hit, cut, and project the apple particles against the walls of the chamber (see figure 6.6). The particles are finally ejected through a grid by centrifugal force. The dimension of the openings of this grid dictates the size of the pomace. Some models have interchangeable grids of different sizes. *Hammer mills* are a type of centrifugal mill where masses rather than blades are used to smash. Large industrial hammer mills have many of these rotating masses side by side (figure 6.7). Centrifugal mills require more powerful motors than grater mills of the same capacity.

Big hammer mills are common in large cider operations both in Europe and in America.

Centrifugal mills are used mainly in Europe for the smaller production of serious hobbyists or small commercial cider makers. Here are some of the most popular models:

• The *Fruit Shark* (figure 6.8) is a Czech mill made by Vares (www.vares.cz). It is especially widespread in England, where there is a distributor (www.ciderworkshop.com/fruitshark .html). It is also distributed in France (www .tompress.com). Rated at 250 to 600 kg/h (depending on the source of information), the mill is supplied only with a 50 Hz motor and so isn't available in America.

• The *Speidel* mill from Germany (www.speidels -hausmosterei.de) is more expensive than the Fruit Shark but has greater capacity, with a rating of one ton per hour (figure 6.9). This makes it powerful enough for small commercial cider making. It is generally available and quite popular in Europe but is not well known in North

Figure 6.6. Chamber and rotor of a Pillan centrifugal mill.

America, even if it is available with a 220 V/60 Hz motor (see morewine making.com), which does require a special outlet.

- *Italian "trumpet"* mills are so called because of their shape and look (figure 6.10). Made of stainless steel, they are produced by different manufacturers under the

Figure 6.7. Rotor of a hammer mill. Photo by Red58bill, Wikimedia Commons.

trade names Zambelli (www.zambellienotech .it), Pillan (www.enotecnicapillan.it), and others. (Note that Pillan bought Zambelli in 2001, and their product lines have now merged.) Some are imported to Canada and the United States fitted with a 60 Hz motor that may require a special 220 V or 240 V outlet; others may be fitted with a 110 V motor. Two models are sometimes sold in wine-making supply stores: the smallest

(Mini Mixer) has a capacity of 800 kg/h and the medium (Mixer), rated 1,500 to 2,000 kg/h. There also is a larger model (Maxi Mixer), rated 3 to 4.5 tons/h.

• The Austrian company *Voran* (www.voran.at) has a line of centrifugal mills ranging from 650 to 4,000 kg/h in addition to a grater mill. All their mills are equipped with 380 V motors. These are industrial-quality mills for professional use.

In addition to the above commercial models made specifically for apples and fruits, some people have adapted machines designed for other purposes. In particular, inventive cider makers have modified kitchen sink disposals and garden shredders into small centrifugal apple mills.

Figure 6.8. Fruit Shark mill. Photo courtesy of Vicky Gorman.

Figure 6.9. Speidel mill. Photo courtesy of Speidel.

Figure 6.10. Italian "trumpet" mill.

KITCHEN SINK DISPOSAL

A kitchen sink (or garbage) disposal is in fact a small hammer mill designed to grind up food leftovers, and many cider makers have adapted one of these to mill apples. As far as I know, this was first done by Don Yellman. He wrote about this in the Cider Digest discussion forum (no. 789, January 27, 1999) and in *Pomona* (vol. 32, Winter 1999), the quarterly publication of the North American Fruit Explorers (NAFEX). We can see in figure 6.11 Yellman's original setup: it is quite simple, with a piece of kitchen counter pierced with a hole to install the disposal, an electrical switch, and a vertical discharge pipe so that the pomace falls into a bucket.

Many others have since taken up Yellman's idea. You can find quite a bit of information on the Internet by searching "disposal apple grinder." Disposals are quite inexpensive, but you should buy a high-end model with internal components made of stainless steel. Large apples must be cut in quarters, and for the best efficiency, two people are required: one to cut the apples, and the other to feed them into the disposal. According to Yellman, it takes some ten to twenty minutes to process a bushel of apples this way. Not only are they relatively slow, but disposals are not designed to run continuously for long periods of time, and they may overheat. Some modifications can be made to ensure proper cooling of the motor—removal of the insulation, installation of a fan—but certainly the best is to install a coil with cold-water circulation. Other cider makers will simply take a break after ten minutes to let the disposal cool down. In general, such a disposal mill may be adequate for very small cider productions, but I wouldn't recommend it for anything much larger than 30 gallons (120 liters) of cider per season. There are exceptions: a member

Figure 6.11. Original setup of a kitchen sink disposal to mill apples. Photo courtesy of Don Yellman.

in a discussion forum reports having milled and pressed half a ton of apples in a day using his highly optimized disposal apple mill.

GARDEN SHREDDER

These shredders are designed to process leaves and small branches into small particles to be transformed into compost. The shredding is done by a high-speed rotating blade, and although there is no grid to control the size of the pomace, this is a true centrifugal mill. They certainly mill apples! They do have drawbacks, however, as some parts are made of non-stainless steel, and they are not designed to process objects that contain as much liquid as apples. Thus, it is necessary to prevent the juice from coming into contact with the motor and the electrical connections. It is also recommended that you use a paint or lacquer on the steel parts to prevent corrosion. On the plus side, their cost is low, and they are efficient. Their capacity is comparable to that of the Fruit Shark described above (which, by the way is also basically a garden shredder, but modified by its manufacturer: the parts that come into contact with the juice have been replaced by stainless steel parts, and it is equipped with a hopper and a receiving container adapted to its function as a fruit mill.)

Comparative Table for Apple Mills

In table 6.1 I present some possible milling solutions for a hobbyist and small commercial cider maker. Note that this list is not exhaustive and that there exist other comparable products. The indicated costs for each mill are approximations and only a comparative index, as there are important price differences from country to country. The capacities are given as approximate time in minutes required to process a bushel of 40 lb. (18 kg) of apples. A mill that has the capacity to process 1 bushel in less than ten minutes might pair well with a press of 1 bushel capacity or less, while a 3 bushel capacity press could be a match for a mill that requires three minutes or less for a bushel. The numbers in table 6.1 were obtained either from the manufacturers' specifications or communication with other cider makers.

Other Alternatives

For very small quantities of apples, a domestic food processor fitted with a grater disk or chopping blade will permit milling apples for making juice tests. It could be sufficient for an amateur cider

TABLE 6.1:

Comparative table for apple mills of small to medium capacity

MODEL	COST	MOTOR	TYPE	CAPACITY (minutes/bushel)	NOTES
Hand-cranked grinder	$250	no	grater	6 to 10	variable according to the person cranking
HVR grinder w/motor kit	$600	1/3 hp	grater	3	North America only
Kitchen sink disposal	$150	1/2 hp	centrifugal	10 to 20	variable according to the model
Fruit Shark	600€	2 hp	centrifugal	3	Europe only
Speidel	$1,150 750€	3 hp	centrifugal	1.25	220 V (50 or 60 Hz)
OESCO HDPE	$1,900	1/2 hp	grater	1.5	North America only
Pillan Mini Mixer	$1,100 1,000€	1.8 hp	centrifugal	1.5	small trumpet Italian mill 110 or 220V, 50 or 60Hz
Pillan Mixer	$1,350 1,200€	2.8 hp	centrifugal	1	medium trumpet Italian mill 220V, 50 or 60Hz
Motorized grinder		1/2 hp	grater	1.5	author's homemade grater mill

maker who wants to make only one small batch of cider and doesn't want to invest in a mill. And as mentioned in the beginning of this article, a heavy piece of wood and a plastic pail may be used as a pestle and mortar to process small batches. However, the freezer method is probably an easier way to process apples for small cider batches.

Freezer

Apples that have been frozen and thawed don't need to be ground before pressing. Once thawed, the apples may be placed whole in the press, and they will yield their juice very easily, as the freezing process breaks the pectin links and rigid structure of the apple. I have even noticed that the yield is higher for apples that have been frozen than with the mill-press tandem. It is, however, necessary for the apples to have been frozen hard and

for a sufficiently long time. My tests suggest that apples should stay in the freezer one week. Also, the apples should be pressed as soon as they are thawed: if left too long, a purée may form in the press, which makes it very difficult to extract the juice. And if the apples are pressed before being completely thawed, then some concentration of the juice occurs. This aspect will be covered in the article on ice cider, section 15.3.

Once they have given their juice, thawed apples simply become flat, as shown in figure 6.12. They usually have a slit in the skin by which the juice escaped. All the solids remain inside the apple. With a basket press it would actually be possible to press the apples without a net inside the basket. An important point is that the pressure should be applied slowly and gradually. If the pressure builds up too fast, this could make the apples explode and project all the internal solids; if pressed

Figure 6.12. Thawed apples, after pressing.

slowly, in contrast, the solids are retained within the skin. Each load, then, should be left longer under the press.

Note that the freezer solution is possible only for making cider, as the juice thus obtained has a mouthfeel and viscosity completely different from normally pressed juice and feels a bit odd to drink. This is due to the degradation of the pectin during freezing. The color is also paler, as no oxidation of the tannins has occurred, and it is much clearer, as it contains fewer particles in suspension. For cider, these effects are not detrimental

to the quality, as the pectins are degraded anyway during fermentation. However, unless you have a huge freezer available, this solution will only be possible for very small production. But on the other hand, the freezer may be a very useful tool to permit blending apples from different seasons of maturity: you may freeze some midseason apples to blend them with late-season varieties. Another useful function of the freezer is for salvation of overripe apples: such apples become very difficult to press, and freezing them permits you to press them much more easily once they have thawed.

◀ 6.2 ▶
Making a Grater Mill

The object of this article is to give some tips on how to build a motorized apple mill of the grinder or grater type. It is based on the grinder I built for myself, which is about as efficient as a comparable commercial unit. I will not give a formal drawing here because in do-it-yourself projects each machine tends to be different, as it is most often made with materials that are available. I hope, however, you will be able to get inspiration from this design to build yourself an efficient mill. Note that this is not an easy project, and it requires some woodworking skills and a minimum of tools.

Background

For my first cider-making years, I used a hand-cranked mill that came with the press I bought in

1989. There are a few pictures of this press and mill in the previous articles. By the mid-1990s, as my cider production was increasing, I decided I had had enough of this slow and tiring hand-cranking, and I built my first motorized grinder. It had a similar geometry to that of the previous manual one, with a rotating drum 6 inches (15 cm) in diameter by the same width. Its performance was OK but no more. The small and hard apples were ground rapidly and without fuss, but the larger and softer apples tended to stick, and I always had to push them with a wooden instrument. Also, the teeth were too long, thus producing a coarse pomace. With this grinder I could process a bushel in four to eight minutes, depending on the apples, which was an improvement over the manual one. I thought I could do better, however. I did try some modifications, like changing the inlet geometry, tinkering with the rotor speed, shortening the teeth, but to no avail really. Only with time did I understand that the rotor diameter was the key to a better design. In effect, if a 6 in. (15 cm) diameter rotor carried small apples easily through the mechanism, then I simply had to make a larger diameter rotor for the bigger apples, so this would scale up the geometry. I started by drawing this new geometry: a 12 in. (30 cm) diameter rotor with a 3.5 in. (9 cm) apple (represented by the red circle in figure 6.13). We can see that there is a space that gets narrower and in which once the apple is engaged it can't bounce back out, which is what was happening with the previous grinder (see sidebar "The Wedge Angle"). So in 2009 I decided to build a new grinder based on this geometry.

There were also a few additional and very important points I wanted to improve:

- Get a finer pomace by making the teeth shorter and controlling the distance between the rotor and stator. Pomace slices or chunks shouldn't be more than ⅛ in. (3 mm) thick. Also, the pomace shouldn't be too fine, as it might then make a slush and render the pressing more difficult.
- Make it easy to clean by having modules that are easily removable. Once disassembled, each module should be cleaned with a hose: there shouldn't be hard-to-reach corners from which apple bits and juice would be difficult to dislodge.
- Decrease the weight of the individual components, again by improving the modularity, so as to make the manipulation and transportation easier.

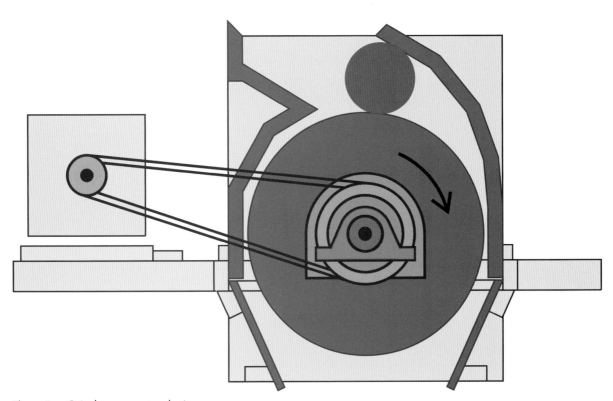

Figure 6.13. Grinder geometry design.

The Wedge Angle

A determinant factor in the overall performance of a grinder is the angle between the two surfaces of contact of the apple with the rotor and stator. I call it the wedge angle by analogy with the mechanical device that may stick or slide depending on its angle and on the friction between the surfaces in contact. The top illustration in figure 6.14 shows the design of my grinder, with a rotor that has a much larger diameter than the apple and a well-shaped stator: the wedge angle is relatively small, less than 30° even with large apples. Such a small angle insures that the apples are carried into the grinder by the friction between the apple and the stator, to be ground without fuss. The lower illustration shows a less efficient configuration, where the rotor diameter is smaller and the stator is a simple vertical surface. The wedge angle in this case is quite large, more than 60°, and an apple will have a tendency to roll over the rotor as it rotates because the friction force will not be sufficient to insure it is carried into the grinder, making it necessary to push on the apples with some instrument to force them in. For a successful design of a grinder or a grater mill, then, it helps to keep this wedge angle small.

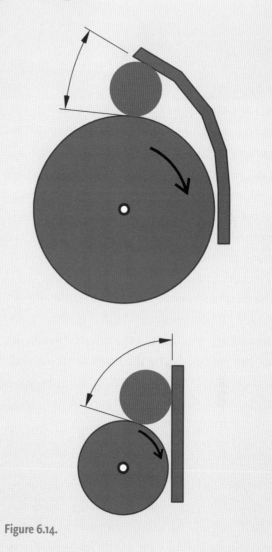

Figure 6.14.

Mechanical Supplies

The mechanical elements required to build a motorized grinder are a motor, two pulleys, a belt, a shaft, and two pillow block ball bearings. I recommend a belt drive for this grinder, since if the rotor jams, the belt may slip, thus protecting the major elements. The motor shown in figure 6.15 on page 106 is from our old washing machine. Such motors are easy to find in flea markets or in shops that repair domestic appliances. This one is ½ hp, which is plenty, and has a rotation

Figure 6.15. Mechanical supplies: motor, shaft, bearings, pulleys, belt.

The Rotor

The rotor is a 12 in (30 cm) diameter wheel a little over 4 in. (10 cm) thick (figure 6.16). I chose this thickness because it corresponds to the diameter of the biggest apples. There is no real reason

speed of 1725 rpm. One with ⅓ hp should also be fine, but I wouldn't recommend going lower than that. The other mechanical elements may be acquired in a specialized store for bearings and other similar supplies. The shaft I used has a diameter of ⅝ in. (16 mm) and a length of 12 in. (30 cm). It doesn't have to be stainless steel, as the juice will not normally come into contact with it. The bearings are of basic quality: there is no need to buy more expensive bearings, as the speed isn't high and the loads are moderate. The pulleys should be chosen in order to get a rotation speed of 600 to 900 rpm on the rotor. I have a 2 in. (50 mm) pulley on the motor and a 4.5 in. (115 mm) one on the rotor. The length of the belt will be determined when the grinder is complete. As for the cost of these elements, you should budget about $15 for the shaft, $25 for each bearing, $5 to $10 for each pulley, and $10 for the belt. And with a little bit of luck, you might be able to find most of these in a flea market for almost nothing.

Tip: The pulleys are fixed to the shaft with a small setscrew, which is tightened with an Allen key. In order to avoid slippage, use a file to make a flat surface on the shaft at the point the setscrew will press.

to make the grinder any wider. I made it in wood since I had some old planks that were well dried. You can't make a wheel that size from a single piece of wood, as it would crack; hence it is necessary to do laminations that are glued together. Note that it is not required to use hardwood for this wheel since it won't be overly stressed. I did as follows: I first prepared six disks from the planks by gluing pieces of wood that had been properly cut—leaving a hole in the center through which the shaft passes. Then I glued the disks one on top of the

Figure 6.16. Finished rotor.

other, making sure joints were alternating (see figure 6.17). I used quite a few C-clamps for this.

Once the gluing was done, I used a circular saw for a rough cutting to a circular shape. For the finishing, I simply fitted the motor with mechanical drive as a lathe, and I could use a chisel to obtain a perfectly circular finish (figure 6.18).

I must say that the amount of work required to make this wheel was more than I had anticipated. If I had to make another, I would probably use HDPE plastic, which is sold in 12 in. (30 cm) diameter bars. I would then simply have to cut a slice of the required thickness (4 in., or 10 cm) and drill a hole in the center for the shaft. Another original solution that has been used by a correspondent in the discussion forums is to glue together about thirty circular saw blades. Other ways are surely possible, depending on your imagination.

THE TEETH

The teeth on the rotor need to be sharp enough to effectively scrape the flesh of the apples but without being razor-sharp. It is preferable that the seeds don't get broken, although one broken pip here or there won't do harm. Stainless steel is best. After having evaluated a number of possibilities, I chose to use pipe collars: they are inexpensive, available in stainless steel, and easy to find and transform into efficient cutters. The largest diameter should be used, as only the solid part is kept. It then simply becomes a question of cutting strips, bending them into an L shape, and drilling a few holes to permit screwing the teeth into the rotor. Stainless steel screws should be used. Figure 6.19 on page 108 shows a new collar and another one ready to cut into strips. You can also see a prototype tooth screwed into the board

Figure 6.17. Setup for gluing the disks one on top of the other.

Figure 6.18. Setup for finishing the circumference by turning.

Figure 6.19. Preparation of the strips from pipe collars.

Figure 6.20. Bending the strips in a vise.

that I used to test its efficiency as a cutter. Figures 6.20 and 6.21 illustrate the bending of the strips in a vise. The strips were inserted ⅛ in. (3 mm) between the jaws, and the free end was hit with a hammer to bend it. The height of the teeth thus obtained is equal to the length inserted between the jaws, in this case ⅛ in. (3 mm), which produces a pomace of pretty much the right size.

TIPS:

Figure 6.21. Bent strip in an L shape.

- For cutting the strips, good-quality sheet metal scissors work fine. And for drilling the holes for the screws, I recommend that you first punch at the hole location to bump the metal so the drill bit stays in place, then use a drill with a sharp bit at low speed but with a good load on it. A drill press is ideal for this.
- On the number of teeth and the pattern for positioning them, much variation is possible. The teeth should be fairly scattered along the circumference and should be at least 2 or 3 in. (5 or 7 cm) apart.

Figure 6.22 shows the rotor complete with the varnish applied. I used an oil-based varnish for furniture and flooring, the most resistant possible.

Figure 6.22. Rotor complete with teeth and varnished.

These are food-safe, but they need to cure for a long time before all the smell goes away—we are talking weeks here, which means the grinder needs to be completed well in advance of the pressing season. You may also notice in figure 6.22 the circular aluminum plate on the side of the wheel. There is one such plate on each side, and their role is to prevent the wheel from slipping on the shaft. For this, they have a setscrew (as with the pulleys). Mine were made by a friend, Marco Béland, who has a small shop and who would accept only a few bottles of cider as payment. I take the occasion here to thank him. An equivalent of these plates could be made by welding a piece of steel pipe to a plate, which could be done in any car repair shop.

Note that I use the rotor with a rotation direction such that the screws lead the cutters. I had first installed it the other way around, but I prefer it this way, as the grind is finer, although this makes the grinder slightly slower.

Frame and Housings

The rotor is really the heart of the grinder, but we need a few elements around it. These are made of wood and consist of:

- The top housing, which incorporates the stator, the back plate, and two sides;
- The bottom housing, which is simply a chute to insure that the pomace is directed into a bucket without too much spill; and
- A frame on which all the elements, including the motor, will be secured.

As I wanted all these elements to be easily removable to facilitate cleaning, I adapted the clips from old ski boots to attach together the two housings onto the frame. One of these clips is seen in figure 6.23. The motor is also attached to the

Figure 6.23. Frame and housings, almost completed.

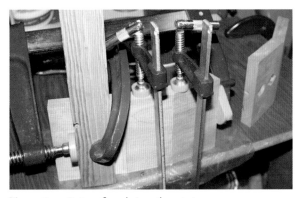

Figure 6.24. Setup for gluing the stator.

Figure 6.25. Top housing assembly: two sides in plywood, the stator on the left and the back plate on the right.

Figure 6.26. Assembling the frame.

frame with such a clip, which makes the removal of these elements very quick.

The top housing is the most complex to build, as it incorporates the stator, whose shape is important to insure the apples are driven inside the grinder, as we have seen at the beginning of this article. I built it out of hardwood, with pieces cut at a precise angle and glued (figure 6.24 on page 109). I added screws for extra strength. The sides are standard plywood, 12" × 14" (30 cm × 35 cm), and the back plate is built in similar fashion to the stator, but it doesn't have to be as precisely made, as its role is simply to guide the apples into the grinder. The width of the stator and back plate needs to be slightly more, ¼ in. (6 mm), than that of the rotor, to leave a clearance between the sides of the rotor and the sides of the housings. Note that the plywood side plate that is vertical in figure 6.25 on page 109 really goes on top of the stator and back plate and is screwed onto these. Also, the squarish apertures provide clearance for the two rotor side plates to make sure the clearance between the side of the rotor and the side plate of the housing may be kept small (at about ⅛ in., or 3 mm).

The bottom housing is also made of plywood, and there is nothing particular about it. As for the frame, it needs to be strong, as it will support all the elements of the grinder. I had a few pieces of oak that I used for this. Figure 6.26 shows the completed frame, whose dimensions are set to accommodate the housings. We see in the middle the reinforcement with holes to fix the bearings. These holes need to be drilled at a larger diameter than the bolts used to maintain the bearings, so as to provide some adjustment: in effect this will permit the operator to precisely adjust the position of the rotor in relation to the stator and keep the gap between the extremity of the teeth and the stator to a minimum.

The Hopper

The hopper is like a large funnel that sits on top of the grinder and into which we pour the apples. It is simply built of four pieces of plywood cut into a trapezoidal shape. A horizontal plate with an aperture inside the hopper holds the apples and prevents all of them from entering the grinder at the same time. The operator may pour about 10 lb. (5 kg) of apples at a time into the hopper and guide them through the opening of the plate. When I work alone, I need about a minute and a half to process a bushel of apples through the grinder. With a helper who pours the apples, the time falls to approximately a minute.

Figures 6.27 and 6.28 show the completed grinder before final assembly and ready for use, with legs attached to the frame and with the hopper on top. Note that for security reasons there should be a protective housing around the belt and pulleys to prevent objects from being caught by the rotation, which isn't shown in figure 6.28.

Figure 6.27. Completed grinder before assembly.

Figure 6.28. Assembled grinder ready for use.

CHAPTER 7

APPLE PRESSES

A press generally consists of two plates on which we apply a load. The pomace is imprisoned between these plates (this is traditionally called the *cheese*) and is thus put under pressure, which forces the extraction of the juice.

In this chapter, we will review the main types of presses that are likely to be used by a cider maker. This will be followed by a guide for those who will want to build their own.

Figure 7.1. Two examples of central stem presses from the end of the nineteenth century. Illustrations, left to right, are from Power (1890–1891) and Jacquemin and Alliot (1902).

◀ 7.1 ▶
Main Characteristics of Presses

We may distinguish the most important traditional types of presses from the following criteria:

- The press may have a central stem or an external frame, in wood or steel. Other presses have a multiple screw system that acts as an external frame.
- The load may be applied with a screw or with a hydraulic cylinder (this is called the *actuator*). Some very old presses had a lever system to apply the load.
- The pomace is contained either inside a slatted basket or by press cloths with separators that permit the draining of the juice (rack-and-cloth press).

In addition to these traditional presses, there is a new type of press, the *hydropress* (also called a bladder, or water, press), which is interesting for cider makers that have small to medium productions and that I describe later. All press types described above are batch presses, meaning that the press is loaded with pomace, pressure is applied, and finally the pressed pomace is removed and the cycle started again. In large juicing facilities, continuous output presses are more often seen. Among these are belt presses, where the pomace is pressed between two large belts that pass between rollers, and continuous screw presses, where the pomace is compressed in a type of Archimedes screw. But large industrial presses are not discussed further here.

Central Stem Presses

The central stem press was much in use by the end of the nineteenth century. Figure 7.1 illustrations on page 113 are from books of that period and show as well the two major methods to contain the pomace: on the left a basket press and on the right a rack-and-cloth press. Some models had a square slatted basket instead. The tightening system could be fairly complex in order to increase the load applied, with the use of ratchets and demultiplication gears. A good description of those systems is given by Power (1891). With the basket presses, in order to facilitate the drainage of the juice, straw was traditionally disposed inside the basket between layers of pomace to form the cheese. Nowadays we would use racks instead of layers of straw.

In these presses the central stem is most often a screw, but it may also be an axis with notches, in which case a ratchet system applies the load (like in older ratchet-type car jacks). Larger presses as in figure 7.1 aren't made anymore, as nowadays we instead use hydraulics for larger capacities, but there are still some in use, chiefly in Europe. However, small and midsize central screw basket presses as shown in figure 7.2 are still being manufactured, mainly in Italy. There are models of different dimensions with capacities ranging from ½ bushel to over 10 bushels of apples. They are generally used for grape pressing but will also work with apples, although the large models are less efficient. These presses are widely available in Europe and America and may often be rented from winemaking supply stores for a day or a weekend.

The central stem presses are simple and relatively inexpensive. However, they suffer from some major inconveniences when compared with external frame presses. First, the stem itself, made of steel, is surrounded with pomace, which is acidic and may cause corrosion of the steel, which may in turn cause blackening of the cider. To avoid this, the stem could be of stainless steel, though this is very expensive, or protected by a coating of paint or lacquer or food-safe grease. For the same reasons, the base, which generally is made of enameled steel or cast iron, needs to be checked regularly to make sure the enamel isn't chipped.

The second inconvenience comes from the annoyance caused by this stem. With a basket press, the use of a drainage bag becomes more difficult, as it will require a hole to let the stem pass. And when the pressing is complete it is far trickier to remove the pressed pomace. With a rack-and-cloth press, again the clothes will need a hole. The racks will also require one, or else they may be made in two pieces. The removal of the pressed pomace will be more laborious. For these reasons, I wouldn't recommend buying or building a press of this type and would suggest instead an external frame press.

External Frame Presses

The external frame press is the most common press system in use for apples nowadays, and the most widely recommended. The load is transmitted through a rectangular frame, which surrounds the cheese that is being pressed. This frame is

Figure 7.2. A modern Italian central screw basket press.

usually made of wood or steel or sometimes a combination of these two materials. Cast iron is also used on some presses. The load is either applied by a screw in smaller presses or by a hydraulic cylinder. As with the previous type of press, the pomace may be held either by a slatted basket or by a rack-and-cloth system.

The concept of the external frame press is quite old, as can be seen from figure 7.3 on page 116 of such a press in the *Vinetum Britannicum* of John Worlidge, dating back to 1676. It is interesting to note here the big wooden screw and the straw basket.

Figure 7.3. A wooden frame press from 350 years ago. Illustration from Worlidge, 1676. Scan from original document courtesy of Andrew Lea.

Most small modern presses for hobbyists in America have a wooden frame with a slatted basket, and a screw is used to provide the load. Figure 7.4 gives a typical example of such a press: this is my first press, which is of a traditional American design. As may easily be seen, all the major elements of this press are quite similar to that from the Worlidge illustration. Another popular design is the double-tub press shown in figure III.2 on page 92. Wooden frame presses are relatively easy to build for someone who has the necessary woodworking tools. It is also possible to buy kits that include the grinder, the screw, and all steel parts. In the United States there are quite a few manufacturers that offer such presses at prices that range between $350 and $1,500, depending on the size and the quality of the craftsmanship, the number of tubs, and whether a grinder is included or not. The capacity of those amateur presses may vary between ½ to 1½ bushels of apples per load. (See, for example, www.correll ciderpresses.com, www.jaffreypress.com, or www.happyvalleyranch.com.) Some manufacturers also offer steel frame presses (www .pleasanthillgrain.com). The yield of these small basket presses is not great, however, and will seldom exceed 60 percent efficiency in weight (i.e., 100 lb. or kg of apples would yield 60 lb. or kg of juice for an efficiency of 60 percent, which would be about 7 gallons from 100 lb. or 57 liters from 100 kg).

At the other end of the spectrum are large, hydraulic, steel frame, rack-and-cloth presses that are used by commercial cider makers. The capacity of such presses may be up to a ton of pomace per load, and they cost tens of thousands of dollars. These presses have a much higher yield efficiency

Figure 7.4. A modern wood frame press.

that may reach 80 percent. There is also an industrial-grade apple press known as the Goodnature Squeezebox, which is an interesting variation on the external frame design where the frame is horizontal and the load also applied horizontally. The layers of pomace are then vertical, in a sort of accordion pattern, with openings on the top for loading. After the pressing is complete, this setup is turned upside down and the dry pomace simply falls and is taken away.

Figure 7.5. A homemade rack-and-cloth press.

The choice is broader in Europe. For example, in England Vigo (www.vigopresses.co.uk) offers a wide selection of steel frame presses whose capacity ranges from ¼ to 2 bushels per load (the smaller models are of the central stem type). Most are basket presses, but the larger model is a rack-and-cloth press. All the Vigo presses use a screw to apply the load. In France Tompress (www .tompress.com) offers a comparable selection of products. And for larger capacities, the products from the Austrian company Voran (www.voran.at) are quite popular with the small and mid-scale commercial cider producers in Europe.

Most of the homemade presses are of the external frame type, in a myriad of designs. Some are made from a modified shop press. Others use a wooden frame or a steel frame. Figure 7.5, showing a small press I built, is a good example: it is a rack-and-cloth press, the frame is welded steel, and the load is provided by a 4-ton hydraulic jack. It has a capacity of 1 bushel of apples per pressing. We can also see, on the left, the wooden square

that is used to form the layers of pomace and, on the right, wooden blocks that are required to increase the stroke of the cylinder.

In my opinion, the external frame press is the best choice for the serious hobbyist cider maker. And since there are many possible variations, I will try here to weigh the advantages and inconveniences of the different configurations.

FRAME MATERIAL: WOOD OR STEEL?

For equal strength, steel is lighter and less cumbersome. On the other hand, wood is easier to work with. This choice will depend a lot on the tooling and materials available, but if you are able to use it, steel has the advantage. Other possibilities would be wooden vertical members and steel or cast iron crossbars or steel threaded rods as vertical members and wooden crossbars, as discussed in the next section. Mechanical shop presses are an interesting option, as they are fairly inexpensive and may easily be modified for pressing apples. Shop presses normally include a hydraulic cylinder.

POMACE RETENTION SYSTEM: BASKET OR RACK-AND-CLOTH?

The main advantage of the basket press is the speed of loading: it is just a question of pouring the bucketful of pomace into the basket of the press. With the rack-and-cloth system, it takes some time to prepare each layer of pomace and build the cheese. A second advantage of the basket press is that there are fewer bits and pieces to clean at the end of the pressing day. On the other hand, the yield efficiency of the basket press decreases as the size of the press increases. This is because the juice that is in the middle of the basket has a long way to travel through the pressurized pomace before it can escape. With a rack-and-cloth system, each layer has a thickness of about 3 in. (8 cm), and the juice can escape more easily and faster. The yield efficiency is thus increased. We may give the advantage to the basket press for small capacities of less than 1 bushel per load. For larger capacities, the rack-and-cloth system would have the advantage.

APPLICATION OF THE LOAD: SCREW OR HYDRAULIC?

The screw is the traditional actuator for the small amateur presses and, as we have seen above, was quite universally used in the old days. Today, however, we can buy inexpensive hydraulic jacks that are available in many capacities between 2 and 20 tons. For do-it-yourselfers who build their own presses, hydraulic jacks are a much more economical solution than the cost of a screw with the nut and a thrust bearing. The only inconvenience of the jack is that its stroke is generally not long enough for a complete pressing, and thus at mid-pressing you must remove the jack, add blocks, and reinstall the jack. If you use a jack with a basket press, you also need to insure the higher part of the basket will not interfere with the lever of the jack. In my opinion, having used both a screw and a hydraulic jack, I think the jack generally has the advantage. But for the smaller basket presses, the screw may be a better choice. And for large rack-and-cloth presses, industrial hydraulic cylinders fed by a pump would be used instead.

Another but less common option is a pneumatic actuator, that is, one that works with compressed air. Figure 7.6 shows how I have modified my old wooden basket press into a much more efficient rack-and-cloth press. In so doing I have

Figure 7.6. Rack-and-cloth press with air spring.

also doubled its capacity: when it was a basket press, I would load a little less than a bushel of apples and would get at most a little over 2 gallons (8 liters) of juice. Now I can press 2 bushels at a time and get 5 gallons (19 liters) per press load. You may notice the actuator, which is like a small tire: this is an air spring, and these are often used in truck suspensions. This air spring is equipped with a valve like the one on a tire, and it is inflated to 90 psi (with the small compressor on the floor) to provide the pressing load. The great advantage of this actuator is that once it is pressurized, the load remains practically constant, even if the cheese retracts. This means I don't need to stay with the press to tighten the screw all the time, and thus I can do something else, like picking or grinding apples. On the other hand, it doesn't provide more than 2 in. (5 cm) of travel, although some models do provide a greater travel than the unit I have. Hence, to make a pressing, I first use the screw to compress the cheese until the pressure builds up. The screw is then retracted and the air spring installed and pressurized for the last part of the pressing. This is the press setup I now use on a regular basis. These air springs are not easily found, and new units are quite expensive, but if you see one at a flea market or elsewhere, it might be worth giving it a try.

The Multiple-Screw Presses

Multiple-screw presses are a variation of external frame presses where the vertical members are threaded rods and the top crossbar moves downward to compress the pomace by the action of the screws or nuts turning. There can be twin-screw, tri-screw, or even quad-screw presses. A good

Figure 7.7. Miniature triple-screw press.

example of a twin-screw press is given in figure III.1 on page 89: an ancient press still in operation on the Isle of Jersey whose screws are made of wood. As these screws are turned with a lever, the load is applied to the cheese. We could more easily imagine such a press in a museum than in a modern cidery. It nevertheless illustrates very well the principle of these presses. Quite a number of twin-screw presses dating from the Victorian era are still in use in England, and a few nice restoration projects have been done on such presses. Some notable examples of multi-screw presses from the end of the nineteenth century had a geared system to insure both nuts turned together and a demultiplication system that was designed so the operator just had to turn a crank to activate the pressing.

Figure 7.7 shows a very small demonstration tri-screw press that I built and use for taking juice samples from small quantities of apples. The screws are tightened with an electric drill equipped with the appropriate socket. One thing, however, with multiple-screw presses is that they are not practical for use as a basket press, because the basket could interfere with the movement of the crossbar, unless the screws are very long and some blocks are used. If you intend to make only a small quantity of cider (for example, because it is your first trial and you are not sure that you want to invest in a press), a small quad-screw press could be the least expensive and easiest press you could have: take two pieces of plywood, about 18 in (45 cm) square; drill a hole at each corner; get four bolts, washers, and nuts to put into each hole; put the pomace in a cloth between the plates; and as you tighten these nuts, you will effectively extract the juice. It is as simple as that. Naturally, you can improve the design a bit by making sides so the juice doesn't spill everywhere, and grooves so the juice flows more easily, and you may get something similar to the small triple-screw press shown in figure 7.7.

Hydropress (Water, or Bladder, Press)

These presses are made in Europe, and some models are available from a few distributors in North America. They consist of a basket—most often in stainless steel grid, though some are slatted wood—inside which there is a rubber chamber or bladder connected to the domestic water system. It is the water pressure that will inflate the chamber and compress the pomace against the grid to extract the juice. These presses are a good solution for intermediate productions and are available in a wide range of capacities, from 1 to 20 bushels of apples, and with price tags from $800 to $8,000 in the United States. Some of the important manufacturers of water presses are:

- Gomark in Slovenia (www.gomark.si), which makes the Lancman presses, distributed in the United States by OESCO (www.oescoinc.com).

- Speidel (www.speidels-hausmosterei.de) in Germany, whose presses are now available in America (morewinemaking.com). See figure 7.8.
- Zambelli (www.zambellienotech.it) of Italy, available through some wine-making supply stores.

Hydropresses are practical, and easy to use and clean. They do, however, have a few inconveniences: the pressure is not as high as with a good hydraulic press, and the yield efficiency will thus be slightly reduced: most often it will be around 50 to 60 percent. Moreover, these presses use a quantity of water, and this water needs to be at a good pressure (45 psi, or 300 kPa, or 3 bars). Thus they can't be used in locations where there is little water or

Figure 7.8. The larger model of hydropress from Speidel. Photo courtesy of Speidel.

low pressure (though it is possible to recapture the water and reuse it with a pressure pump). The durability of the rubber chamber is not really known. I imagine that with time the rubber may lose its elasticity and watertightness. Are you sure you will be able to get a replacement chamber fifteen years from now? And finally, these presses will work well only if filled to capacity. This can prove annoying, for example, when there is only a small quantity of a certain variety of apple and you would like to obtain pure juice from this variety to measure its properties. A smaller press would have to be used on those occasions.

I don't personally use one of these presses, but here are a few tricks I gathered from reports given by users: when only a partial load of pomace is available for pressing, it is then possible to fill-up the press with pressed pomace from the previous load, and it works fine this way. Another important recommendation is that the press should not be overfilled as it then loses some of its efficiency: it should just be loosely filled to capacity.

◀ 7.2 ▶
Designing and Building a Press

Once you have decided to make your own press, the first step is to define its main parameters: type, capacity, applied load, and general dimensions. I will concentrate the discussion here on rack-and-cloth presses with an external frame, as these are easiest to make, the most efficient, and the most generally recommended for serious hobbyist as well as small commercial cider makers. Later we will examine in more detail the different bits and pieces that you will need to build to complete the press. And, as examples, I will develop the design of two simple presses, a small and a medium—one of these should meet the needs of most readers:

- The small press has a capacity of about 40 lb. (18 kg) of pomace (1 bushel of apples) and is recommended for a cider production of up to 150 gallons (600 liters) per year, which would require processing about a ton of apples (50 to 55 bushels). This is really the smallest press size that is worth doing as a rack-and-cloth press, and it is large enough for most hobbyists. Even if you make less cider, I would not recommend making a press any smaller than that, unless you need something very small for making juice tests, and in that case it would be preferable to make something other than a rack-and-cloth press. You could, for example, build the same frame but use it as a basket press, which would reduce its capacity and permit faster loading and unloading cycles. The recommended actuator for this press would be a 4- to 6-ton hydraulic jack.

- The medium press has a capacity of about 120 lb. (54 kg) of pomace (3 bushels of apples) and is recommended if your cider production is from 100 to 500 gallons (400 to 2,000 liters) per year. This press would use an 8- to 12-ton jack.

This is a serious hobbyist's press that could also meet the needs of a very small commercial cider maker. If you think you need a larger press than this, it could still be made on the same model but scaled up. However, I would then recommend making the crossbeams out of steel rather than wood. Also, buying and adapting a shop press could be a better alternative for larger pressing needs.

Press Components

A press comprises a number of elements that you will need to either make or procure:

- **Frame.** This is the structural part of the press, for which some strength calculations need to be made (see the following section). The frame consists of two vertical beams that we call the *uprights* and two horizontal ones that we call the *crossbeams*.
- **Actuator.** The actuator is the mechanical element that will produce the compressive load on the pomace. The most common actuators are the screw and the hydraulic cylinder, but other types, like compressed air actuators, could be used. For the two presses we propose to make here, a hydraulic jack would be the least expensive and most efficient actuator.
- **Stand.** This component provides the feet to the press and keeps it in a vertical position. It also holds the tray.
- **Tray.** The role of the tray is to collect the juice escaping from the cheese and to guide it toward a receiving container.
- **Racks.** These are used as separators between the layers of pomace. Racks are preferably

grooved so as to facilitate the drainage of the juice. A first rack should be placed on the bottom of the tray unless the tray itself is grooved.
- **Press cloths.** The pomace is contained in fabric press cloths that let the juice escape.
- **Cheese form.** This is a square form that is used to build up the cheese. It is not used during the actual pressing.
- **Top plate.** This square plate is put on top of the last layer, receives the load from the actuator, and distributes the pressure evenly on the cheese.
- **Spacing blocks.** These are blocks that are used between the top plate and the jack to adjust for the jack extension, which will not be long enough for a complete press.
- **Receiving bucket.** This is the container where the juice flows from the tray.

Basic Parameters of the Press

Let us first determine the basic parameters for the press: these are the height and width of the frame, the capacity, and the load required to obtain a good yield efficiency.

Press width

The free width between the uprights is the first important parameter to look at. This controls the size of the tray and the racks.

The tray exterior width will be equal to the press free width minus a small clearance of ⅛ to ¼ in. (3 to 6 mm).

The tray interior width is obtained by subtracting twice the thickness of the sides. If you make your tray out of wood, these sides would usually be ¾ in. (19 mm) thick.

The racks should be smaller than the tray width to insure no juice falls outside of the tray. This should also allow for small misalignments. Usually the rack width would be 1.5 to 2 in. (35 to 50 mm) less than the tray interior width for smaller presses and 2 to 4 in. (50 to 100 mm) less for larger presses.

The layers of pomace should be formed smaller than the racks, as they will expand under the pressure, and we don't want them to protrude too much outside of the racks. Hence the cheese form should be about 1.5 in. (38 mm) smaller than the racks if the layer height is about 2.5 to 3.5 in. (63 to 90 mm), which is the recommended height range. With thinner layers, the form could be made wider. And knowing the form width and height, we can obtain the volume capacity of a layer of pomace.

LOAD

The load required from the actuator is a function of the rack surface area, because it is the racks that transmit the pressure from one layer to another. The minimum recommended pressure for a good pressing is 50 psi (350 kPa). Large industrial presses may develop pressures above 100 psi (700 kPa), but the gain over 80 psi (550 kPa) is quite marginal. Hence, in general, for a homemade press we aim at 50 to 80 psi (400 to 550 kPa). The required load (P) is obtained from:

$$P = (\text{pressure}) \times (\text{rack width})^2$$

In US customary units, the load thus obtained will be in pounds if the rack width is in inches and may be converted into tons by dividing by 2,000. In SI units, if the rack width is in cm and the pressure in kPa, the result has to be divided by 100,000 to obtain the load in tons.

PRESS HEIGHT

Once the width is established, the height of the press will determine how many layers of pomace we will be able to fit in the press and hence its volumic capacity. So let's look at what we need to fit in the free available height between the two crossbeams of the frame. Starting from the bottom, we have a base board, which would be ¾ in. (19 mm) thick plywood; the tray board, which is ¾ in. (19 mm) plywood; racks and layers of pomace in alternation; the top plate; and the jack. Most jacks are approximately 8 in. (20 cm) high when retracted. As for the top plate, it needs to be thicker as the load is increased. For small presses, a thickness of 1.5 in. (38 mm) is fine, but for larger presses this may be doubled.

I would not recommend building a stack higher than the width of the racks, as this could make the stack unstable: some racks could slip, and the cheese would become impossible to press. We should first determine the number of layers we will have in our cheese: taking our medium press example, with a rack thickness of ½ in. (12 mm), a rack width of 17.5 in. (45 cm), and a cheese height equal to the rack width, we see we could have:

- 4 layers each 4.4 in. (11.3 cm) thick, making the cheese form height 3.9 in. (10.1 cm)
- 5 layers each 3.5 in. (9 cm) thick, cheese form height 3 in. (7.8 cm)
- 6 layers each 2.9 in. (7.5 cm) thick, cheese form height 2.4 in. (6.3 cm)

I would choose the five-layer configuration in such a case, although the six-layer configuration would also be good. Building the five-layer cheese will take slightly less time, but the yield could be slightly better with the thinner layers.

CAPACITY

The maximum volume capacity (*V*) of the press would then be given by:

$$V = \text{(number of layers)} \times \text{(form height)} \times \text{(form internal width)}^2$$

where *V* will be expressed in cubic inches or cubic centimeters. Now, you could make a smaller press if you wish, for example, by making fewer layers or with thinner layers, but I would still recommend

sizing the height of the press so it may accommodate the maximum capacity as defined above.

Finally, from the volume capacity, we may approximate the capacity in mass (or weight) of apples from the volumic mass of the pomace, which is approximately 0.03 lb./cubic inch or 0.8 kg/liter. (Note that 1 liter is 1,000 cubic centimeters.) From this, we obtain the press capacity in bushels, each bushel containing 40 lb. (18 kg) of apples.

The juice yield efficiency from such a press may vary from 45 percent to 70 percent in mass, depending on the juiciness of the apples, the

TABLE 7.1:
Basic parameters for the example presses

		SMALL PRESS		MEDIUM PRESS	
		US UNITS	SI UNITS	US UNITS	SI UNITS
Frame, free width	in./cm	16	41	21	54
Frame, free height	in./cm	24	60.5	30.5	77
Tray, external width	in./cm	15.75	40.4	20.75	53.4
Tray, internal width	in./cm	14.25	36.6	19.25	49.6
Rack, width	in./cm	12.75	32.8	17.5	45.1
Number of layers		4		5	
Form, internal width	in./cm	11.25	29	16	41.3
Form, height	in./cm	2.7	7.0	3.0	7.8
Top plate, thickness	in./cm	1.5	3.8	3	7.5
Capacity, volume	cu in./L	1361	23.5	3,840	66.7
Capacity, mass	lb./kg	41	19	115	53
Capacity, bushels	bu	1		3	
Juice yield (45 percent efficiency)	gal./L	2.1	8.1	5.9	22.9
Juice yield (70 percent efficiency)	gal./L	3.3	12.6	9.2	35.6
Juice container	gal./L	3.6	13.8	10.1	39.1
Load	tons	4 to 6		8 to 12	

fineness of the pomace, the pressure applied, and the amount of time under pressure. Hence, we could obtain from 2 to 3.2 gallons (7.7 to 12 liters) of juice per bushel of apples. Ideally, the juice-receiving container should be large enough to contain all the juice from a complete pressing; otherwise, it will invariably happen one day that you will forget to empty it and some juice will spill (this is Murphy's law). For this, we may take the higher figure above and give an extra allowance of 10 percent for the capacity of the container.

Table 7.1 gives the basic parameters for the example presses described in the beginning of this article.

Building the Press

Now that the basic parameters are defined, it's time to build the press. I will discuss here methods to make the components described above,

and to illustrate this I have built a smaller-scale press of similar design and taken pictures of the main steps. This is truly a miniature press that I intend to use for demonstration only. It has a capacity of just 6.5 lb. (3 kg) of apples. However, it has all the same features as the larger press that you will be making. I have a small, 1.5-ton jack that I will use with it.

FRAME

I propose building a frame that consists of hard-wood laminated crossbeams and threaded rods for the uprights. This represents the simplest way to assemble a frame and requires the least special tooling and equipment. Figure 7.9 shows the completed frame of the demonstration press.

The crossbeams are made by a laminate of hardwood planks (oak or maple). Note that for the demonstration press shown in figures 7.9–7.14, I

Figure 7.9. Frame of the demonstration press.

Figure 7.10. Crossbeam gluing setup.

TABLE 7.2:
Dimensions for the press frame

		SMALL PRESS		MEDIUM PRESS	
		US UNITS	SI UNITS	US UNITS	SI UNITS
CROSSBEAMS:					
Number of planks		4	4	6	6
Plank thickness	in./mm	0.75	19	0.75	19
Plank height	in./mm	5.5	145	7.5	195
Crossbeam length	in./cm	20.5	53	27	72
Rod position C/C	in./cm	18.25	47	24	63
THREADED RODS:					
Rod diameter	in./mm	0.75	20	1	24
Rod length	in./cm	40	100	50	128

used softwood. These planks are glued together with a standard carpenter's glue. It is important to clamp the planks together solidly while the glue dries. Screws may also be used.

Four planks, nominal 1 × 6s, are used for the small press and six planks, nominal 1 × 8s, for the medium press. Thus the finished crossbeams for the small press will be 3 in. (76 mm) wide by 5.5 in. (145 mm) high and for the medium press 4.5 in. (114 mm) wide by 7.5 in. (195 mm) high. These dimensions have been calculated to handle the higher recommended loads of 6 and 12 tons, respectively. For other sizes of presses, the methods to determine the strength of the frame are explained in the following section. The necessary dimensions to make the frame are given in table 7.2.

To facilitate the assembly (and avoid having to drill through the crossbeams), groove the two middle planks before gluing so as to create a hole through which the rods will pass (figure 7.11). These grooves should be made at the rod position center given in table 7.2 (Rod position C/C, center to center), and their width should be equal to the rod diameter, while their depth should be half the width. Note that if you use an odd number of planks for the crossbar (as is the case with the demo press), the middle plank may be cut shorter to achieve the same result.

The uprights will be threaded rods whose size and length are given in table 7.2. In addition to the two rods, eight nuts and washers are required for the assembly. Choose the largest and thickest washers available, as these will help spread the load over a larger surface of wood. To further help in spreading the load, the use of load distribution plates is essential (figure 7.12). These are planks of hardwood, or preferably steel plates, that will distribute the load over the whole width of the crossbeam.

Figure 7.11. Groove in the crossbeam plank to allow passage for the threaded rod.

Figure 7.12. Assembly of the rod with a load distribution plate.

Figure 7.13. Steel plate to distribute the load from the jack.

In a similar fashion, a load distribution plate should be installed at the center of the top crossbeam, where the jack will apply the load. Remember up to 12 tons will push on this point, and it is essential to spread this load over a large area. This plate should also be marked to indicate the middle position of the crossbeam, so that the jack will be well aligned with the frame. This plate should be in steel and of a sufficient thickness: I would recommend ½ inch if a 12-ton jack is used. With a smaller jack, a thinner plate may be used, and for the demo press I have a ¼-inch steel plate, which is amply sufficient, as may be seen in figure 7.13.

STAND

The stand holds the press at a certain height above the floor and gives it stability. It is normally built around the lower crossbeam or sometimes is an

Figure 7.14. Three-legged stand for the demo press.

extension of the uprights, and it provides the feet to the press. It needs to be sturdy enough so that when you work on the jack, the press remains stable. It also supplies a platform that maintains the tray in place and provides some structural strength so the tray doesn't bend under the load.

For the small demonstration press, I made the very simple three-legged stand shown in figure 7.14. However, I found out that this stand, although very cute for this miniature demonstration press, is not stable enough for real pressing use. Hence, for the press you are building, I would suggest instead a design as per the drawing of figure 7.15, where the crossbeam is represented by a large X. The top plywood board should be ¾ in. (19 mm) thick. The dimensions of this board are:

length: same as width of tray, so for the small press 15.75 in. (40.4 cm) and for the medium 20.75 in. (53.4 cm);

depth: same as width of racks, so for the small press 12.75 in. (32.8 cm) and for the medium 17.5 in. (45.1 cm).

The vertical legs should be of a length sufficient to accommodate the height of the juice-receiving container that you will use. They may be made with the same type of planks used for the crossbeam. Note that the joints between the plywood board and the legs, circled in red in figure 7.15, need to be strong to resist the load and keep the tray from bending. Hence, they should be glued and screwed. And finally, it is useful to make this stand slightly tilted toward the front: this improves the drainage of the juice, as it will flow naturally to the exit.

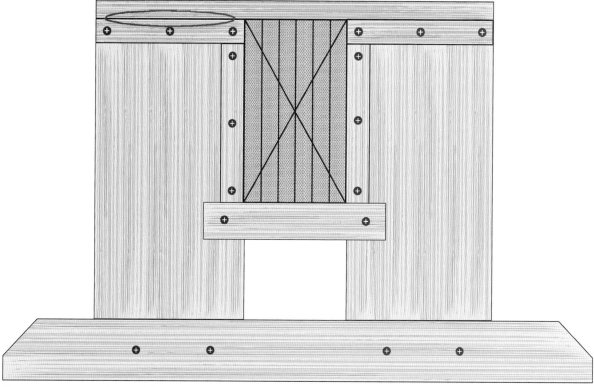

Figure 7.15. Suggested stand design.

TRAY

The bottom of the juice-collecting tray is made of a plywood board, and its side walls are planks that may be either soft- or hardwood. The width of the tray for the small press is 15.75 in. (40.4 cm) and for the medium 20.75 in. (53.4 cm). Its length may be 1 to 2 in. (25 to 50 mm) or so longer. For the side walls, a height of 1.5 to 2 in. (40 to 50 mm) is fine, and the thickness would be ¾ in. (19 mm). The base plywood should be stiff enough, so a thickness of ¾ in. (19 mm) is recommended. A hole needs to be drilled to permit the juice to drain toward the receiving container.

If you like to be fancy, you may shape the front of the tray at an angle, as in figure 7.16, but this is not really necessary.

RACKS

The racks are separators between the layers of pomace. The number of racks you will need is

Figure 7.16. Juice-collecting tray with a rack.

equal to the number of layers you will make to build the cheese—four or five, respectively, for the two example presses, unless your tray is grooved, in which case you will need one less rack. They should be made square, with the side length (or width) as given in table 7.1: 12.75 in. (32.8 cm) for the small press and 17.5 in. (45.1 cm) for the medium.

The two most common materials to make them are wood and HDPE plastic. Some cider makers simply use plain boards as racks, but I personally think that if the rack is grooved on one side, this improves the drainage of the juice, thus permitting a faster press and increased yield. I have used two different methods to make racks: the first is by gluing strips of wood on a thin plywood board, as illustrated by figure 7.17. Once all the strips are glued, the rack is cut to final dimensions. This method requires quite a bit of time but makes very nice racks. The plywood

Figure 7.17. Racks made by gluing strips of wood on plywood.

thickness may be ¼ in. (6 mm), and the strips may be ¾ to 1.5 in (19 to 40 mm) wide by about ¼ in. (6 mm) thick, with spacing also ¼ in. (6 mm).

The second method is to cut grooves (on one side only) on a plywood or HDPE plastic board. The thickness of the board may be ½ in. (12 mm);

Figure 7.18. Grooved plywood rack and cheese form.

the depth and width of the grooves should be about ¼ in. (6 mm). The distance between the grooves would be about 1 in. (25 mm). A router table would be preferred for this, but a table saw may also be used; however, two passes are then required for each groove to obtain the width, and the shape of the grooves thus obtained may render the rack more prone to breakage. This is much faster than the first method, and the racks made this way are just as good, only not quite as handsome. Such a rack is shown in figure 7.18 with the cheese form.

For the bottom rack, i.e., the one that sits in the tray and on which you build the first layer, it may be made slats on slats instead of on plywood: this improves the draining of the juice as it can flow under the rack. It would then be a bit like a trellis. The rack shown in figure 7.16 is of the slat-on-slat type.

Cheese form

The cheese form is a simple square wood frame made from four planks, as shown in figure 7.18 with a rack. The interior width and height of this frame are given in table 7.1 on page 124. However, if you use planks ¾ in. (19 mm) thick, you may then make this frame with its external size equal to that of the racks. This also makes the stack-building operation easier, as the form will automatically be centered with the underlying rack.

Press cloths

The pressing cloths are square pieces of fabric. They are placed diagonally in the cheese form, so their diagonal dimension is equal to twice the internal form width plus height, plus some

Figure 7.19. Three types of fabric for press cloths.

overlap, which should be about three-quarters of the cheese width. The side should then have a length of approximately:

(2 × internal width) + (1.5 × form height)

For the small press, this gives 27 in. (69 cm) and for the medium press 37 in. (94 cm). You will need one cloth per layer, but I suggest you have a few extras on hand. Even though they don't tear very often, it is annoying if it happens and you have no spare.

Figure 7.19 shows three types of fabric I have used for press cloths. On the top is a nylon fabric, which is sold specifically for this usage and can be ordered online but is quite expensive. The two other fabrics come from a fabric store, where they were sold as curtain material. They work just as well. Look for a white or undyed fabric that will let the juice flow easily and resists tearing. And if you are comfortable using a sewing machine, you may finish the edges.

Historically, these cloths were made of horsehair, and from this the name *hair* has been given to a layer of pomace between two racks. Another name for a single layer of pomace contained within a press cloth is a *pillow*. The origin of this name is not clear, but some people actually use pillow cases filled with pomace between racks for pressing.

TOP PLATE AND SPACING BLOCKS

The top plate is made from square plywood boards glued one on top of the other. For the small press, the thickness should be 1.5 in. (38 mm) (i.e., two boards, each ¾ in. thick) and for the medium press 3 in. (75 mm) (four boards). I like to make the width of the top plate slightly larger than the

Figure 7.20. Top plate and spacing blocks.

racks at the inside of tray dimension, that is, 14.25 in. (36.6 cm) for the small press and 19.25 in. (49.6 cm) for the medium.

The spacing blocks can be made from scrap pieces of wood. It is nice to have blocks of various heights, but they should all have the same width: 5.5 to 6 in. (14 to 15 cm) for the small press and 7.5 to 8 in. (19 to 20 cm) for the medium. One thing I do is to put a pin on one side of each block and a hole on the other. The pins I use for this are sold to hold shelves in furniture. On the one side the hole is slightly tight, so the pin is forced in and stays there, while on the other side the hole is big enough so that the pin from the adjacent block would fit into it quite loosely. This way, when I stack blocks one on top of the other, I don't have to bother centering them, as the pins automatically do it. And the top plate also has a hole to insure a good alignment with the first block. Note in figure 7.20 the dirty block on the right. This is the one on which the jack is placed. It has pieces of wood glued on it so that the jack will always be in the same position, with its axis on the center of the block. (It is dirty because one day the jack lost some oil.) I highly recommend making such a block, as it insures the jack is always well centered on the top plate. Note that this block has a pin underneath that will fit the hole in the center of the top plate. I call this one the jack base block.

PROTECTION OF THE WOOD

The question of whether we should coat the wood or not often arises in discussion forums. Both opinions have their proponents. There was even one correspondent recently who said he uses new,

Figure 7.21. Completed demo press.

uncoated plywood racks every year and throws them away once the pressing season is over. For my part, I prefer to use a good-quality, oil-based varnish to coat all wooden parts that may come into contact with the juice. This makes the cleaning much easier, as the dried juice won't stick as much. However, this varnish needs a lot of time to cure completely to ensure that there will be no odor left. The coating has to be completed three or four weeks before the beginning of the pressing season. I would like to emphasize that the wood and glue used for manufacturing plywood is not food safe and may taint the cider. Thus, varnish should be used on all plywood parts that may come into contact with the juice (racks and tray in particular). Moreover, these parts should be checked regularly for wear of the varnish and recoated if required. You can see in figure 7.21 of the completed demo press that the stand, tray, lower crossbeam, rack, cheese form, and top plate are varnished, while the spacing blocks and top crossbeam are not, as these will not come into contact with the juice.

Using Your New Rack-and-Cloth Press

The use of this press is quite straightforward. You first need to build the cheese with pomace that has been previously milled. Place the tray on the press and a first rack centered in the tray with the grooves facing upward. Then place the cheese form on the rack and a cloth diagonally inside the form (see figure 7.22 on page 134). Next, fill the form with pomace. You may compress the pomace a bit as you do this. Bring the four corners of the cloth over the pomace. Press down a bit so the juice will make the cloth stick (see figure 7.23).

Figure 7.22. **Preparing the first layer.**

Then remove the form, place another rack (always with grooves facing upward) over the pomace and the form on this new rack. Make sure everything is well centered, and make the second layer as you did the first. Repeat for the other layers until you have completed building the cheese. Install the top plate over the cloth of the last layer, the jack base block, and the jack. Adjust the length of the jack with the screw so that you have contact with the load distribution plate on the top crossbeam. Add spacer blocks if necessary (figure 7.24).

Before applying the load, make sure all the layers are well aligned and centered. Check that the axis of the jack is parallel with the uprights. When you start pumping the jack, there will be very little resistance in the beginning, and the juice will flow abundantly. Pump slowly, as you don't want much pressure during the first pressing phase.

Figure 7.23. First layer completed.

You will reach the end of the stroke of the jack quite quickly, within a couple of minutes. You then need to remove the jack, retract the piston, place some spacer blocks between the top plate and the jack base block, and reposition the jack (figure 7.25). The pressing will then enter its second phase, where things go slower. You should start to feel some resistance to the pumping of the jack, indicating that the pressure is building up in the cheese. At this stage you can start doing something else, like milling apples, for example. You need only check the press every five minutes and tighten the jack. However, when the resistance starts to build, it means the forces in play become important, and you need to insure all elements are well aligned. If the press makes funny noises or starts to twist somehow, it probably means alignment is wrong and you should investigate.

After about twenty minutes, most of the juice will have been extracted. But the longer you keep on pressing, the more juice you will get. The decision when to stop is yours. It is always difficult to decide to stop a pressing when there is still some juice flowing, even if the flow is very thin. Once finished, you need to undo the pressed cheese and start again for a new load.

On the question of when to stop, if you have little time and lots of apples, twenty minutes under the press may be sufficient. But on the other hand, if you have lots of time and no apples to spare, you might prefer to leave the pomace under press for one or even two hours. You would then obtain 10 to 15 percent more juice from the same quantity of apples. Another way to improve the yield is to make a second pressing of the pomace. Set the pressed pomace aside, but break up the layers.

Figure 7.24. Installing the jack.

Figure 7.25. Jack repositioned with spacer blocks.

Once you have accumulated enough, you may build a new cheese with this dry pomace. You can usually combine the dry pomace from two to three press loads into a new load for repressing. Some cider makers add water to the dry pomace before repressing, but I prefer not to, as this dilutes the juice and doesn't really improve the extraction, according to tests I have done. So a possible strategy, if you go for the two-pressing option, is to have a relatively quick first pressing (fifteen to twenty minutes) followed by a long second pressing (an hour or more). This permits the maximum extraction in the least time. Such a second pressing may yield about 20 percent of the juice obtained with the first pressing.

Now there remains the question of what to do with the dry pomace. I guess the best solution is to compost it and to return this organic matter to the orchard. The dry pomace may also be fed to some domestic farm animals, like cows and pigs, who are very fond of it (sometimes they may be too fond of it, hence moderation is recommended).

◄ 7.3 ►
Strength of the Press Frame

Structurally speaking, the frame consists of an assembly of two vertical beams (the uprights) and two horizontal ones (the crossbeams). The uprights are stressed axially, while the crossbeams are stressed in bending, hence the sizing will be different for the two types of beams. It may be noted that many presses are overdesigned and thus bulkier than they really need to be. In this article we will use sound mechanical engineering principles to determine the size these beams need to have to resist the load applied by the actuator, which may be either a screw or a hydraulic cylinder.

Properties of the Materials

When a beam is subjected to a load, some stress is induced in the material. Stress is defined as a force per unit area of material. In US customary units, the stress is expressed in pounds per square inch, abbreviated as *psi*, or in *ksi*, which are each 1,000 psi. These are the same units as for pressure. In SI units the stress is expressed in newtons per square millimeter, or *megapascals* (MPa), with 1 MPa = 145 psi. (For more on units, see Appendix 1.)

In engineering the stress is denoted by the Greek letter sigma (σ). Different materials will have different resistance to the stress; for example, wood may not sustain as high stress as steel. So for each material considered, I will use an allowable stress (σ_a), which is the maximum recommended stress for the material in question. This σ_a is lower than the failure stress of the material, as it includes a security factor, which I have set at a value of 2. Table 7.3 gives the recommended allowable stress for the most likely materials to be used in a press frame. I have also included the volumic mass relative to water to permit calculation of the weight of the frame.

TABLE 7.3:
Allowable axial stress for common press frame materials

MATERIAL	VOLUMIC MASS (relative to water)	FAILURE STRESS MPa	RECOMMENDED ALLOWABLE STRESS MPa	psi
Ordinary structural steel	7.9	250	125	18,000
Cast iron	7.2	170	85	12,300
Hardwoods (maple, oak)	0.65	55	27.5	4,000
Soft resinous woods (pine, spruce)	0.4	35	17.5	2,550

Note that for wood the properties are given for compression with the load in the same direction as the fibers of the wood, which is conservative, as wood is stronger in tension. When the load is applied perpendicular to the fibers, wood has much less resistance—approximately ten times less. So if you use plywood, keep in mind that the plies are in alternating directions; half of the plies will be perpendicular to the load, hence practically useless for the resistance, and this should be taken into account by dividing the allowable stress by 2.

Sizing of the Uprights

The calculations for the uprights are quite straightforward, as the stress is simply given by the ratio of the axial load through the upright by the material area. Hence, the following formula will permit us to calculate the required material area, which I denote A_u, knowing the load (P) provided by the actuator and the allowable stress (σ_a) for the material taken from table 7.3:

$$A_u = 0.5\, P / \sigma_a$$

where the factor 0.5 is used because only half of the load is transmitted through each upright.

Example: For a hardwood press frame where the actuator delivers 6 tons:

In US customary units the load P = 6 tons × 2,000 lb. = 12,000 lb. and

$$A_u = 0.5 \times 12,000 / 4,000 = 1.5 \text{ sq. in.}$$

hence, uprights 1.5 in. by 1 in. would sustain this load.

In SI units the load P = 6 tons × 10,000 N = 60,000 N and

$$A_u = 0.5 \times 60,000 / 27.5 = 1,100 \text{ mm}^2$$

hence, uprights 30 mm by 36 mm would sustain this load.

The value of A_u thus obtained should always be taken at the smallest section of the upright. If there are grooves or holes in the upright, the actual area should be corrected accordingly.

Sizing of the Crossbeams

Calculation of the bending stress in the crossbeams is a bit more complex. We first need to determine the bending moment, denoted by the letter M, which depends on the width (W) of the frame (this width should be taken center to center of the uprights and is larger than the frame free width) and the load (P):

$$M = P W / 4$$

The moment M is in lb-in or N.mm, and hence the width should be expressed in inches or millimeters, while the load is in pounds or newtons. Note that the bending moment varies along the crossbeam and will be at its maximum value at the center, at the point where the load from the actuator

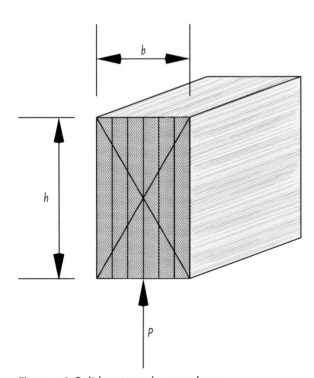

Figure 7.26. Solid rectangular crossbeam.

is applied. It is important, then, not to weaken the crossbeam, for example by drilling a hole at its center. Thus, when using a screw, it is better to use two beams with a spacing in between for the screw.

To calculate the maximum bending stress, the following formula is used:

$$\sigma = M h / 2 I$$

where h is the height of the crossbeam and I is a property of the section called the moment of inertia. For a simple rectangular section (figure 7.26), the value of I is given by

$$I = b h^3 / 12$$

where b is the base of the rectangle, that is, the thickness of the crossbeam. Note that h has to be the dimension in a direction parallel to the load line of action (P). We will see in the sidebar "Value of I for Different Shapes of Beams," how to calculate I for more complex sections.

Now, what we normally want to determine are the dimensions b and h of the crossbeam for known values of the load, width, and allowable stress. We will then use the following:

$$B h^2 = 1.5 P W / \sigma_a$$

which is valid for a rectangular and solid crossbeam.

Example: Taking the medium-size press example of the previous section, with W the center-to-center distance between the threaded rods, $W = 24$ in (630 mm), a load of 12 tons, and a crossbeam made of hardwood:

In US customary units the load $P = 12$ tons × 2,000 lb. = 24,000 lb. and

$b\,h^2 = 1.5 \times 24{,}000 \times 24\,/\,4{,}000 = 216$ cu. in.

thus a crossbeam 7.5 in. high by 4.5 in. thick would support this load, as

$4.5 \times 7.5^2 = 253$, larger than the required value of 216.

In SI units the load $P = 12$ tons $\times\,10{,}000$ N = 120,000 N and

$b\,h^2 = 1.5 \times 120{,}000 \times 630\,/\,27.5 = 4{,}000{,}000$ mm³

thus a crossbeam 195 mm high by 114 mm thick would be strong enough.

Assembly of the Frame

The corners where the crossbeams are assembled to the uprights may be a weak point if not well designed. I review here some common systems of assembly but can't hope to cover all the numerous assembly possibilities. Note that each corner will have to support half of the nominal load P, as this load is split between the two uprights.

WELDED STEEL FRAME

This is probably the sturdiest assembly method for an all-steel frame and is the method I used on my small steel press, as shown in figure 7.27. The inconvenience is that it can't be disassembled and requires a welding machine or a welder. The calculation of the strength is simple: 1,000 lb. per linear inch of weld. For example, on my small press the crossbeam is rectangular tubing 3 in. × 1.5 in., while the uprights are 1 in. square. The length of the weld seam is 3 + 3 + 1 + 1 = 8 linear

inches; thus it may resist 8,000 lb., which is plenty for the load in this press. In SI units the strength would be 180 N per linear mm of weld.

WOODEN FRAME ASSEMBLY

A good way to build a wooden frame is to notch the uprights (approximately ¼ in [6 mm] deep) and use two beams for each crossbeam, as shown in figure 7.31 on page 141. For this to work, the uprights need to extend the position of the crossbeam. The eventual failure of such a joint would be by shearing of the upright extensions along the two red lines that may be seen in figure 7.31. To calculate the strength, we use the shearing area to determine the shearing stress. And the allowable shearing stress in wood is approximately one-fourth the allowable axial stress as given in table 7.3 on page 137; hence, for hardwoods it would be

Figure 7.27. Welded steel frame.

Value of *I* for Different Shapes of Beams

While wooden crossbeams will most often be of rectangular shape and solid, steel crossbeams will normally not be a solid bar, as this would be unnecessarily heavy. The most useful steel beam shapes for this sort of application are the rectangular tubing, the I or H beam and the C beam. Normally, the moment of inertia for these steel beams is obtained from specialized tables, but we can obtain sufficiently good approximations from the following simple relations:

RECTANGULAR TUBING

This is simply a case of taking the value of *I* for the external dimensions of the beam and subtracting the value for the internal void.

We thus obtain:

$$I = [(b\,h^3) - (b_i\,h_i^3)] / 12$$

where b_i and h_i are the width and height of the internal void in the beam (figure 7.28).

H AND I BEAMS

Similarly, for the H and I beams, we will subtract the value for the two internal voids from the value for the external dimensions:

$$I = [(b\,h^3) - 2(b_i\,h_i^3)] / 12$$

Note that H beams are wide-flange I beams (figure 7.29). Both are much stronger in bending when installed as per the illustration, that is, with the central web vertical, and should always be used in that way.

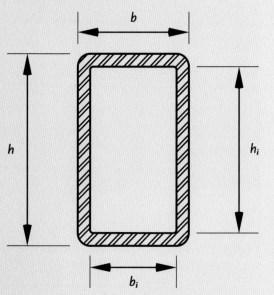

Figure 7.28. Rectangular tubing steel crossbeam.

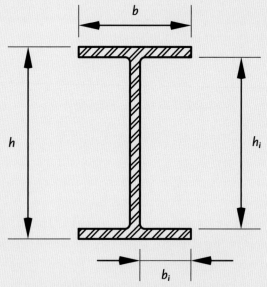

Figure 7.29. H beam steel crossbeam.

C BEAM

For a press crossbeam, C beams would be used in pairs as shown in figure 7.30. You may leave a free space between the two beams, for example, if you use a screw actuator or for facilitating the assembly with the uprights, but this will not change the value of the moment of inertia. We use the same principle for the calculation. For a crossbeam made of a pair of C beams as illustrated:

$$I = [2(b\,h^3) - 2(b_i\,h_i^3)] / 12 \; = [(b\,h^3) - (b_i\,h_i^3)] / 6$$

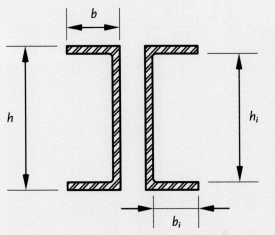

Figure 7.30. Pair of C beams for a steel crossbeam.

1,000 psi (6.9 MPa). For example, on my wood frame press the upright extensions are 1.875 in. (48 mm), and the width of the uprights is 3.5 in. (90 mm). The shearing area is thus 2 × 1.875 × 3.5 = 13 sq. in. (the factor 2 is used because there are two shearing planes on each extension), so the joint may resist 13 × 1,000 psi = 13,000 lb., which is plenty for this press. With the SI units, the shearing area is 2 × 48 × 90 = 8,600 mm², multiplied by the allowable stress 6.9 MPa, which gives 60,000 N for the resistance of the joint.

Note that in this type of assembly some bolts are used, but their role is mainly to insure the crossbeams are well tightened against the uprights, and they will not hold any substantial part of the load. It is really the notching that carries the load.

THREADED ROD ASSEMBLY

Using threaded rods as uprights for the press makes one of the easiest assemblies with the crossbeam. This assembly system will work fine with a wooden crossbeam and also with a rectangular tubing steel crossbeam. This simply consists of drilling a hole for the rod in the crossbeam

Figure 7.31. Wood frame assembly with shearing lines.

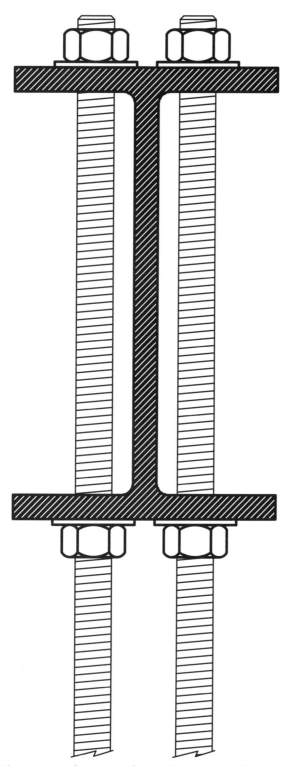

Figure 7.32. H-beam steel crossbeam assembly with threaded rods.

and using two nuts and washers. It also has the advantage of being easily disassembled at the end of the season for storage of the press. There are no stress verifications to do for such a joint, as the nuts are designed to bear all the load that the threaded rod can take. So as long as these uprights can each handle half of the jack nominal load, it will work. You may check table 7.4 or 7.5 on page 147 to verify how much load the threaded rod can handle. And since the hole in the crossbeam is not in the middle, where the bending stress is greater, this doesn't weaken the crossbeam. For photos, see the previous section discussing the building of such a press.

Another popular design is an assembly consisting of H- or I-beam steel crossbeams with two threaded rods at each end, as shown in figure 7.32. In this case you would need four rods because of the central web of the beam: you wouldn't want to drill through it. Note that in this design even if there are four rods supporting the load, it is preferable that each rod be strong enough to hold half of the nominal load, because if the jack is not perfectly aligned in the middle point of the beam, this load will not be split equally between the rods.

ASSEMBLY BY BOLTS OR PINS

Bolts or pins may be used to assemble an all-steel frame. Most shop presses have their crossbeams retained that way, as the height adjustment of the crossbeam is thus made easy. The bolts or pin resists the load by shearing of the shank, hence a shear stress is induced in the shank that is equal to the shear load divided by the section area of the shank. Usually there are two shear planes, so the effective area is doubled. For steel, the allowable shear stress is approximately 60 percent of the allowable axial stress given in table 7.3 on page 137. Note that both bolts and pins are normally made in high-strength steel and would have an allowable stress higher than this. However, calculating as if they were made of ordinary steel makes the design more conservative and is recommended.

Example: A crossbeam is retained by one pin at each end with a diameter $D = 1$ in. (25 mm), and there are two shearing planes. The nominal press load $P = 6$ tons.

In US customary units, we have the load $P = 12,000$ lb., and half of it (6,000 lb.) is taken by each pin. The shank section area is $\pi D^2 / 4 = 0.8$ sq. in. There are two shear planes, so the effective area is twice that value (1.6). The shear stress will then be 6,000 / 1.6 = 3,750 psi. We see from table 7.3 that this is much lower than 60 percent of the allowable axial stress for steel (18,000 psi) and is an acceptable stress.

In SI units the load $P = 60,000$ N, half of which is 30,000 N. The shank section area is 490 mm², which is doubled to 980 because of the two shear planes. Shear stress is 30,000 / 980 = 31 MPa, which is compared with 60 percent of the allowable axial stress (125 MPa).

Concluding Remarks

As can be seen, there are many ways to build a press frame, and the method you use will depend mainly on the material and tooling available. In this book I have chosen to take as an example the configuration with threaded rod uprights and wood crossbeams because this approach is the one that requires the least special equipment and is the easiest to build, and the calculations are very simple. If you have any doubts concerning the strength of your own design, please consult an engineer.

◀ 7.4 ▶
Screw Mechanics

If you opt for a screw actuator, you may already have a screw that you intend to use with your press or you may wish to buy the required screw. It is also sometimes possible to find a good screw in objects at hand, like an old piano stool that uses such a screw for height adjustment. In any case the screw should have a size that is well adapted to the capacity and size of the press. The mechanical equations for screws are relatively simple, and a few calculations will permit you

to do all necessary verifications. In technical terms, this screw is often called a *threaded rod*. Tables 7.4 and 7.5 on page 147 contain important parameters for the screw types and sizes most likely to be used in a press, in US and SI units. These tables include some load calculations and thus should help determine the maximum recommended load a given screw may provide or, conversely, what size of screw would be required for a given load.

Screw Types and Designations

Let's first look at the shapes of threads that may be used. For press actuators, a trapezoidal shape thread is popular. This is called an Acme thread in the United States. However, regular threaded rods have a triangular thread, which is the normal thread used for bolts (this is the UNC type in the United States). These rods will be easier to find and less expensive than rods with trapezoidal threads. Other thread types that may be found are the square thread and the modified square thread: they are not as common but work very well for presses. There is also a fine thread (UNF in the United States), but it is not recommended for presses, as it requires too many rotations to obtain the same travel from the screw.

Square and trapezoidal threads are bigger than regular triangular threads. This means that their pitch is longer (fewer threads per inch), hence less turning is required to obtain the same travel of the screw. These bigger threads are also less susceptible to wear. For a screw to be used as a press actuator, square or trapezoidal threads are preferable. For a screw to be used as uprights in a press frame, a threaded rod with regular triangular threads should then be used, as it is less expensive and may carry more load.

In North America screws will most often be specified in US units, that is, inches, although metric screws are also available in specialized shops. Their dimension is given by the nominal diameter, which corresponds to the diameter that is measured on the exterior of the thread—also called the major diameter. The second parameter is the pitch of the thread, which in the US system

is specified by the number of threads per inch. Hence, a screw specified as ⅞-6 has a diameter of ⅞ inch on the exterior of the thread and six threads per inch, which means we have to turn six complete rotations for the screw to advance one inch. For the metric or ISO screws, both the nominal diameter and the pitch are given in millimeters, and a screw specified as, for example, M20 × 4, would have an external diameter of 20 mm and a pitch of 4 mm, indicating that the screw will advance 4 mm for each complete rotation. Note that in metric thread specification, the letter(s) that precede the diameter indicates the type of thread: M for triangular thread, Tr for trapezoidal, and Sq for square; and a × is used between the diameter and the pitch values.

Screw Calculations

Following are the engineering equations that are used to build the tables 7.4 and 7.5 on page 148. Chances are slim that you will ever need them—most likely if you wish to use a screw size that is not covered by the tables 7.4 and 7.5.

THE LOAD CAPACITY

The strength of bolts and screws is specified by the class (ISO/metric) or grade (US). The lowest grade or class that may be found corresponds approximately to the strength of ordinary structural steel and is specified as ISO class 4.6 or as US grade 2. This is the quality you are most likely to find if you buy a threaded rod at the hardware store. At a specialized shop you could find (at higher cost) a stronger screw. This question of steel quality influences the recommended allowable stress

($σ_a$) in the screw. For the current discussion, I will assume the lowest grade of steel, as this will ensure the calculations made here will be safer and adequate for any screw quality. We will thus use the same values for $σ_a$ as seen in the section on the strength of the frame, that is, 18,000 psi (125 MPa), which corresponds to the strength of ordinary steel with a security factor of 2.

The equation for the maximum load capacity of the screw (P_M) is:

$$P_M = σ_a \, π \, D_r^2 \, / \, 4$$

where:

P_M is obtained in pounds (US units), and should be divided by 2,000 to obtain the load in tons. In SI units the load is obtained in newtons (N) and should be divided by 10,000 to obtain tons.

D_r is the diameter of the rod at the root of the thread (in. or mm). This diameter corresponds to the solid core of the rod and is normally obtained from specialized tables or calculated from the geometry of the thread.

Note that this maximum load may be used for a rod that is in a pulling position, as in the uprights of the frame, or in a multiple-screw press. If the rod or screw is in a pushing position, as for the actuator of a frame press, the situation is different, and we will see just below that in this case it is preferable to reduce the load.

BUCKLING AND ACTIVE LENGTH

When a long beam is pushing and thus is in compression, it may be subjected to an instability phenomenon called *buckling*. You may demonstrate this easily using a long, thin rod (a plastic ruler works fine for this). If you try to push on something with such an elongated rod, it will bend very easily under a small load. The same may happen with a threaded rod, which is long in relation to its diameter. We use Euler's equation to calculate the critical condition of a beam subjected to compression. I have modified it slightly below so its result gives directly the active length and to include a security factor of 2 on the load. Note that buckling is not dependent on the allowable stress of the steel, hence a higher-grade steel is not an advantage for a rod in pushing condition:

$$L_a = (D_r^2 \, / \, 8) \, \sqrt{(π^3 \, E) \, / \, (2 \, P_P)}$$

where

L_a is the maximum recommended active length for the screw (in. or mm)

E is Young's modulus, which is a property of the material. For steel, E = 29 million psi (which we also write as 29,000 ksi) or 200,000 MPa

D_r is the root diameter, as seen above

P_P is the pushing load (lb. or N), which will be discussed below

The active length is calculated between the nut and the end of the threaded rod that press on the top plate, as shown in the drawing (figure 7.33). This length will be at its maximum at the end of the pressing, when the apple pomace is well compressed.

We can see from the equation that to obtain a longer active length, the load has to be reduced. If

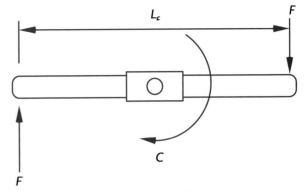

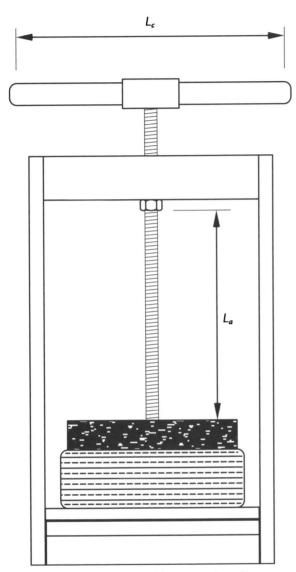

Figure 7.33. Active length and lever-arm length.

Figure 7.34. Screw handle viewed from the top.

plate and the screw to reduce the active length. For the calculations of the active length in the tables, I have used:

$$P_P = 0.8 \ P_M$$

TORQUE APPLIED TO THE SCREW AND LEVER-ARM LENGTH

A torque is defined as a force multiplied by the lever-arm length upon which it applies to give a rotation to an object. In the case of our screw, we want to calculate the torque needed to obtain the axial load specified. Note that the torque will be lower if there is a thrust bearing at the end of the screw than if the screw presses directly on a steel plate because of the friction between the screw and the plate. I have done the calculation for the worst case, but if you do have a thrust bearing, the required torque and lever-arm length would then be about 30 percent lower.

The equation giving the exact relation between the torque and the axial load in a screw is quite complex and requires some parameters that may be difficult to obtain. A much simpler equation that still gives a good approximation of the torque (within 1 or 2 percent) is used here:

you use a pushing load equal to the maximum load computed above, the permissible active length may not be long enough for your pressing needs. Hence, I would recommend using a pushing load of no more than 80 percent of the maximum load. If the active length is not long enough for your press, you may reduce the pushing load further or use a bigger screw with a reduced load. Another alternative would be to use blocks between the top

TABLE 7.4:
US system screw parameters

Type of thread	Triangular (UNC)					Trapezoidal (Acme)				Square/Modified Square			
Designation	3/4-10	7/8-9	1-8	1⅛-7	1¼-7	3/4-6	7/8-6	1-5	1¼-5	3/4-5	7/8-4.5	1-4	1¼-3.5
Nominal diameter (in.)	0.75	0.875	1	1.125	1.25	0.75	0.875	1	1.25	0.75	0.875	1	1.25
Pitch (threads per in.)	10	9	8	7	7	6	6	5	5	5	4.5	4	3.5
Root diameter (in.)	0.63	0.74	0.85	0.95	1.07	0.55	0.67	0.77	1.01	0.55	0.65	0.75	0.96
Load, maximum (tons)	2.8	3.9	5.1	6.4	8.2	2.1	3.2	4.1	7.3	2.1	3.0	4.0	6.6
Load, pushing (tons)	2.1	2.9	3.8	4.8	6.1	1.6	2.4	3.1	5.5	1.6	2.3	3.0	4.9
Active length (in.)	16	19	22	24	28	14	17	20	26	14	17	19	25
Torque (ft.-lb.)	37	59	89	126	179	28	49	72	159	28	46	70	144
Lever arm length (in.)	10	16	24	33	48	7	13	19	42	7	12	19	38

TABLE 7.5:
ISO system screw parameters

Type of thread	Triangular					Trapezoidal				Square			
Designation	M16×2	M20×2.5	M24×3	M30×3.5	M36×4	Tr20×4	Tr24×5	Tr28×5	Tr32×6	Sq20×4	Sq24×5	Sq28×5	Sq32×6
Nominal diameter (mm)	16	20	24	30	36	20	24	28	32	20	24	28	32
Pitch (mm)	2	2.5	3	3.5	4	4	5	5	6	4	5	5	6
Root diameter (mm)	13.8	17.3	20.8	26.2	31.7	15.5	18.5	22.5	25.0	16.0	19.0	23.0	26.0
Load, maximum (tons)	1.9	2.9	4.2	6.7	9.8	2.4	3.4	5.0	6.1	2.5	3.5	5.2	6.6
Load, pushing (tons)	1.4	2.2	3.2	5.1	7.4	1.8	2.5	3.7	4.6	1.9	2.7	3.9	5.0
Active length (cm)	35	44	53	67	81	40	47	58	64	41	49	59	67
Torque (N.m)	32	62	107	212	372	50	85	146	206	53	89	153	223
Lever arm length (cm)	16	31	53	106	186	25	42	73	103	26	45	76	111

$C = 0.14\ P_p\ D$

where

P_p is the pushing load (lb. or N)

D is the nominal diameter of the screw (in. or mm)

C is the torque in lb-in (divide by 12 to obtain ft-lb) or N.mm, considering the end of the screw is cut flat and is turning against a flat steel plate.

The lever-arm length, which in fact is the length of the handle, will then be obtained by:

$L_c = C\ /\ F$

where

L_c is the length of the lever arm (in. or mm)

C is as described above

F is the force applied on the handle (lb. or N). Naturally, F will depend on the strength of the person who is tightening the screw. For the calculations of the table, I have assumed a force of 45 lb (200 N, or 20 kg). Note that as shown in the drawing (figure 7.34), two forces F, equal and opposite, are required to produce the torque: this is the natural way to operate the screw, pushing on one side of the handle and pulling on the other.

Concluding remarks

As may be seen in tables 7.4 and 7.5 on page 147, with a load of 4 tons or more, the torque required quickly becomes very large and the lever arm requires such proportions that it may be awkward to use. Further, with such a great torque, the press will want to turn, and so it will be necessary to anchor it to the floor to prevent its rotation. For these reasons, nowadays screw presses are used only for small hobbyist presses, and a hydraulic actuator is preferred when the load becomes greater than 4 tons.

⦀ PART IV ⦀

The Apple Juice or Must

The apple juice, which we may now refer to as the *must,* as it is destined for fermentation, is a fairly complex liquid that contains a great number of substances. Some time ago I was reading the web site of a French cider specialist and author from Brittany, Mark Gleonec, and he mentioned the fact that the apple juice contains all the elements necessary for its transformation into cider. This is very true, and it even contains those necessary for its ultimate transformation into vinegar if the cider maker doesn't take appropriate action to stop the process at the cider stage. Apart from water, there is sugar, some of which will be transformed into alcohol and some of which may remain as residual sugar in the finished cider. There is also acid, which gives a sensation of freshness; tannins, which provide color, body, astringency, and bitterness; pectins, which can also contribute to the texture or mouthfeel; enzymes, which

will transform this pectin; and microorganisms (yeasts and bacteria), which will actually perform the transformation of the juice; as well as food for these microorganisms in the form of nitrogenous substances, amino acids, and vitamins. The juice also contains oxygen, mineral salts, fat, starch, fibers, some volatile oils that give aroma, color pigments, and many other constituents. Actually, some studies have isolated more than one hundred aromatic and volatile compounds that contribute to the flavor and aroma of juice and cider. Many of these are present only in the parts per million (ppm) range, which makes their measurement extremely difficult. The quantity of each of those substances will vary from one sample of juice to another and from year to year, depending on such factors as the variety of apple, the cultural practices, the *terroir,* and the weather during the growing season. Following is an approximate range of the proportions that the more abundant of these substances may have in the juice:

Water	80–85 percent
Sugar	7–18 percent
Acid	0.1–3 percent
Tannins	0.1–1 percent
Pectic substances	0.1–1 percent
Nitrogenous substances	0.01–0.1 percent

And all the other substances taken together may account for about 2–3 percent of the total. Let me now introduce two useful measures that we will use in the following sections:

- **Total solids** (TS), sometimes also called **dry extract** (DE), is the sum of the substances that would remain if the liquid were evaporated. This means the water, volatile compounds, and alcohol (in the case of cider) are removed, and, in theory, what is left is weighed. The TS and DE are expressed in grams per liter at a reference temperature, generally 20°C (68°F). Most often, we see the term "total solids" for the juice, while "dry extract" is used for a cider, but they are the same in practice. The sugar, acid, tannin, and pectin will form the bulk of the TS. On average, the sugar will account for approximately 82 percent of the total solids, but this proportion may vary substantially from one juice sample to another.
- **Sugar-free dry extract** (SFDE) is the total solids or dry extract with the sugar removed. So these are the nonfermentable solids in the juice. What is interesting about this measure is that it doesn't change much during the fermentation: if we have, for example, 25 g/L of SFDE in a juice sample, we will have about the same

quantity in the finished cider. Note that for a perfectly dry cider where all the sugar has been fermented, the SFDE would be equal to the DE.

Often in the literature, the TS/DE and SFDE are expressed as grams of equivalent sugar per liter rather than their measured mass per liter. This means that the given quantity of solids would raise the density of the must or cider by the same amount as this equivalent sugar quantity.

A cider maker should understand what the most important substances within the total solids may bring to the cider and how their concentration may affect its taste, balance, mouthfeel, and appearance. Thus, I discuss questions relative to sugar, acidity, tannins, nitrogen, and pectins individually in the following articles.

First, though, a quick examination of a few of the other elements.

Microorganisms

The must contains many types of living microorganisms, among which are yeasts and bacteria.

- **Yeasts** are unicellular fungal organisms measuring between 2 and 10 microns. They are of utmost importance, as they will actually perform the alcoholic fermentation that will yield the cider. There are many types of yeasts, including some that are considered spoilage yeasts. More details are given in the article on yeasts, section 14.2. Yeasts come in good part from the apple's skin but also from its flesh and core cavity. Hence, washing the apples prior to pressing may remove some of the yeast from the skin, but there will be plenty left. Some yeasts are also picked up from the surrounding air during pressing and from the pressing equipment, which, mainly if it is old, may be highly contaminated with yeast spores.

• **Bacteria** are simpler unicellular organisms that are much smaller than yeasts, measuring less than 1 micron. Two types of bacteria are particularly noteworthy for the cider maker: lactic acid bacteria (LAB) and acetic bacteria. Some LAB are responsible for the malolactic fermentation that transforms the malic acid into lactic acid. These are discussed further in section 14.4. Some other LAB, however, are responsible for cider disorders and off-flavors. The acetic bacteria, for their part, are responsible for the transformation of the alcohol into vinegar. These two last subjects are discussed in the article on cider troubles in chapter 16.

Microorganisms may or may not require oxygen to grow a population and perform the work they are destined to do. The temperature and other parameters of the must, in particular the acidity, also influence their development.

Oxygen

Molecular oxygen, O_2, will be present in solution in the must. The better part of this oxygen will have been picked up from the ambient air, either by the pomace, if it has been left for maceration, or simply by the contact of air with the juice.

Oxygen reacts chemically with a great number of compounds, these reactions being generally called *oxidation*. One of the first visible signs of a reaction of this type is the rapid browning of the pomace after milling: this is oxidation of the tannins that is taking place. Such a browning would not occur in a medium deprived of oxygen. Some chemical substances are called antioxidants: these will react with the free oxygen, thus scavenging it and leaving none for other reactions. We will see later on that sulfite has an antioxidant effect.

Oxygen is also required by some microorganisms for their growth and development. Depending on whether oxygen is present or not, we talk about an aerobic or anaerobic medium. In the case of cider, the must is an aerobic medium, and the yeasts will use the initially present oxygen for their development and growth of the population. In subsequent phases all the oxygen becomes consumed, and if no new air is permitted to come into contact with the fermenting cider the medium becomes anaerobic, and the yeasts will continue their work anaerobically to transform the sugar into alcohol. The lactic acid bacteria are also anaerobic, while the acetic bacteria and some of the so-called spoilage yeasts are aerobic only, and this is the reason air should not be permitted to come into contact with the cider during the later phases of the fermentation.

CHAPTER 8

THE SUGARS

For an apple to merit being considered good, it first needs to be rich in sugar, and to contain about 150 grams per liter of must, or to mark 1.075 on the hydrometer. It is the sugar that gives the alcohol and thereafter its strength to the cider.

G. LANGLAIS, 1894

Like Langlais, I believe that richness in sugar is the first quality for an apple destined to make cider. I do not, however, ask as much as he does and will accept lower sugar concentrations than those he suggests. In effect, if we kept only the apples containing that much sugar, we wouldn't make much cider, as there are very few apples that would qualify as good. As this is such an important property, in the following pages we will look in more depth at the sugar content of the must and the properties of this sugar.

◀ 8.1 ▶

Generalities on Sugars

So, yes, the sugar concentration is the first property of a juice, the one we avidly measure as soon as the juice flows from the press—and for good reason, because when the juice is rich in sugar, this gives the promise of a good-quality cider for the following reasons:

• A high sugar level in the juice translates into a good degree of alcohol after fermentation, which lends strength to the cider, but also ensures a good keeping quality and protection against infection.

TABLE 8.1:
Classification of apples according to their richness in sugar

Sugar content	Specific gravity	Remarks
Low	1.045 and less	Summer apples and cooking apples; not recommended for cider unless they have other desirable qualities
Medium	1.045–1.060	Good
High	1.060–1.070	Ideal for cider
Very high	over 1.070	Exceptional; crabapples sometimes have such high sugar content

- The apples that contain the most sugar are also very often those that have the most flavor and produce a richer cider.
- High-sugar apples tend to be the ones that ripen later in the season and that contain smaller amounts of nitrogenous substances—and this is beneficial for a slow fermentation, which will give a high-quality cider.

I use a hydrometer to evaluate the sugar richness of juice and usually put a limit at a specific gravity (SG) of 1.045: when the juice from a certain variety is rich enough to give a density that is regularly higher than this limit, I consider the variety has some potential for cider, depending also of course on its other properties, such as tannins, acid, flavor. Table 8.1 gives an idea of the value of apples according to their sugar content.

It is important to note that such evaluation should be done over the course of several years because the sugar concentration will vary from year to year and from one location to another. After a very wet summer, the apples will be larger and contain more water, and consequently the sugar will be diluted; whereas after a dry summer the apples will be smaller but richer in sugar.

The Different Sugars

There are numerous types of sugars in nature. In apple juice there are three main fermentable sugars present:

- *Fructose* (aka *levulose* or *fruit sugar*) is the most abundant. Its concentration may vary between 7 and 11 percent in mass. It is a simple and reducing sugar. The term *reducing* refers to the capacity of this type of sugar to interact chemically with some other compounds and hence indicates it is easier to transform. The term *simple* refers to the chemical structure, which is a *monosaccharide*.
- *Glucose* (aka *dextrose* or *grape sugar*) is in much lower proportion, between 1 and 3 percent. It is also a simple and reducing sugar. The concentration in glucose decreases as the apple ripens.
- *Sucrose* (aka *saccharose* or *cane sugar*), the granulated white kitchen sugar, is a double sugar (*disaccharide*) and nonreducing. However, it may be inverted, in particular by the yeasts. This is a chemical reaction where the sucrose combines with a bit of water to give equal amounts of glucose and fructose. Note that as some water is

used in the reaction, the mass of the obtained glucose and fructose is 5.26 percent more than the mass of the original sucrose. The concentration of sucrose in the juice may vary between 2 and 5 percent.

In addition, there may be some very low concentrations of other fermentable sugars. Plus, apple juice contains some *sorbitol* (aka *glucitol*) in a proportion that may vary between 0.2 and 1 percent. Pear juice normally contains more sorbitol than apple juice, up to 2 percent. This substance is unique, as it has a sweetening effect (about half that of the same amount of true sugar) but technically is not a sugar but a *polyol*, also called *sugar alcohol*. Hence, the sorbitol is part of the SFDE (see beginning of part IV), and its presence increases the density of the finished cider. The presence of sorbitol is one of the reasons why a dry perry is never as dry as a bone-dry cider. Another important property of sorbitol is its laxative effect, which has lent a certain reputation to perry, at least when it is consumed in too great a quantity.

Measurement of the Sugar Content

The sugar total (S) of a juice or cider is normally expressed in grams of reducing sugar equivalent per liter of juice or cider (g/L) at a reference temperature of 20°C (68°F). Sometimes however, in older publications, we may see 60°F or 15°C as reference temperature. The exact measurement of S is done in a laboratory and is a fairly complex manipulation that requires chemicals not easily available to home or small-scale cider makers. It was a German chemist, Hermann von Fehling, who in 1849

developed a test to measure the sugar concentration, by titration with a solution called Fehling's reagent. Different manipulations are required to test the reducing sugars and the nonreducing sugars, as the latter need to be chemically inverted.

The first known measurements of the sugar concentration in cider-apple juices by the Fehling test were done by de Boutteville and Hauchecorne, as reported in their book *Le Cidre* of 1875. Unfortunately, it was shown later that these authors did not correctly take into account the reducing and nonreducing sugars present in the juice, thus their results were not valid. Their followers, however, did manage to settle this issue correctly, and in subsequent books and articles the reported sugar concentrations of analyzed juices were exact.

Fehling test kits are available from specialized suppliers of oenology equipment. Nowadays, though, in most laboratories the Fehling test has been superseded by modern equipment, in particular high-performance liquid chromatography (HPLC), which provides very precise measurement of the sugar.

Cider makers use two simple and relatively inexpensive instruments to estimate the sugar content of a juice: the *refractometer* and the *hydrometer*. In fact, these two instruments will give a fairly accurate measurement of the total solids in the juice, and the sugar is estimated from the average proportion of sugar in total solids. This will be discussed further in section 8.3.

THE REFRACTOMETER

The refractometer (figure 8.1) is a small and portable instrument that uses the refraction of light to estimate the sugar concentration of a solution. You place a drop of the juice to be tested on the

Figure 8.1. Refractometer.

sensor plate, place the transparent plastic cover flap over it, and look in the eyepiece toward light, revealing a scale indicating the Brix of the juice. The principle of this instrument is that light is bent or refracted as it passes from one medium to another, as, for example, when light crosses the surface of water or a lens. The angle of the deviation changes with the nature of the medium and in particular with the sugar concentration of a solution. So by measuring the angle of deviation as the light goes through a sample of apple juice, the instrument will estimate the amount of sugar in that juice sample.

You need only a few drops to take a measurement, an advantage in the orchard, as you can simply pick an apple, extract a drop of juice, and take a measurement. The downside is that such a small sample may be unrepresentative of the overall crop's sugar level. Thus, it is recommended that you make several measurements with the refractometer. Also, the refractive index is a property that varies with temperature, and a correction is required when the temperature of the sample is different from the calibration temperature of the

instrument. Some refractometers include an automatic temperature compensation; otherwise you will need a correction table.

Once the refractive index has been measured by the instrument, a table may be used to obtain a corresponding sugar concentration, generally as *degrees Brix,* which represent the percentage by mass of the sugar (the Brix scale will be discussed further below). Some models of refractometers are directly calibrated in the Brix scale, which is more practical. However, the Brix reading given by the instrument doesn't correspond to the true sugar content of an apple juice: it is a theoretical concentration of pure sucrose in pure water. The reality of apple juice is quite different, as we have seen with the number of different substances present, many of which have an influence on the refractive index. Thus the refractometer will give us the sugar concentration of a pure solution of sucrose and water that would have the same refractive index as the juice we are testing. Actually, this measurement will estimate the total solids present in the juice quite accurately, but the accuracy is not as good for the true amount of sugar.

The cost of a refractometer used to be in the range of $150 to $200 for a good-quality model without temperature compensation, which cost another $100. I have, however, recently seen on the Internet some models offered for a much lower price, and I am told that such basic instruments, which may be bought from wine-making supply stores, are quite dependable. There are also some models with a digital display that are easier to use, but the price is higher. The refractometer is very useful in the orchard to estimate the ripeness of the apples and the ideal date of harvest. On the other hand, this instrument doesn't give an accurate measurement when there is some alcohol present in the solution, which makes it less appropriate for most cider-making operations and in particular for monitoring the fermentation, where the hydrometer is preferable.

THE HYDROMETER

In cider making we tend to use a simple and inexpensive instrument: the *hydrometer*. This instrument gives an indirect estimation of the sugar concentration in a solution by measuring its density. This is because as there is more sugar in a solution, its density increases. And the hydrometer is in fact a graduated floater that floats higher as the solution is denser. It may be graduated with different scales; in general, in North America and England, it is the specific gravity (SG) scale that is preferred. In France a volumic mass scale is preferred. Hydrometers calibrated with a Brix scale are also often seen (see "Expression of the Sugar Content" for an explanation of all these scales). But whatever the scale of the hydrometer (and some even have three scales built in), we can use a table that will give an approximate value for the sugar content of the juice from the reading. As the hydrometer is such an important instrument in cider making, I have devoted a full article to its use in the next section.

Expression of the Sugar Content

We have seen above that the sugar content (S) is expressed in grams of sugar per liter of solution (g/L) but that we may also estimate it via degree Brix or density. In everyday cider-making operations, it is the density that is the most-often-used index to express the sugar content. Let us now define in a more rigorous way the various ways to express the sugar content of a juice and look at some simple rules that relate them.

VOLUMIC MASS

The *volumic mass* (often denoted by ρ, the Greek letter rho) of a substance is defined as its mass (M) per unit of volume (V):

$$\rho = M \,/\, V$$

This property is sometimes called *density* or *mass density*. It is usually expressed in grams per liter (g/L) or sometimes in kg/m³. It is important to note that the volumic mass of a substance changes with the temperature because of the thermal expansion: a certain quantity of water, say 1 lb., will occupy a larger volume when at higher temperature. Below, I give a table of the volumic mass of water and of some sugar-water solutions at different temperatures for a standard atmospheric pressure.

TABLE 8.2:

Volumic mass of pure water and of sugar-water solutions

TEMPERATURE		ρ (g/L)				
°C	°F	Water	2.5°Bx	5°Bx	10°Bx	16°Bx
0	32	999.8	1,009.9	1,020	1,041	1,067.1
5	41	1,000.0	1,009.9	1020	1,040.7	1,066.6
10	50	999.7	1,009.5	1,019.6	1,040.1	1,065.8
15.56	60	999.0	1,008.8	1,018.7	1,039.1	1,064.6
20	68	998.2	1,007.9	1,017.8	1,038.1	1,063.5
25	77	997.0	1,006.7	1,016.5	1,036.7	1,061.9
30	86	995.7	1,005.3	1,015	1,035.1	1,060.2

Important: When the volumic mass of a substance is given, the temperature at which the property applies should always be indicated.

SPECIFIC GRAVITY

The *specific gravity* (SG) is the ratio between the volumic mass of the substance considered and the volumic mass of water (ρ_w), normally taken at the same temperature:

$$SG = \rho / \rho_w$$

This is a dimensionless number, usually expressed with three decimals.

On some occasions we use the concept of points of gravity or degrees of gravity (°SG), most often when we want to express the difference between two readings of SG. This then consists in taking only the decimal part of the SG. We will express it as follows:

$$°SG = 1,000 (SG - 1)$$

For example, if the SG is 1.050, it is equivalent to 50°SG.

Note that there exists an equivalent scale used for wine in some European countries: the *Oechsle* scale (°Oe), whose definition is given by the difference between the volumic mass of the juice and that of water at the same temperature:

$$°Oe = \rho - \rho_w$$

For all practical purposes, these are equal to the °SG, hence:

$$1°Oe \approx 1°SG$$

Strictly speaking, SG should be accompanied by two temperature numbers for the two volumic masses: for example, SG(60°F/60°F) is the volumic mass of the liquid considered at 60°F divided by the volumic mass of water at 60°F. In a similar fashion, in Europe it will generally be specified as SG(15°C/15°C) or SG(20°C/20°C). This is rarely enforced in cider-making practice, though, because

The Sugars **159**

(and this is a very useful property) SG doesn't vary much with temperature within cider-making usage. This is because both apple juice and cider have a coefficient of thermal expansion close enough to that of pure water so that the SG doesn't change more than one- or two-tenths of a °SG within a usual temperature range. This, however, becomes less and less true as the alcoholic strength or the sugar concentration increases to higher values than are seen in normal cider making.

If the SG of a juice or cider is known, we can obtain the volumic mass by multiplication with the volumic mass of the water at the temperature of the substance in question:

$$\rho = \rho_w\,SG$$

For example, let's assume we have a sample of apple juice that is at a temperature of 68°F and has a SG = 1.055. From table 8.2, we see that, at this temperature, the water has a volumic mass of: ρ_w = 998.2 g/L. Then the volumic mass of our juice sample will be given by the equation above and we obtain ρ = 1,053.1 g/L. Thus, one liter of this juice at 68°F will weigh 1,053 grams or 1.053 kg.

Note that the volumic mass is commonly assumed to equal 1,000 multiplied by the SG, which in the case of the example above would have given the weight of our liter of juice to be 1.055 kg. The difference is 2 g, or 0.2 percent. This is a small discrepancy, but when it comes to the evaluation of the sugar content, this difference in density may cause an error on the order of 5 percent.

THE BRIX SCALE

The Brix scale is commonly used in North America to express the sugar concentration of a solution. It is based on a table relating the sugar concentration to its SG that was first developed by Karl Balling in 1843. It was subsequently improved upon by the German scientist Adolf Brix, and again, in the early 1900s, by Fritz Plato, who improved its precision to the 6th decimal point. Hence we may see in the literature sugar concentrations expressed in either of these three scales: Balling, Brix, or Plato. Nowadays, the Balling scale may be considered obsolete, and the Plato scale is mostly used in the brewing industry. They are however essentially the same, the differences between them being much smaller than the precision of any measuring instrument a cider maker is likely to have. From the reading of the instrument, we obtain *degrees Brix* (°Bx), which represents the sugar concentration in percentage of mass. For example, 15°Bx corresponds to 15 g of sucrose diluted in a solution of pure water and sucrose whose total mass is 100 g. For pure sucrose solutions, there exists an exact relation between the Brix and SG scales, and this has been tabulated by the National Bureau of Standards (NBS) in the United States (Circular C440). This table is easy to find on the Internet. A very rough relation between these two scales is:

$$°Bx \approx °SG\,/\,4$$

which is a useful formula as a calculator is not required for the conversion. A better approximation of °Bx is given by the following simple formula:

$$°Bx \approx 261.3\,(1 - 1\,/\,SG)$$

which is accurate to about ±0.05°Bx up to 26°Bx, or SG 1.110. This accuracy is sufficient for most of our cider-making uses, and this is the formula I will usually use in the following discussions. With higher sugar concentrations (for example, when making ice cider), the error increases markedly, however. If more precision is required or if the sugar concentration is higher, the following third-order regression based on the NBS C440 table may be used:

$$°Bx = 258.58 \, (SG - 1) - 225.7 \, (SG - 1)^2 + 173.5 \, (SG - 1)^3$$

which is accurate to ±0.003°Bx up to 44°Bx. Note that the values of SG in this table are defined as SG(20°C/20°C). And conversely, the SG may be computed from the Brix to within ±0.03°SG with the following:

$$°SG = 3.8687 \, (°Bx) + 0.013048 \, (°Bx)^2 + 0.0000487 \, (°Bx)^3$$

and: SG = 1 + °SG / 1,000

Putting the formulae to use: if, for example, we assume a sample of juice of SG 1.060, or 60°SG, the first rough formula would give 15°Bx. The simple formula gives 14.8°Bx, and the third-order regression gives the exact value of 14.74°Bx. And if we calculate the SG corresponding to a Brix of 14.74 from the last formula, we obtain SG 1.06002, a discrepancy of 0.02°SG from our starting value.

TOTAL SOLIDS

In apple juice, as there are other matters in solution apart from sugar, the Brix relates better to the *total solids* (TS) than to the sugar in solution. Hence, we may obtain a good approximation of the TS from the °Bx multiplied by the volumic mass to transform this reading into g/L:

$$TS \, (g/L) = ρ \, °Bx / 100$$

we may then combine this result with the simple formula for °Bx above, and this permits us to express the TS as a function of the SG (valid up to SG 1.110):

$$TS = 2.613 \, ρ_w \, (SG - 1)$$

with, at the reference temperature of 20°C, $ρ_w$ = 998.2 g/L. Hence:

$$TS = 2608 \, (SG - 1) \text{ at } 20°C$$

POTENTIAL ALCOHOL

The *potential alcohol* (A_P) is a scale that is often used in cider, wine, and beer making. It represents the strength of the alcohol by volume in percent (%ABV) at 20°C that would be obtained if all the sugar present in the juice were fully fermented and transformed into alcohol. If we know the exact concentration of sugar in a juice, we may deduce quite precisely its alcoholic potential from the following formula (we will see more on this in section 14.5), which is given by Warcollier in *La Cidrerie* (1928):

$$A_P = 0.06 \, S$$

where S is the fermentable sugar content in g/L. We also often see a rule to the effect that the alcohol is equal to the sugar divided by 17 (i.e., A_P = S/17), which is essentially the same, since 1/17 = 0.059. Most of the time, however, S is not known, and we will use an average value, as will be seen in the article on the amount of sugar in apple juice, section 8.3.

The following two simple relations are often seen in the literature and give rough estimates of the potential alcohol. They may be useful for a first approximation:

$$A_P \approx {}^\circ Bx \; / \; 2$$

and

$$A_P \approx {}^\circ SG \; / \; 8$$

◄ 8.2 ►
The Hydrometer

The value of fruits, for the manufacture of cider, may be judged of from the specifick gravity of their expressed juices. The best cider and perry are made from those apples and pears that afford the densest juices; and a comparison between different fruits may be made with tolerable accuracy, by plunging them together into a saturated solution of salt, or a strong solution of sugar: those that sink deepest, will afford the richest juice.

JAMES THACHER,
The American Orchardist, 1822

The objective of this article is to improve the precision of density and specific gravity readings for apple juice or cider. The density gives an indication of the sugar concentration in an apple juice and the potential alcoholic strength the cider will have. This was already understood in Thacher's time, but his way of evaluating the density of the fruit, by plunging it into a solution of high-density salt or sugar and recording how low the fruit sank, was surely not very accurate. The measurement of the density also permits us to monitor the evolution of the fermentation and to evaluate the amount of

residual sugar present in the cider. However, the hydrometer is not a very accurate instrument, and so we will try here to minimize its imprecision.

Use of the Hydrometer

A hydrometer is, in fact, a graduated floater. The greater the volumic mass of the liquid, the higher the hydrometer floats. So what the hydrometer really measures is always the volumic mass of the liquid in which it floats. However, depending on the way the instrument is calibrated, the graduations may correspond to specific gravity or to another scale.

There are different types and qualities of hydrometers. Figure 8.2 on page 162 shows three of my instruments:

- The shorter one on top is a low-cost hydrometer often called a *triple-scale hydrometer,* sold in all wine-making supply stores. These have three scales: one for specific gravity, one for degrees Balling or Brix, and one for the potential alcohol. This last scale is normally calibrated for beer or wine and thus should not be used

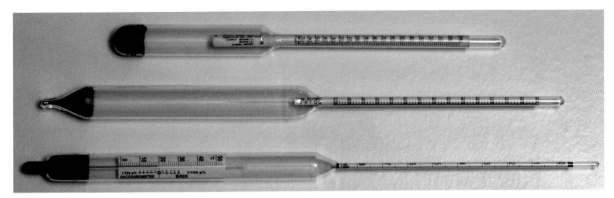

Figure 8.2. Three models of hydrometers

for cider. The SG scale has a range from 0.990 to 1.170, with a resolution of 0.002 (i.e., from one graduation to the next, there will be 2°SG). These hydrometers are not very precise.

- In the middle is a more precise hydrometer for specific gravity, whose range covers from 1.000 to 1.070, with a resolution of 0.0005 (or four times better than the triple-scale hydrometer). The precision of the reading is much improved with such a hydrometer.
- The longer one on the bottom is a thermo-hydrometer, which incorporates a thermometer in the body of the instrument, thus avoiding the necessity of using and cleaning two different instruments when taking an SG reading. This particular one is calibrated to give Brix degrees, and the range is from 0 to 8°Bx, with a resolution of 0.1°Bx . In SG, this corresponds approximately to a range of 1.000 to 1.032, with a resolution of 0.0004. This one is my favorite and most precise hydrometer, and I find it indispensable when I need to evaluate slow speeds of fermentation. The thermometer gives a precise reading of the temperature, and the SG is obtained by an appropriate conversion from Brix to SG. Note that once the hydrometer is calibrated with the procedure given below,

the calibration will automatically take care of the scale conversion.

As mentioned above, it is very easy to purchase a triple-scale hydrometer; the two others are available from specialized oenology or laboratory supply stores and can be ordered online. In addition to these models, other types of hydrometers may be useful for a cider maker: a precision volumic mass hydrometer or an alcohol hydrometer, for example.

Figure 8.3 shows a hydrometer indicating a specific gravity of 1.017. To make a precise reading, it is necessary to look at the actual level of the liquid and not to take into account the *meniscus* (the curve in the liquid near the stem of the hydrometer). In this reading, the top of the meniscus would have been 1.0165, while the bottom is 1.017. I have also seen some hydrometers sold in France that were calibrated for a reading on the top of the meniscus, but such hydrometers are not common.

TEMPERATURE CORRECTION

For a hydrometer that is calibrated to give the specific gravity, we would normally take the reading at the calibration temperature, which is written on the instrument. In North America it is usually 60°F, and the instruments that are from Europe may be calibrated at 15°C or 20°C.

As mentioned above, the hydrometer in fact measures the volumic mass of the liquid, but the scale is calibrated as a function of the volumic mass of the water at the calibration temperature—thus, we can read the specific gravity directly on the scale. That is why an exact reading is possible only at the calibration temperature. When the liquid temperature deviates too far from the calibration temperature, a correction is necessary:

Let us assume a hydrometer calibrated at 60°F and some apple juice at a temperature of 77°F. The hydrometer gives a reading of $SG_{read} = 1.055$.

The volumic mass (ρ) of the juice is then

$$\rho = \rho_{60}\, SG_{read}$$

where ρ_{60} is the volumic mass of water at 60°F (the calibration temperature), given by table 8.2 on page 158: $\rho_{60} = 999$ g/L

which gives for the volumic mass of the juice $\rho = 1053.9$ g/L.

And we will obtain the true specific gravity (SG_{true}) by dividing this last result by the volumic mass of the water at 77°F: $\rho_{77} = 997$ g/L, also given by table 8.2 on page 158.

$$SG_{true} = \rho\, /\, \rho_{77} = 1053.9\, /\, 997 = 1.057$$

The temperature correction for this liquid at 77°F is thus +.002 (i.e., 1.057–1.055)

In general, the following relation may be used:

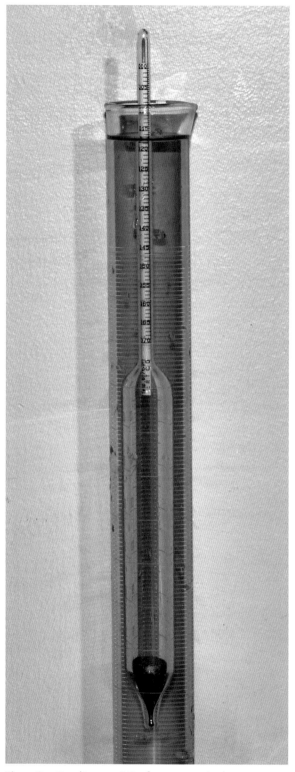

Figure 8.3. Reading an SG of 1.017 on a hydrometer.

TABLE 8.3:
Temperature correction table, hydrometer calibrated at 60°F

TEMPERATURE	< 43°F (< 6°C)	50°F (10°C)	53°F (12°C)	60°F (15.6°C)	65°F (18.5°C)	70°F (21°C)	77°F (25°C)	84°F (29°C)
CORRECTION	-0.001	-0.0007	-0.0005	0	+0.0005	+0.001	+0.002	+0.003

$$SG_{true} = SG_{read} \left(\rho_{cal} / \rho_T \right)$$

where ρ_{cal} is the volumic mass of the water at the calibration temperature of the hydrometer, and ρ_T is the volumic mass of water at the temperature of the juice or cider. The value of ρ_T is taken from table 8.2 or obtained from the following regression formula, where T is in °C:

$$\rho_T = 999.9 + 0.0364\,T - 0.006\,T^2$$

Although the above relation will give a more exact correction for temperature and is preferable when maximum precision from the hydrometer is required, table 8.3 will be precise enough on most occasions.

Calibration of the Hydrometer

As long as I had only one hydrometer, I was always confident of the reading I obtained and never thought of cross-checking it. This was a standard triple-scale hydrometer. One day, however, I bought a more precise hydrometer, with an SG scale from 1.000 to 1.070, and I noticed there could be quite a difference between the measurements obtained from the two instruments—something like four points of density difference when both were in the same liquid. Naturally, I

trusted the better-quality instrument and stopped using the triple-scale hydrometer. But with time I bought more hydrometers—some with a thermometer in the body, some with a close range—to the point where I now have about a dozen of them. And since even the better-quality instruments didn't always give the same values of SG when put into the same liquid, I decided I had to calibrate them so I could use any of them and still obtain consistent values of SG.

THE PRECISION OF A MEASUREMENT

No instrument exists that will give an absolutely exact measurement, and hydrometers are no exception. In general, when doing experimental work that involves instrumentation and measurement, we consider that the precision of an instrument is approximately equal to its resolution. This means that we assume the uncertainty from the instrument is more or less the value of one division. This is the *instrumental error*. For example, for a standard triple-scale hydrometer, the graduations are 0.002 on the SG scale, which corresponds to its resolution, so the instrumental error in this case would be ±0.002. Other hydrometers may have resolutions of 0.001 or 0.0005 on the SG scale. This, however, as long as the instrument is well calibrated and doesn't show any bias of measurement—which unfortunately is not always the case. Moreover, besides the instrument's imprecision, there is also the possible error that comes from the way the measure was taken. This is called the *manipulation error*. For example, the temperature may have affected the measurement or some carbon dioxide gas bubbles may have stuck to the instrument and changed the reading. Because of this, it is generally recommended when doing measurements to double the instrumental error in order to take into account the manipulation error. This means that if we have an apple juice for which we measure an SG of 1.050, and this measure was taken with a triple-scale hydrometer that has a resolution of 0.002, the total uncertainty of the measure would be ±0.004, and the true SG of the juice should be between 1.046 and 1.054 if the instrument is correctly calibrated. If the measure was taken with a precision hydrometer that has a resolution of 0.0005, then the total uncertainty would instead be ±0.001, and the true SG of the juice would then be between 1.049 and 1.051. These uncertainties are quite large, and when monitoring a slow fermentation where there may be an SG drop of 0.001 in ten days, we can easily see it is just about impossible to do if the uncertainty of the measure is ±0.004. In order to reduce this uncertainty, here are a few recommendations:

- Use a good-quality hydrometer that has a resolution of 0.0005 on the SG scale. Make sure the instrument is dry and clean.
- Always make sure there are no bubbles that stick to the instrument.
- Make sure the instrument and the liquid are at the same temperature. Leave the hydrometer in the liquid at least a couple of minutes before taking the reading.

- Always measure the temperature: use a separate thermometer if you don't have a thermo-hydrometer.
- For maximum precision, use a cylinder (see figure 8.3 on page 163) and look carefully at the level of the liquid.
- If you have more than one hydrometer, take the same measurement with each one and check the consistency of the measures.
- Calibrate the hydrometer according to the procedure that follows.

CALIBRATION PROCEDURE

This procedure involves the preparation of some reference sugar or salt solutions that will have a measured concentration and thus will have a known specific gravity. Distilled water will also be a reference solution for SG 1.000. By checking the reading from a hydrometer with these solutions, it is possible to make a correction for this hydrometer that will make it more accurate. I recommend making at least three points of calibration within the range of the hydrometer: one in the low part of the range, one in the middle, and one near the top. For example, if you have two hydrometers, one that has a range of 1.000 to 1.050 and the other with a range of 1.000 to 1.100, you would use distilled water for a reference solution of SG 1.000, then a 6°Bx solution for a reference at SG 1.024, a 12°Bx solution for a reference at SG 1.048, and a 22°Bx solution for SG 1.092 would finally cover the high end of the second instrument.

When I tested my dozen hydrometers against such reference solutions, I found that about a third of them didn't really need any correction: the reading I got from them was always within 0.0005 of the reference SG. Another third needed only an offset correction: by adding or subtracting a constant value on the whole range of the instrument, I could get within 0.0005 of the reference SG. This offset was as large as 0.004 in one case (this was a triple-scale hydrometer), but for the others it was only one or two points of density. And for the last third of my hydrometers, a constant offset didn't do the job, as there was a slope (or linearity) error. For example, in one of my instruments I need to subtract 0.002 from the reading when I measure in the bottom of the scale, but at the top of the scale the instrument is accurate and I don't need to make a correction anymore.

REQUIRED MATERIALS

In order to prepare the reference solutions and calibrate the hydrometers, the following materials will be required:

- Distilled water. A gallon will be enough. Give preference to true distilled water rather than purified water, and check the ppm of minerals. Choose the one that has the lowest number. The one I use indicates less than 2 ppm of minerals.
- A balance or scale with a resolution of 0.1 gram and a minimum capacity of 600 g (1 kg would be better; see Appendix 1). The reference solutions will be obtained by measuring a certain weight of sugar or salt in a weighted amount of solution. Precision is required, and with such a balance you can insure the SG error on the reference solutions will be less than ±0.0002 in SG. The cost of these is relatively reasonable; I was able to buy one for under $60.
- Granulated white sugar. I recommend getting a fresh pack, as older sugar may have absorbed some humidity. Such sugar contains over 99.9

percent chemically pure sucrose and less than 0.1 percent impurities (mostly ashes). See further if you prefer to use salt.
- A thermometer, ideally with a precision of 1°F (0.5°C) or better.
- A hydrometer jar or cylinder, of the right size for the hydrometers that will be calibrated.
- Two beakers (1L size) or other clean and dry containers to mix the sugar and water.
- A syringe (1 or 3 mL) or eyedropper for the final water additions.

PREPARATION OF THE REFERENCE SOLUTIONS

Preparation of the solutions is quite straightforward. For example, if you want a solution at 12°Bx, this is 12 percent sugar in weight, so you need 12 g of sugar for 100 g of solution. I suggest making 500 g of solution, although only about 250 g will really be needed. This is to improve the precision. In effect, if the error on the balance is ±0.2 g, this will translate into an error of ±0.0002 in SG for 500 g of solution and an error of ±0.0004 in SG for 250 g of solution. So the more solution you make, the more precise it will be.

To make the solution, first put a container (clean and dry) on the balance and reset the scale to zero. Then add the amount of sugar: in the case of 500 g of a 12°Bx solution, this would be exactly 60.0 g. Then add distilled water until you reach about 499 g. To complete the amount of water, use a syringe or an eyedropper to reach exactly 500.0 g of solution. One mL of water will add 1 g, and one drop about 0.1 g. The best way to insure the mix is homogeneous is to pour the solution from one container to another four or five times before using it. Make sure all the sugar is well dissolved in the water.

TABLE 8.4:
Reference sugar solutions

°Brix	SG (20°C / 20°C)	SG (60°F / 60°F)	GRAMS OF SUGAR for 500 g of solution
2.5	1.0098	1.0098	12.5
6	1.0237	1.0238	30
12	1.0484	1.0485	60
16	1.0654	1.0656	80
22	1.0919	1.0922	110
30	1.1291	1.1296	150

TABLE 8.5:
Reference salt solutions

% MASS concentration	SG (20°C / 20°C)	SG (60°F / 60°F)	GRAMS OF SALT for 500 g of solution
1	1.0071	1.0072	5
4	1.0286	1.0290	20
6	1.0431	1.0437	30
9	1.0652	1.0659	45
13	1.0952	1.0961	65
17	1.1260	1.1271	85

Table 8.4 gives some useful data for the preparation of reference sugar solutions. Depending on the hydrometers to be calibrated and the applications, those solutions won't all be needed. For example, the 30°Bx solution will be necessary only if you are making some ice cider; otherwise, juice will never approach such densities. This table was constructed using the National Bureau of Standards' 1942 circular C440, *Polarimetry, Saccharimetry and the Sugars,* which gives the SG of sugar solutions at a reference temperature of 20°C. I computed the SG at a reference temperature of 60°F, taking into account the difference in thermal expansion between water and sugar solutions. We can see that at Brix of 16 and lower, the difference is negligible, as low-concentration sugar solutions have almost identical thermal expansion as pure water. However, for higher Brix values, this factor becomes more important.

USING SALT FOR THE REFERENCE SOLUTIONS

Reference solutions for SG may also be made with salt instead of sugar. The advantage of salt is that the solutions may be kept without fear that they will begin to ferment. You should use coarse salt sold for pickling, as this type of salt doesn't contain iodine and thus is purer than normal table salt. And just as for sugar, use a fresh pack, because salt absorbs humidity. Table 8.5 was built from data published by the Salt Institute and gives the density of brines for different concentrations and temperatures. We can see that in the case of salt there is more difference between the SG at the two reference temperatures. This is because brine has a larger coefficient of thermal expansion than that of water or sugar-water solutions. Hence, if you use salt for your reference solutions, it becomes more important to make the measurements at the closest possible temperature to the reference temperature of the hydrometer.

MEASURES AND INTERPRETATION

Once the reference solutions are prepared, install yourself in a well-lit area at a temperature as close as possible to the reference temperature of your hydrometers. Allow enough time for the solutions

TABLE 8.6:

SG measurements for hydrometer calibration

REFERENCE SOLUTION	SG 1.000		SG 1.0238		SG 1.0656	
	#1	#2	#1	#2	#1	#2
Hydrometer 1.000–1.070	1.0015	1.0020	1.0245	1.0250	1.0660	1.0655
Triple-scale hydrometer	1.004	1.004	1.027	1.028	1.070	1.069

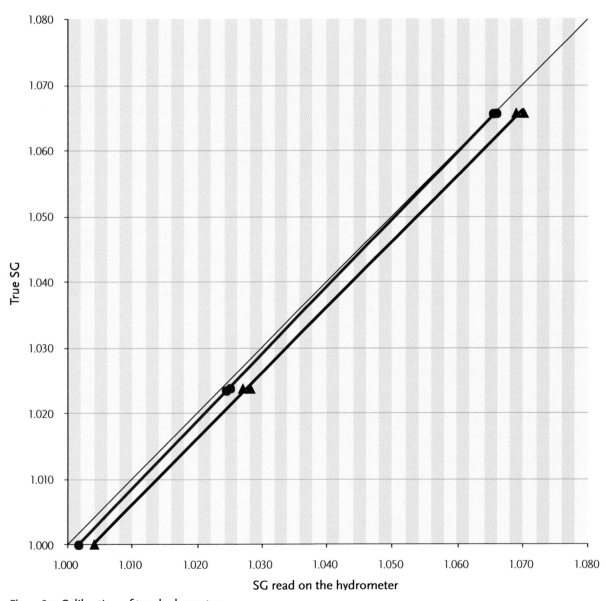

Figure 8.4. Calibration of two hydrometers.

and hydrometers to reach the ambient room temperature. Then take the readings from the hydrometers in each of the solutions, and note also the temperature of the solutions. It is preferable to measure twice in each solution to avoid errors. Before inserting a hydrometer into another solution, rinse it and dry it so as not to alter the concentration of sugar with a bit of liquid that would come from another solution. If the temperatures differ from the reference temperature, you may apply the temperature correction to your readings, as discussed above.

Additionally, in order to minimize the possibility of errors, I would recommend doing the whole process of preparing the reference solutions twice. If the hydrometer gives the same reading both times, it is much more reassuring. And finally, you can put your results into a graph and make a calibration line between the SG reading on the instrument and the true SG.

Table 8.6 presents a calibration example from two of my hydrometers, the first having a range from 1.000 to 1.070, and the second being a standard triple-scale instrument.

The result appears in figure 8.4, where the 1.000–1.070 hydrometer is represented by the blue line and the triple-scale hydrometer by the brown line. The thin black line would correspond to an ideal hydrometer. Once your graph is constructed, it may be used as in the following example: if I read an SG of 1.035 with my 1.000–1.070 hydrometer, I find this value on the bottom scale and go up to the blue line, which I intersect at a value of 1.034 on the left scale. Thus, the corrected SG is 1.034. It is also possible to make this correction process automatic with the help of a computer and a spreadsheet. You will find such a spreadsheet, named Hydromtr.xls, with the companion material of this book described in Appendix 2.

◀ 8.3 ▶
The Amount of Sugar in Apple Juice

As there can't be a mathematical relationship between the density of the juice and the corresponding amount of sugar, tables can only give approximations; we can't expect exact figures; for a given density, the amount of sugar indicated by the table may differ in some cases by 10 or 15 grams from the real number given by chemical analysis.

G. WARCOLLIER, *La Cidrerie*, 1928

Knowing the true amount of sugar in the juice is of considerable interest for a cider maker, as it permits us to evaluate the strength of alcohol of the cider and the amount of residual sugar. However, as Warcollier writes in *La cidrerie*, this exact amount of sugar can't be obtained by the measurement of the density, nor, as a matter of fact, by the measurement of the Brix with a refractometer. Only a chemical analysis of the juice can indicate the true value of sugar concentration. This is due to the fact that apple juice contains many different constituents besides sugar and water, as we saw in a previous article. Each of these substances—tannins, acids, pectins, and others—will influence the density of the juice, each in its own way. Additionally, the respective proportions of these substances will vary from one variety of apple to another, from one specific terroir to another, and from year to year as a function of the climatic conditions and cultural practices. Hence, the hydrometer or the refractometer will give a good evaluation of the total solids in solution in the juice, but the corresponding amount of sugar is only an estimation based on the average taken from the analysis of a large number of samples.

The Sugar Content

This being said, most if not all books on cider since the end of the nineteenth century have included either a table or a mathematical relation that gives the amount of sugar from the density of the juice. And for a very simple reason: the density is an easy property to measure. After the development of the Fehling test for sugar dosage, some scientists of that era, and in particular Truelle, Lechartier, Power, and Warcollier in France, made some complete chemical analyses of cider apple juices and built a bank of data that included the density, sugar, acidity, and tannins of a large number of samples. To build a table, these scientists would plot the data on a graph and draw a best-fit line from which the points of the table could be taken. Truelle built such a table using analysis he had done on cider apples from Normandy, while Lechartier did similar work with cider apples from

Brittany. These two tables were then merged into a new table that has been called the *Dujardin-Salleron* table by some and the *Truelle-Lechartier* table by others, and which appears in the important book by Warcollier (1928) mentioned above. This table is still used, almost unchanged other than minor corrections, in most actual works on cider, for example in Proulx and Nichols (1980), Lea (2008), and Moinet (2009). One notable exception, however, is in the book by Bauduin (2006), where the table presented has been constructed from more recent analysis: G. Bohuon, P. Perrin, and J. M. Le Quéré, *Note sur la détermination de l'extrait sec total du cidre* (1991). The sugar table that appears in Bauduin's book gives sugar concentration values that are slightly above those from the Dujardin-Salleron table, and it also has the merit of providing a minimum, average, and maximum value for a given juice density.

What stands out as significant in all of this is that the sugar tables found in most of these cider books have been built from chemical analysis performed at the turn of the twentieth century on French cider apples. Hence, it is quite legitimate to question such tables on their validity for other types of apples. For example, the North American apple varieties used to make cider have very different properties, as they contain more acidity and less tannins than typical French cider apples. Does the Dujardin-Salleron table still apply to juice obtained from such apples? To answer this question and also to be able to evaluate the magnitude of the possible error when using such tables, I started to collect data from published works. I found the following:

- Warcollier, *Le Pommier à cidre* (1926): A table presents the results of analysis done on 144 samples of juice from different French cider apples. Thesc analyses were done by scientists of that period: Truelle, Lechartier, Power, Warcollier himself, and possibly a few others. These data points are probably the basis for the Truelle and Lechartier tables.

- Lloyd, *Report on the Results of Investigations into Cidermaking, Carried Out on Behalf of the Bath and West and Southern Counties Society in the Years 1893–1902* (1903): A total of 109 data points from tables giving the composition of the juice of various apples grown in England, mostly English cider apples but also some table and culinary apples.

- Alwood, *A Study of Cider Making in France, Germany and England* (1903): In this publication, tables give the composition of German (61 data points) and American apples (31 data points). This is particularly interesting, as the apples from these countries contain more acidity and less tannins than traditional French or English cider apples.

In addition to these resources, I was able to gather some additional data points from a few publications that are more recent: Smock and Neubert (1950) and a few others; plus a few more from other old books. So in total I was able to gather the results of 403 analyses of the sugar content in a juice sample, as a function of the known value of the density. In many cases the data had to be converted to specific gravity when the density was expressed as the volumic mass.

These data points are summarized in table 8.7. The slope in this table represents the ratio of the sugar in g/L to the decimal part of the specific gravity (i.e., SG − 1). This slope was calculated for each data point, and the average value is given. The standard deviation is calculated on the slope. This is a statistical indicator for the scatter of the data. In particular, when a certain set of data follows the normal distribution, then statistically 95 percent of the data will be between bounds defined by the average more or less twice the standard deviation. In other words, if we take the combined data set with an average slope of 2,130 and a standard deviation of 120, we may say that, statistically speaking, 95 percent of the data would be bounded by two lines, with respective slopes of 1,890 and 2,370, as 2,130 − (2 × 120) = 1,890 and 2,130 + (2 × 120) = 2,370. Thus, we may calculate the average and the lower and upper bounds of the 95 percent confidence interval for the sugar content of an apple juice from the following relations:

$$S_{avg} = 2130 \ (SG - 1)$$
$$S_{min} = 1890 \ (SG - 1)$$
$$S_{max} = 2370 \ (SG - 1)$$

TABLE 8.7:
Data points from the analysis of the sugar concentration of apple juices

COUNTRY OF ORIGIN	FRANCE	UNITED STATES	UNITED KINGDOM	GERMANY	COMBINED
Number of data points	171	44	127	61	403
Average slope	2,140	2,030	2,160	2,110	2,130
Standard deviation	100	120	120	110	120

Then, if we take as an example a juice sample with an SG of 1.050, we may say that there is a 95 percent probability that the true sugar concentration (S) will be between these two bounds:

$$S_{min} = 1890 \ (1.050 - 1) = 94.5 \ g/L$$
$$S_{max} = 2370 \ (1.050 - 1) = 118.5 \ g/L$$

And the average value of S for a large number of samples tested would be:

$$S_{avg} = 2130 \ (1.050 - 1) = 106.5 \ g/L$$

We see in this example case that the possible variation of S (which we write ΔS) would be ±12 g/L from the average value, considering a 95 percent confidence interval. This compares very well with the assertion from Warcollier, cited at the beginning of this article: "the amount of sugar indicated by the table may differ in some cases by 10 or 15 grams from the real number given by chemical analysis." Another way of seeing this is by the uncertainty in the percentage of the sugar content. In this case we could then say the sugar concentration is given by the relation for S_{avg} above, more or less ΔS, which is 11.3 percent of S_{avg}.

By way of comparison, for a volumic mass of 1,048 g/L at 20°C (equivalent to SG 1.050), the Bauduin table mentioned earlier gives 108 g/L of sugar, with minimum and maximum of 103.9 and 112.1, respectively. And for a volumic mass of 1,049 g/L at 15°C (equivalent to SG 1.050) the Dujardin-Salleron table gives 104.5 g/L of sugar. So all these numbers are quite close. However, it seems that Bauduin underestimates slightly the possible error when compared with the present analysis, as the variation ΔS is only ±4.1 g/L with this table.

It is interesting to compare this slope for S_{avg} with the relation we obtained earlier for the total solids (TS) from the density reading (see section 8.1):

$$TS = 2608 \ (SG - 1)$$

We can thus see that the average sugar content from a large number of tests would equal 82 percent of the value of the total solids.

An interesting feature of the data presented in table 8.7 is that the slope for the data from the United States is 5 percent lower than the combined average. This is still within the 95 percent confidence interval. The average slope for the data points from Germany is also slightly below the combined average. The fact that both American and German apples have higher acidity content than French and English cider apples could be an explanation for this, as if there is more acid for a same amount of total solids, the amount of sugar has to be reduced. It should also be noted that the more modern data points showed excellent correlation with the points taken from old publications, both for the slope and for the scatter of the data, and this indicates that the old measurements are as accurate as the more modern ones.

In order to be able to visualize all these data points and draw a best-fit line, I plotted them in figure 8.5, using different markers for the different countries of origin, to which I added the following:

- The brown solid line above the data points is the total solids. This is the sugar concentration that a pure water-sugar solution would have at a given SG and represents a high limit for S.
- The white line is from the standard Dujardin-Salleron table as published in most cider books.

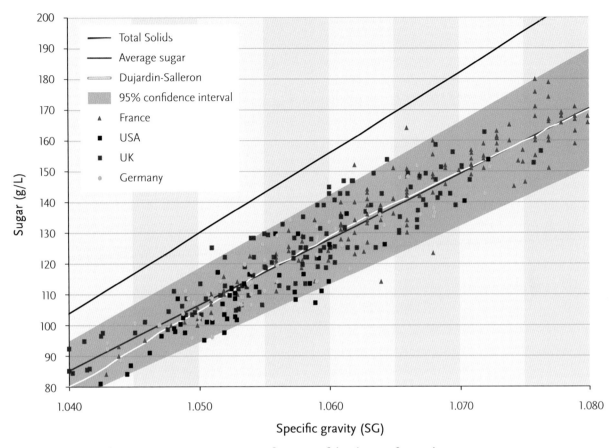

Figure 8.5. Graph of the sugar concentration as a function of the density for apple juice.

- The thick blue line is the average sugar obtained by the relation above for S_{avg}.
- The shaded area represent the bounds of the 95 percent confidence interval and is defined by the relations above for S_{min} and S_{max}.

From this graph, we can note the following:

- The line representing the Dujardin-Salleron table is very close to the line for S_{avg} for high densities (SG > 1.052) but gives lower values at low densities. The reason for this behavior of the Dujardin-Salleron table in the low densities isn't known and doesn't appear to be supported by the actual data.

- There are about 15 data points outside the shaded area, which represent a bit less than 5 percent of the complete data set. This is in accordance with the 95 percent confidence interval.

Sugar-Free Dry Extract (SFDE) and Potential Alcohol

The influence of the substances other than sugar and water can easily be seen on figure 8.5. These substances, the sugar-free dry extract (SFDE), include the acids, tannins, pectins, minerals, amino acids, and so on. For instance, we can see that a pure water-sugar solution at a concentration of 130 g/L would have an SG of approximately 1.050 (from the brown line). But for this same amount of sugar, an apple juice would on average have an SG of about 1.061. Hence, the SFDE would in this case have raised the SG by 0.011. Another way to look at this is that a juice at an SG of 1.050 on average will contain approximately 107 g of sugar per liter. Then the difference between 130 and 107 is 23 g/L, which may be considered an equivalent weight of sugar brought by the SFDE. The SFDE itself will not weigh exactly 23 g, as the substances of which it is constituted do not necessarily influence the density in the same way sugar does. We may, however, say that the SFDE is 23 g/L of sugar equivalent. And a cider sample that contains more sugar than the average will contain less SFDE, and vice versa. It is possible to evaluate the SFDE once all the sugars have been fermented and transformed into alcohol. We simply then have to evaporate this alcohol, and the density of the remaining solution gives an indication of the SFDE. We will see more on this in Section 14.5 on alcohol and evaluation of the alcoholic strength. In general, we will simply evaluate the SFDE as the difference between the total solids and the sugar content:

$$SFDE = TS - S$$

And if we only know an average value for S, the value thus obtained for SFDE would also be an average for a large number of samples. As we have seen earlier, on average S is 82 percent of TS; so then SFDE is on average 18 percent of TS.

We may note that the total solids represent an upper limit for the value of S. In effect, if a sample of juice had such a high sugar content that S would be equal to TS, then the SFDE would be equal to zero, and we would have a pure water-sugar solution. But the SFDE couldn't be negative.

The *potential alcohol* (A_P) is a scale that we have seen earlier for the expression of the sugar content in the cider. It is expressed as a function of the sugar content in the juice:

$$A_P \text{ (\%ABV)} = 0.06\, S$$

From the work above, we may use the value of S_{avg} in this relation, thus obtaining an average value for $A_{P\text{-avg}}$:

$$A_{P\text{-avg}} \text{ (\%ABV)} = 127.8\,(SG - 1)$$

Note that for cider the potential alcohol scale is different from that for beer or wine (essentially because the average ratio of SFDE is different); thus, a table or a hydrometer calibrated for either of these will give an inaccurate value for cider.

The Sugar Table

Table 8.8 was compiled with the relations above and those from section 8.1. It gives as a function of the specific gravity (SG):

- ρ, the volumic mass of the juice at 20°C
- Brix, in % (i.e., g per 100 g of juice)
- TS, total solids or dry extract per liter
- S_{avg}, the average sugar concentration, as discussed above
- ΔS, the bounds of the 95 percent confidence interval on S
- $A_{P\text{-avg}}$, the average potential alcohol in %ABV at 20°C

TABLE 8.8:
Sugar table for apple juice

SG	ρ (g/L)	Brix (%)	TS (g/L)	S_{AVG} (g/L)	ΔS (±g/L)	$A_{P\text{-}AVG}$ (%)
1.035	1,033.1	8.78	90.7	74.5	8.4	4.47
1.040	1,038.1	9.99	103.7	85.2	9.6	5.11
1.042	1040.1	10.48	109.0	89.5	10.1	5.37
1.044	1042.1	10.96	114.2	93.7	10.6	5.62
1.045	1043.1	11.19	116.8	95.8	10.8	5.75
1.046	1044.1	11.43	119.4	98.0	11.0	5.88
1.047	1045.1	11.67	122.0	100.1	11.3	6.01
1.048	1046.1	11.91	124.6	102.2	11.5	6.13
1.049	1047.1	12.15	127.2	104.4	11.8	6.26
1.050	1048.1	12.39	129.8	106.5	12.0	6.39
1.051	1049.1	12.62	132.4	108.6	12.2	6.52
1.052	1050.1	12.86	135.0	110.8	12.5	6.65
1.053	1051.1	13.10	137.7	112.9	12.7	6.77
1.054	1052.1	13.33	140.3	115.0	13.0	6.90
1.055	1053.1	13.57	142.9	117.1	13.2	7.03
1.056	1054.1	13.80	145.5	119.3	13.4	7.16
1.057	1055.1	14.04	148.1	121.4	13.7	7.28
1.058	1056.1	14.27	150.7	123.5	13.9	7.41
1.059	1057.1	14.51	153.3	125.7	14.2	7.54
1.060	1058.1	14.74	156.0	127.8	14.4	7.67
1.061	1059.1	14.97	158.6	129.9	14.6	7.80
1.062	1060.1	15.21	161.2	132.1	14.9	7.92
1.063	1061.1	15.44	163.8	134.2	15.1	8.05
1.064	1062.1	15.67	166.4	136.3	15.4	8.18
1.065	1063.1	15.90	169.1	138.4	15.6	8.31
1.066	1064.1	16.13	171.7	140.6	15.8	8.43
1.068	1066.1	16.59	176.9	144.8	16.3	8.69
1.070	1068.1	17.05	182.2	149.1	16.8	8.95
1.072	1070.1	17.51	187.4	153.4	17.3	9.20
1.075	1073.1	18.20	195.3	159.8	18.0	9.58
1.080	1078.1	19.33	208.4	170.4	19.2	10.22
1.085	1083.1	20.46	221.5	181.1	20.4	10.86

Table for apple juice only. Properties in g/L at 20°C (68°F).

For concentrated apple juices, table 15.5 with SG from 1.090 up to 1.180 is given in section 15.3 on ice cider on page 286.

A NOTE ON CHAPTALIZATION

This sugar table will not give a correct estimate of the SG after *chaptalization* (the technical term for the addition of sugar to the must before primary fermentation) because the SFDE is not increased in the same proportions as the sugar. In fact, the SFDE remains constant as the amount of sugar is increased, yielding a final SG lower than what could be anticipated. The table may, however, be used in the following manner to give an estimate of the SG of the chaptalized juice:

Assume that a juice has an SG of 1.040, containing 85.2 g/L of sugar, which is the average sugar amount for this density. Such a juice has a potential alcohol of 5.11 percent. If 40 g/L of sugar is added, this would bring the amount of sugar to S = 125.2 g, from which we could read an erroneous value for SG at 1.059 and a potential alcohol of 7.5 percent.

The correct way to evaluate the SG of this sweetened juice is to add the amount of sugar to the amount of total solids: with an initial SG of 1.040, the TS is 103.7 g/L, to which we add 40 g/L, for a total amount of 143.7 grams per liter of juice we had at the beginning. Besides, the volume and mass will also change because of this sugar addition. The original mass of one liter of juice is given by the value of ρ for an SG of 1.040, or 1,038 grams. After addition, this is also increased by 40 grams, hence we have 1,078 grams. From this, we compute the new Brix: 143.7 / 1,078 = 13.33 percent, and the table gives us the correct SG of the chaptalized must at 1.054. We can see that the original estimation for SG was in error by 0.005. The new volume is the mass (1,078 g) divided by the new value of ρ, which is 1,052.1 g/L: this gives 1.024 liter. The sugar concentration is the original value of S, 85.2 g/L, plus the added sugar, 40 g/L, divided by the volume, 1.024 L, which gives 122.2 g/L. The corresponding potential alcohol is 7.3 percent.

CHAPTER 9

THE ACIDS

After sugar, the other most important property of a must is its acidity, which has a great influence on the gustative sensation we get from drinking the cider. Additionally, acidity is connected to the biochemical reactions that happen during the cider-making process, and it is important for the cider maker to understand those.

◄ 9.1 ►
Total or Titratable Acidity

Malic acid is an organic acid that on average makes up 90 percent of the total of acid components in fresh apple juice. In the remaining portion, there is some *quinic acid* (up to 10 percent), some *citric acid* (1 to 2 percent), and a few other acids in smaller proportion. Once fermented, however, the cider may contain a relatively important proportion of *lactic acid* and a (hopefully) lesser proportion of *acetic acid,* both of which are produced during the fermentation process. Note that the word "malic" has the same root as the Latin word *malus,* which is also the botanical name for the entire apple genus. In effect, malic acid was first extracted from apple juice in the late eighteenth century. Malic acid is, however, also found in many other fruits besides apples, as well as some vegetables.

The acidity of a juice or cider is a property that is easily measurable. It is important to have a good idea of its quantity in our cider and to control it if necessary, because the acidity has an important influence on the taste perception of the cider: when the acidity is too low, the cider will lack freshness and will seem dull. On the other hand, too much acidity may render the cider too tart or sharp and unpleasant to drink. We need to make a well-balanced cider that will feel just right when drunk, and this is normally done by blending different varieties.

Another important property depends on the acidity: the pH, which I discuss below in section 9.3. For now, let us look at the type of acidity responsible for the gustatory sensation, the *total acidity*.

Because the total acidity of an apple juice or cider is measured by titration it is also (and perhaps more correctly) called *titratable acidity* (TA). Kits are sold in all wine-making supply stores for taking this measurement. For apple juice and cider, the total acidity is normally expressed in grams of malic acid equivalent per liter (g/L) of juice or cider at 20°C. More details on titration are given in the next section.

The acidity concentration of apple juice differs greatly by variety: some sweet apples may give a juice that will contain only 1 g/L of malic acid, while the juice from very acidic crabs may have thirty times that much. For the apples used in cider making, the range is not as great, and we will usually avoid the varieties whose acidity is more than 12 g/L (although some English cider apples of the *sharp* type, and most notably the Fox-whelp, may have an acidity of the order of 20 g/L). Naturally, the higher the acidity number, the more pronounced the acidic taste sensation. To give an

TABLE 9.1:
Apple classification according to their acidity

Acidity	TA (g/L as malic acid)	Type
Low	less than 4.5	Sweet apples
Medium	4.5 to 7.5	Balanced: ideal for cider
High	7.5 to 11	Many table apples
Very high	more than 11	Cooking apples, crabs

idea for comparison, lemon juice has an acidity of about 40 to 50 g/L.

Other factors, such as climate, influence the acidity content of apples as well. In Australia, where the summer temperatures are hot and the growing season long, the acidity level for a given variety is sensibly lower than it would be if the same variety were grown in a cool climate. And even in the same location there are important seasonal variations: whether it has been more or less rainy, sunny, hot, and so forth. The degree of maturation, too, has an influence on the acidity: the longer the apples are stored and the riper they are at the moment of pressing, the less acid the juice will contain. On the other hand, cultural practices have relatively little effect on acidity.

We may classify apples according to their acidity as shown in table 9.1.

An important objective of blending is thus to mix juices or ciders from different varieties of apples in order to obtain a well-balanced blend in terms of acidity. It is important to understand that fresh apple juice is rich in sugar, and when we drink it this sugar counterbalances the perceived acidity, thus giving us an overall pleasant gustatory experience. However, as this juice is transformed into cider, the sugar is converted into alcohol, and the acidity becomes much more prominent, to the point where it may render the cider unpleasant to drink if its concentration is too high. On the other hand, if there is not enough acidity, the cider will seem to lack "freshness." Note that the alcohol will also counterbalance the acidity somewhat, but to a lesser degree than sugar. Experience shows us that a well-balanced cider should maintain an acidity concentration within the following limits:

- For a fresh, dry, and festive sparkling cider, the acidity should be between 6 and 7.5 g/L of malic acid.
- If the finished cider is to be a medium-sweet or a sweet style, the acidity could be higher, as the residual sugar will counterbalance the extra acidity. Ice ciders, for example, have very high acidity levels, but since the residual sugar is also very high, the balance is maintained.
- For a European-style cider with a high tannin content, the recommended acidity is lower, as the tannins compensate for the lack of acidity by giving body and bitterness to the cider. For such a cider, the recommended acidity is generally between 4.5 and 6 g/L.

These acidity levels are usually obtained by blending, as very few apples naturally have the ideal acidity concentration. Blending may be done either with fresh juices prior to fermentation or with ciders after the fermentation is complete. Thus, blending is one of the most important operations for creating great ciders; for more on this, see chapter 13.

A way to express the acidity balance of the apple juice is by the ratio of sugar to acid. This ratio is obtained by dividing the sugar content S (in g/L) by the total acidity TA (also in g/L). It thus gives the number of grams of sugar present for each gram of malic acid. This ratio is more useful for juice that is to be drunk fresh than it is for making cider. When the ratio is high, over 30:1, the juice will be very sweet and will lack acidity when consumed fresh, but it would be good in blending for cider. For a good apple juice, this ratio would ideally be between 15:1 and 20:1. And when this ratio is less than 10:1, we get a very sharp juice, too acidic to be pleasant.

The acidity, as measured by titration, may vary somewhat during and after the alcoholic fermentation, as some of the malic acid is transformed into lactic acid. This causes a reduction of the titratable acidity because lactic acid is a simple acid, while malic acid is a double acid (diprotic). Thus, for an equal number of molecules, malic acid gives twice as much acidity. The main phenomenon that causes this transformation is called *malolactic fermentation* (MLF), which may occur after the alcoholic fermentation is completed. As this is quite important in cider making, I have written an entire article on malolactic fermentation, section 14.4. Other biochemical reactions will also affect the acidity of the cider: for example, a small quantity of acetic acid is produced by bacteria. Some types of yeast are known to provoke either an increase or a diminution of the acidity as well (as we will see when we discuss yeasts further).

◄ 9.2 ►
Measurement of Acidity by Titration

Titration is a simple and inexpensive method for the measurement of acidity in a fresh juice or cider.

REQUIRED MATERIALS

- A test tube or small glass.
- Alkali solution (base): *sodium hydroxide* (NaOH). The concentration, or normality, of NaOH used for titration is usually 0.2 N (N/5) or 0.1 N (N/10). It may also be an adjusted value for a given kit. The concentration should be written on the bottle.
- Indicator: *phenolphthalein* (pink-red) or *bromothymol blue* (blue-green).
- A burette and/or syringes to measure small quantities of liquid.

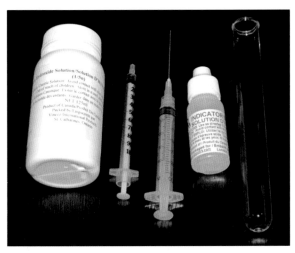

Figure 9.1. Titration kit for acidity: from left to right, a bottle of NaOH at N/5, a 1 mL syringe for titration, a 3 mL syringe for measuring the sample volume, a bottle of phenolphthalein, and a test tube.

Kits containing all the necessary materials are sold in wine-making supply stores. Figure 9.1 shows a sample kit.

MANIPULATION

If you are testing a cider (either fermenting or finished), you should first take and aerate a sample to eliminate the carbon dioxide gas. Alternatively, you may put the sample in a microwave oven for a few seconds to evaporate the gas.

- Measure a precise quantity of the juice or cider to test with a syringe and put it in the test tube or glass.
- Add a few drops of the indicator solution.
- Do the titration by adding small quantities of the alkali solution until the indicator starts changing color.
- Shake the sample well: the indicator color should vanish the first few times. Continue adding the alkali solution until the color change persists after shaking. If you are using phenolphthalein as an indicator for testing fresh juice, the final color change may be subtle, the juice appearing slightly more brownish once the indicator has changed color.
- Note the quantity of alkali solution added (in mL).

EXPRESSION OF THE RESULT

There are many possible ways to express the result of titration, and this may lead to some confusion.

In the following formulae, I use K for the number of mL of NaOH that was added and L for the number of mL of the sample tested. Then the general formula to obtain the total, or titratable, acidity (TA), expressed in molar acid equivalents per liter (eq/L) is:

$$TA \ (eq/L) = N \ K \ / \ L$$

where N is the normality of NaOH, usually 0.1 or 0.2. Note that for NaOH, the normality is equal to the molarity, that is, the number of moles per liter.

For apple juice and cider, however, I recommend having the acidity in grams of malic acid per liter, as this is the main acid found in apples. For this, we need to use the molar mass of malic acid (134 g/mol). Each mole contains 2 acid equivalents because malic acid is diprotic. Hence, for malic acid, there are 67 grams per acid equivalent. We then need to multiply the above equation by 67 to obtain the total acidity in grams of malic acid:

$$TA \ (g/L, \ malic \ acid) = 67 \ N \ K \ / \ L$$

and this result may be divided by 10 if a total acidity in percent is desired. For example, a TA of 5 g/L is equivalent to 0.5 percent of acidity.

Expressing the acidity in g/L of malic acid is in my opinion the most logical for cider making and is the method I use throughout this book. It is also that most often used by professionals and researchers in the cider industry. There are, however, other ways to express the acidity. In North America the total acidity is sometimes given in tartaric acid equivalent, probably because the kits easily bought in wine-making supply stores are designed for wine, and tartaric acid is the main acid compound found in grapes. In this case, we

TABLE 9.2:
Conversion factors for total acidity (TA)

TYPE	COUNTRY	TO OBTAIN g/L, malic acid
g/L, tartaric acid	America	multiply by 0.89
g/L, sulfuric acid	France	multiply by 1.37
meq/L	France	multiply by 67/1,000

would proceed as above but use the molar mass of tartaric acid (150 g/mol) divided by 2 (tartaric acid is also diprotic) to obtain a multiplication factor of 75 grams of tartaric acid per acid molar equivalent:

$$TA \ (g/L, \ tartaric \ acid) = 75 \ N \ K \ / \ L$$

With the standard wine acidity kits, the concentration of NaOH is usually 0.2N, and the volume of the sample is 15 mL. The total acidity in g/L is then simply equal to the number of mL of NaOH required to provoke the color change of the indicator.

In books from continental Europe, in particular from France and Spain, two other ways to express the total acidity are used: one is with sulfuric acid equivalent (same principle as above, with 98 g/mol, 49 g/eq) and the other is in milliequivalent per liter (meq/L).

Table 9.2 summarizes the conversion factors required to obtain the total acidity in grams per liter of malic acid.

When you consult a work giving values for total acidity in apples, make sure you know how the acidity is expressed. Although the author usually indicates the units within the text, you may have to deduce them from the country of origin.

To conclude, it may be useful to mention that we may modify to our advantage the recommended quantities of liquid with titration kits. Here are two examples:

- If your kit is calibrated for tartaric acid, you can modify the number of mL of the sample tested. These kits usually require a sample of 15 mL. If you instead use a sample of 13.4 mL, the titration will directly give the correct value in malic acid.
- You can also reduce the quantity of liquids you use. For example, if a kit calibrated for tartaric acid requires a 15 mL sample and dosing the NaOH with a 10 mL syringe, the same result may be obtained with a 1.5 mL sample and a 1 mL syringe. Such small syringes are easy to obtain in drugstores, and it will then be possible to do ten times as many analyses with the same kit.

And my personal favorite procedure is as follows:

- Measure a sample of 2.68 mL of the juice or cider to test with a 3 mL syringe. (In practice, there is no graduation at 2.68, so I take just a bit short of 2.7 mL.)
- Add two or three drops of phenolphthalein. A little more doesn't hurt, however, and gives the color change more contrast.

- Use a small 1 mL syringe for titration of the NaOH.
- The total acidity in grams of malic acid per liter will be equal to the number of mL of NaOH multiplied by 5 if the concentration of the NaOH is 0.2N.

NOTE ON THE PRECISION OF THE MEASURE

Titration done as described above is not very precise, and errors on the order of 0.2 to 0.4 g/L are normal. Such errors are caused by imprecision in measuring the volumes, by the fact that the alkali solution may not be exactly at the right concentration, by the presence of carbon dioxide in the cider, or by not seeing the exact point of color change of the indicator. It is important to have a fresh bottle of the alkali solution and to renew it regularly. Some procedures do give more exact results, and the use of a pH meter instead of the indicator solution also improves the accuracy. For this, we add the alkali until we reach a pH of 8.2–8.3, which is the pH for which the phenolphthalein changes color. However, for normal cider-making practice, the precision of this measure is not critical; the approximate result given by the normal procedure is usually good enough.

◄ 9.3 ►
The Acidity and the pH

As noted above, in addition to expressing the acidity of a juice or cider as the total, or titratable, acidity, we can also express the acidity as pH, or potential hydrogen. This is a distinct property with its own role

in the cider-making process. Most notably, it influences the biochemical reactions that occur during fermentation. In practice, the pH is related to the protection of cider from spoilage microorganisms:

a cider that has very little acidity will be much more susceptible to being spoiled by such organisms.

The pH is an acidity scale that measures the concentration of free hydrogen (H+) ions in a solution. The pH scale is an inverse logarithmic scale that goes from 0 to 14. We say of a pH equal to 7 that it is neutral: this corresponds to pure water. The pH values lower than 7 are acids, and those higher than 7 are bases. The lower the value of pH, the more acidic the solution. And since the scale is logarithmic, when the pH is reduced by one unit, the actual acidity is multiplied by ten.

The measurement of pH may be done with a pH meter or indicator strips. The pH meter is a fairly costly instrument that needs to be regularly calibrated. (There are some inexpensive pH meters, but these may be of rather poor quality and durability.) A pH meter normally has a digital display, and you just put the probe into the solution to obtain the pH reading. For the majority of amateur cider makers, however, indicator strips are good enough (although not as precise as a good pH meter). They are easy to find at low cost and are sold in different ranges, the most useful in cider making covering from 2.8 to 4.6. You simply dip the end of the strip into the juice and compare the color to a chart giving the values of the pH. Most apple juices have a pH between 2.8 for the more acidic juices to about 4.5 for juices that contain very little acidity. For a more precise evaluation, be sure to compare the strip with the color chart in daylight.

The pH and the Cider

As mentioned earlier, the pH is related to the biochemistry of the fermentation. From 1960 to 1980, researchers, most notably at the Long Ashton Research Station in England, studied this relationship. For practical cider-making purposes, we can glean from this research the following important guidelines:

- When the pH is lower or equal to 3.0, the acidity is normally sufficient to protect the cider from spoilage due to unwanted microorganisms.
- If the pH is between 3.0 and 3.8, the acidity alone would not be enough for protection, and the addition of sulfite (SO_2) is recommended to complete the protection. The suggested dosage of SO_2 varies from 50 ppm when the pH is closer to 3.0 up to 180 ppm when the pH reaches 3.8.
- If the pH of the juice is higher than 3.8, it is advisable to lower the pH to 3.8 either by blending or adding some malic acid, and then adding the recommended SO_2 dosage for a pH of 3.8. See the article on sulfite, section 14.1.

The Relation between pH and Total Acidity

There has been considerable discussion in the cider-making community as to whether we could substitute one of the acid measurements for the other. In other words, can we use the result of a total acidity titration to assess the level of protection of a cider? Or can we use the pH measurements in blending different varieties when seeking a certain level of acidity in the juice or finished cider?

Before we go further, I need to explain a few basic things about acid solutions. What is called a *strong acid* is a substance that, when in solution in water, will release one H+ ion for each molecule of the acid. We then say it is fully dissociated. And if we know the dilution, we can compute the number of molecules and thus the mass of acid and the TA; we can also compute the number of H+ ions and the pH. So there will be a predictable and exact relationship between pH and TA for a particular strong acid, and this relationship will be such that when the TA is multiplied by 10, the pH will be reduced by one unit, as this is how the pH scale is defined.

Apple juice, however, is quite different: we are dealing with mostly malic acid, mixed with a few other acids present in lower concentrations. These acids are organic weak acids that can release either zero, one, or two H+ ions per molecule depending on the conditions, and thus they are only partly dissociated. The difficulty is that we can't predict the extent of dissociation, which depends on many factors (and I will skip these, as the discussion would become too complex). So even if we know how many molecules of acid we have, we don't know how many H+ ions they will have released. Hence, we can't compute the pH from the TA. Thus, the original question now recurs: Although we can't theoretically obtain a predictable and exact relationship between pH and TA for apple juice, could there be some sort of empirical relationship, meaning that the extent of dissociation of the acids would be fairly constant from one sample of juice to another?

As there was no definitive answer to this question, I started gathering some data points to either confirm or reject this possibility. Each data point had to give both measurements (i.e., TA and pH) from the same sample of juice. I found some from the following references:

- Four data points of commercial table apple varieties from the United States, unspecified origin and date in table 38, p. 338, of Smock and Neubert (1950).

- Nine data points from English cider apples in Beech, F.W. and Wood, D.E.S. (1979), (in the Proceedings of The Second Cider Workshop, 3rd October, 1979, Long Ashton Research Station, UK).

- Nine data points from table apples grown in British Columbia in 1934–1945 and eight data points from tests done in New England, from tables 6.3 and 6.5 in *Apple Juice*, by Moyer, J. C. and Aitken, H. C. (1980), (in Nelson, P. E. and Tressler, D. K. (editors), *Fruit and Vegetable Juice Processing Technology*, 3rd edition. Westport, CT: The AVI Publishing Co).

- Forty data points from "Cider Apple Data" on Andrew Lea's web site, *The Wittenham Hill Cider Pages*. The measurements would probably have been done around the end of the 1970s from cider apples and standard eating apples grown at the Geneva Agricultural Experiment Station in New York.

- Twenty-two data points from Spanish cider apples, given in Dapena and Blazquez Noguero (2009).

In addition to these ninety-two published data points, I was able to gather quite a number of points from cider makers in England and North America after making requests through the Cider Workshop and the Cider Digest Internet discussion forums. I added these to data points I had taken myself, giving me a total of 187 points, taken from different areas in North America and England from the 1930s to 2010, and from a diversified range of apple varieties and types.

I then plotted these data points on a semi-log graph (figure 9.2). I chose the semi-log because the pH is a logarithmic scale, and thus the resulting graph was linear. I was then able to draw a best-fit straight line through these points with the slope adjusted so the pH would decrease by one unit when the total acidity is multiplicd by 10, as per the theory of pH. This is the brown line on the graph. Its equation is:

$$pH = 4.3 - \ln(TA) / \ln(10)$$

which can also be written:

$$pH = 4.3 - 0.4343 \ln(TA)$$

Now, it can easily be seen that there is a lot of scatter of the data points around this mean line. To evaluate the amount of scatter, we compute the standard deviation of the data in relation to the mean line, which turns out to be 0.17 in pH units.

Then, if this data follows a normal distribution curve, we may be able to say that 95 percent of the data points should be within two times the standard deviation from the mean line. The shaded area on either side of the brown line represents the mean plus or minus two times the standard deviation. The equations deliminating this shaded area are:

$$pH_{min} = 3.96 - \ln(TA) / \ln(10) ;$$
$$pH_{max} = 4.64 - \ln(TA) / \ln(10)$$

and the area between pH_{min} and pH_{max} is called the 95 percent confidence interval. And in effect, we can see that there are only a few data points outside this interval. So what this tells us is, if this data sample is truly representative, when we

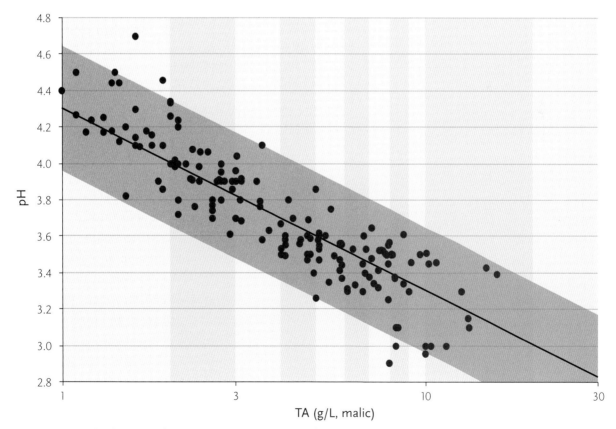

Figure 9.2. Graph of pH as a function of titratable acidity for 187 data points.

measure TA we could say that there is a probability of 95 percent that the pH would be between pH_{min} and pH_{max}, and there will be a difference of 0.68 in pH units between the two values. For example, with a TA of 7 g/L (or 0.7 percent) as malic acid, this will tell us that the pH should be between 3.11 and 3.79, with a probability of 95 percent.

Unfortunately, in practice this is not very useful, because it could not help us in the dosage of the SO_2 required to protect the cider. With our example and a pH of 3.11 (the minimum value), a very small dose of SO_2 is required, while at a pH of 3.79 a dose near the maximum is required. The standard deviation is too large, and in consequence the graph and equations cannot be used to dose the sulfite and skip the pH measurement.

Now, if we look at it the other way around, let's say we have a juice sample for which we have measured a pH of 3.6. Could this be any help in blending this cider? If we turn the equation around, or if we look at the graph, we find that for this pH of 3.6, the 95 percent confidence interval would go from a TA of 2.3 and up to 11 grams per liter. Again, this is way too wide to be of any practical use, as a TA of 2.3 g/L is very low acidity and 11 g/L is very high acidity. It cannot help us in figuring the best blend for this juice, and we would still have to measure the total acidity of this juice in order to be able to make a good blend with it.

This analysis confirms that both a pH and a TA measurement of acidity are necessary in cider making. These two measures each have their own use, and one cannot be substituted for the other. On a more positive note, this graph may be helpful to double-check the acidity measurements. If we take both measurements (pH and TA) and plot this point on the graph, then see that the point is quite far from the mean line, we might take the measurements a second time to be sure they are accurate.

CHAPTER 10

THE TANNINS, OR PHENOLIC SUBSTANCES

What we call *tannin* in the context of cider (and also of wine) is in fact a group of phenolic substances that have two important properties:

- **Astringency**, which provokes an effect of shrinkage of body tissues, followed by a dry sensation in the mouth. This results from the binding of the lubrication proteins of the saliva with the tannins, resulting in a decrease of the quantity of lubricant in the mouth and a rough sandpaper sensation. We also talk about puckering mouthfeel. This property (in a moderate amount) is a much-sought-after characteristic of some classic red wines such as Bordeaux or Chianti.
- **Bitterness**, one of the basic tastes our taste buds recognize. Highly bitter substances are generally considered of acrid and unpleasant taste. However, a slight bitterness may be rather pleasant and, in a drink, is thirst-quenching,

as in some quality beers that are well hopped and in tonic water (where bitterness is given by quinine).

In fact, the tannins really are compounds called procyanidins, which are responsible for the bitterness and astringency in fruit. These molecules may be of varying length, the shorter types being bitter, while the longer types are rather astringent. Depending on the apple variety, there may be more or less of the shorter or of the longer types, hence giving the corresponding character to the juice. This is covered with more details in the book *Fermented Beverage Production* by Lea and Piggot (2003).

In cider a moderate amount of tannins adds to the complexity and gustatory persistence. Tannins give body and consistency to cider, and when the pleasant sensation lasts for a sufficiently long time we may say of such a cider that it has a "long mouthfeel." Tannins also add to the color of the cider. In contrast, an insufficient level of tannins may render the cider insipid or uninteresting.

Most of the tannin in cider comes from the apples, and the concentration varies greatly with the variety. Table apples generally contain very little tannin. Cooking apples contain a bit more, and some crabs have an appreciable quantity. But it is among the special cider apples from some cider-making regions of England and France that we find most of the high-tannin varieties.

The use of wooden barrels for the fermentation and maturation of cider also adds to the tannin content, and Andrew Lea, on his web site (*The Wittenham Hill Cider Pages*; www.cider.org.uk), reports on experiments he has done that show that fertilization of apple trees may reduce the tannin concentration in the juice. Seasonal variations may be important, too, more so in fact than for the sugar or acidity content. Other processes controllable by the cider maker may act on the tannins as well. Most notably, maceration of the pulp between milling and pressing will induce some oxidation of the tannins, darkening the juice and the resulting cider. And in general the faster the extraction of the juice, the paler the juice and the cider will be.

Different cider-producing regions of the world have their own traditional cider-apple varieties, and the tannin content of the cider may vary considerably from one region to another, thus influencing greatly the type of cider produced. In the northwest of France (Normandy and Brittany) and the southwest of England (the West Country), the ciders traditionally contain a lot of tannins because of the special cider-apple varieties grown in these areas. In most other cider-producing regions, including the East of England, Spain,

Germany, Switzerland, and North America, high-tannin cider apples are not grown to a large extent, and hence the ciders produced are rather low in tannin.

However, the situation in North America in particular is changing. More and more high-tannin apple varieties are now being grown in commercial quantities: certain varieties (mainly English but also French as well as some genuine American ones like the Hewes or Virginia Crab) are garnering considerable interest among cider makers and orchardists, after having been almost forgotten for decades. Additionally some newly discovered varieties are exhibiting higher tannin levels and other good attributes. Many American cider makers now realize that the addition of these varieties in a blend improves the quality of the cider, especially its body or "structure." Steve Wood, whom we met earlier in this book, was one of the pioneers of this trend toward using European cider apples in North America.

Measurement and Expression of the Tannin Content

Even professional cider makers do not generally undertake to measure tannins, as this is better left to a well-equipped laboratory. There are two main tests to measure the tannin content in a juice or cider (note that the same tests are used for wine):

- The *Lowenthal method*, also called the *permanganate index* or *titration method,* was used at the Long Ashton Research Station. The result of this titration, total tannins, is usually expressed as tannic acid equivalent, either in percent, parts per million, or grams per liter.

- The *Folin-Ciocalteu index* is now the standard method in the wine industry. It is based on a colorimetric reaction and requires the use of special equipment to analyze the optical density of a sample. The result of this test is expressed as a concentration of gallic acid equivalent.

Complete descriptions of these methods appear in good reference works on wine analysis. On his web site Andrew Lea also gives a description of both methods; moreover, he has done some comparative tests between them, showing a very strong correlation between the results. This indicates that we may express the total tannin content either in tannic acid or gallic acid equivalent without appreciable difference. In the present book I use the tannic acid equivalent expressed in grams per liter because most of the data we have on cider apples comes either from the LARS analyses or from data presented by Boré and Fleckinger (1997) for French cider apples, and data in both are expressed in tannic acid equivalent.

In the absence of a test, a cider maker may have a fairly good idea of the tannin content by tasting the juice or cider, since the two main effects of tannins, bitterness and astringency, are very easily detectable by tasting. With a little bit of practice, you can evaluate if a sample has low, medium, or high tannin concentration. Besides, tasting allows a further discrimination between hard tannins, which are rather bitter, and soft tannins, which are more astringent.

For practical purposes in cider making, we will use the following values for tannin concentration in apples:

- Low tannin: less than 1.5 g/L of tannic acid equivalent. Sample is mild, with almost no noticeable bitterness or astringency.
- Medium tannin: between 1.5 and 2.5 g/L. Some mild bitterness or astringency is perceived, generally at a pleasant level.
- High tannin: over 2.5 g/L. Sample is very bitter and/or astringent, mouth-puckering, unpleasant. Apples with such a high tannin level would generally be considered "spitters."

The ideal concentration for a cider that would be rich in tannins, typical of the West Country in England or the north of France, would be around 2 to 2.5 g/L. Most of the ciders from other producing regions would be around 1 g/L or below.

CHAPTER 11

THE NITROGENOUS SUBSTANCES

It is a well-known fact that the speed of fermentation is, within some limits, directly proportional to the amount of nitrogenous matters in the medium and that in a juice deprived of nitrogenous matters, the fermentation stops.

G. Warcollier, *La Cidrerie*, 1928

Nitrogen (designated by the chemical symbol N) is an element that we often forget to consider when discussing cider making, although its importance has been recognized for many decades, as this excerpt from Warcollier shows. Andrew Lea even calls it "the forgotten element." Its importance is great, and the control of its concentration will considerably affect the quality of the cider.

First, nitrogenous compounds are essential to life and, in particular, to the growth of apple trees. Nitrogen is one of the important constituents of compost, manure, and other fertilizers used in agriculture. In a well-fertilized orchard, the apple trees are vigorous in part due to a plentiful supply of nitrogen, and the fruit production will be more abundant than in an unfertilized orchard. It is interesting to note that nitrogen is also the main constituent of air, but most plants can't absorb it easily in gaseous form, and it is essentially from the soil that apple trees extract the nitrogen required for their growth.

Second, a part of those nitrogenous matters that contributed to the growth and productivity of our apple tree will end up in the apples themselves. Some studies have in effect shown that the juice of apples from fertilized trees contains more nitrogen than juice from unfertilized trees, which is sort of obvious (Smock and Neubert, 1950; Lea, www.cider.org.uk). The inconvenience, however, is that these same nitrogenous substances are also very nutritive for the yeasts and thus will promote a rapid fermentation.

The main nitrogenous substances in apples are proteins, soluble nitrogen, amino acids, and a few others in lesser proportions (Smock and Neubert, 1950). Of these, proteins account for a sizable portion (in the order of 20 percent) of the total nitrogen, and these can't be used by the yeasts. What yeasts need to grow and multiply are amino acids, ammonium salts, and thiamin (vitamin B_1). If these compounds are abundant in the must, the fermentation will be rapid and complete. And if this kind of rapid fermentation is the goal, as it is, for example, in the industrial production of cider, these substances will be routinely added (such a mixture is often called *yeast nutrients*). On the other hand, if the must contains insufficient quantities of nitrogenous materials, the fermentation will be slow and may even stop before completion.

The cider maker who seeks quality prefers a slow fermentation. In effect, this permits the complex flavors and aromas to develop themselves and allows the acids and tannins to smoothen, all of which enhance the cider. To maximize the quality of the cider, then, it may be necessary to compromise the productivity of the orchard by adopting cultural practices that reduce the nitrogen content in apples, as we have seen in chapter 4.

The measurement of the amount of the nitrogenous matters in a must may be done by formol titration (also called formol index), a test originally developed by the Danish chemist S.P.L. Sørensen in 1907. Nowadays there are many variants of this test and many ways to express its result. It is notably used in the wine industry, and a complete description of the procedure may be found in any reference book on wine analysis. While formol titration is a relatively simple procedure for a well-equipped lab, it is quite challenging for a hobbyist to find the required

reagents and do it accurately. In the context of wine and cider making, the result of the formol titration would give the yeast-assimilable nitrogen (YAN) or the easily assimilable nitrogen (EAN) in milligrams of N per liter (mg/L), which are equivalent to ppm (1 ppm = 1 mg/L). Typical values for a cider must would be:

- 50 mg/L, for a must that is poor in nitrogen and thus would have a fermentation that is very slow and possibly incomplete
- 80 to 120 mg/L, the range of most cider-apple juices and about right for a good, slow to medium-speed, complete fermentation
- 120 to 150 mg/L, for a must rich to very rich in nitrogen
- 300 mg/L, a very high value seen in juice from fertilized young dwarf trees—not recommended for making a high-quality cider

As a side note, the YAN from wine-grape juices is naturally much higher than the values considered normal for apple juices.

Another way to measure the nitrogen is by the Kjeldahl method, which is considered the most accurate test but gives a result as total nitrogen, a value that includes some nitrogen that is not assimilable by the yeast. Alessandro Nogueira and his colleagues measured the total nitrogen measured with this method before and after fermentation of a typical French cider-apple must ("Slow Fermentation in French Cider Processing Due to Partial Biomass Reduction," *J.Inst.Brew.* 114, 2 [2008]: 102–110). They found 130 mg/L before fermentation and 25 mg/L in the fermented cider, and they concluded that this remaining 25 mg/L consisted of the nonassimilable nitrogen, essentially in protein form. Thus, this must contained a little more than 100 mg/L of YAN, and its fermentation lasted two months. And in this particular case, the non-assimilable nitrogen accounted for 20 percent of the total nitrogen initially present in the must.

Without such test results, most hobbyists can get an idea of the nitrogen content in the must by observing the following points:

- The nitrogen content will vary with the apple variety. Such information may be obtained by observing the speed of fermentation of single-variety musts. In particular, early-maturing varieties contain much more nitrogen, and their juices ferment very quickly. And in general we may observe that the latest-maturing varieties are the ones that ferment the slowest, thus indicating that these varieties contain less nitrogen. Also, according to Lea (2008), the cider-apple varieties said to be of vintage quality would contain less nitrogen than others.
- Apples from old trees of low vigor will be smaller and contain less nitrogen and amino acids than those from young and vigorous trees.
- The big, handsome apples from commercial orchards contain more nitrogen.
- I have also observed that apples that are dead ripe or slightly overripe at the moment of

pressing yield a juice that will ferment more slowly. This may be explained by the fact that as the maturation proceeds, the soluble nitrogen compounds (i.e., the YAN) are used to synthesize proteins that are not assimilable by yeasts (Smock and Neubert, 1950), without changing the total nitrogen content.

In summary, for the apples to have a low content in yeast-assimilable nitrogenous substances and thus promote a slow fermentation for a high-quality cider, choose apples of late-maturing varieties, from trees that are older and have little vigor, growing in an unfertilized orchard, and press them at the latest possible date, when they have started to become soft or are slightly overripe.

As a final word, a technique called *keeving,* routinely used in France for traditional cider, is being used more and more in the hobbyist cider-maker community. Keeving (or *défécation* in French) enables the cider maker to reduce the quantity of nitrogenous matters in the must before the start of the fermentation. After a successful keeve, it is also possible to control the speed of fermentation and to effectively stop it by lack of nutrients while there is still some residual sugar. We will discuss this procedure in detail in section 15.1.

CHAPTER 12

THE PECTIC SUBSTANCES

The mucilage. The pectic substances to which we give this name have a gummy aspect; their role has still not been well studied; we only know that they give smoothness to the liquid, that they seem very useful to the keeping quality, and that the musts that give superior ciders have a relatively high content of them.

G. POWER, *Traité de la culture du pommier et de la fabrication du cidre*, 1890

Apple juice contains a small quantity of pectin—or, more precisely, pectic substances— usually in the range of 0.1 to 1 percent, or 1 to 10 g/L. These carbohydrate derivatives (polysaccharides) influence certain aspects of cider making, as Power recognized already in 1890, although, as he says, at that time they had not yet been sufficiently studied. Now we know that

- they are in part responsible for fruit firmness and the facility with which the fruit yields up its juice;
- they are responsible for the formation of the *chapeau brun* (brown cap) in the keeving process (section 15.1);
- they can cause pectic gels and pectic hazes, which are defects of the cider and can be rather annoying (chapter 16).

The chemistry of pectins is a vast and complex subject, for which I don't have the qualifications to present a complete discussion. Because of their importance, however, I prepared the following short summary, which is mostly inspired from the book *The Pectic Substances* by Z. I. Kertesz (New York: Interscience Publishers, 1951).

Within the group of pectic substances are:

- *protopectin*, parent pectic substances that are water-insoluble. These protopectins most notably occur in cell walls of plants and give some firmness to fruits.

- *pectinic acids* and *pectic acids*, forms of polygalacturonic acids that are water-soluble. The difference between the two comes from the presence or absence of *methyl-ester* groups in the molecule. Pectic acids do not have such groups and are said to be demethylated or deesterified, while pectinic acids do contain a proportion of methyl-ester groups.

Pectins as used in the kitchen are esterified pectinic acids that have the property of forming gels with sugar and acid, as in fruit jellies, for example.

In general, pectic substances are degraded by pectolytic enzymes called *pectinase*. This name, in fact, is a general term for a group of specialized enzymes that work to break the pectic molecules. Among the most important of these enzymes are:

- *protopectinase*, which transforms protopectins into pectinic acids;
- *pectinesterase* (PE), also often called *pectin methyl-esterase* (PME), which strips the methyl-ester groups from the pectinic acids to transform them into demethylated pectic acids;
- *polygalacturonase* (PG), which depolymerizes the demethylated pectic acid and cuts it up into small soluble bits of simple galacturonic acid; and
- *pectin lyase* (PL), which works in a fairly similar fashion as PG.

All these enzymes work together to degrade the pectin and eliminate its sticky effect. They exist naturally in plant tissues and are also produced in large quantities for the food industry.

After harvest, during apple storage, the protopectins within cell walls are naturally broken down into soluble pectinic acids. During that process, the apples get softer. According to Smock and Neubert (1950), the concentration of soluble pectic substances may easily triple during that period. Later, as the apples become overripe and mealy, the soluble pectins are degraded into nonpectic substances.

As a practical effect, then, if the apples are pressed while very firm soon after harvest, they will have a maximum level of protopectins and a minimum level of soluble pectinic acids. Since the protopectins are water insoluble, they will precipitate with the lees without causing trouble. On the other hand, if the apples are pressed fully ripe or slightly overripe, the juice will have a maximal level of soluble pectin and thus may be more at risk of developing pectic haze or gel. Such fresh juices will also have more viscosity, making the pressing more difficult and the juice yield lower.

There is a simple test to assess the level of soluble pectin in a juice. These pectins precipitate in the presence of alcohol, and this explains why the pectic troubles usually happen when the cider is done. The test involves taking a sample of juice and mixing it with two or three times its volume of strong alcohol (a good and inexpensive alcohol for this test is 70 percent rubbing alcohol made of ethyl alcohol or denatured spirit or methylated spirit). The liquid should be well mixed and left for a few minutes. After that time, if the juice has a high level of soluble pectinic acids, these should precipitate and form a gel, which may be more or less solid if the concentration is not so high, only strands of pectin will be seen. This alcohol test is actually a cooker's test that is done to check if a juice contains enough pectin so it can make a jelly. Its results are not easily interpreted into useful information for cider making, unfortunately.

Certain laboratory methods permit a better estimation of the pectin content, but these are not easily done on a kitchen counter.

Pectic Enzyme Treatments

In cider making we generally prefer to completely degrade the pectic substances right at the start of the process so that they won't cause problems later on. For this, we use commercially available pectinase, sold in all wine-making supply stores. These are, in fact, mixtures of pectolytic enzymes, which usually include PME, PG, and PL, and sometimes others. Note that there exist different pectinase blends that are optimized for a certain usage. In particular, we may find in a wine-making supply store a general purpose fruit pectinase or a grape-optimized blend. Other blends, optimized for apples or pears, may be somewhat difficult to find but are more efficient for cider-making applications. There are three pectic enzyme treatments that may be done on the must before fermentation:

- **Simple pectinase addition.** This is the simplest treatment. It consists of adding pectinase to the must after pressing and before doing the yeast-culture inoculation. The enzyme does its work degrading the pectin during the fermentation. Pectinase addition is like taking out insurance against pectic troubles that could happen later. The procedure for doing this was given in chapter 1.
- **Debourbage**, or **depectinization.** This takes things one step further. It starts as a simple

pectinase addition, to which a fining agent such as Cold Mix Sparkolloid may be added to help the juice to clear. We then let the enzyme do its work before the start of the fermentation. After the pectinase is added to the must, it is left to stand for a few days: it should clear more or less quickly depending on the temperature, and a sediment will deposit on the bottom of the container. Most pectinases don't work well at low temperatures and need to be around 60°F (15°C) to be active. The risk to this method is having a natural fermentation start within this period, but if you have also sulfited the must, the chances for this are slim. The cleared must is racked into a new vessel, and the yeast culture may then be added. This pre-fermentation clarification is routinely done by many commercial cideries. It allows us to start the fermentation with a clean pectin-free must, which will facilitate the clearing of the cider once it is done.

- **Keeving.** This is another type of pre-fermentation clarification process. Done traditionally in France and to a lesser degree in England, it enables us to obtain a cider that retains some natural sweetness. In this case we don't use a pectinase, which is a mixture of different enzymes, but only one type, the PME, which in combination with calcium produces the *chapeau brun* (brown cap). The juice under this cap is very clear and purged from all the pectin and impurities. This clear juice is racked into another vessel, and the fermentation then proceeds. I discuss this procedure further in the article on sweetness in cider, section 15.1.

PART V

Fermentation and Beyond

In this last part of the book, we look at the cider-making procedures that occur between the pressing of the juice and the opening of the bottles of cider. Topics include blending, monitoring, and control of the fermentation for different styles of cider: sweet, sparkling, and ice cider. There is also a short review of the most common troubles or sicknesses of the cider. The discussions are more detailed than in chapter 1 in an attempt to bridge the gap between basic cider-making books and advanced oenology works.

For several reasons, most of the material presented in these chapters is based on personal experience. When I did presentations at the annual Cider Days festival, the audience was far more interested in hearing about my own cider making than what I had merely read about. I am also somewhat reluctant to discuss subjects I haven't experienced myself. Some readers may think this book is thus incomplete. True, one cannot possibly be good at and have tested everything! I hope, though, that the subjects covered here fulfill the needs of most readers.

CHAPTER 13

BLENDING

A well-done cider is a subtle blend of different varieties, adapted to their terroir, each bringing a touch of acidity or bitterness, its richness in sugar and its perfume.

FRANÇOIS MOINET,
Le Cidre—Produire et vendre, 2009

When planning the cider blend, you must consider the apples available to you. Sometimes the assortment will not allow for the preparation of a quality cider. Sometimes you may be limited to certain styles: for example, you can't make an English-style cider if you don't have English bittersweets.

In this article I examine techniques that permit us to predict some characteristics of a cider obtained from a blend of different varieties of apples. Note that there are different methods and times to blend:

- **Blending of juices before starting the fermentation.** This approach is most suitable when many varieties of apples are grown. One or more blends may be prepared from each pressing session with apples that ripen during the same season.
- **Blending "as it goes" (i.e., during the primary fermentation).** This would generally be practiced by a cider maker who makes just one batch of cider every year: he or she would have one large fermentation vessel, start the fermentation with the earlier pressings, and add more juice to the fermenting cider as more pressing sessions are completed, ending when the latest-maturing apples are finally pressed.
- **Blending of ciders after the fermentation is completed.** This case is better adapted when only a few apple varieties are grown and do not come to maturity at the same moment. Each variety may then be fermented individually and the blend done once all these batches are fully fermented.

It is also possible to prepare some blends before the fermentation and to make a second blending once the fermentation is completed. This is often done in commercial cideries. For hobbyists, the blending of juices before fermentation is the most recommended approach.

Caution: When you use low-acidity apples, in particular if you are considering fermenting them as a single-variety cider, remember not to ferment one batch that would have too high a pH because of the risks of spoilage. In all cases the pH needs to be 3.8 or lower, which should be attained by either blending with higher-acidity apples or adding acid.

Our Objective Is to Produce the Best Possible Cider

The most important objective when making cider is to obtain a product of great quality. This quality will be the best compensation for your efforts. And in this search for quality, the selection of apples and the way to assemble them certainly is a most crucial step.

So let's first see what factors go into making an ideal cider blend:

- **A high sugar content.** This, in my opinion, is the first quality to consider in a blend destined for cider making. I like to aim for a specific gravity (SG) of 1.060 or higher for the late-season cider blends and 1.055 for the first-season ciders. Naturally, this is not always possible, because some years the sugar content is not as high, and furthermore, in some terroirs such high sugar concentrations can't be obtained. In any case, it is always advantageous to maximize the sugar richness, even if it means discarding the apples of some varieties that are lacking in sugar.
- **A balanced acidity.** We should ideally maintain the total acidity (TA) of the blend between 5 and

7 g/L of malic acid, although acidities as low as 4 g/L and as high as 8 g/L may be acceptable for some special types of blends. The higher values will go with a refreshing cider, one that is sparkling and festive, or with a cider that will remain sweet. The lower values are adequate for a cider that contains more tannins, of the traditional English style, for example.

- **A tannin content corresponding to the desired style.** In general, North American ciders have a rather low tannin content, while most European ciders have a lot more. These tannins bring body to the cider, as well as some bitterness and astringency. This element probably is the most important in determining the style of cider.
- **A low content of nitrogenous matters.** Remember that these are nutrients for the yeast and low concentration allows a slow fermentation. Hence, we should reject apples that mature very early in the season and those that are grown using intensive orcharding practices.

The attentive reader will have recognized here most of the fundamental elements that have been discussed in chapter 4. For the sugar and acidity, these properties are easy to measure, and we can predict the values for the blend if we know them for the individual varieties. For the tannins, we need to taste the juice and, ideally, also the fruit before pressing; experience here is irreplaceable. And for the nitrogenous substances the only way to estimate them is by the knowledge of the cultural practices in the orchard.

I have already mentioned this point, but I will repeat it here: I insist on the sugar concentration of the apples. There are many reasons for this. First, yes, it is the sugar that gives the alcohol, and we always want enough alcohol to insure the cider will keep well. But also, the apples that are rich in sugar are those that ripen later and have more flavor. Most of the time a high sugar content goes hand in hand with a low nitrogen content, because the cultural practices that produce highly nitrogenous apples also produce diluted apples in terms of sugar.

Which brings us again to the notion of the quality of the apples for cider. We have discussed this issue in chapter 2, but it can't be overemphasized that the quality of the cider is first and foremost dependent on the quality of the apples used to make it. We have seen just above what would be an ideal blend in terms of content of the important constituents. Now let's look again at the ideal blend, but in terms of the apples needed to obtain the maximum quality:

- **Apples of late maturation.** These apples have the best flavor and the most sugar. Note that certain varieties of midseason apples are also of high quality for cider.
- **Apples that are fully ripe or even at the limit of being overripe.** This is when we get the maximum flavor, combined with a reduction of the nitrogenous matters. Well-ripened apples ferment more slowly but may be harder to press and yield a little less juice. We sometimes use the term "sweating" for apples that have been kept for maturation.
- **Apples from old standard and unfertilized trees.** This insures a low nitrogenous content and a slow fermentation.
- **Small and scabby apples.** Some scab may even increase the quality of the juice by concentrating the sugars and flavors, but it will reduce the yield. All other things being equal, smaller apples always have more flavor than larger ones.

Blending for Sugar and Acidity

Figure 13.1 on page 204 is a new version of the sugar-acidity graph I first presented in the article on cider-apple classification, section 5.1, with the grouping that was defined in that article (note that the "perfect apples" group has been removed for clarity). In addition, I have indicated on the graph the areas for different qualities of blends.

- The *ideal blend* should be our target. This blend would have an SG over 1.060 (and thus a potential alcohol of over 7.7 percent), and its acidity would be between 5 and 7 g/L of malic acid.
- The *good blend* is when the apples don't have quite enough sugar whatever we do. We can still make an excellent cider, but it will not have as much alcohol. I do, however, require an SG of 1.050 (potential alcohol 6.4 percent) or better for the blend to be considered a good one.
- On the left, we can see an area for low-acidity blends, which would be typical for a cider from the southwest of England, for example. For such a blend to make a good cider, however, the tannin needs to be high and compensate for the lack of acidity. Slightly lower SGs are also seen in such blends.
- On the right, we have an area for sharp blends, which have an acidity slightly higher than the ideal. This would be acceptable for a festive sparkling cider with little tannin or for a cider that retains some residual sweetness.

We also see on the graph a brown line that represents the possible blends from two juice

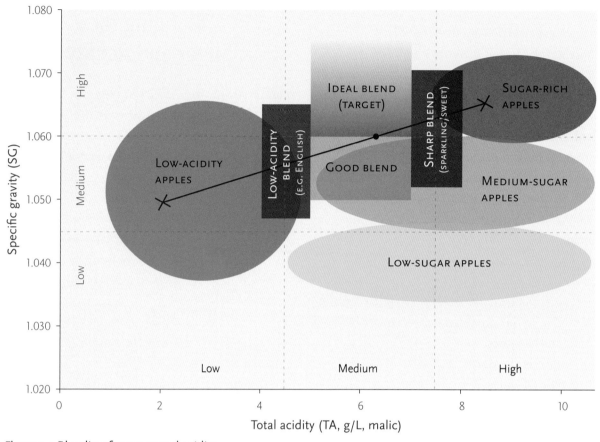

Figure 13.1. Blending for sugar and acidity.

samples: a low-acidity juice, SG 1.050, TA 2 g/L, and a sugar-rich juice, SG 1.065, TA 8.5 g/L. The line represents the location of the possible blends of these two juices. A half-and-half blend would be exactly at the midpoint of the line. But I would prefer a blend of two-thirds sugar-rich juice with one-third of the low-acidity juice, represented by the brown dot located at a third of the length of the line.

It can easily be seen from this graph how difficult it is to integrate some low-sugar apples into a blend while maintaining an overall good blend. Hence, apples in this group would not be used in a quality cider blend except in special circumstances, where such an apple has a

particular character that we want to integrate in the cider.

With such a graph, it becomes possible to plan a blend and determine the proportions of each apple type to obtain the ideal blend. Naturally, it is necessary to know the properties of each variety, and for this a sample of juice will have to be pressed in order to measure the SG and TA. Fortunately, we get to be able to anticipate those numbers from previous years' experiences. This graphical approach for planning a blend will, however, become overly confusing when there are many varieties to blend. In general, it is more practical to use a computer with the spreadsheet that will be presented a bit later.

Blending for Tannins

Blending for tannins is more difficult than for sugar and acidity because we don't have numbers indicating the tannin content of the juices we will blend. Most of us only have our taste buds to evaluate if a certain sample has high or low tannin and if this tannin is rather hard/bitter or soft/astringent—although the indications given in the directory of varieties in chapter 5 may help. Also, when tasting a variety to assess its tannin, it is not sufficient to taste only the apple. Some apples are true spitters, but their juice may be more palatable, and a better evaluation of the tannin may be obtained from tasting both the fruit and the juice. Further, the amount and type of tannin is the dominant factor in determining the style of cider. The only real guide that we have is to look at typical blends from different producing regions:

- Ciders from southwestern England and from Normandy and Brittany in northern France are usually blends containing 40 to 70 percent apples with high tannin content, that is, bittersweets and bittersharps in England, *douces amères* and *amères* in France. Ciders from Brittany usually have somewhat more tannin than those from Normandy and would be in the higher range.
- Ciders from Spain are typically blended with 20 percent of apples that are rich in tannins (*dulce amarga* and *amarga*).
- Ciders from North America and from the eastern regions of England are most often made without any tannin-rich apples, using essentially eaters and cookers.

The other difficulty is to balance the astringency and bitterness. Some cider makers prefer a cider that has relatively more bitterness than astringency, and others prefer it the other way around. Each cider maker has his or her favorite recipe, which will make their cider slightly different from those of their neighbors.

The good news, however, is that if the tannin blending doesn't turn out as expected, it won't make the cider unpalatable: at worst it won't be according to the expected style. The only thing that really counts is not to overdo it. Too much hard or bitter tannin may render the cider unpleasant: we want only a slight touch of bitterness to give an interesting character.

As a last point, if you blend a cider with a high tannin content, it is better to make it low in acidity. It seems that the tannins and the acids complement one another: if there is a lot of one, there should be relatively less of the other.

The Blending Wizard Spreadsheet

As I mentioned earlier, I tend to blend the juices before fermentation. Generally, I press the varieties individually and record the SG and TA from each. As each pressing session advanced, I often found myself wondering if the resulting blend would be well balanced, and if it wouldn't be preferable to add some low-acidity or maybe some high-sugar varieties to complete the blend. For this, we need to make what is called a weighted average. For example, if I have three juices in quantities Q_1, Q_2, and Q_3, and these juices are at SG_1, SG_2, and SG_3, respectively, then the weighted average for SG would be:

TABLE 13.1:

Blending Wizard

Variety	Quantity	Sugar	Acid	Percent of blend
Variety name 1	6	1.063	8.5	30%
Variety name 2	5	1.055	9.5	25%
Variety name 3	3	1.049	4	15%
Variety name 4	6	1.058	3	30%
				0%
				0%
				0%
				0%
Blend	20	1.057	6.43	

$$SG_{avg} = (Q_1\, SG_1 + Q_2\, SG_2 + Q_3\, SG_3) / (Q_1 + Q_2 + Q_3)$$

And the same calculation would be done for the TA. This is exactly what the spreadsheet I have developed does. This is an Excel spreadsheet that will also work with Open Office and Libre Office. You will find it with the companion materials of this book under the name BlendWiz.xls in Appendix 2.

Hence, if we know the SG and TA of the juices from the different varieties we intend to use for our blend, we may use the spreadsheet to predict the values we will obtain for the blend. And it will make the work easier to adjust the quantities of each juice to obtain the best possible blend. Table 13.1 is a facsimile of what it looks like:

We use the fields in light peach to enter the data:

- The variety name is optional, as it is only for reference.

- The quantity may be expressed in gallons, liters, or any unit as long as the same unit is used for all entries. Naturally, the result will be in the same unit.
- The sugar and acid are entered in their usual units. Note that you could use Brix or SG for sugar, but the program will not function with pH values for acidity because the pH is a logarithmic scale and can't be averaged, hence TA is used.

The fields in yellow—that is, the total quantity of must, its average SG, and its TA—are calculated by the program. Further, in the column on the right, the respective proportion of each variety in the blend is given.

In the example blend given above, we see that variety 1 is sugar-rich, 2 is medium-sugar, and 3 and 4 are low-acidity varieties. The blend would have an SG of 1.057, which is quite good and close to the ideal, and the TA would be 6.43 g/L of malic acid, an excellent value.

Some Blend Examples

I present here two examples of typical blends that I do for my ciders.

First-Season blend

This blend is made with apples that ripen by September 10 to 15th and are pressed on the last days of September or beginning of October. I have three varieties of low-acidity apples that ripen in that period (Douce de Charlevoix, Bulmer's Norman, and Muscadet de Dieppe), and together these will represent about 40 percent of the blend. These apples are also quite rich in tannin. The sugar is increased mainly with the Bilodeau (high sugar and medium tannin) and, depending on the availability, sometimes with other crabs like the Chestnut. I may use about 25 percent of these sugar-rich apples in the blend. And to complete the blend, I use some neutral apples of the season, which are generally in the medium-sugar group, like Lobo. The resulting blend is usually around SG 1.055 and TA 5 g/L of malic acid, which puts it on the left part of the good blend area. The tannin content is quite high, with over 50 percent of the blend coming from tannin-rich apples. The ciders are fermented to dryness and have a slight bitterness and an excellent mouthfeel given by the astringency.

Late-Season blend

This blend is made with my late-ripening varieties, which are harvested in October. The pressing may be done by mid-November. First, we have the russet group of apples, which have a very high sugar content with high acidity and low tannin. This group includes varieties such as Golden Russet, Reine des reinettes, Belle de Boskoop, and a few others and may account for about 30 percent of the blend. Second, we have the later-ripening, low-acidity apples, Yarlington Mill and Banane amère, which usually account for about 20 percent of the blend and bring most of the tannins. Yarlington Mill has soft and astringent tannin, while Banane amère's tannins are rather hard and bitter. For the rest, I use apples that have medium to high sugar, moderate acidity, and low tannin—mostly Cortland and other similar varieties like Fameuse or Liberty, plus Honeygold. The resulting blend normally has a high SG, up to 1.065 in a good year. The acidity is usually also quite high, some years close to 8 g/L of malic acid, which puts it in the sharp blend area. I usually make a keeve with this juice, which permits me to produce a medium cider (see the article on sweetness in ciders, section 15.1), and this sweetness will balance the high acidity of the blend. These ciders have a rather low but still present tannin content.

CHAPTER 14

THE FERMENTATION PROCESS

The fermentation, where the must transforms into cider, is really the essence of cider making. Whatever actions they may take during the fermentation process, cider makers can't improve upon the quality of the raw material (i.e., the must), but they can work to get the maximum from it. On the other hand, wrong actions taken during fermentation can ruin a must that would otherwise have had a great potential. We begin this chapter with a discussion of the sulfite, because this chemical compound has such an influence on the smooth progress of the fermentation. Then with the yeast addition, we really see the beginning of this fermentation, which we follow and try to control in order to obtain a cider of the highest possible quality. We close this chapter with a look at the alcohol: how much is produced and how we can estimate its strength.

◀ 14.1 ▶
The Sulfite

The chemical compound that we commonly call *sulfite* is in fact *sulfur dioxide*, and its chemical formula is SO_2. Sulfite is used extensively in the making of cider and wine because it has some very useful properties: Sulfite is an *antiseptic* that kills microorganisms when used in a sufficient dose and in an acid medium. Bacteria are the most sensitive to its action, followed by yeasts of the apiculate type, and finally yeasts of the genus *Saccharomyces*, which are more resistant. Sulfite is also an *antioxidant,* which binds chemically with oxygen and with other molecules produced by primary oxidation. Once bound with an SO_2 group, a molecule that could potentially cause some oxidation becomes deactivated and cannot interact anymore with the other cider constituents. This effectively protects the cider against oxidation and also against some disorders that need some oxygen to develop.

In practical terms for cider making, we use sulfite for the following reasons:

- **Sanitation of the material before use.** We use the antiseptic property of sulfite to kill germs and bacteria that are in the carboys before filling them or on the material that will be in contact with the cider, like a hydrometer. We simply need to rinse the material in question with a concentrated sulfite solution to which some acid is added. Although acceptable for an amateur cider maker, this use of sulfite will probably be banned within a couple of years for commercial cider making in Europe. In general, larger-scale cider makers would rather use an antiseptic solution sold for this purpose.
- **Sterilization of the must**, a day or two before inoculating some cultured yeast. And since microorganisms don't all have the same sensitivity toward sulfite, it is possible to adjust the dosage in such a way as to eliminate only the bacteria or, if the dose is strong enough, all the wild yeasts.
- **Protection of the cider once the fermentation is complete.** During active fermentation, the carbon dioxide gas that is produced, being heavier than air, acts like a blanket to prevent oxygen from coming into contact with the cider. However, when the fermentation is complete, air could then come into contact with the cider surface. The antioxidant property of sulfite will then give some protection.
- **Curative effect.** When the cider is attacked by some bacteria or fungus, we may sulfite it to kill and eliminate the organisms in question and to protect the cider against further attack.

How Sulfite Works

When we add a certain amount of SO_2 to the apple juice or cider, a good part of it combines more or less rapidly with certain constituents in the juice and with the products of the fermentation. This is referred to as the *bound* SO_2. The rest is said to be *free*, meaning that it remains active. It is through the action of combining, or binding itself, with different molecules that the free SO_2 protects the cider.

As the fermentation progresses, more and more of the SO_2 that was initially free becomes bound with some products of the fermentation, such that once the fermentation is complete, there may not be any free SO_2 left, or very little of it. Some cider makers will add a second dose of SO_2 as they rack at the end of fermentation or at bottling time to insure the protection of the cider during maturation. When such an additional dose is given, there is a larger proportion of the SO_2 that remains free, but still not all of it. The chemical equilibrium between free and bound SO_2 is dynamic and quite complex, in fact, and beyond the scope of this discussion. The following graph (figure 14.1) illustrates the evolution of the different forms of SO_2 during a fictive fermentation.

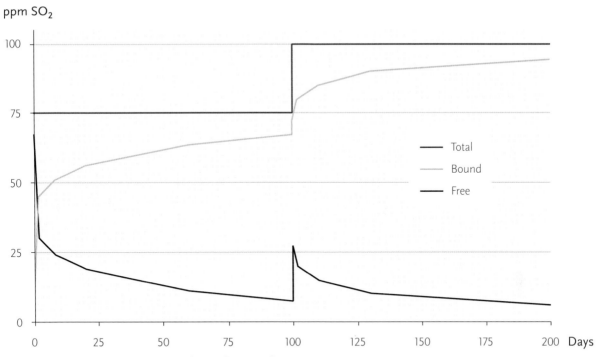

Figure 14.1. Graph of the evolution of SO_2 during a fermentation.

We assume here that at day zero, that is, just after pressing, we sulfited the juice at an initial dose of 75 ppm of SO_2. At this moment and for a short while, almost all the SO_2 is in the free state, but it will combine rapidly with the juice constituents. It is during this period that the sulfite has its maximum sterilization effect and can kill bacteria and yeasts present in the juice. After a day, half or more of the initial SO_2 is already in the bound state, and the free part is greatly reduced. The juice is thus much less toxic for the yeasts and can be inoculated with a selected strain of yeast; the fermentation may then proceed.

During the fermentation (from day 1 to day 100 on the graph) the free SO_2 decreases slowly as it binds itself with products of fermentation, and the bound part increases. Note that for simplicity, the total SO_2 value on the graph remains constant at 75 ppm, which is the sum of the free and bound parts, and equal to the quantity initially added. In reality, this is not exact, as some SO_2 may be produced or removed by the action of the yeasts during fermentation.

When the fermentation ends (day 100 on the graph), the cider is racked, and we assume an additional dose of 25 ppm SO_2 is added to give some protection during maturation. The total SO_2 then steps up to 100 ppm and remains there. At the moment of this second addition, again most of it is in the free state for a short while, which is most useful, as during racking the cider may come into contact with air. Then, during maturation, the SO_2 combines itself slowly with the cider constituents, until there will be practically no more free SO_2 left at the moment the cider is drunk.

This model is extremely simplified and doesn't take into account many factors, in particular the fact that the total quantity of SO_2 varies, even if the cider maker doesn't add any sulfite. Different biochemical reactions that occur during fermentation will interact with SO_2 and this may increase or decrease the quantity of SO_2. Some yeasts under certain conditions may produce up to 30 ppm of SO_2. For these reasons, the graph cannot be used to evaluate the quantity of free SO_2 you have in your cider. The only way to know the true concentration of free SO_2 is by chemical analysis as described below.

A last word on the dynamic equilibrium between the different forms of SO_2: in the bound state, part of the sulfite is permanently bound, but another part is bound in a reversible way, meaning that some of the bound SO_2 may become free again when the concentration of free SO_2 decreases. Also, in the free state there are two forms, and the important one is said to be *molecular* or *soluble,* as it is really this form that is active. The fraction of the free SO_2 that is in the molecular form is dynamic and variable, most notably in relation to the pH, the temperature, and the alcohol concentration of the cider. The effect of pH is very important: the fraction of the active molecular form may be ten times higher at pH 3 than at pH 4, and this means that the lower the pH (i.e., the more acidic the cider), the more efficient the SO_2. This explains why the dosage of SO_2 in the must is done in relation to the pH. The concentration of the molecular form of SO_2 required to obtain an antiseptic action is around 0.5 to 1 ppm, depending on whether we want a selective effect on only some sensible organisms or a total effect.

The Dosage of Sulfite

We usually specify the dosage of sulfite in parts per million (ppm) of SO_2 (see Appendix 1). Usual doses are generally between 20 and 200 ppm. In many countries the law forbids adding more than 200 ppm of SO_2 to the cider.

As mentioned earlier, the recommended dosages of SO_2 are given as a function of the pH, because when the pH is high, the free SO_2 is less efficient, and we need to add a lot more sulfite to obtain the same effect. Figure 14.2 gives the recommended initial dose to add to freshly pressed juice, before the start of fermentation. This comes from research work done in England during the years 1960 and 1970 (from Lea, 2008). See also section 9.3 on acidity and pH.

The sulfite dose obtained from this graph is calculated to provide 1 ppm of molecular SO_2 in an average apple juice and should normally be sufficient to give complete control of wild yeasts. Then, one or two days after introduction of this sulfite, it will be possible to inoculate a cultured yeast. When the juice pH is 3 or lower, the acidity is considered high enough to protect the cider, and thus sulfite addition is not required. When the juice pH is higher than 3.8, it is recommended to blend in more acidic apple varieties or add some acid to increase the acidity and lower the pH to 3.8 or less. This is because the amount of sulfite that would be required to efficiently protect such a low-acid cider would be more than the maximum legal dose of 200 ppm.

In practice, most small-scale cider makers use indicator strips to measure the value of the pH. These strips don't have great precision; an uncertainty on the order of pH 0.2 to 0.3 would be normal. Considering this, a three-level recommendation would often be more appropriate:

pH between 3.0 and 3.3: addition of 50 ppm of SO_2
pH between 3.3 and 3.6: addition of 100 ppm of SO_2
pH between 3.6 and 3.8: addition of 150 ppm of SO_2

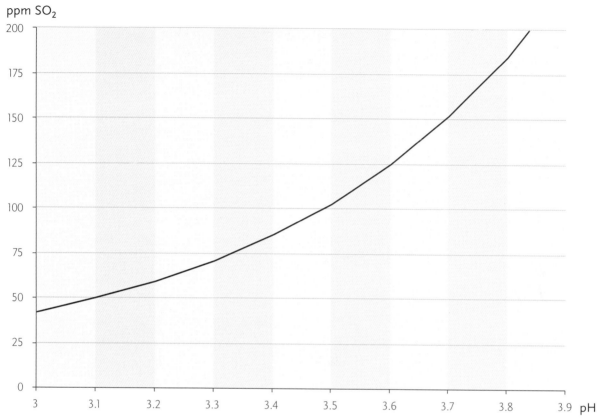

Figure 14.2. Recommended dosage of sulfite as a function of must pH.

For a natural yeast fermentation, the above-mentioned dosages will be too high, as this would kill off the wild yeasts that are naturally present in the must, and thus the fermentation would not start. It is then recommended to use only half the normal dosage, which would be sufficient to kill the bad bacteria while letting apiculate and wild *Saccharomyces* yeasts survive. These will still be able to multiply and start the fermentation (see section 14.2 on yeasts). In a similar way, if a malolactic fermentation is desired, the initial sulfite dose has to be reduced because the SO_2 would kill the lactic bacteria that make this fermentation possible (see section 14.4 on malolactic fermentation). On the other hand, if the apple lot used to make the juice contains a lot of rotten fruit, the sulfite dose would then need to be increased, because such apples contain more compounds that will combine with the SO_2, with the result that the concentration of free SO_2 will be lower than expected. For making a perry, it is recommended to increase the dosage by 50 ppm over the standard guidelines given above, because pear juice contains more sulfite binders than apple juice, thus a smaller fraction of the total SO_2 will remain in the free state.

When sulfite is added at the end of the fermentation, the objective is to insure a sufficient level of free SO_2 to protect the cider during maturation. The dose doesn't need to be strong enough to kill microorganisms, as it does for the first addition. The difficulty is in adding the right amount, which involves making an analysis of the free SO_2

remaining in the cider and then calculating the required amount to bring the quantity of free SO_2 to the desired level, which will vary depending on the pH and the cider maker. In general this ideal level will be somewhere between 10 and 50 ppm. This procedure is usually done only in a larger-scale operation, however. Small-scale and amateur cider makers most often use a dose defined as a fraction of the initial SO_2 addition, such as a third or a half, for example. Experience is required here, as there can't be a general recommendation. If you can taste the sulfite when drinking the finished cider, this means you have added too much, and next time you need to add less.

The Preparation of Sulfite

In the old days, sulfur wicks were burned inside the barrels before use. The fumes impregnated the wood and this provided the SO_2 to the cider. This technique is still used by some cider makers who ferment their cider in wooden barrels, but it is pretty hard to obtain a precise dosage this way.

Caution: When manipulating sulfite powder or a sulfite solution, always avoid inhaling the fumes, as they are very irritating.

For the small-scale cider maker, the main sources of sulfite will be potassium metabisulfite, sodium metabisulfite, and Campden tablets. These products are easily found in any wine-making supply shop. The professional may use other forms better adapted to large volumes of production.

- **Potassium metabisulfite** is a white salt that theoretically contains 57 precent of its mass in SO_2. In practice, we generally consider this half of its mass, and thus 100 grams will give 50 g of SO_2.

- **Sodium metabisulfite**, also a white salt, theoretically contains 64 percent of its mass in SO_2, but, as for the previous compound, we count a little less in practice: about 55 to 60 percent. It also contains about 25 percent sodium. Although the quantity of sodium is very small, some cider makers object to using it to sulfite the must, preferring potassium metabisulfite. As a sterilization solution, both forms are equivalent.

- **Campden tablets** are in fact made of potassium metabisulfite and calibrated to give 50 ppm of SO_2 in 1 imperial gallon (1.2 US gal, or 4.5 L) of juice or cider. Hence, four tablets are required to dose 50 ppm in a 5-gallon batch. Personally, I don't like these tablets very much because they first need to be reduced to a powder with a mortar, and they are difficult to dissolve.

STOCK SOLUTION

One of the most practical ways to use sulfite is in the form of a 5 percent SO_2 stock solution. To prepare it one needs to dissolve 10 grams of potassium metabisulfite (approximately 2 teaspoons) for 100 mL of solution. One mL of this stock solution will yield 50 ppm of SO_2 to 1 liter of juice or cider. A word of caution: this solution and its fumes are corrosive and require appropriate containers. Glass and plastic are OK, but thin metal closures will not last, as these will get attacked and pierced by the corrosion.

Another way is to use the metabisulfite powder and dissolve just the required quantity in a bit of water or juice when needed. For example, if we want to add 50 ppm of SO_2 in a 5-gallon carboy, we will need 50 mg/L × 19L × 2/1000, which makes

1.9 grams of potassium metabisulfite (slightly less than ½ teaspoon) to add in the carboy.

ANTISEPTIC SOLUTION

To prepare a sterilization solution for the cider-making equipment, we can make an SO_2 solution of 0.5 percent in water (this is equivalent to 5,000 ppm), to which we can add a quantity of malic or citric or tartaric acid (we have seen that SO_2 is more efficient in an acidic solution). The concentration doesn't need to be exact: some use a 0.2 percent solution, while others prefer to use a 1 percent solution. So, to prepare 1 liter of this antiseptic solution, we need about 10 grams (2 teaspoons) of potassium or sodium metabisulfite and 5 to 10 grams (1 to 2 teaspoons) of acid that we dilute in 1 liter of water. This solution may be reused quite a few times and can be kept for a month, but with time it will lose some of its strength. There are many uses for this solution: it is ideal for sanitizing the pressing equipment just before pressing and to rinse out a carboy before filling it. I also pour some in the racking tube before racking. For those who prefer not to add sulfite to the cider (see the discussion that follows), the material may be subsequently rinsed with water. As for the stock solution, this cleaning solution will have to be kept in a container that cannot rust.

The Advantages and Inconveniences of Adding Sulfite to the Must

Sulfite has been used in wine and cider making for centuries, and it has been a very important factor to obtain a good-quality product. However, its use does have some inconveniences:

- Sulfite is a toxic and corrosive product. It is important for the cider maker to avoid inhaling its fumes and to manipulate it with caution. It may even provoke asthma attack.
- Some people are very sensitive to sulfite and may detect it in the finished cider even if the dose is not excessive. When a cider that still contains free SO_2 is drunk, it is then relatively easy to detect, having something of the taste of sulfur or burnt matches, and in my opinion this is a defect.
- Many people believe that sulfite in wines and ciders is a cause of headaches and hangovers after an evening when a bit too much has been drunk. As far as I know, this has never been scientifically proven, but I think it is plausible, in particular if the sulfite was overdosed.
- Sulfite may prevent the malolactic fermentation, which is desirable for some cider styles.

For all these reasons, many cider makers prefer not to add sulfite to the must and to the cider. However, when making this decision, it is important to weigh all the factors and to accept a higher risk of getting a spoiled cider batch. Among the factors that plead in favor of not adding sulfite, there are:

- The fact that many yeasts naturally produce SO_2 during fermentation, some strains more than others. For example in the documentation for Lalvin's EC-1118 yeast, it is said that this strain may produce up to 30 ppm of SO_2 when the cider is low in nutrients. Thus, if the juice was fairly acid, as is often the case with North

American apples, this may be sufficient to fully protect the cider.

- Modern equipment, in particular glass carboys and stainless steel vats, are much easier to clean and sterilize than were the wooden barrels used in the old days. Further, if careful precautions are taken to prevent air from coming into contact with the cider and if the cider room is kept perfectly clean, the risk of proliferation of a bad microorganism is greatly reduced.

- Many modern selected yeast strains have a dominating effect and will not let another type of population develop in the same medium. After inoculation of a strong yeast population, then, and as long as this population is active, there is little to fear from contamination by another microorganism.

- Almost all commercial wines and ciders contain added sulfites. However, if we are making our own cider for our own consumption, it is justified to desire a product that would be the most natural possible and thus that would not contain any chemical additive.

- For a commercial cider maker, the fact of not adding sulfite may become a sales argument and give some added value to the product for a certain market niche. On the other hand, the economic loss from a spoiled batch of cider could be very important.

For those cider makers who choose not to add any sulfite to the must, it is then very important to control the quality of the apples used, to wash them, and to eliminate all rotten apples before pressing. It is also preferable to pick the apples from the tree rather than off the ground. I would recommend rapidly inoculating a strong population of a dominant strain of yeast and then monitoring the cider regularly so that intervention could be rapid if a problem occurs. The most critical period for an unsulfited cider is when all sugars have been fermented: at this point there is no more carbon dioxide gas produced that would protect the cider from air, and the yeast population decreases and cannot remain dominant. Protection from air contact is then the key to avoiding contamination. See the article on cider troubles in chapter 16 for some tricks to doing this.

Some types of ciders will be more at risk in the absence of sulfite. For example, traditional craft cider in England is usually made with apples that have little acidity (i.e., high pH) and that have been picked from the ground. These ciders are often fermented with natural yeasts. Such ciders would be much more at risk than a North American cider made with high-acidity apples that have been picked from the tree, and inoculated with a cultured champagne yeast. Hence, a careful cider maker might choose to add sulfite only to those batches he considers to be more at risk.

For my part, I use the sulfite-based sterilization solution to clean my materials and equipment before use, as described earlier. I only occasionally add sulfite to the must—for example, when I judge a certain batch is more at risk because the pH is too high or because the sanitary condition of the apples leaves something to be desired (after a wet and scabby year, with apples that are very ripe, for instance, there is often some fungus on the scab lesions). Most of my ciders are thus unsulfited, but I do about fifteen batches of 5-gallon carboys every year, so if I lose one it wouldn't be catastrophic. Still, the only problems I've had were a few occurrences of film yeast, which were easily cured.

Other Products That May Play a Role Similar to Sulfite

A few additives have an action similar or complementary to that of sulfite. These generally permit us to reduce the use of sulfite.

- *Potassium sorbate* has some antifungal properties and in particular some inhibiting effect on yeasts and other microorganisms, such as those responsible for film yeast. It isn't used by itself but in combination with sulfite, thus permitting the cider maker to reduce the sulfite dose. In particular, sorbate is often used with ciders that contain some residual sugar, since it helps prevent a restart of the fermentation. Sorbate will not stop an active fermentation. But if the yeast population has been greatly reduced by some other means (a cold shock, for example), it will help prevent the population from rebuilding itself. The maximum permitted dosage of sorbate is 200 ppm of sorbic acid, which corresponds to 275 ppm of potassium sorbate. When sorbate is used, malolactic fermentation has to be avoided, because the combination of sorbate and lactic acid produces some molecules that smell somewhat like geranium and would thus spoil the cider. This means that some free SO_2 is required to prevent malolactic fermentation (between 10 and 50 ppm, depending on the pH).
- *Ascorbic acid* (vitamin C) is an antioxidant that may help to protect a cider as it "captures" the oxygen that could come into contact with the cider. It is most often used at bottling time in association with sulfite, dosage of which can then be reduced. The maximum dose of ascorbic acid allowed is 150 ppm, but it is not

recommended that you exceed 80 ppm, as ascorbic acid can be detected by taste when the dose is higher.

Testing of SO_2

Testing of SO_2 may be important for two reasons:

- The amount of free SO_2 should be measured before adding more SO_2 during the maturation of the cider or before bottling, in order to add the right amount for the desired protection.
- The amount of total SO_2 may be checked in a commercial cider to make sure the value doesn't exceed the maximum legal dosage, which is 200 ppm in many countries. This is required only if the cider maker has added an amount close to this limit, as some may be naturally produced by the fermentation, but this natural SO_2 would not normally exceed 30 ppm.

Different methods exist to test the concentration of free and total SO_2 in a cider. The most accurate method, and the one that would be used in specialized laboratories, is the Ripper titration with iodine. This method is well documented in most oenology books but requires some chemicals that are not easily obtainable by a hobbyist as well as sulfuric acid, which is potentially dangerous. Kits for the Ripper titration are sold by specialized merchants, but most cider makers use either titrets or small electronic analyzers, which are much easier to use.

Titrets are ampules containing chemicals into which you add a measured quantity of the cider to be tested. Titrets test only for free SO_2, its concentration being indicated by a color change. The accuracy is approximately ±10 ppm of SO₂ over a range of 10 to 100 ppm. The cost of these titrets is quite reasonable, at approximately $2 per test.

Electronic analyzers are available at different prices, the more expensive the more accurate. For example, the Hanna titrator, which uses the Ripper titration method, costs approximately $700, plus $2 per test for the reagents, and it permits free and total SO₂ analysis with an accuracy within 5 percent of the reading. Another popular and less expensive analyzer is the Vinmetrica, which also permits free and total SO₂ analysis.

◄ 14.2 ►
The Yeast and Yeast Nutrients

Yeast is an essential element for the making of cider. It consists of unicellular fungus microorganisms that actually transform sugar into alcohol. They are visible in the cider under a microscope with a ×400 magnification. Their spores are present in the air, and in the flesh and skin of the apples. In any old cider house, all the pressing equipment, the walls, and the floor are highly contaminated with spores of the local yeast flora, thus insuring that the fermentation will start by itself. The yeasts had been doing their work without anyone noticing them until Louis Pasteur demonstrated their essential role in the fermentation process, publishing many important papers on the subject between 1857 and 1870.

Following the work of Pasteur, Georges Jacquemin published his first works on selected pure yeasts for alcoholic fermentation by the end of the 1880s. Jacquemin succeeded in selecting some pure yeast strains of premium quality that could be subsequently inoculated into a must, thereby permitting added control over the final product. In *La Cidrerie moderne ou l'art de faire le bon cidre*

(1902), he even recommends sterilizing the must by adding sulfite prior to the inoculation of the selected yeast strain, just like current recommendations. At the time, however, most cider makers ignored his recommendations and kept on making cider with the wild yeast strains that were present in their terroir. It took another fifty years before cultured yeast strains became widely available and used by cider, beer, and wine makers.

Nowadays there are four main yeasting options for the cider maker: a wild yeast ferment, like in the old days; a fully controlled ferment, involving sulfite for sterilization of the must followed by a pure yeast inoculation; and two intermediate options, one a pure yeast inoculation on an unsterilized must, and the other a partial sterilization of the must followed by a wild yeast ferment. I review these in the following discussion.

Wild Yeast Fermentation

In nature there are many yeast species and many different strains within each species. And each of these has distinct characteristics, most notably concerning the conditions for their survival and proliferation: temperature, tolerance to alcohol, tolerance to SO_2, and also the flavor profile they impart to the cider.

A detailed description of yeast strains and species would be beyond the scope of the present book and may be found in a good oenology reference. For the purposes of this discussion, I classify the different yeast types in a very crude way:

- **The *Saccharomyces* group**. This family of yeasts is the most important for the complete transformation of sugar into alcohol. Thus, they are considered strong fermenters. In cider it is *S. cerevisiae* that is the most common. These yeasts generally have a high tolerance to SO_2, meaning that a normal sulfite dose will not kill them. They are also tolerant to alcohol, some strains being able to ferment up to 17% ABV (whereas a wild strain would likely not tolerate such a high alcohol strength). They are also efficient fermenters, producing more alcohol per given quantity of sugar than other yeasts. These yeasts are not present in great numbers in the apple itself but colonize the juice from spores that are in the press cloths, the air—in fact, everywhere in the cider house.
- **The non-*Saccharomyces*, or starting, yeasts**. These are often referred to as the *apiculate* yeasts, and the most important species of this group is *Kloeckera apiculata*. We call them "starting yeasts" because they are abundant on the apple skin and in the flesh, so they can start their fermentation work very quickly after pressing is done. However, their alcohol tolerance is low, and they will die when the alcohol strength reaches 2 to 4 percent. They

are also sensitive to SO_2, and a normal sulfite dose will eliminate them. For the fermentation, they are not as efficient as *S. cerevisiae*, producing about 20 percent less alcohol from the same quantity of sugar, so overall their contribution to the total alcohol of the cider is relatively small. However, many authors and also many cider makers consider their contribution to the flavor and bouquet of the cider very important, because the action of these yeasts adds some complexity and richness to our favorite drink.
- **The spoilage yeasts**. These are the unwanted yeasts. In this group are the yeasts responsible for the film yeast sickness (*Pichia* and *Candida* species), and the *Brettanomyces*, which give some off-flavors. In general these spoilage yeasts need oxygen to colonize a cider, thus the recommendation to keep air out of the fermentation vessel is intended to keep these unwanted yeasts under control.

Typically, a wild yeast fermentation will start within a few days if the temperature is over 50°F (10°C) because of the action of the non-*Saccharomyces* starting yeasts. During that time, the wild *Saccharomyces* yeasts are starting to grow a population that will soon take control of the fermentation. Even if their lifespan is short, though, the apiculate yeasts will also have given some of their flavor profile to the cider.

Another important point is that the wild strains of *S. cerevisiae* will generally not be as strong fermenters as the cultured strains, so fermentation by wild yeasts alone will be slower and may not go all the way to full dryness. This might be of interest to cider makers who want a cider with some residual sugar.

WILD YEAST FERMENTATION IN A PARTIALLY STERILIZED MUST

An alternative to the fully wild fermentation is a fermentation in a partially sterilized must. This approach is very popular among the community of craft cider makers. It involves adding half of the normal dose of sulfite to the must (see the preceding section on sulfites to evaluate the sulfite dosage). This would eliminate the spoilage yeasts and bacteria, as well as most of the apiculate yeasts, but would leave the wild *Saccharomyces* yeasts unharmed. The benefit would be to profit from an added complexity by allowing wild strains to do the fermentation while at the same time reducing the risks of spoilage. The *lag phase,* during which the yeast population grows and establishes itself, is, however, much longer with this approach, and often an inexperienced cider maker will get nervous and pitch a cultured yeast when the wild yeasts appear to be taking too much time to give obvious signs that the fermentation has started.

Cultured Yeast Fermentation

Numerous strains of yeast have been isolated and are available as pure cultured yeast. The main advantages of using such yeasts are the reliability and predictability of the final product, as well as the reduced risk of a stuck fermentation, as cultured yeasts are usually strong fermenters. Another important point is that their features are documented, and a fairly complete data sheet should be available for all the strains sold by major companies. These data sheets will normally give information on such characteristics as:

- Species and subspecies. Most often this is *Saccharomyces cerevisiae cerevisiae,* though for champagne yeasts the subspecies would be *S. cerevisiae bayanus.* The latter is considered a *finishing* yeast, and it is more tolerant of high alcoholic strengths.
- Production of SO_2. Some yeast strains are known to produce a relatively large quantity of SO_2, up to 30 ppm for the Lalvin EC-1118, for example.
- Competition (or killing) factor. This indicates that the particular strain produces a toxin that impedes other species and strains of yeasts from colonizing the medium and competing with the main yeast. Yeasts can be positive (contain the toxin), sensitive (no toxin and are killed by the toxin), or neutral (no toxin but are not killed by the toxin). Note that this toxin only affects other yeasts and will not act against bacteria.
- Temperature range at which the yeast will thrive.
- Fermentation speed.
- Alcohol tolerance.
- Production of hydrogen sulfide (H_2S), an unwanted compound that smells like rotten eggs. Some yeasts are known to produce higher levels of H_2S or to do so more commonly.
- Interaction with malic acid. Some yeasts (e.g., Lalvin 71B) are known to metabolize up to 20 percent of the malic acid present in the must, thus softening the cider.
- Flocculation. This indicates that the yeast will deposit as large flocs and yield compact lees on the bottom of the container. This property is sought mainly for champagne yeasts used for in-bottle fermentation.

The standard method of cultured yeast fermentation is to do a sterilization of the must by a full sulfite dose (see the preceding section on sulfites), followed, a day or two later, by the inoculation of a strong population of the selected yeast strain. This procedure thus eliminates the spoilage yeasts and the non-*Saccharomyces* as well as most wild *Saccharomyces* yeasts, so that the strain used for inoculation will clearly dominate the fermentation and leave its characteristic flavor profile. The main criticism concerning this approach is that the flavor profile is considered unidimensional and lacking in complexity, and in particular lacking in the flavor compounds produced by the apiculate yeasts. Many commercial cideries will, however, use this approach because of its reliability and consistency, as well as the decreased risk of spoilage. This approach would also be the most recommended one for a novice cider maker, as it will insure consistent results from the fermentation while the cider maker gains experience in the other aspects of cider making.

Cultured yeast fermentation in an unsterilized must

Many cider makers are reluctant to use sulfites for must sterilization for the reasons explained in the preceding section on sulfites. Another reason not to sterilize the must is to profit from the wild yeasts. For example, some cider makers wait until the non-*Saccharomyces* yeasts start a wild ferment and only after that inoculate a strong culture of pure selected yeast. This way the cider gets some of the flavor profile from the apiculate yeasts, and once inoculated the cultured yeast would dominate the fermentation against weaker, wild *Saccharomyces* strains and insure a good, strong ferment to dryness. This approach will not protect against spoilage yeasts and bacteria, but it is still possible to sulfite the cider once the fermentation is completed, and this will protect it during the more critical period of maturation.

Selection of a yeast strain

Most of the cultured yeast strains have been isolated from wine-producing regions and thus are wine yeasts. There are additionally a few cider yeasts that have been isolated. (Beer yeasts are also available but are generally not recommended for cider.) Pure selected yeasts are available either in dried or liquid form. Dried is more common and less expensive (at least for the most popular strains), but it requires the yeast to be rehydrated before inoculation to the must. Personally, I tend to use the Lalvin dried yeasts, largely because they are readily available from a store just five minutes from my home. Here are characteristics of the yeast strains I most often use:

- Champagne yeast (Lalvin EC-1118, Red Star "Pasteur Champagne," Red Star "Prise de Mousse/Première Cuvée"). These three yeasts are quite similar and considered all-purpose yeasts. They are strong fermenters that will ferment to dryness unless the must is very poor in nutrients. They are also used to restart a stalled (or stuck) fermentation. Champagne yeast tolerates cold temperatures, and it gives a very clean, neutral, slightly sharp flavor to the cider. It is my classic and most often used strain.
- Lalvin 71B-1122. This yeast strain is generally recommended for making primeur wines or *vin nouveau,* that is, a very young wine. It gives a fruity character and is also used for making semisweet wines. One of its useful documented features is that it metabolizes some malic acid, thus reducing the total acidity by 15 to 25 percent. I use it mainly when a blend has more acidity than I would like.

I once tested the Wyeast 4783 "Rudesheimer," a strain used for Riesling wines. There are quite a few other strains from the Wyeast catalogue that I intend to try in the future—in particular the 4766 Cider. Other Lalvin yeast strains commonly used and recommended for cider making are the ICV D-47 and the DV-10. Another company that produces a good selection of yeasts is White Labs. I have not yet tried their products, but their WPL 775 English Cider yeast would surely be worth a trial. An Australian wine yeast strain, AWRI 350, was extensively used and well appreciated by the now defunct Long Ashton Research Station in England and is still used by cider makers in England and Australia. In addition, there are many other yeast manufacturers and distributors that have valuable products. In the old days we would stick with what was available in the closest store, but nowadays, with Internet orders, it has become much easier to get any yeast from anywhere, and this creates a large playground for a cider maker who enjoys experimentation.

PREPARATION
OF A YEAST CULTURE

Dried yeast needs to be rehydrated before inoculation to the must. Instructions for this are given on the package, but personally I prefer to make a small starter culture, as I think it introduces a stronger population to the must and insures a more vigorous start to the fermentation: I use 2 to 3 cups of juice in a beaker that I heat slowly in a water bath up to the rehydration temperature; then I stop the heating and introduce the contents of the yeast package. I do not stir and simply put a plate on top of the beaker for protection. The juice will stay warm for a while and slowly cool down to

Figure 14.3. Yeast culture.

room temperature. After twelve to twenty-four hours, a vigorous culture develops (see figure 14.3) that can be introduced into the must. If the must is very cold, the culture may be brought to the same cold temperature gradually before inoculation to the fermentation vessel: this reduces the thermal shock for the yeasts. If you have chosen to add sulfite to the must, you may start such a yeast culture at the same time you add the sulfite, but make sure you have removed the juice required for the culture before sulfiting. The next day your culture will be ready when the sulfite has become less toxic for the yeasts.

COMPARATIVE YEAST TESTS

As we've seen, there is no perfect yeasting method that will provide the optimal flavor profile while at the same time insuring protection against spoilage organisms. Each approach has some advantages and also some drawbacks. It comes down to each cider maker to make his or her own choices according to personal taste and to judge the risks related to a spoiled batch. The best way to evaluate yeasting approaches and to find which is your favorite is to do some side-by-side tests of identical musts fermented with different yeast strains. This really allows you to assess the influence of the yeast on the final cider, and even more when one of the test batches is made with a previously used known yeast strain as a control. And, in addition, making such a comparative test is a fun part of cider making, as when it's time to compare the batches, it is necessary to invite tasters over, and interesting discussions arise as to which is the best. There is not always a consensus!

I have performed quite a few such yeast tests. For example, in a side-by-side comparison of Lalvin 71B-1122 with EC-1118, I was able to confirm the 20 percent acidity reduction capacities of the 71B, which is quite useful for a must that is a bit too acidic. In another test with the Wyeast 4783 "Rudesheimer," I didn't find any advantage with this yeast over the Lalvin EC-1118. On a few occasions I also did side-by-side tests of a wild yeast with a cultured yeast, and on all occasions the cultured yeast was stronger and faster to reach dryness. Wild yeast ferments have always been easier to stop, thus making it easier to obtain a cider with natural residual sugar.

The Yeast Nutrients

We have seen in chapter 11 that the nitrogenous substances present in the apple juice are a natural nutrient source for the yeast. However, their concentration may vary greatly as a function of the apple variety, cultural practices, terroir, and seasonal conditions. Further, apple juice is generally poorer in natural nutrients than other fruit juices, like grape juice, for example. Hence some cider makers will want to supplement the naturally occurring nutrients with chemical nutrients to insure a strong and reliable fermentation that will rapidly go to dryness. On the other hand, many cider makers prefer a slow fermentation and will even be grateful if the fermentation stops before completion, hence yielding a cider with residual sugar. For this second category of cider makers, nutrient addition is definitely out of the question except in special circumstances or if there is a specific problem. For example, yeast nutrient may be added to a stuck cider when we want the fermentation to go a little further, or in some special bottling procedures when a sweet and sparkling cider is desired. These applications will be discussed further in sections 14.3 and 15.2. In wine-making supply stores, we generally find two substances that may be used as nutrients for the yeast:

- **Diammonium phosphate** (DAP) is a chemical compound containing ammonium ions that release nitrogen: 21 percent of the weight of DAP is nitrogen in an assimilable form by the yeast. It is sold in the form of a water-soluble, white crystalline salt.
- **Thiamine,** or vitamin B_1, referred to as a yeast energizer. A very small quantity of thiamine is essential for the yeast to perform its work of turning sugar into alcohol, but it is very unlikely that this small quantity will not already be present in the juice.

Sometimes we find mixed packs that contain both of these compounds.

Now, the question is: How much nutrient is required for fermentation of a cider? On the package of DAP that I can buy in my wine-making supply store, it is recommended to use 1 teaspoon per imperial gallon of cider. This is approximately 1,000 ppm of DAP, a massive dose that would be more than sufficient to insure a strong and complete fermentation in a must that would contain absolutely no natural nutrients. The first and only time I used such a dosage on a cider, the fermentation picked up like a rocket and finished to dryness in no time—not what I had wanted. After that, I decided I needed to make some tests to assess the response of a cider to a small quantity of added nutrients, for this when I had a stabilized or stuck cider at a certain SG, I would introduce a small quantity of nutrients and observe the resulting drop of SG. The outcome of those tests indicated that for each 10 ppm of DAP I would add to a stuck cider, the fermentation would restart slowly, causing an SG drop of approximately 0.004, and after a few months the fermentation would stop again at this new lower SG. This was interesting, as it enabled me to anticipate the amount of fermentation I could get from a controlled amount of added DAP.

Some time after having made those tests, I had a discussion with Andrew Lea on the Cider Workshop forum, in which he mentioned that during the 1950s at the Long Ashton Research Station, they did tests to evaluate the amount of nutrients required to restart a stuck fermentation, and they came to a recommendation that 50 ppm of ammonium sulfate or phosphate should be used for each 0.010 drop of SG required, plus

a fixed 0.2 ppm of thiamine. This dosage is about twice the amount obtained from my own tests, but their work was based on the assumption that a full fermentation to dryness was required; hence, it makes sense to use more nutrients in those circumstances.

We may also compare these numbers with the amount of YAN naturally present in the apple juice, as seen in the article on nitrogenous substances (chapter 11). We can see there that the minimum quantity of YAN required for a complete but very slow fermentation would be around 50 ppm or possibly a little more. If we assume the original must has an SG of 1.060, complete fermentation means an SG drop of 0.060. Also, considering that DAP is 21 percent nitrogen, those 50 ppm of YAN would be equivalent to 238 ppm of DAP. Then, to obtain an SG drop of 0.010, this indicates we would need about 40 ppm of DAP, which is quite consistent with the previous findings.

From all of this, we may conclude that if we want to restart a stuck fermentation and have the cider ferment to dryness, then a dosage of 40 to 50 ppm of DAP per each 0.010 of required SG drop would be fine. But if we want the fermentation to stick again at a lower SG, then we should use less, and 25 ppm of DAP per each 0.010 of required SG drop would in this case be recommended from the outcome of the tests I have done. I would, however, encourage you to do your own tests before applying this recommendation to a large batch of cider. Note that these amounts apply when no yeast is added, as the addition of a yeast culture also means some nitrogenous substances are added with the biomass of this yeast. Hence, if you wish the cider to stick again at a lower SG, you should not add yeast.

◀ 14.3 ▶
The Monitoring and Control of the Fermentation

In this section, we look at the evolution of the cider between the beginning of the fermentation and the moment it is ready for bottling. We have briefly seen in the third chapter that, as the fermentation proceeds, it goes through different phases: after a primary, or turbulent, phase comes a quieter secondary phase and a maturation period during which a malolactic fermentation may occur; finally, the cider clears and we can bottle it. These phases will now be reviewed in greater detail. Our objective is to provide the conditions that will maximize the quality of the cider. For this, we take actions to insure a slow but regular fermentation, which will permit the cider to develop its bouquet. A slow fermentation is beneficial to the cider flavor because many of the flavorful molecules are volatile, and hence they will have a better chance to stay in the cider rather than escape to the atmosphere if the fermentation is slow and quiet and done at low temperature. Additionally, some interventions done at the right moment may permit us to keep a part of the original sugar unfermented, hence yielding ciders that naturally retain some sweetness.

We will reach our objectives by first monitoring the fermentation carefully. This means that we will regularly measure the specific gravity (SG) of the cider and determine how fast the fermentation is proceeding, which we can present graphically. The monitoring will help us take the right step at the right moment to control the fermentation, depending upon the type of cider we want to make.

The Speed of Fermentation

All through the following discussions, I use the notion of *speed of fermentation*. There may be many ways to define it, but I introduce here a handy *fermentation speed unit* (FSU), which is defined as follows:

1 FSU is the speed of fermentation that corresponds to a drop in SG of 0.001 in 100 days.

Hence, a speed of 100 FSU is equivalent to an SG drop of one point per day. To measure the speed, we need two measurements of SG (SG_1 and SG_2) distant by a certain number of days (N). The speed is computed from:

speed (FSU) = 100,000 ($SG_1 - SG_2$) / N

As an example: on February 12 the SG measured for SG_1 is 1.012, and on April 3 SG_2 is 1.008. The number of days N is 50. The average speed between February 12 and April 3 is then 8 FSU. The same speed could be noted as 0.08 point of gravity per day, but I find the FSU units are more convenient, in particular for the low speeds of fermentation, as in the case of this example.

The Phases of the Fermentation

1.
PERIOD OF ESTABLISHMENT OF THE YEAST POPULATION

During this period the yeast will multiply its population, but we observe very little activity, as there is no significant variation in the density or production of the carbon dioxide gas. The measured speed of fermentation is close to zero. When the cider has been inoculated with a strong yeast culture and the temperature is relatively high, this period may be very short, only a few hours. But generally, if the temperature is lower than 55°F (12°C), this establishment period may need a couple of days. And in the case of a wild yeast fermentation, a week or even more could be required if the must has been sulfited.

While the population is establishing itself, the yeast needs oxygen, and the fermentation vessel used should be wide enough to provide a good contact surface between the air and the must. The vessel may still be closed, as long as there is a good layer of air under the lid. Some cider makers will stir the cider during this period to aerate it, but I have never found this to be necessary.

2.
PRIMARY OR TURBULENT FERMENTATION

The fermentation will start gradually as the yeast population gets established. A white to light brown foam forms on the surface of the must. After a few days this foam may be an inch or more thick, and the top becomes browner in color as the fermentation carries some solid deposits to the surface. There is an important production of carbon dioxide during this phase, which will be easily noticed if the fermentation vessel is hermetically closed and equipped with an airlock.

The turbulent fermentation may last between ten days to over a month, depending on the type of apples, how late in the season they were harvested, the ambient temperature, the nutrient content of the must, and the strain of yeast used. It is during this period that the speed of the fermentation is at its maximum, and between one-third and three-quarters of the initial sugar of the must will be transformed by the fermentation. Here are a few real-life examples:

- A first-season cider prepared with midseason-maturing apples and containing plenty of nitrogenous nutrients will usually have a fast fermentation. If the initial SG is 1.055, we could, for example, have a turbulent fermentation that would last twelve days and end up with an SG of 1.015. This would be an average speed of 330 FSU during this phase. Generally, my first-season ciders have fermentation speeds between 250 and 350 FSU during their turbulent phase.
- For a late-season cider, fermentation is slower. If, for example, we have a must with an initial SG of 1.060, the turbulent phase may last twenty days, and the SG may be 1.034 at the end. In this case the speed would have been 130 FSU. For this type of cider, fermentation speeds on the order of 100 to 200 FSU would be considered normal. If this is a wild-yeast ferment, however, the speed could be slower.

When the turbulent phase quiets down, the foam vanishes gradually, leaving some brown deposits on the surface. This indicates the end of this phase. It is then possible to proceed to the first racking (see further on the interventions of the cider maker).

3.
SECONDARY FERMENTATION PHASE

There is no set point of transition between the turbulent phase and secondary phase unless you have opted to make an early first racking, in which case the moment of this racking would mark the beginning of the secondary phase. The secondary fermentation will last until the alcoholic fermentation is finished. It is in our interest that this fermentation proceed as slowly as possible, and for this we will try to have a cool temperature in the cider room, 50°F (10°C) or even less. When everything goes smoothly, the cider maker doesn't have much to do during this phase, but it is recommended to monitor things. If a first racking was done and was effective, the speed of fermentation should be much lower now than it was during the turbulent phase. I like it to be around 50 FSU or slightly less. And as it goes along, we observe a gradual decrease in speed. For all practical purposes, we may consider the secondary phase complete and the cider stabilized when the speed of fermentation is about 3 to 4 FSU or lower over a period of a month, which would correspond to an SG drop of 0.001 during this month. For a cider that was started in late fall, the end of the secondary phase usually occurs by late the following spring or around the beginning of the summer.

4.
MALOLACTIC FERMENTATION

Malolactic fermentation (MLF) is considered a phase in this process even though it doesn't happen for all ciders. It may happen spontaneously at the end of the secondary phase or be caused by the inoculation of lactic acid bacteria. I discuss this in greater detail in the next section.

5.
MATURATION AND CLEARING OF THE CIDER

During this last phase of the fermentation, the cider is very quiet. Carbon dioxide is not produced anymore, as there is no more alcoholic fermentation. Small quantities may still be produced by malolactic fermentation, but when we see some activity in the airlock, the most probable cause is that the cider is warming up (we are in the beginning of summer by then), and some of the carbon dioxide that was in solution escapes in gaseous form and may cause a bit of activity in the airlock. This is because the solubility of carbon dioxide in water decreases as the temperature rises. In any case, this is the most critical period for the cider, as it is no longer protected by the blanket of CO_2 that is produced by active fermentation. Hence, it is important to make sure there is as little air as possible in the vessel. It may be necessary to top up the fermentation vessel, and the airlock must be checked regularly. Even if the cider is very calm in appearance, there are still chemical and biochemical reactions happening, and these may enhance the flavor and aroma of the cider as well as smoothen it. Additionally, this period of calm will allow the particles in suspension to form a deposit on the bottom of the vessel, as the cider clears naturally. Once the cider has cleared, we consider this maturation phase complete and the cider ready to bottle, but we still may let the cider sit on its lees for a while before bottling.

6.
REFERMENTATION FOR CARBONATION

If you choose to prepare a sparkling cider by natural carbonation, then there may be an ultimate phase of fermentation in bottles or in a hermetically closed vessel. See section 15.2 for details.

Fermentation Vessels

The criteria for vessels for the primary fermentation phase are quite different from those for subsequent phases. For the primary phase, a larger vessel is needed, as it is useful to have some extra cider. Further, a good headspace is required over the must to allow for the foam that will be produced, otherwise this foam will overflow and spill onto the floor. Typically, there will also be a relatively large area of contact between air and the must, and this is quite acceptable at this stage because the yeast needs oxygen during the population establishment period. This vessel doesn't have to be hermetically closed, nor does it need to be equipped with an airlock, although these two features may still be desirable.

For the secondary and subsequent phases, we want to minimize the contact with air, since less carbon dioxide is produced as the fermentation slows. When there is a lot of this gas, it protects the cider, but in the later phases there is not

enough to insure protection anymore. Hence, the fermentation vessel should have a hermetic lid and an airlock so no oxygen can enter and reach the cider. It should also provide a reduced area of contact between the cider and the gas in the headspace on top of the cider and a minimal volume of headspace. Cider makers typically use containers completely full of cider or tanks equipped with lids that are adjustable in height. Alternatively, you can remove the air from a headspace by injecting carbon dioxide into the top of the tank to act like a protective blanket over the cider.

We have seen in the first chapter of this book that a novice or small-scale cider maker might use a large plastic pail as a primary fermentation vessel, followed by a carboy for the secondary fermentation. Carboys are excellent for this, as they have a narrow neck, and when they are filled to the top, there is only an area of about a square inch (5 cm²) of contact between the cider and the gas in the headspace. Further, the volume of this headspace is very small. This sort of setup remains acceptable for serious hobbyists: with about a dozen carboys of different sizes and a consequent number of large pails, it is possible to have a decent production, on the order of 100 gallons (400 L) per year. Note that glass carboys are available in capacities of up to 14 gallons (54 L). Further, such a setup has the advantage of great flexibility, as a combination of containers of different sizes may accommodate any batch size with a minimum of loss.

When scaling up, however, some other types of fermentation vessels may be considered. For the primary fermentation, food-safe plastic (HDPE) drums are available in many capacities, ranging from about 10 to 100 gallons (40 to 400 L), with the standard 55 gallon (208 L) being very common. For larger volumes, intermediate bulk

Figure 14.4. Stainless steel tanks at Farnum Hill Cider.

containers (IBCs) are reasonably priced and quite popular among small- and medium-scale commercial cider makers. IBCs are large, cube-shaped plastic containers enclosed in steel cages and are designed to be moved with a pallet truck. They come in different sizes, but 250 gallons (1,000 L) is a fairly common capacity. Drums and IBCs may be easily acquired secondhand, but in that case it is necessary to be very selective as to what they have previously been used for. For example, a drum that has contained olives may smell relatively strong, but this will not transmit to the cider, and after a good wash it will be fine to use. But if it has contained something like concentrated orange juice, this taste will transfer to the cider. Needless to say, if this container has been used for nonfood products, it shouldn't be used for cider.

For the secondary fermentation, considering the requirements mentioned above, it is preferable to use dedicated plastic or stainless steel fermentation tanks. Such tanks are made for the wine and brewing industries and are available in varying capacities for everyone from serious hobbyists up to large commercial operations. And since such tanks are specifically made for fermentation, they are equipped with the right apertures for cleaning, racking, airlocks, and so on. Some have a conical bottom that makes separation from the lees easier.

Some stainless steel tank models are of a variable capacity with a lid that may be installed at any height (a floating lid), usually with an inflatable seal. Other models have a refrigeration coil built in, which makes it possible to control the temperature with a simple thermostat. Plastic would generally be used for capacities between 15 and 50 gallons (55 and 200 L). For over 50 gallons, stainless steel tanks such as shown in figure 14.4 are the norm.

WOOD BARRELS

Some cider makers like to use barrels for the secondary fermentation and the maturation of the cider, perhaps a holdover tradition from the days when wooden barrels were the only large vessels that could be made. (See figure 14.5.)

Those who use barrels do so mainly because the cider will take some tannin from the wood, thus the barrel modifies the flavor of the cider. A second reason is that it is much easier to obtain a spontaneous malolactic fermentation in a barrel (see section 14.4). However, barrels do have some drawbacks: they are difficult to clean and disinfect, and the wood pores may host some spoilage microorganisms. They also need good care to keep them from drying out and leaking. For these reasons, many cider makers wouldn't use a barrel under any circumstances, now that there are modern materials like stainless steel, glass, or plastic that are more convenient.

One thing is sure, though: barrels are not for beginners, if only because of their size. Small ones are 55 gallons (200 L), a hefty batch size for a novice.

Figure 14.5. Barrel room at Farnum Hill Cider.

And although some smaller sizes do exist, they are not recommended for cider making because the ratio of the wood surface to the volume of cider is too large and makes the cider excessively woody.

For a successful cider operation with barrels, the secret is cleaning and sanitation, as usual, but even more so in this case. Some products are specially formulated for barrels and can be found in a wine-making supply store.

Monitoring of the Fermentation

Good monitoring of the evolution of the fermentation is important, as it helps you make the right intervention at the right moment. In its simplest form, this monitoring will just be notes of the date, the measured SG, and the speed of fermentation at some more or less regular time intervals. The temperature measurement is also necessary, as it allows you to make the correction to the SG reading. And a few acidity measurements during the evolution of the cider may help identify whether a malolactic fermentation is actively occurring.

WHEN SHOULD MEASUREMENTS OF SG AND ACIDITY BE TAKEN?

I suggest the following schedule, which in my opinion is a minimum. Naturally, it is always possible to take measurements more often and get a better grasp of how things are going.

- After pressing of the apples: SG and TA of the fresh juice. This value of SG is particularly important, as it will permit you to evaluate the alcoholic strength of the cider.

- At the end of the primary fermentation: SG and calculation of the average speed during the primary fermentation.
- At the moment of a racking and approximately two weeks later: SG and calculation of the fermentation speed to assess the effectiveness of the racking.
- During the secondary fermentation and the maturation: a measurement of SG and calculation of the fermentation speed once a month. During the later phases, when the fermentation has slowed down, once every two months will be sufficient.
- By the end of winter, before the temperature starts to rise in the cider room: TA once or twice so see if there are variations of the acidity due to the fermentation.
- During malolactic fermentation, if it occurs: a few measurements of TA, to view its evolution.
- At the moment of the last racking, before bottling: SG and TA.

USING A SPREADSHEET FOR MONITORING

I like to use a spreadsheet to automatically do the calculations of the speed of fermentation and also for the temperature and calibration corrections of the hydrometer. Once the data have been entered, it is easy to produce nice-looking graphs for the evolution of the SG, temperature, speed of fermentation, and TA. Table 14.1 is an example spreadsheet for a batch I called Demo. I made entries on the light peach fields, while the yellow fields are automatically calculated by the system. These include the number of days elapsed since the beginning of the fermentation, the corrected SG, and the fermentation speed in FSU.

TABLE 14.1:

Fermentation monitoring on a spreadsheet

		Year:	**2010**				Batch:	**DEMO**
DATE	**TEMP (°C)**	**SG READ**	**TA**	**DAYS**	**SG CORR**	**FSU**	**INTERVENTIONS**	
2010.10.01	17	1.062	7	0	1.0622		Pressing	
2010.10.03	17	1.062		2	1.0622	0	Yeast inoculation	
2010.10.20	16	1.035		19	1.0351	160	First racking	
2010.11.20	12	1.025		50	1.0245	34		
2011.01.25	9	1.015		116	1.0143	16		
2011.03.30	12	1.008	6.5	180	1.0075	11	Stabilization racking	
2011.06.30	18	1.005		272	1.0054	2		
2011.09.20	17	1.004	4.5	354	1.0042	1	Bottling	

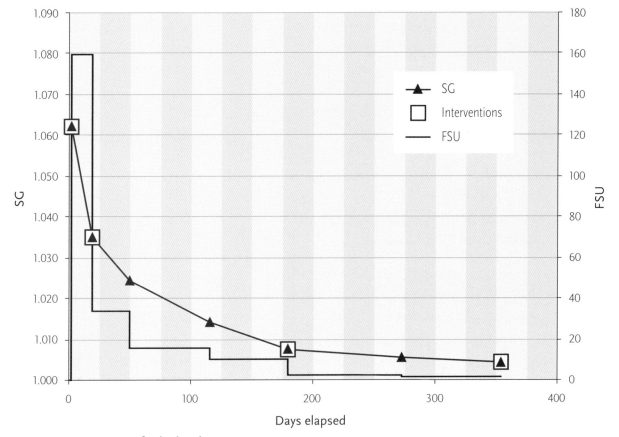

Figure 14.6. Monitoring of cider batch: Demo 2010.

A graph such as the in figure 14.6 may then easily be produced. In this particular one, I have plotted the evolution of the SG in blue, with the interventions that were done appearing as larger squares. The speed of fermentation is represented by the brown line. This is an approximate representation, where it is assumed the speed is constant and equal to its average during a period between two measurements. A spreadsheet program similar to table 14.1 is provided with the companion materials (Appendix 2).

Interventions by the Cider Maker during the Fermentation

Once the fermentation is started, the cider maker usually doesn't have much to do. Apart from the monitoring described above and a couple of interventions, you need to check the airlock regularly and renew the antiseptic liquid. By the end of the fermentation, you should watch for the possible outbreak of some spoilage, such as a film yeast (see chapter 16 on cider troubles). But mainly you simply have to be patient and let the cider take its time to make itself.

TEMPERATURE CONTROL

A professional cider maker might let the cider ferment in a cider house where the temperature is controlled to about 50°F / (10°C). A hobbyist cider maker who lives in an area where there are cold winters should have a small room which, ideally, should be unheated and have a window as a temperature-control method. It is not necessary to control the temperature precisely, and some fluctuations are normal, but it would be good if the temperature in this room could drop to 40–50°F (5–10°C) during the colder part of winter, so that the fermentation maintains a slow pace. An unheated room in the basement would be ideal, as it stays cooler during summer. A spot in a garage is another possibility. An air-conditioning unit may used for the cider room if there is no way to cool it naturally. In places where it is not so cold in winter, as in France and England, cider makers can leave the cider outside to ferment with minimal protection. In these regions the cider may freeze, but not for very long, and the fermentation restarts when the temperature heats up a bit. In colder parts of North America, this would not be possible, however, as the cider would become a solid ice cube from December to April. What we need to remember is that cider doesn't fear cold, but excessive heat should be avoided.

RACKING

Racking is an operation by which we separate the cider from its lees by moving the cider from one fermenting vessel to another without disturbing the lees, which remain in the first vessel. An important effect of racking is to reduce the biomass of the cider. By *biomass* we mean the organic matters that feed the yeast, as well as dead and live yeast cells. The dead ones contain some nitrogenous nutrients that would be released back to the cider by autolysis to feed the new generation. Hence, a racking decreases the number of active yeast cells and lowers the essential yeast nutrients in the cider, with the result that the fermentation slows down. In order to maximize the effect of a racking, it is preferable to do it when the cider is relatively cold, as the activity of the yeast is then reduced and there is less agitation in the cider. With less yeast and fewer nutrients in suspension in the cider, the separation from the biomass will thus be more effective. As racking is generally done during winter, it is possible to open a window the day before to cool the cider room. Traditionally, even if they didn't know the scientific reasons for this, European cider makers would choose a cold and clear day to perform the racking because they had observed the cider was clearer on such days. Some farmers even took into account the moon phase before deciding for the best moment to perform a racking. And, naturally, it is very important not to disturb the lees before or during the racking, and to rack off only the cider into the new vessel.

We distinguish three types of racking that may be done on a cider: the *first racking*, which is done relatively early; the *stabilization racking*, which is optional and may be done during the later phases of the fermentation to reduce its speed; and the *final racking*, which is done once the fermentation is complete.

FIRST RACKING

The object of the first racking is to move the cider from its primary fermentation vessel to its secondary vessel, where it will be protected from air contact during the later phases of fermentation. However, this racking will also reduce the speed of fermentation, as mentioned above.

There are two schools of thought as to the best moment for the first racking. We may call them early and late first racking. An early first racking is done soon after the foam from the turbulent fermentation has settled, while the SG is still relatively high. This might be anywhere from ten days to four weeks after the start of fermentation, and the SG may be somewhere between 1.020 and 1.040. The point in making the first racking as soon as possible is to profit from the speed reduction effect early on: this increases the chances of getting a stuck fermentation, which would leave the cider with some residual sugar. A late first racking, on the other hand, is performed when most of the fermentation is done and the SG is approaching the point of dryness, typically around SG 1.005. And actually, this first racking may be done at any time between these two moments. For a dry cider, a late first racking may be just fine.

In figure 14.6, plotting the monitoring of an example cider, we can see the speed reduction effect caused by an early first racking. The average speed between days 2 and 19 was 160 FSU. The first racking was done on day 19, and the average speed between that day and day 50 has fallen to 34 FSU. Thus, this racking was successful in reducing the rate of fermentation.

Whichever moment you choose for your first racking, you should check the SG and compute the speed of fermentation. Note that it may be difficult to measure the SG during the turbulent fermentation because the foam makes the reading difficult. Hence, often the first SG check is done during this racking.

STABILIZATION RACKING

In some circumstances we may do one or more additional rackings during the secondary fermentation phase. We call this *stabilization racking*. Its aim is to reduce the speed of fermentation to eventually obtain a cider that is stable while still containing some sugar. By "stable," we mean that the fermentation can no longer proceed because the cider doesn't contain the necessary nutrients to sustain a yeast population. A stable cider may thus be bottled even if it contains some unfermented sugar without fear that this sugar will re-ferment in the bottles. Stabilization racking, then, is an essential operation to obtain a medium or a sweet cider by natural methods. This will be discussed further in the articles on sweetness and ice cider making in chapter 15. Note that if the objective is to make a dry cider, there is generally no point in doing a stabilization racking unless there is a particular reason to slow the fermentation.

If we observe the example graph in figure 14.6 on page 232 for the fermentation monitoring, we can see that a stabilization racking was done on day 180 (this was the end of March). The SG was then 1.0075 and the speed 11 FSU. At this rhythm the cider would have attained dryness in a little more than two months (7.5 × 100 days / 11 FSU = 68 days). However, I was aiming for an off-dry profile with this cider. The stabilization racking was effective and permitted me to reduce the speed to 2 FSU, and the cider stabilized itself nicely at a SG of 1.004—just right for an off-dry cider. Note that for a cider that contains a lot of nitrogenous nutrients, more than one stabilization racking may be required before the cider becomes stable.

FINAL RACKING

A final racking is done once the maturation and clearing of the cider is complete and it is ready to bottle or keg. The object is simply to separate the cider from its lees. The aim is not to slow fermentation, as it is normally complete and the FSU already at or very near zero. The final racking is a preparatory step for the bottling procedure, so this is the moment to add yeast or sugar (if you want a sparkling cider) so these will get well mixed with the cider.

INCREASING THE SPEED OF FERMENTATION

Usually, the cider maker is mostly interested in slowing the fermentation in order to obtain the best ciders. However, sometimes we overdo it. One too many stabilization rackings may make the fermentation overly slow and even make it stick while the cider is still too sweet. When this happens, the first thing to do is to increase the temperature of the cider, as this will activate the yeast. If it is small enough to move, simply bring the carboy into a warmer location, where the temperature would be between 60 and 70°F (15 and 21°C). A small dosage of yeast nutrients, of about 25 to 30 ppm of DAP, could also help at this stage. (Note that 30 ppm is equivalent to ⅛ teaspoon in a 5-gallon carboy; see section 14.2 for a discussion on yeast nutrient dosage.) These measures are generally sufficient, and within a couple of weeks the fermentation will gain some strength and you will start to see more bubbles in the airlock. After about a month in this warmer location, an SG measurement should show an increase of the fermentation speed. If not, see the following information on stuck fermentations.

RESTARTING A STUCK FERMENTATION

It may sometimes happen that the fermentation stops completely while there is still a lot of sugar to ferment. This may be due to a must that is exceptionally poor in nutrients or a very weak wild yeast population, or it might occur if a cultured yeast was nonviable for one reason or another. A stuck fermentation is an extreme example of the case seen above for slow fermentation, and the recommendations given there should first be applied. In order to diagnose a true stuck fermentation, you should have two equal SG readings taken one month or more apart while the temperature is at least 60°F (15°C). If at this moment the cider has reached a sufficient alcoholic strength to conserve itself, that is, at least 4% ABV, you will then have obtained a naturally sweet cider without effort. Let's take a hypothetical cider whose juice's original SG was 1.065 and where the fermentation stuck at an SG of 1.025. The cider would then have a strength of 4.5% ABV, and it would have about 5 percent residual sweetness, which would make it a sweet cider. If you go that route, read section 15.1 on sweetness in cider. On the other hand, if this same hypothetical cider had stuck at an SG of 1.040, its alcoholic strength would not be sufficient to insure its keeping quality. You would then have to restart the fermentation. Assuming you have already increased the temperature and added some yeast nutrients as recommended for speeding up a slow fermentation, the possible remaining options would be to aerate the cider and to inoculate a new yeast culture.

Aeration will provide oxygen to the yeast. To do it, you may rack a part of the cider, but make it splash when you transfer it into the receiving container. Then put it back into the carboy and don't worry about disturbing the lees; this may only improve the efficiency of the treatment. Aeration will be more efficient if combined with addition of yeast nutrients, and you may add another small dose at this point, depending on the dosage you added previously. You might aim for a total dosage of 100 ppm, which would be sufficient to insure an SG drop of 0.020 in the cider.

The above treatment will not work instantly. Presumably, the yeast population was very small at the moment of aeration and nutrient addition, so it will take a while before a new population builds up again. It may be a good month before you can see that some fermentation activity has started again. If after that period nothing happens —still no visible bubbles of carbon dioxide and no change in SG—then as a last resort you can inoculate a new yeast culture to the cider. Champagne yeast is usually recommended to restart a stuck fermentation.

ULLAGE: TOPPING UP THE FERMENTATION VESSEL

Ullage refers to the headspace volume on top of a wine or cider and is a term used mainly in the context of barrel fermentation. Some evaporation occurs through the wood, and it is necessary to regularly fill up the void caused by this evaporation in order to prevent the air from coming into contact with the cider. Nowadays most cider makers prefer to use fermentation vessels made of modern materials like plastic, stainless steel, or glass. With these materials, there is no evaporation; however, there is always a quantity of cider that is lost during the racking operations. For example, if you do a stabilization racking from a 5-gallon carboy into another one of the same dimension, you will lose about a quart (or liter) in the operation; hence, you will need this same quantity to fill up the receiving carboy. Also, you will notice that as the fermentation proceeds there is a slight reduction of volume that occurs. Even if you don't do a stabilization racking, then, you might need to fill up a void in the carboy when the cider reaches the maturation phase.

The preferred method is always to have some extra fermenting cider at hand. For this, some planning is required. Before starting the fermentation, insure there is more juice than will be required to fill the secondary fermentation vessel. Then when you do the first racking, the extra cider may be kept in a 1-gallon (or whatever size you have on hand, considering the quantity of extra cider) jug equipped with an airlock. This cider will ferment at approximately the same rhythm as the bulk of the cider and may be used as necessary for ullage fill-up. Another possibility is to freeze some of this extra partially fermented cider in small containers.

Other methods are possible for reducing the ullage, which I list here by order of preference:

- If the void to fill is small, put some glass marbles or other filling objects (previously sanitized) into the carboy.
- Add some cider from a previous year's batch.
- Add fresh apple juice.
- Add water, though this will slightly dilute the cider.

An alternative is to use CO_2 for blanketing on top of the cider. This is described in the sidebar "Working with a CO_2 Tank" in section 15.2, on pages 276–278.

◀ 14·4 ▶
The Malolactic Fermentation

The *malolactic fermentation* (MLF) is a biochemical transformation of the malic acid present in the cider. We have previously seen that the malic acid is the main acid component in apple juice. This organic acid has a very pronounced and sharp taste. When MLF occurs, the malic acid is transformed into lactic acid, which is much less aggressive and smoother. Some carbon dioxide is also produced during the transformation. The malolactic fermentation is caused by *lactic acid bacteria* (LAB), which are much smaller organisms than the yeast responsible for the alcoholic fermentation. It usually occurs when the alcoholic fermentation is getting close to completion, during spring or summer, as the temperatures get warmer in the cider house. It may happen spontaneously or be provoked by the cider maker by inoculation of a strain of LAB.

This fermentation is generally considered favorable for ciders that have high acidity, as it will reduce it noticeably. Moreover, MLF mellows and gives some roundness to the cider, improves mouthfeel, and often gives some buttery notes. The bouquet and aromas are also modified and are more spicy. Some English ciders require a malolactic fermentation to develop a particular and sought-after character called (affectionately) "old horse." Other characteristic aromas given to the cider by the MLF are described a little further.

CONDITIONS THAT ARE FAVORABLE OR UNFAVORABLE TO THE DEVELOPMENT OF MLF

- **Temperature.** Depending on the strain of LAB considered, a temperature of at least 60°F (15°C), plus or minus a few degrees, is generally believed necessary for the malolactic fermentation to proceed. The MLF will thus often start spontaneously by the end of spring, as the temperature heats up in the cider house, and at a moment where the alcoholic fermentation is complete or almost so. In the old days, before scientists discovered all the factors involved, people would say that the cider would again start to "work" when the apple trees were in bloom: this was the time MLF would be active, and this produced some bubbling in the cider as carbon dioxide gas escaped. Note that as the temperature rises in spring, some of the dissolved carbon dioxide is released by the cider because the solubility of this gas decreases at higher temperatures. Seeing gas bubbles in the airlock, then, is not necessarily a sign that MLF is occurring.

- **Acidity.** Different strains of LAB have varying tolerance to pH, although in general they prefer a medium that's not too acidic (i.e., at a pH higher than 3.5). Some strains will develop only at high pH, while others may still work at relatively low pH. But a very low pH of the order of 3.0 will inhibit any strain of the bacteria and prevent malolactic fermentation.
- **Sulfite.** LAB have little tolerance to sulfite, and a relatively weak dosage, on the order of 10 ppm free SO_2, will be enough to inhibit them. Hence, if MLF is not wanted, a dosage of approximately 50 ppm of sulfite may be added by the end of the alcoholic fermentation and before the temperature gets milder. Conversely, if MLF is desired, sulfite should be limited to the minimum dosage and added to the must only once the MLF is completed.
- **Aging in wood barrels.** Because of the porosity of the wood, old wooden barrels will retain spores from the bacteria population of the previous year's malolactic fermentation even if they are

cleaned and sanitized. Hence, cider makers who use barrels for maturation of their ciders will obtain a spontaneous MLF without difficulty.

The transformation takes quite a bit of time before it is completed. Three months is a good average. It will take longer when the temperature is lower or when the medium is more acidic. Often, too, the transformation will only be partial.

CHEMICAL REACTION

During the malolactic fermentation, a molecule of malic acid transforms into a molecule of lactic acid plus one molecule of carbon dioxide:

$$C_4H_6O_5 \rightarrow C_3H_6O_3 + CO_2$$

Malic acid: $C_4H_6O_5$
    molar mass: 134 g/mol
    volumic mass: 1.61 g/mL approximately, at 20°C (68°F)
    volume for 1 mole: 83 mL

Lactic acid: $C_3H_6O_3$
    molar mass: 90 g/mol
    volumic mass: 1.25 g/mL approximately, at 20°C (68°F)
    volume for 1 mole: 72 mL

Carbon dioxide: CO_2
    molar mass: 44 g/mol

Malic acid is a diprotic acid, which means that each mole contains two acid equivalents. Lactic acid is monoprotic, so each mole contains one acid equivalent. This means that if all the malic acid is transformed, and considering that malic acid constitutes approximately 90 percent of the original total acidity, then there would be a 45 percent reduction of the titratable acidity.

From the reaction formula above, we see that for each mole of malic acid transformed, one mole of carbon dioxide will escape, thus reducing the total mass of the cider by 44 grams. Additionally, from the volumic masses of malic and lactic acids, we see there will be a slight reduction of the volume of the cider, of 11 mL per mole of malic acid transformed. Note that this last number is indicative only because when in solution the change in volume could be different. These two effects combined will cause a slight decrease of the SG of the cider, of one or two points. If the MLF occurs inside a hermetically closed container, such as a bottle, then the carbon dioxide will stay in solution instead of escaping, and this will cause a slight sparkle in the cider.

THE LACTIC ACID BACTERIA (LAB)

Two main genuses of bacteria that are involved in the malolactic fermentation of cider have been identified:

- *Oenococcus*. Formerly known as *Leuconostoc*, a coccus type of bacteria. The species involved is *Oenococcus oeni*.
- *Lactobacillus*. Rod-shaped bacteria. This genus contains many species, some of which are considered spoilage bacteria.

Additionally, a third genus, **Pediococcus**, is known to be involved in the natural MLF of wines, but I haven't seen it mentioned in relation with cider. The *Oenococcus* bacteria feature a better tolerance to acidic pH. They are quite efficient in reducing the acidity but have less effect on the flavor and mouthfeel of the cider than the *Lactobacillus*. The *Lactobacillus* will be more dominant at higher pH, around 3.5 to 3.8, with ciders that contain a good proportion of bittersweet apples. It is a *Lactobacillus* that gives the "old horse" character to some English ciders. English cider makers will generally prefer a spontaneous MLF obtained from wild bacteria, as they consider the cider so obtained to have more complexity, due to the diversity of bacteria at work. The commercial cultured MLF strains that may be bought in the trade are most often monocultures of the *Oenococcus* type.

FLAVOR CHARACTERS GIVEN BY MLF

In addition to the "old horse" character, there are quite a few other typical flavors that may be given to the cider by the MLF. In an effort to standardize the scoresheets used in cider competitions, the Beer Judge Certification Program (BJCP) has defined the following descriptors for MLF character in the cider:

- **Farmyard**: Manure-like (cow or pig) or barnyard (horse stall on a warm day).
- **Phenolic**: Plastic, band-aid, and/or medicinal.
- **Spicy/Smoky**: Spice, cloves, smoky, ham.

Additionally, the following descriptors (also defined by the BJCP) apply to characters given by some other types of LAB, which are considered as different from those causing MLF:

- **Acetaldehyde**: Green apple candy aroma/flavor
- **Diacetyl**: Butter or butterscotch aroma or flavor
- **Mousy**: Taste evocative of the smell of a rodent's den/cage.

The mousy character is considered a fault, and is discussed in chapter 16. A little of acetaldehyde and/or of diacetyl may be acceptable in some ciders.

CALCULATION EXAMPLES

Following are a few examples of the sort of calculations we can do on malolactic fermentation.

We may detect if the MLF has happened by monitoring the titratable acidity (TA). Let's denote by TA_1 the acidity before the beginning of the transformation. Then, after a complete transformation of the malic acid, a measurement of the acidity should give TA = 0.55 TA_1 if the malic acid constituted 90 percent of the original acidity. We may then roughly estimate the fraction of the transformation in percent by the following calculation:

Transformation % = 222 [1 − (TA / TA_1)]

Note that TA_1 may be different from the acidity of the must before the start of the fermentation, because the alcoholic fermentation may increase or decrease the acidity somewhat. Hence, the value of TA_1 should be measured when the alcoholic fermentation is complete or almost so, but before the MLF has started, which may be tricky.

For example, a cider is prepared from a must that originally had a TA of 6.5 g/L as malic acid. During the alcoholic fermentation, the TA is monitored, and by the end of the winter the SG is getting close to 1.000, while the TA has increased to 7 g/L. This last value would be taken as TA_1. Then by midsummer, if the TA has decreased to 4.5 g/L, from the above calculation we would estimate that the MLF is approximately 80 percent complete.

We can also estimate the variation in mass, volume, and SG of the cider due to the MLF. If we use the same case as above, with a reduction of TA from 7 to 4.5 g/L due to MLF, this indicates that 5 g/L of malic acid has been transformed (this is 80 percent of 90 percent of 7 g/L). Using the molar masses seen above, we may deduce that these 5 grams produce, per liter of cider:

5 × 90/134, or 3.36 g of lactic acid and
5 × 44/134, or 1.64 g of carbon dioxide.

If the carbon dioxide gas escapes to the atmosphere, then there is a net loss of mass of 1.64 g. There would also be a slight change in volume, which could be estimated as:

volume occupied by 5 grams of malic acid:
83 mL × 5 / 134 = 3.1 mL

volume occupied by 3.36 grams of lactic acid:
72 mL × 3.36 / 90 = 2.69 mL

The difference between these two values, 0.41 mL per liter, is the reduction of volume attributable to the MLF. To calculate the variation of SG, we could proceed as follows: if the SG of the cider before MLF is 1.000, its volumic mass is 998.2 g/L. After the MLF the original liter is reduced by 0.41 mL and becomes 0.99959 L. The mass is reduced by 1.64 g to 996.56 g, hence the volumic mass after this transformation is 996.56 g / 0.99959 L = 996.97 g/L, and this last number divided by the volumic mass of water (998.2) gives SG = 0.9988. Hence, in this example, where MLF is completed at 80 percent, the SG would be reduced by 1.2 points of gravity.

Another possibility is that the malolactic fermentation occurs in the bottle. The 1.64 grams of carbon dioxide would then remain trapped in the bottle and would dissolve in the cider. This is a small quantity, though, corresponding to 0.83 volume of CO_2 in solution (see section 15.2 on sparkling ciders), and would not cause any appreciable increase of the internal pressure, nor much sparkle.

TESTING FOR MALOLACTIC FERMENTATION

For hobbyists and small-scale commercial cider makers, the Accuvin malic acid test kit is a simple tool to test for malolactic fermentation. These are strips on which there is a spot of reagent that changes color with the concentration of malic acid, and the color of the reagent is compared with a color chart to estimate the malic acid concentration. They are somewhat similar to pH strips, but their cost is higher, about $3 to $5 per test strip. The measurement range is from 30 to 500 mg of malic acid per liter.

It should be noted that this range is a bit short for cider. If we take the cider that was given in the example above, it is only when the transformation is completed at 92 percent that the concentration of malic acid falls to 0.5 g/L (i.e., 500 mg of malic acid/L). Hence, this test may be useful to identify

the moment the MLF is complete but not for monitoring its evolution during the early stages.

Another test cider makers may do is the paper chromatography test. Kits for this test are sold in wine-making supply stores for $60 to $80. Such a kit contains about twenty-five sheets, each of which, depending on its size, can be used for a certain number of simultaneous analyses. The manipulation is more delicate for this test, and some eight to twelve hours are required before the result sheet may be interpreted. The interpretation is qualitative more than quantitative: the presence of lactic acid is revealed, and it is possible to see that the concentration of malic acid has decreased. The lower detection of malic acid is 100 mg/L, so the test doesn't show accurately when the MLF is complete; however, it is good at monitoring its evolution during the early stages. It is a good complement to the Accuvin test.

Other, more accurate methods do exist but would be used in a laboratory rather than at the home or small-scale commercial cidery. For reference, we may mention the analysis with a spectrophotometer to measure the concentration of malic acid and the use of high-pressure (or high-performance) liquid chromatography (HPLC), both of which necessitate the purchase of costly equipment.

◀ 14.5 ▶
The Alcohol

We have already seen that it is the yeast that transforms the sugar into alcohol. The biochemistry of this transformation is complex and goes through

many intermediate stages that I will not discuss here: this would be covered in an advanced oenology treatise. The alcohol in question here is *ethyl alcohol*, or *ethanol*, which shouldn't be confused with *methyl alcohol*, or *methanol*, also known as wood alcohol. The first is the product of the fermentation of sugar; its chemical formula is C_2H_5OH and boiling point 173°F (78.5°C). The second is produced by pyrolysis of wood, has the chemical formula CH_3OH, is toxic to humans, and has its boiling point at 148° F (64.6°C).

We are interested mainly in determining the quantity of alcohol produced from a certain quantity of sugar and studying how this alcohol influences the final gravity of the cider. For this, I built a simple model that predicts the alcoholic strength and SG of a finished cider. I started the research that led to this model because I wanted to understand why some ciders, when fermented to dryness, have an SG of 1.000, while others may have an SG as low as 0.995. What causes this difference? And more important, if we have a finished cider at an SG of 1.000, how do we know how much residual sweetness it contains, and how do we know that it won't ferment down to 0.995 once bottled?

At the end of this article, I also give a few methods that allow us to estimate or measure the alcoholic strength of a cider. This alcoholic strength is by convention expressed as a percentage of alcohol by volume (% ABV) at a reference temperature of 20°C (68°F) and is denoted as A_V.

The Pasteur Relation

A primary element to consider is how much alcohol is produced from a certain quantity of sugar (the sugar considered here is a reducing sugar, that is, glucose or fructose). The first scientific estimation of the rate of production of alcohol is attributed to Joseph-Louis Gay-Lussac at the beginning of the

nineteenth century. Gay-Lussac obtained the following rule from the molecular masses of sugar, ethanol, and carbon dioxide: 100 grams of sugar would transform into 51.1 g of ethanol and 48.8 g of carbon dioxide. Later, while doing his work on yeast, Louis Pasteur demonstrated that the Gay-Lussac relation was too optimistic, as other substances or byproducts are produced during the fermentation, thus reducing the rate of production of alcohol. According to Pasteur, 100 grams of sugar transform into:

48.4 g of ethanol
46.6 g of carbon dioxide
3.2 g of glycerin
0.6 g of succinic acid
1.2 g of yeast cells

More recent works have shown that other substances are also produced in very small quantities but without influencing in any significant way the rate of production of the alcohol and carbon dioxide. Different studies done by the middle of the twentieth century with wine yeast give measured rates of alcohol production between 47.8 and 48.2 grams per 100 grams of sugar, with an average value of 48, slightly less than evaluated by Pasteur (in fact, Pasteur's 48.4 is a maximum that may be attained in ideal fermentation conditions). For carbon dioxide, these same studies show a slightly higher rate than estimated by Pasteur, at an average of 47 grams per 100 grams of sugar.

The Volumic Contraction of a Water-Alcohol Mixture

When I started to study this question, one of the first things I discovered is that the total volume of a mixture of water and alcohol can't be obtained by simple addition of the volumes of each component: if, for example, we mix 1 liter of water with 1 liter of pure alcohol, we will not obtain 2 liters of a mixture at 50% ABV. The final volume will in fact be slightly less than 2 liters and the alcohol concentration slightly more than 50 percent. This is because when alcohol and water are mixed together, there is a volumic contraction that occurs due to a sort of fusion between the two liquids as they make a solution. For cider, this means that the volumic contraction will slightly reduce the volume of the finished cider and increase its density. It is necessary, then, to use an alcoholometric table to determine the resulting total volume of a mixture and its density. The tables I use here, by the International Organization of Legal Metrology (OIML), are available on the Internet. Note that the complete document contains fifty-five pages of tables for the density and alcoholic strength at different temperatures.

First, we may extract from these tables the values of the volumic mass (ρ) of water, alcohol, and alcohol-water mixtures at different temperatures, for a standard atmospheric pressure. These will be of use for us later, and I have put them in table 14.2.

Let's look at an example: Say we mix 70 mL of pure alcohol with 930 mL of pure water. If no volumic contraction would occur, we would obtain 1 liter at an alcoholic strength of 7% ABV, a typical strength for a cider. And we could predict $\rho_{mixture}$, the volumic mass of the mixture, by simple weighted average as follows:

$$\rho_{mixture} \neq (\rho_{alcohol} V_{alcohol} + \rho_{water} V_{water}) / (V_{alcohol} + V_{water})$$

If we make all the calculations for a temperature of 20°C, the volumic masses of alcohol and water are, from table 14.2: $\rho_{alcohol} = 789.2$ g/L and $\rho_{water} = 998.2$ g/L. The volumes are: $V_{alcohol} = 70$ mL and $V_{water} = 930$ mL. The equation would give an erroneous result of 983.6 g/L, quite different from the value given in table 14.2, which is 988.4 g/L

Table 14.2: Volumic mass of pure water, pure alcohol, and alcohol-water mixtures

TEMPERATURE		ρ (g/L)					
°C	°F	Pure alcohol	40% ABV	10% ABV	7% ABV	5% ABV	Pure water
0	32	806.2	960.6	987.1	990.4	992.8	999.8
5	41	802.0	957.6	987.0	990.4	992.9	1000.0
10	50	797.8	954.5	986.6	990.1	992.6	999.7
15	59	793.5	951.3	985.8	989.4	992.0	999.1
15.56	60	793.0	951.0	985.7	989.3	991.9	999.0
20	68	789.2	948.1	984.7	988.4	991.1	998.2
25	77	785.0	944.7	983.4	987.2	989.9	997.0
30	86	780.7	941.2	981.8	985.7	988.4	995.7

for 7% ABV at our calculation temperature. This result is wrong because the final volume will be smaller than the sum of the volumes of water and alcohol; hence I have used the symbol ≠, which means *not equal* in the equation above.

If we now use the alcoholometric table to determine the final volume, we proceed as follows:

First we determine the alcoholic strength by mass of the mixture, because although the total volume isn't equal to the sum of the parts, the total mass is equal to the sum of the parts in mass because of the mass conservation laws:

Mass of alcohol : $M_{alcohol} = \rho_{alcohol} V_{alcohol}$
Mass of water: $M_{water} = \rho_{water} V_{water}$

Taking the same values as above, we then obtain the masses of alcohol and water: $M_{alcohol} = 55.25$ g and $M_{water} = 928.33$ g, and the total mass of the mixture, which is the sum of the parts:

$$M_{mixture} = M_{alcohol} + M_{water} = 55.25 + 928.33 = 983.58 \text{ g}$$

From this we have the alcoholic strength by mass (noted A_M) as the mass of alcohol divided by the mass of the mixture:

$$A_M = M_{alcohol} / M_{mixture} = 5.62\% \text{ in mass}$$

Table IIIa of the OIML alcoholometric tables gives us the volumic mass at 20°C of a mixture as a function of the alcoholic strength by mass:

$$\rho (5.6\%) = 988.41 \text{ g/L} ; \rho (5.7\%) = 988.26 \text{ g/L}$$

An interpolation between these values gives the searched value for 5.62%:

$$\rho_{mixture} = 988.38 \text{ g/L}$$

Finally, knowing the total mass and the volumic mass of the mixture, we obtain the total volume:

$$V_{mixture} = M_{mixture} / \rho_{mixture} = 0.9951 \text{ L}$$

And as expected, this last value is slightly smaller than 1 liter. The contraction is 4.9 mL, or 0.49 percent of our initial estimation obtained by the sum of volumes. And because of this contraction, the alcoholic strength by volume, instead of being 7% ABV, as initially expected, is really 7.03% ABV. These differences are slight, but it is essential to take this volumic contraction into account if we want to obtain a correct SG estimation for an alcoholic mixture. In the following, I denote the volume variation as ΔV (Δ is the Greek letter *delta*, universally used in the scientific world to express a difference), which will have a negative value to indicate this is a reduction of volume. So we may write:

$$V_{mixture} = V_{alcohol} + V_{water} + \Delta V$$

If we repeat this calculation for different values of the alcohol concentration, we can build a table of the volumic contraction as seen in table 14.3.

To use table 14.3, we first need to determine the volumic ratio. In the case of our example above, the volumic ratio was equal to 7 percent, that is, the volume of alcohol divided by the sum of the volumes. Table 14.3 indicates that the volume variation is −0.49 percent. We thus need to subtract 4.9 mL from the sum of the volumes to obtain the true volume of the mixture: 995.1 mL. And once we have this result, it is an easy task to compute the SG of the mixture:

TABLE 14.3:
Volumic contraction of alcohol-water mixtures

$V_{ALCOHOL} / (V_{ALCOHOL} + V_{WATER})$ Volumic ratio	$\Delta V / (V_{ALCOHOL} + V_{WATER})$ Volumic variation
%, AT 20°C (68°F)	%, AT 20°C (68°F)
1%	−0.06%
2%	−0.12%
3%	−0.19%
4%	−0.26%
5%	−0.33%
6%	−0.41%
7%	−0.49%
8%	−0.57%
9%	−0.66%
10%	−0.74%
11%	−0.83%
12%	−0.93%
13%	−1.02%
14%	−1.12%

$$\rho_{mixture} = M_{mixture} / V_{mixture} =$$
$$983.58 \text{ g} / 995.1 \text{ mL} = 988.4 \text{ g/L}$$

$$SG_{mixture} = \rho_{mixture} / \rho_{water} =$$
$$988.4 / 998.2 = 0.990$$

In the following model, I use regression coefficients instead of the table. We can calculate the volumic contraction as follows:

Defining R as the volumic ratio in percent:

$$R = 100 \, V_{alcohol} / (V_{alcohol} + V_{water})$$

then the volumic contraction in percent will be given by:

$$\Delta V / (V_{alcohol} + V_{water}) =$$
$$0.0000315 \, R^3 - 0.002135 \, R^2 - 0.0561 \, R$$

which is valid for values of R up to 18 percent.

Note that this relation and table are strictly valid only for pure mixtures of water and alcohol. In the case of cider, if it is dry, the values obtained will be practically exact. For a sweet cider, the sugar may slightly affect the result.

Model for Calculation of the Product of Fermentation

Now that we have laid the foundations of our model, we can study the transformation of the juice into cider and calculate the properties of this cider. Here is how it goes: First, we need to separate the components of the must. We will take 1 liter at the reference temperature of 20°C of this must and determine the quantity in grams of the total solids, fermentable sugar, and unfermented solids. We will analyze separately what happens with the fermentable sugar and the rest of our initial liter of must.

From the mass of fermentable sugar, using the Pasteur relation (but the slightly modified coefficients of 48 percent alcohol and 47 percent CO_2, which correspond better to the reality of a fermenting cider), we obtain the amount, in grams, of the alcohol, carbon dioxide, and the other products of fermentation. From this we can compute the volume of the alcohol, as we know its volumic mass at the reference temperature. Most of the carbon dioxide will escape to the atmosphere and thus is lost. There may be a small quantity that will remain in solution in the cider, but we will ignore it. As for the other products of the fermentation, which include the succinic acid, glycerin, and others, we don't know how these will influence the volume of the mixture. We will simply assume they have the same volumic mass as pure water. This is probably not exact, but the error would be slight, as the quantity involved is small.

Then we need to analyze the mass and volume of what is not alcohol: the water, the unfermented solids, and the other products of the fermentation, which, as mentioned above, are given the same volumic mass as water, and thus whose mass is simply added to that of water. By convention, the unfermented solids are expressed as sugar equivalent; hence, they mix with water in the same way sugar would. We can calculate an equivalent Brix for this mixture and determine its volumic mass and volume using the relations seen in section 8.1 on sugar.

And finally, we will mix everything together and apply the volumic contraction seen above to find the volume and mass of the finished cider. Once we know these, it is easy to find the specific gravity and alcoholic strength by volume. This is the second important assumption of the model: that the volumic contraction with this mixture is the same as it would be with pure water combined with the same quantity of alcohol.

Sample calculation

As an example, we will apply the model to three different ciders and find their respective final SG and alcoholic strength:

- Cider A is fermented to dryness from a fresh juice that has an initial SG of 1.056 and a sugar

content equal to the average for this SG, as seen in the article on sugar (section 8.1)—in this case S = 119.3 g/L and is equal to the fermented sugar. The total solids would be 145.5 g/L, and the unfermented solids would represent the difference, 26.2 g/L.

- Cider B is the same, but now we will assume there will remain 7 g/L of residual sugar in the finished cider for an off-dry cider. Hence, in this case the amount of sugar fermented is decreased by this amount, to 112.3 g/L, while the amount of unfermented solids is increased to 33.2 g/L.
- Cider C is from a chaptalized must, where the fresh juice SG was 1.044, and sugar was added to raise the SG to 1.056. We assume this cider is fermented to dryness. From the procedure described in section 8.3, it can be shown that 34.4 g/L of sugar are required to raise the SG to 1.056. This will increase the amount of fermentable sugar to 125.5 g/L, the total solids to 145.5 g/L, and the unfermented solids would in this case be 20 g/L.

The model results are shown in table 14.4, with all relevant calculations.

It is interesting to note that Cider A has a final gravity exactly equal to 1.000 when fully fermented. Cider C, in comparison, has a final gravity of 0.997, the difference being caused by the fact that Cider C was chaptalized. We have seen in section 8.3 that on average the amount of fermentable sugar relative to total solids comes to 82 percent. Such a must will have a final SG very close to 1.000, whatever the initial gravity. However, if a must contains more sugar than this average relative amount, then the final SG at dryness decreases to values smaller than 1.000. In

TABLE 14.4:
Calculations for model of cider final conditions

	CIDER A	CIDER B	CIDER C	FORMULA
MUST INITIAL CONDITIONS				
SG	1.056	1.056	1.056	
TS (total solids) (g)	145.5	145.5	145.5	
Fermented sugar (g)	119.3	112.3	125.5	
Unfermented solids (g)	26.2	33.2	20.0	
M_1 (total mass) (g)	1054.1	1054.1	1054.1	$1\,L \times SG \times 998.2\ g/L$
PASTEUR RELATION—PRODUCTS OF FERMENTATION				
Mass of alcohol (g)	57.26	53.90	60.22	Fermented sugar $\times$ 48 / 100
Carbon dioxide (g)	56.07	52.78	58.96	Fermented sugar $\times$ 47 / 100
M_2 (other products) (g)	5.97	5.62	6.27	Fermented sugar $\times$ 5 / 100
V_1 (volume of alcohol) (L)	0.0726	0.0683	0.0763	Mass of alcohol / 789.24
WATER WITH UNFERMENTED SOLIDS AND OTHER PRODUCTS OF FERMENTATION				
Mass (g)	940.8	947.4	934.9	$M_1 + M_2$ − Fermented sugar
Equivalent Brix (%)	2.785	3.504	2.144	Unfermented solids / Mass
SG	1.0109	1.0137	1.0084	per regression (section 8.1)
V_2 (volume) (L)	0.9323	0.9363	0.9288	Mass / (SG $\times$ 998.2)
VOLUMIC CONTRACTION AND FINAL VOLUME OF CIDER				
V_3 (sum of volumes) (L)	1.0049	1.0046	1.0051	$V_1 + V_2$
Volumic ratio (%)	7.22%	6.80%	7.59%	V_1 / V_3
Volumic contraction (%)	−0.505%	−0.470%	−0.535%	per regression
ΔV (L)	−0.0051	−0.0047	−0.0054	$V_3 \times$ Volumic contraction / 100
Final volume of cider (L)	0.9998	0.9999	0.9998	$V_3 + \Delta V$
FINAL MASS OF CIDER, SG, ABV				
Final mass of cider (g)	998.03	1001.32	995.14	M_1 − Carbon dioxide
Volumic mass (g/L)	998.22	1001.47	995.37	Final mass / Final volume
Final SG	1.0000	1.0033	0.9972	Volumic mass / 998.2
Alcoholic strength (%ABV)	7.26%	6.83%	7.63%	$100 \times V_1$ / Final volume

the case of Cider C, the percentage of fermented sugar as part of the TS is 86 percent. The alcoholic strength is also slightly higher because there is more sugar that has been transformed into alcohol.

The case of Cider B is given as an example to show how to use the model with a cider that doesn't ferment all the way to dryness. In that case, as expected, the final gravity is higher and the alcoholic strength is lower.

Finally, we may note that the final gravities obtained above could be lower if we would take into account the malolactic fermentation. As seen in a previous article, MLF may reduce the final SG of the cider by one to two additional points, which, in the case of Cider C, would bring the final SG close to 0.995. The malolactic fermentation would not, however, modify the alcoholic strength.

CONCLUDING REMARKS

This model does enable us to answer some of the questions mentioned in the beginning of this article. In particular, it helps us understand the influence of different parameters on the final gravity of the cider. It doesn't answer everything, though, as we would need to know the exact value of the sugar content of the must to be able to predict exactly the conditions of the finished cider, and for this only a chemical analysis of the must would provide the precise figure.

Estimation of Alcoholic Strength by Gravity Drop

The simplest and most commonly used method to estimate the alcoholic strength (A_v) of a cider is by using the difference between the SG of the initial must and the SG of the finished cider, which we will denote here by ΔSG. We then have:

$$A_v = K \Delta SG,$$

where K is a proportionality factor. Values for this factor vary in the literature, from approximately 125 to 130 for cider and up to 136 for wine and beer. Whether we use 125 or 130 or any intermediate value will not have a very significant effect on the result, as most cider makers are usually only interested in knowing the alcoholic strength within about 0.5 percent. For example, if we assume a must whose initial SG was 1.050, and the finished cider has an SG of 0.998, the SG drop would be ΔSG = 0.052. With K = 125, this would give A_v = 6.5% ABV, while with K = 130 we would obtain A_v = 6.76% ABV. The difference between the two values for A_v is 0.26%, well within the required precision.

Note that the model described above predicts a value between 129 and 130 for the factor K. This is slightly more than the value I used in section 8.3 (on sugar) for establishing the potential alcohol in the sugar table, based on Warcollier's work, which was 127.8. However, as mentioned above, with even a partial malolactic fermentation, we could easily have an additional drop of one point of gravity without changing the alcoholic strength, and thus the factor K would be reduced to 127 or 128. From this we may conclude that for a cider that hasn't had a malolactic fermentation, the use of a higher value for the factor K, of 129 or 130, would give an excellent estimation of the alcoholic strength. And for a cider that has had an MLF, a value of K that is slightly smaller, around 126, 127, or 128, would give a more accurate estimation.

A Simple Method for Measuring Alcoholic Strength

Many methods for the measurement of the alcoholic strength of a wine, beer, or cider have been proposed since the beginning of the nineteenth century. A complete review would be far beyond the scope of this book, but some of these methods may still be useful for a cider maker. This first one, which we call the *residue method*, is well adapted for hobbyist cider makers, as it is easy to set up, doesn't require any expensive equipment, and gives quite acceptable results.

The origin of this simple method may be traced to the French chemist Louis-Émile Tabarié, who in 1829 invented an instrument called the oenometer that used this method. He reported his invention in the *Annales de chimie et de physique* (vol. 45, 1830). This method and some variants have been described in the literature under the names *extract* or *spirit indication,* the *boiling* method, and, more recently, the *Honneyman* method, after a paper William Honneyman published in 1966, *"Calculating Alcohol Yields from Specific Gravities: A Lecture of considerable interest to winemakers who rely on the hydrometer alone for estimating alcohol yields."*

The principle of the method is quite simple: We take a measured volume of cider of known SG, from which the alcohol is boiled off. During this boiling process, some water will also have evaporated, but since the alcohol has a lower boiling point than water, by the time a fraction of the water has gone (about a third), then all the alcohol will have evaporated. Once the alcohol is removed, distilled water is added to reconstitute the original volume of the cider sample and the SG is measured. This solution is called the residue, and its SG will be higher than that of the original cider since alcohol is lighter than water. The difference between the two values of SG gives us an indication of the alcoholic strength of the original cider. As an illustration, if we look at table 14.2 for a pure mixture of water and alcohol at a strength of 7% ABV at 60°F, we have: $\rho_{mixture}$ = 989.3 g/L and ρ_{water} = 999 g/L, so we compute the SG of this mixture as:

$$SG_{mixture} = \rho_{mixture} / \rho_{water} = 0.9903$$

Now, if we remove the alcohol from this mixture and replace it with distilled water, we will be left with pure water, which has an SG of 1.000. Hence, removal of water causes an increase of SG of 1.000 − 0.9903 = 0.0097. The assumption of this method is that any cider (or beer or wine) that has an alcoholic strength of 7% ABV, whatever its density and residual sugar, would have this same SG increase of 0.0097 if the alcohol were removed and replaced by water.

Using the alcoholometric tables, it is then a simple task to build a table that will give the alcoholic strength by volume (A_v) as a function of the increase of SG in the residue. Table 14.5 on page 250 is from Honneyman's paper.

It is also relatively easy to establish a regression from this table, and this allows us to program it on a spreadsheet. The alcoholic strength may thus be obtained from the following equation:

$$A_v \ (\% \ ABV) = 8{,}040 \ (SG_2 - SG_1)^2 + 640 \ (SG_2 - SG_1)$$

In practice, if we want an acceptable accuracy from this method, we need to use a good precision hydrometer. In effect, we can see from the table that an error of 0.001 on the difference of SG would

TABLE 14.5:
Honneyman's table for
alcoholic strength by volume

SG_2-SG_1	A_v	SG_2-SG_1	A_v	SG_2-SG_1	A_v
0	0	0.009	6.4	0.018	14.1
0.0015	1	0.010	7.2	0.019	15.1
0.002	1.3	0.011	8	0.020	16
0.003	2	0.012	8.8	0.021	17
0.004	2.7	0.013	9.7	0.022	18
0.005	3.4	0.014	10.5	0.023	19
0.006	4.1	0.015	11.4	0.024	20
0.007	4.9	0.016	12.3	0.025	21
0.008	5.6	0.017	13.2	0.026	22

induce an error of approximately 0.8 percent on the alcoholic strength. If we wish to measure A_v with an accuracy better than 0.5% ABV, then we must be more precise with the measure of SG.

REQUIRED MATERIALS

- Precision hydrometer with a resolution of 0.0005 on SG or better
- Thermometer
- Boiling flask (a coffeepot will do)
- Volumetric flask or graduated cylinder, 250 mL
- Distilled water (approximately 300 mL)

PROCEDURE

- Make sure the distilled water and cider sample are at room temperature.
- Measure the SG and temperature of the cider sample. This will be SG_1.

- Measure exactly 250 mL of cider and pour into the boiling flask.
- Rinse the volumetric flask or graduated cylinder used above with a bit of distilled water and pour into the boiling flask.
- Boil the cider until about half is evaporated. The kitchen stove will do for this.
- Let cool until room temperature is reached, then pour back into the volumetric flask or graduated cylinder. There should be between 100 and 150 mL of liquid.
- Rinse the boiling flask with a bit of distilled water and pour into the measuring flask.
- Top up the volume of the residue with distilled water until it is exactly 250 mL.
- Measure the SG and temperature. Ideally, the temperature will be the same as measured on the sample. If it is still too warm, you may wait a bit more or do a temperature correction as discussed in the article on hydrometers, section 8.2. This will be SG_2.
- Compute the SG difference and obtain the alcoholic strength from the table or regression formula.

A variant of the method is to use $(1 - SG_1 / SG_2)$ in table 14.5 instead of $(SG_2 - SG_1)$. This variant is called the *division formula*, while the original is called the *subtraction formula*. There was quite a bit of discussion in the late 1800s in the scientific community as to which of the two formulae was the most accurate; as far as I know, a consensus was never reached. For normal cider-making practice, however, the difference is quite negligible, as may be seen from this example:

Assume a dry cider with an SG_1 of 1.000 and SG_2 of the residue 1.0097. We have seen that the subtraction formula will yield a value of 7% for

A_V. The division formula in this case will give: $(1 - SG_1 / SG_2) = 0.0096$, for a value of A_V of 6.9 percent. However, with a sweet cider that could have an SG of 1.025, for example, the difference between the results from the two formulae would be larger and could attain 0.3 percent.

Other Methods for Measuring Alcoholic Strength

VINOMETER

The vinometer is a simple and inexpensive glass apparatus that looks roughly like a small funnel with a long, thin stem. It gives an estimation of the alcoholic strength using the properties of capillarity and surface tension of the wine or cider. However, a vinometer will give an accurate result only if a pure solution of alcohol and water is tested. The residual sugar and other solids in solution in the cider will alter the result substantially. The tests I have done with a vinometer on cider didn't yield sufficiently satisfying results to warrant its recommendation.

HYDROMETER AND REFRACTOMETER METHOD

This method uses a reading of the Brix of the cider sample with a refractometer, combined with a reading of its SG with a hydrometer, to obtain the estimated alcoholic strength of the cider. The principle is that the refractive index and the density respond differently to the alcohol presence in a solution: the density is reduced by the alcohol, while the refractive index is increased. The method is thus very quick and inexpensive, since many cider makers already have the required measuring instruments.

The alcoholic strength is deduced from an empirical relation. Many such relations have been proposed by different authors, but most are applicable to wine. The selection of an appropriate one for cider analysis is surely not a simple task, and I have never seen that such relations had been specifically derived for cider. One of the popular relations for wine has been published on the Internet by Werner Roesener and goes as follows (after slight rearranging):

$$A_V \text{ (\% ABV)} = 1.518 \, Bx - 365 \, (SG - 1)$$

This method is usually considered to be accurate to within ±0.5% ABV for wine. However, since the residual solids in cider have a different composition from those in wine, and considering that these constituents may influence the refractive index, it would be surprising if the same accuracy could be attained. We can also see from the relation that the result has more sensitivity to a measurement error in Brix than in SG: an imprecision of 0.5°Bx with the refractometer measurement will give an error of 0.75% ABV, and an imprecision of 0.001 in the measure of SG would cause an error of 0.36% ABV in the result. In conclusion, I doubt that this method would provide an accuracy better than ±1% ABV for cider, and though it may be used for a very rough and quick estimation of the alcoholic strength, it would not be accurate enough to satisfy a commercial cider maker's labeling requirements.

EBULLIOMETER

The ebulliometer relies on the principle that the boiling point of an alcoholic solution will vary with the alcoholic strength. The Dujardin-Salleron

Figure 14.7. Dujardin-Salleron ebulliometer.

strength would continuously decrease as the alcohol evaporates if the vapors were left to escape, and it would be impossible to take a measurement. Nowadays there are electronic ebulliometers that have a digital reading, but the old traditional model still sells. It is important to note the ebulliometer will give an accurate measurement only on dry wine or cider because the presence of sugar changes the boiling point of the solution.

To take a measurement, you must first make a run with pure water, since the boiling point is influenced by the atmospheric pressure. You record this and then test the samples. If the session is long, it is good procedure to retest a pure water sample once in a while to make sure the atmospheric pressure hasn't changed. The disk seen in figure 14.7 allows you to translate the temperature reading into an alcoholic strength.

The ebulliometer is routinely used in many commercial cideries, as it is not too expensive (from a commercial point of view) and is quick and sufficiently accurate for legal labeling requirements. The precision obtained on the alcoholic strength is better than ±0.5% ABV and would probably be within ±0.2% ABV most of the time.

Secondhand ebulliometers are easily found for a good price on the Internet, particularly from eBay France. I was able to get a 1932 Dujardin-Salleron in perfect working condition for $140 plus shipping from France. Another type is also often seen, the Malligand ebullioscope, which features a thermometer bent in an L shape. I must say I find the Malligand instrument more elegant, but its disadvantage is that it is not made anymore (although a copy still is in Italy), making it more difficult to obtain spare parts for it. There is also some evidence that the Dujardin-Salleron instrument is more accurate.

ebulliometer shown in figure 14.7 sells today for about $800 and is practically unchanged since its development in late 1800s. The instrument includes an alcohol burner that heats a sample of the cider, a precision thermometer, and a condensing system for the vapors, since the alcoholic

DISTILLATION

Distillation is the most accurate method of measuring alcoholic strength and is often used in research laboratories. A good, dedicated distillation apparatus costs less than $1,000, and this isn't really expensive for a commercial cidery. However, the manipulation requires precision and is time consuming, which is the main reason why it is not routinely used in cider making.

It is relatively easy for a hobbyist to build a distillation kit for less than $100 from a boiling flask (a glass coffeepot could work for this), a condenser, some rubber stoppers, and tubing. Such a kit would probably not be as precise as the dedicated apparatus of the trade, mainly because it would lack a splash guard, the joints could leak slightly, and the condenser could let some vapors go through, but it might still give quite accurate results if carefully made and used. (A splash guard is a sort of barrier at the exit of the boiling flask that prevents tiny drops of the boiling liquid to be carried with the vapors and subsequently altering the result.)

The procedure to make a measurement would be as follows:

- Measure a quantity of cider to test and note its temperature. Usually 250 mL is sufficient, but this depends also on the boiling flask capacity, the hydrometer, and the hydrometer jar you have. A volumetric flask would be preferable for this measure, but a graduated cylinder will also do. Pour the measured cider into the boiling flask.
- Rinse the volumetric flask or graduated cylinder used above with a bit of distilled water and pour into the boiling flask.

- Install the tubing and condenser, start heating, and put a receiving container under the exit of the condenser for the distillate. This receiving container could be the same you used for the measure.
- Boil the cider until about half is evaporated. Stop the heat.
- Complete the distillate with store-bought distilled water to exactly the same volume you measured in the beginning (i.e., 250 mL). Make sure this volume measurement is made at the same temperature as for the first measure.

You now have a solution that contains all the alcohol that was in the cider this time diluted in pure water. From the density of this distillate, then, you can obtain the cider's alcoholic strength. In the case of a cider, the SG of this solution would be between 0.988 and 0.994. You may use:

- A close-range precision SG hydrometer and alcoholometric table to obtain the strength in alcohol, or
- A special hydrometer graduated for alcohol measurement. There are on the market hydrometers with a range of 0 to 20 proof, or 0–10% ABV, with a resolution of 0.1% ABV that are perfect for this and are sold at a very reasonable price (around $30).
- At a much higher cost (around $100 each), there are thermohydrometers for alcohol that are more precise than the previous one and that have a shorter range (i.e., 0 to 5% ABV, 5 to 10%, 10 to 15%, and so on). These would be primarily for research.

As a cross-check, once you have finished you may take the residue that remains in the boiling flask and test it according to the simple procedure seen earlier.

A final word about volatile acidity (see also chapter 16 on cider troubles): if the cider contains a sizable amount of volatile acidity, this acidity will distill with the alcohol and be present in the distillate, thus altering slightly its density and the result. For a hobbyist, this error may be neglected, but for the most accurate results the acidity of the cider should be neutralized with a base before proceeding with the distillation.

When done in a laboratory environment with a high-quality distillation apparatus, this method yields a result with an accuracy of approximately ±0.1% ABV. When done by a hobbyist with a do-it-yourself kit, the same accuracy cannot be reached, but probably ±0.5% ABV or even better could be achieved.

CONCLUDING REMARKS

For a hobbyist, the estimation by gravity drop or the use of the model described earlier is generally sufficient. The simple residue method may also prove useful as a cross-check. For a commercial cider maker, something better is required, mainly because of the legal requirement to give a more or less accurate alcoholic strength on the label. The accuracy required varies from one country to another, and tax rates may change with the alcoholic strength, so it is important to take into account the local laws on this matter. For example, in the United States, although the alcoholic strength as given on the label doesn't need to be very accurate, the cider maker needs to know for sure if the cider is above or below 7% ABV, as the tax rate changes once this level is crossed. Hence, for a commercial cider maker the ebulliometer could be a valuable investment. The alternative would be to send cider samples to a dedicated laboratory that does such analyses for wineries and cideries. And, by the way, such a laboratory probably wouldn't use one of the methods described here but rather some new generation of electronic wine analyzer that may have an accuracy of ±0.1% ABV and can analyze up to thirty samples in an hour. There are a few such instruments that also permit many other analyses, but unfortunately their cost puts them out of reach for most cideries.

CIDER DIVERSITY

As the fermentation is complete, we are left with a fermentation vessel containing a still and usually dry cider, that is unless some stabilization rackings were done to make the fermentation stop while there is still some residual sugar. It should then be racked to separate the cider from its lees (this is the final racking) and may be bottled as is, using the simple bottling procedure seen in the first part of this book, or it may be kegged or put in bulk storage, for example if we wish to do some post-fermentation blending. We may already have quite a bit of diversity from such still ciders: from different types of blends and apple varieties, different yeasting strategies, from whether malolactic fermentation has occurred or not. . . . However, cider makers often like to have different styles for different occasions. Also, as we cider makers drink cider rather often, it is nice to have a lot of diversity in our batches: sweet ciders, sparkling ciders, and even ice ciders. This way we don't so much have the impression of always drinking the same thing!

◀ 15.1 ▶
Sweetness in Cider

Many cider makers would like to produce a cider that retains some residual sugars, as such mild sweetness counterbalances the natural acidity of the cider and makes it smoother. Unfortunately, the way things normally go is that the yeasts will keep at their work until all the sugars are fermented, leaving a bone-dry cider at the end. Further, if sugar is added at bottling, this sugar, too, will ferment in the bottles, and the final product will be a sparkling dry cider, unless some other methods, like pasteurization or the addition of chemical compounds (sulfite, sorbate) or unfermentable sweeteners are used to prevent such an in-bottle re-fermentation. All these methods have their drawbacks. But there is another approach that consists of creating a nutrient-depleted medium where the yeasts will not find the minimum requirements that would permit them to perform their task completely. This process involves a pre-fermentation clarification of the must called a *keeve* (*défécation* in French), where the pectins present in the juice are modified under the action of an enzyme to develop into a gel that rises on top of the must and forms a gelatinous crust called a *chapeau brun* (*brown cap*). In the English cider makers' community, keeved ciders are sometimes regarded as a sort of Holy Grail of cider making. In France cider makers have traditionally made cider this way since the nineteenth century, and it is still commonly made with a modernized version of this process even in large commercial operations.

The Sweetness Perception

The amount of residual sugar present in the cider at the time of consumption will determine the sweetness perception. We use three main categories for cider: dry, medium, and sweet, and the dry and medium may be further divided into two subcategories. Table 15.1 indicates the approximate amount of residual sugar required (in grams per liter) to give the sweetness perception corresponding to each of these categories.

The approximate specific gravity (SG) in the last line of the table is based on a cider that would have an SG of 1.000 at complete dryness, which is normally the case if it was made from a juice that had the average amount of sugar for its density (see section 14.5 on alcohol), that wasn't chaptalized, and that didn't undergo malolactic fermentation. Otherwise, the SG at complete dryness may be as low as 0.995, and a correction should be done accordingly.

The boundaries between the different categories are somewhat arbitrary and may vary depending on the source. For table 15.1, I have set them in accordance with the Beer Judge Certification Program (BJCP) guidelines, which are used for most cider competitions in North America, such as GLINTCAP. (Note the BJCP Guidelines are currently undergoing revision, and there might be minor differences in the names of the categories.) The Quebec cider regulations have slightly different boundaries, in particular for the definition of a sweet cider, which should contain 50 g/L of residual sugar. And some countries have very strict regulations on the sweetness indication that may appear on a label. In France, for example, this is ruled by the "Décret du 29 juillet 1987," which specifies the following categories:

- **Brut**: residual sugar less than 28 g/L (we can see that this covers from the very dry category up to medium-sweet),
- **Demi-sec**: residual sugar between 28 and 42 g/L,
- **Doux**: more than 35 g/L residual sugar, but with an alcoholic strength of less than 3% ABV.

In England the dry-medium-sweet categories are also used, but there is no consensus as to the boundaries between these. I have looked at the rules from three well-known competitions held in the southwest of England, and for two of them the break

TABLE 15.1:

Sweetness categories for cider

	DRY		MEDIUM		SWEET
	DRY	**OFF-DRY**	**MEDIUM**	**MEDIUM-SWEET**	
RESIDUAL SUGAR in g/L	0 to 4	4 to 9	9 to 20	20 to 40	more than 40
RESIDUAL SUGAR in percent	0 to 0.4	0.4 to 0.9	0.9 to 2	2 to 4	> 4
SG (approximate)	1.000 to 1.002	1.002 to 1.004	1.004 to 1.009	1.009 to 1.019	> 1.019

point between dry and medium was at SG 1.005, while it was at SG 1.008 for the third. Similarly, the break point between medium and sweet was set at SG 1.012 for one and SG 1.015 for the two others.

In any case, sweetness perception varies from one individual to another. Someone who usually drinks and enjoys very dry wines and ciders will often consider a cider to be sweet even if it contains relatively less sugar. Table 15.1, then, should serve as just a rough guide. Further, the acidity will also influence the sweetness perception: a cider with a high level of acidity may give a dry perception even if it contains 10 g/L of sugar, and, conversely, a cider with low acidity may give a medium perception at 8 g/L of sugar.

The Keeving Process

In the traditional French method, the ground pomace was left for maceration until the next day before pressing. This permitted the action of the enzymes pectin methyl-esterase (PME), which are naturally present in the apple flesh, to start the transformation of the pectinic acids into demethylated pectic acids (see chapter 12 on pectins). Later, a few days after pressing, the cider maker would add some calcium, usually in the form of chalk or ashes, and a bit of table salt. The calcium combines with the demethylated pectic acids to produce calcium pectate, an insoluble gel that traps the tiny bubbles of carbon dioxide produced by the fermentation slowly starting. This gel is then pushed upward by the gas bubbles and compacts itself into a sort of thick, brown, gelatinous crust: the *chapeau brun*. This gel also traps most of the impurities present in the must, a good part of the nitrogenous substances that act as yeast nutrients, as well as many yeast cells, including most of the apiculate and spoiling yeasts. Once the *chapeau brun* has fully formed, the must underneath it is perfectly clear and is then racked off into a new vessel. At that point, the must contains far fewer yeast cells and yeast nutrients and undergoes a much slower fermentation that ideally becomes "stuck" at the desired density to yield a stable cider that retains some residual sweetness.

The success of this traditional method relied heavily on the amount of natural PME present in the apple flesh. And it can be assumed that older

French cider apples were selected on their ability to keeve naturally. Nowadays, however, PME is produced microbiologically and is available for purchase. The use of this enzyme removes a lot of the randomness associated with keeving. The PME enzyme is used by the food industry and up until recently was still quite difficult to procure in the small quantities required by cider makers (and even more so for the hobbyist), except in France, where it is distributed in a special formulation with a calcium salt solution for cider makers under the trademark Klercidre and distributed by Laboratoires Standa (www.standa-fr.com). But things are changing, and now some North American suppliers have started to distribute PME in small quantities through the Internet (cidersupply.com).

FAVORABLE CONDITIONS FOR A SUCCESSFUL KEEVE

Even with the use of added PME and calcium salt, the success of a keeve is not assured. The two most common reasons for failure are that the fermentation starts before the *chapeau brun* has had time to form and that there are not enough pectins in the juice. It may also happen that a must that has gone through a successful keeve still has enough nitrogenous nutrients so that the fermentation may proceed to dryness. So to insure the maximum probability for success, the following guidelines are aimed at delaying the start of natural fermentation, reducing the nutrient content of the juice, and insuring an adequate level of pectic substances:

- Varieties that are known to contain less nitrogen and more pectins should be chosen. These will generally be late-maturing apples, as late varieties are slower to start a natural fermentation.

Some experimentation is, however, still required in order to assess these qualities among North American apples. In England the varieties described as vintage usually have those qualities.

- The apples should be fully ripe and even at the point of being overripe (i.e., starting to become soft), as the concentration of soluble pectinic acids increases with the ripening process, and the concentration of soluble nitrogenous substances decreases.
- Cultural practices that decrease the nitrogen concentration should be preferred (i.e., apples from unfertilized older standard trees rather than apples from an intensive high-production orchard).
- The temperature in the press room and cider room should be around 46–50°F (8–10°C). Over 54°F (12°C) there is a much-increased risk of a rapid start of fermentation. Under 43°F (6°C) the reactions will be much slower, and the *chapeau brun* will need more time to form. However, according to Warcollier (1928), temperatures as low as 40°F (4°C) are still adequate for a successful keeve.
- Maceration of the pulp (see beginning of Part III) is recommended, although not considered absolutely necessary. Modern French publications suggest between two and eight hours of maceration (Bauduin, 2006), but only if the temperature is low enough. Otherwise, maceration could promote a rapid start of fermentation. As mentioned above, the naturally present PME enzyme will start working during maceration, and among other things this makes it possible to extract more of the pectins present in the flesh. Some cider makers even spray some PME on the pulp just after milling. During maceration there will also be some oxidation of the tannins, and this will give color to the cider.

- Of the juice properties, it is often said that juices should be high in density, as this makes it easier for the gel to rise and float. And although a minimum SG of 1.055 is sometimes recommended, I have made successful keeves with juice that had an SG as low as 1.050. Also, I have seen mentioned that only low-acidity juices obtained from bittersweet apples can be keeved successfully. However, based on my tests, this doesn't seem to be an issue, as I have had successful keeves from Cortland and Liberty apples, which have quite high values of acidity.

My keeves have always been successful when I have used later-maturing apples, and in particular the Cortland variety. I do in general leave the pulp to macerate for a couple of hours. The few failures that I had always occurred when I tried a keeve with a first-season blend of earlier-maturing varieties. A good practice would be to prepare the keeved cider as one of the last batches of the season: the temperature is then colder, and the apples are fully ripe. It should be noted, however, that if the keeve fails, the must may still be fermented in the usual way to yield a very good dry cider.

PREPARATION OF THE KEEVE

The vessel for the keeve should be higher than it is wide, though some French publications advise against a height over 6 feet (2 meters). The vessel should be filled to no more than 85 percent of its capacity, as some space is required for the *chapeau brun*. It should also be kept in mind that about 20 percent of the juice will be lost in the *chapeau brun*; hence, a provision should be made as a function of the size of the fermenter. Some extra juice should also be set aside for filling the carboy after the rackings have been done. For example, if a 5-gallon carboy is to be used as fermenter, the required quantity of juice should be at least 6.5 gal (25 L), and an 8-gallon (30-liter) plastic pail would make an adequate vessel for the keeve. A hermetic lid is not required for the keeve vessel, but some cover should be used to protect the must while keeving.

Just after pressing, the PME enzyme should be added to the juice, ideally as the keeve vessel is filled. The quantity required is very small: 7 to 10 grams or mL depending on whether it is in powder or liquid form, for 100 liters of juice, which makes 70 to 100 ppm. Hence for a 5-gallon batch, you need 6.5 gal (25 L) of juice and would use 2 to 2.5 grams of PME. If the enzyme is old (one or two years), this dosage may be increased, as the PME loses some of its activity after a while. The oldest PME I have used was three years old, and a dose of 150 ppm yielded a successful keeve. The enzyme should be kept in the refrigerator to maximize its shelf life.

A day or two later, the calcium salt should be added to the must and well mixed. The ideal is calcium chloride ($CaCl_2$) at a dosage of 400 to 500 ppm. Calcium chloride may be procured either as an aqueous solution of varying strength or as a salt. In the latter case, it will usually be a hydrated salt, with the chemical formula $CaCl_2-2H_2O$ or $CaCl_2-6H_2O$. Depending on the form, the dosage would be as follows to obtain 450 ppm of $CaCl_2$:

- Aqueous solution, 33 percent in weight: 140 mL per 100 L of must
- Hydrated salt, $CaCl_2-2H_2O$: 60 grams per 100 L of must
- Hydrated salt, $CaCl_2-6H_2O$: 90 grams per 100 L of must

Food-grade calcium chloride is not commonly found except in cheese-making supply stores. An easier-to-procure alternative is a mixture of calcium carbonate (ground chalk) and table salt. The dosage would then be 40 grams each per 100 L of must. I have used this alternative a few times when I didn't have calcium chloride on hand, and it worked perfectly.

Should the juice be sulfited? There is no definitive answer to this question. The standard method, as done in France, is to use unsulfited juice. However, if you usually sulfite your juice before starting the fermentation and prefer it that way, you may still do so, but with a dosage of about half the normal amount (see the articles on sulfite and yeasts, sections 14.1 and 14.2), so that you would then have wild yeast fermenting in a partially sterilized must. In all cases sulfite will delay the start of the fermentation, and if for some reason you think the fermentation might start before the *chapeau brun* has had time to form, then sulfite might save your keeve. In particular, if the temperature in the cider room is too high, sulfite could be a way to retard the start of the fermentation and allow time for the rise of the *chapeau brun*.

A second question is, how about using cultured yeasts? Here I would have to say no, because the whole point of doing a keeve is to promote a slow fermentation that will become stuck when there is still some residual sugar. Adding a cultured yeast goes against this objective. Actually, I did it once on a cider whose fermentation was much too slow: after two months, the SG had dropped by only 3 points, so I thought I had to do something and added a cultured yeast with a very small amount of nutrients. The result was that I was never able to stop the fermentation after that, and it proceeded all the way to dryness, even though I did some stabilization rackings in an attempt to slow it.

THE RISE OF THE *CHAPEAU BRUN*

The following pictures illustrate the formation and rise of the *chapeau brun*. Within about a week after introduction of the calcium salt, a gel should start to form in the must (see figure 15.1). The time required for this gel to form will vary depending on the temperature and the quantity of pectins in the juice. This particular photo was taken eight days after the addition of calcium. In figures 15.2 and 15.3, the gel has begun to rise. For this to happen, there has to be a start of fermentation that produces some carbon dioxide gas. The gas gets trapped by the gel, and this is what makes the gel float on top of the cleared must. The first three photos were taken at intervals of two days between each.

Figure 15.1. Chapeau brun, day 8.

Although the photo of day 12 shows a *chapeau brun* that seems well formed, it is not yet ready for racking, and it is a common mistake to rack too early. Before racking, the cider should be checked with a turkey baster inserted through the *chapeau brun* to make sure it is clear of gel. In figure 15.4 of day 16 it can be seen that the *chapeau brun* is more compacted and drier. I could then proceed with racking (figure 15.5). We call this first racking the *keeve racking*.

When all goes well, the keeve racking will yield a nice, translucent must that will ferment slowly under the action of the natural wild yeasts. Figure 15.6 on page 262 shows two carboys of fermenting ciders: the one on the left is a keeved cider, and the one on the right is a cider prepared the usual way. The light from the camera flash goes right through the keeved cider, while the other one is opaque. Sometimes, however, things happen a bit differently. Figure 15.7 on page 262 shows a cider that started to ferment before the *chapeau brun* had time to rise. After the primary, or turbulent, fermentation, I racked the cider as I usually do for an unkeeved cider, and, surprisingly, a gel formed a few days after the racking, and the cider cleared beautifully. I was then able to rack the cleared cider, and, finally, this failed (or delayed) keeve yielded an excellent cider, very similar to the result of a successfully keeved cider. Such a gel may also form when the keeve racking was performed too soon, which is an easy mistake to do, but which doesn't have serious consequences.

Figure 15.2. Day 10.

Figure 15.3. Day 12.

Figure 15.4. Day 16.

Figure 15.5. Keeve racking.

Figure 15.6. Cleared and opaque ciders.

Figure 15.7. Late keeve.

THE FERMENTATION

The fermentation phases in the case of a keeved cider are slightly different from those of an un-keeved cider (described in section 14.3). In particular, there is no turbulent fermentation. After the keeve racking, the cider enters a mode of fermentation that is rather like a secondary fermentation phase, very quiet, and with a slow fermentation speed that should be around 40–80 FSU and slowing down as the fermentation proceeds. If the fermentation is faster than that, a stabilization racking should be done rather quickly. And if the fermentation is much too slow, you may follow the tips I give in section 14.3 for increasing the speed of fermentation. A cultured yeast inoculation

should, however, be done only as a last resort, as there is a risk that it will ferment the cider all the way to dryness.

Once the density has dropped to an SG of about 1.030, the fermentation speed should have decreased to about 10–20 FSU. If it is higher than that, a stabilization racking is necessary to slow it down at this stage. It might also be necessary to lower the temperature. The fermentation speed should be reevaluated about ten to fifteen days after the racking, and an additional racking might have to be done if the speed is still too fast.

Assuming the fermentation speed is well under control, the density should drop slowly and eventually approach the target SG you have for this cider. For example, if you wish to make a medium-sweet cider that would have a finished SG of 1.015, a stabilization racking should be done when the density is about 2 to 4 points higher than this target SG: at 1.018 would be good in this case. After this racking, the fermentation speed should be around 5 FSU (twenty days for a drop of 1 point of density), and the cider may be left another two to three months, by which time it will have matured and slowly stabilized to a density close to the target. It will then be time to bottle it. Note that if the fermentation speed is lower than 4 FSU at bottling time, the cider will stay pretty flat in the bottle, or it might develop a little bit of carbonation, but not much. To get a sparkling sweet cider, you would have to bottle it while the speed is slightly higher than that number. See section 15.2 on sparkling ciders for more details.

CONCLUDING REMARKS

Obtaining a naturally sweet cider by the keeving process may be tricky, and success is not always assured. The method relies heavily on a successful keeve followed by some rackings done at the right moment. You should plan to make about three rackings, and after each of these you will need to fill the carboy to the top. Thus, it is important to have some spare cider from the keeve racking that may be fermented separately, in a small half-gallon bottle, for example, or kept in the refrigerator for topping up. An extra carboy will also be required for the rackings. Another point is that all this is very slow: the whole process is designed to reduce the speed of fermentation, so a keeved cider may need a full year before it is ready for bottling. The cider maker's patience is essential.

A hobbyist cider maker generally uses racking only as a tool to manage the fermentation, with sometimes help from some control of the temperature. It is important to realize that this will not always permit you to attain your exact target SG. We have to accept that sometimes the cider decides for us, and there is not much we can do, whatever our skill. In large commercial operations in France, additional tools are used, including filtering and centrifugation, that yield more reliable results. Unfortunately, the cost of the equipment that's necessary to do these methods usually puts them out of reach for a hobbyist.

Other Methods to Obtain a Sweet Cider

In the beginning of this article, I briefly mentioned other methods to obtain a cider that retains some residual sugar. I now review these in a little more detail.

SUGAR ADDITION

The most obvious method would be simply to add either table sugar or dextrose to dry cider at bottling time. However, there will always be some yeasts left in the cider, so eventually this added sugar will re-ferment in the bottle to yield a dry and sparkling cider. In technical terms this would be called an unstable sweet cider. One way to overcome this problem is to keep the sweetened cider cold and drink it quickly before the re-fermentation has had time to kick in. In the refrigerator such a cider may keep for about a month, while at room temperature ten days would be the maximum recommended shelf life.

MULTIPLE RACKINGS

This is a method that I use fairly regularly. In general it will not produce a cider as sweet as is possible with the keeving method, but it yields some excellent off-dry or medium-dry ciders. Because I have old, standard apple trees, and my orchard is not fertilized, when I started making cider I quite regularly had some stuck fermentations from my later cider batches of the season. At the time I took measures to restart those stuck fermentations in order to obtain dry ciders. It took me some time before I realized that these were in fact a gift of the gods, as they allowed me to make ciders of excellent quality that contained a good amount of natural residual sugar. And eventually I started to encourage these stuck fermentations by doing multiple stabilization rackings, as described in section 14.3.

Note that this method will not work with all ciders, and the conditions that are favorable for a successful keeve, outlined above, are also required here. If you see that your cider starts fermenting at high speed, then the odds are slight that you can stop it by multiple stabilization rackings. But if at the moment of the first racking you see that the speed has been reasonable since the start of fermentation, say, 120 FSU or less, then there is an excellent chance that the method will work. The first racking should be done at relatively high SG, as soon as the turbulent fermentation is finished. Then if the speed reduces to somewhere between 20 and 50 FSU while the SG is still above 1.030 after the first racking, you are on a good track. Once you have been successful in controlling the speed, you may treat this cider in the same way you would a keeved cider and follow the tips given above.

PASTEURIZATION

One way to achieve a stable sweet cider by sugar addition is to kill the yeast cells remaining in the cider by pasteurization after bottling. Such a pasteurized cider may then have a long shelf life without fear of re-fermentation. I will not enter here into a description of a pasteurization unit. Good instructions and models can be found on the Internet, and a hobbyist can easily construct a simple stovetop unit. The recommended pasteurization temperature for cider is 149°F (65°C), so the unit should have the capacity to heat the cider inside the bottle to that temperature, maintain this temperature for about ten minutes. Then the bottles may be taken out of the bath for cooling. An easy way to monitor the cider temperature is to keep an open bottle filled with water in the bath with the bottles of cider: you can then measure the temperature in that bottle and assume the temperature in the bottles of cider (which are sealed) is the same. A drawback of pasteurization is that, if overdone, it affects the flavor, giving a slight cooked taste to the cider. Hence, the temperature should not exceed the recommended value given above.

ARTIFICIAL SWEETENERS

The use of artificial sweeteners (or sugar substitutes) is an easy way to obtain a cider that gives a perception of sweetness and is a method adopted by some craft cider makers, notably in England. These sweeteners are not fermentable by the yeasts, thus the cider will remain stable. They are added to the mature dry cider at bottling time. An interesting feature of artificial sweeteners is that they do not increase the density of the cider; hence, you may measure an SG of 1.000 while having the perception of a medium-sweet cider that should normally have an SG of 1.015 (see table 15.1 on page 257). The most-recommended sweetener for use in cider is *sucralose* (sold under the trade name Splenda). Since its sweetening effect is 600 times that of table sugar, only minute amounts are required to sweeten a large quantity of cider. We are talking here of adding only about 50 ppm of pure sucralose to achieve a medium cider. This is 50 mg per liter, or 1 g (approximately ¼ tsp) for a 5-gallon carboy. It is, however, difficult to procure pure sucralose in reasonable quantities for cider making, and Splenda, which is easy to get, contains only an infinitesimal quantity of sucralose. The other sweetener often used for cider is *saccharin*. It has half the sweetening effect of sucralose, but this is still 300 times more than table sugar. Saccharin has been around for a much longer time than sucralose and has been used for sweetening cider in England for over 100 years, to the extent that it is now considered "traditional." Some cider drinkers, however, dislike the aftertaste given by saccharin, and many craft cider makers on the Internet discussion lists strongly object to it. I have never tried it, so I can't judge.

COLD-STOPPED FERMENTATION AND STERILE FILTRATION

This method calls for arresting the fermentation by refrigerating the cider to a temperature close to the freezing point when it has reached the desired sweetness. In practice this is done in tanks equipped with a refrigerating coil. After a few days, the yeast drops to the bottom of the tank and the cider is then filtered. Many stages of filtration may be necessary to finish with a half-micron filter pad, which will remove the remaining yeast cells. The cider may then be bottled. The filtration and bottling head need to be sterile, otherwise the cider could pick up some microorganisms (after the last filter) that would restart fermentation in the bottles. Normally, some additives will also be used, such as sulfite and sorbate, to insure stability and a long shelf life. This is a method that is also used for stabilization of ice cider, and it requires equipment beyond what a hobbyist is likely to have. On the other hand, this is the technique most often used in commercial cideries, as once the required equipment is acquired, the process is quite straightforward and reliable.

◀ 15.2 ▶
Bubbles in the Cider

Sparkling wines like Champagne have always been associated with celebrations. There is something festive about bubbles! And ciders are no exception. Visually, a sparkling cider features bubbles that rise to the surface, where they may make a white foam, thicker as we pour the cider and generally vanishing after a while. But there is more to a sparkling cider than just the sight of the bubbles: the aroma and taste perceptions are also affected, as we will see below.

The *effervescence* is the feature of a sparkling, *pétillant*, or fizzy cider. This effervescence is provoked by a gas, carbon dioxide, which is in solution in the cider. The gas induces pressure in the bottle, which thus needs to be robust enough to withstand that pressure. As the bottle is opened, the pressure is relieved: this decreases markedly the solubility of the gas almost instantly. Thus, what was initially in solution in the liquid changes to a gaseous state and escapes the liquid as bubbles that rise toward the surface. Depending on the quantity of carbon dioxide in solution, this process may be fairly quiet, as in a slightly *pétillant* cider; or quite intense, as in a fully sparkling one; or even explosive, if you overdo it. Also noteworthy: a small part of the carbon dioxide in solution is transformed into carbonic acid, which modifies the taste of the cider, giving it a slightly biting and pleasant flavor. The smell is also modified, as the bubbles contain some of the aromatic qualities of the cider, which is thereby enhanced.

The Effervescence

There are two principal ways to obtain carbon dioxide in solution: by fermentation or by injection.

Natural carbonation, or *prise de mousse* in French, is a technique that permits the retention of some CO_2 produced by fermentation. There are many variants, but in most cases it involves provoking a controlled fermentation that will produce the desired quantity of CO_2 in a hermetically sealed vessel. As this gas can't escape, it will stay in solution. This approach is discussed in more detail below.

Forced or *artificial carbonation* is a process by which CO_2 is injected under pressure until saturation. This is the technique used in the industry to give the sparkle in carbonated drinks, including mineral water and soft drinks. The method is well adapted for industrial production but may also be used on a small scale by hobbyist cider makers. Once carbonated, the cider may be bottled, but most often small-scale producers will instead serve the cider directly from the pressurized vessel: we then have a draft cider, which is popular in England in particular. For hobbyists and small-scale producers, it is relatively easy to procure secondhand *Cornelius kegs* that are used for soda and are available in a 5-gallon size. Beer kegs can also be used. Note that when the cider has been artificially carbonated, many laws require that it be indicated on the label. Such ciders generally will not have the delicacy and quality of those obtained by natural carbonation: the bubbles are larger and the foam vanishes more quickly. See the sidebar on use of CO_2 on pages 276–278 for more details.

VOLUMES OF CO_2 AND CARBONATION

There may be different levels of effervescence depending on the amount of carbon dioxide dissolved in the cider. An often-used unit of measurement is the number of *volumes* of dissolved CO_2, which is defined as follows:

One volume of CO_2 (designated 1 vol) corresponds to the quantity of CO_2 in gaseous form at 0°C and atmospheric pressure that would occupy the same volume as the liquid in which it is dissolved. For example, if we want to carbonate 1 liter of cider to 1 volume of CO_2, we need 1.977 grams of CO_2 in solution, as the density of gaseous CO_2 is 1.977 grams per liter at 0°C under atmospheric pressure.

Then, expressed in volumes of CO_2, the classes of carbonation as defined by the Quebec "Regulation respecting cider and other apple-based alcoholic beverages" and also used by the BJCP for competitions in North America are:

- **Sparkling** (*mousseux* or *bouché* in French), when the cider contains between 3.5 and 5.5 volumes of CO_2. Such a cider will form a good foam as it is poured. In France the term *cidre bouché* is more often used for a traditionally made farm cider, which can be slightly cloudy and may contain lees, whereas a *cidre mousseux* will normally be perfectly clear and without deposits.
- *Pétillant*, crackling or semisparkling, when the cider contains between 1.5 and 2.5 volumes of CO_2. This cider produces a little foam that vanishes quickly when poured into a glass, but the sparkle is easily seen by the bubbles rising to the surface.
- **Still** (*tranquille* in French), when the cider contains no or up to 1 volume of dissolved CO_2. This cider doesn't produce any foam when poured into a glass, but it may be saturated with CO_2 (i.e., 1 vol of CO_2), and in that case there might be a few rising bubbles indicating a very slight effervescence (these would usually be seen a little while after pouring, as the cider warms up). This is called *perlant* by the French, and there is no proper English word to qualify it. *Perlant* ciders are very agreeable to drink, with a minimal carbonation that enhances the flavor.

In this book I consider the *perlant* category of ciders as distinct from the *still* ciders. And although this distinction is not officially recognized in the United States, my hope is that this will change in the future, because *perlant* ciders have their own personality, different from that of a cider with no carbonation at all.

Pressure Calculation

We may use Henry's law of gas solubility to predict the pressure in a closed container of sparkling cider. This same law will also permit us to determine how much pressure of CO_2 we need to force-carbonate a cider. Henry's law states that at constant temperature, the quantity of gas dissolved in a liquid is proportional to the partial pressure of this gas on top of the liquid. The mathematical formulation is:

$$c = k_H \, p_p$$

where:

p_p is the partial pressure of the gas (in our case, of the CO_2),

c is the concentration of the gas in solution,

k_H is the proportionality constant of Henry's law. Note that its value varies with temperature and also differs from one gas to another.

For us cider makers, the most practical way to use this law is by expressing the concentration in volumes of CO_2 (vol) and the pressure in atmospheres (1 atm is 14.7 psi or 1.013 bar or 101.3 kPa). The value for the k_H constant is normally given at a reference temperature, and there exist equations to calculate the value at different temperatures. From these I obtained table 15.2 on page 268.

This permits us to determine that, for example, in a cider that would contain 4 volumes of CO_2 in solution, the partial pressure of carbon dioxide in

TABLE 15.2:

Value of Henry's law constant for carbon dioxide as a function of temperature

°C	0	5	10	15	20	30	40	50	65
°F	32	41	50	59	68	86	104	122	149
k_H (vol/atm)	1.58	1.35	1.16	1.00	0.87	0.66	0.51	0.41	0.29

the container would be 2.5 atm at 32°F (0°C) and of 6 atm at 86°F (30°C). This helps us understand that as the bottle is opened, the pressure of the gas in the airspace under the stopper decreases suddenly, meaning the concentration of CO_2 in solution has to decrease proportionally: the gas that was in solution thus escapes the liquid, provoking the effervescence. Also, we can see that the warmer the bottle will be at the moment of opening, the less CO_2 may remain in solution, so there will be more escaping and sparkling.

Now, this partial pressure of CO_2 is not the same as the real, or effective, pressure the container (i.e., the bottle) will have to endure. On one hand, the partial pressure is an absolute pressure, and we want a relative pressure: we need to deduct the atmospheric pressure that surrounds the exterior of the bottle, 1 atm. On the other hand, at the moment of bottling there was some air in the bottle, also at a partial pressure of 1 atm. However, about half of this air will dissolve in the cider (still according to Henry's law, but this time applied to oxygen and nitrogen), so that at the end the combined partial pressure of oxygen and nitrogen is around 0.5 atm for a standard-size bottle. Hence, in total, we need to subtract approximately 0.5 atm from the partial pressure of CO_2 to obtain the pressure effectively endured by the bottle. We may then rearrange the equation seen above to obtain P, the effective pressure:

$$P = (c \, / \, k_H) - 0.5 \text{ atm}$$

This pressure calculation is interesting, but it is only really useful if we know the resistance of the bottle. For example, a good *champenoise* bottle is designed to resist 12 atm, and its weight is about 2 lb. (more precisely, between 860 and 900 grams). For the other types of bottles containing carbonated drinks, for example, beer, mineral water, or soda bottles, glass or plastic (PET), it is recommended that the effective pressure stay under 6 atm. And in all cases it is wise to maintain a good safety margin.

If we look again at our previous example of a cider carbonated to 4 volumes of CO_2, the effective pressure the bottle would have to resist would be 5.5 atm at 86°F (30°C), which is reasonable for a champagne-type bottle. It wouldn't be advisable to use a beer bottle for this cider, though, as the pressure is too close to the limit for such a bottle. However, we might want to pasteurize this cider to conserve some residual sugar. In this case, for a typical pasteurization temperature of 149°F (65°C), we use a value 0.29 for k_H, and we would obtain an effective pressure of about 13 atm in the bottle. At such a pressure, even the most robust bottles become potential bombs. This is why it is generally recommended to limit to 2.5 vols of CO_2 the carbonation for ciders that will be pasteurized and to use only top-quality champagne-type bottles.

Natural Carbonation, or *Prise de Mousse*

Natural carbonation by fermentation may be done in tanks or bottles by many methods. Patricia Howe (see "Sparkling Wines" in Lea and Piggott, 2003) describes a good dozen. I discuss only a few that are more often seen for cider.

BOTTLE CONDITIONING WITHOUT CLARIFICATION

This is the simplest method and the one I use for my own sparkling ciders. It is simply done by bottling the cider with some fermentable sugar. This sugar may be added at the moment of bottling (we then call it *priming sugar*) or may be some residual sugar remaining from an incomplete fermentation (see below on sugar dosage). Depending on the situation, yeast may be added to insure a good in-bottle re-fermentation. This method has the inconvenience that there remain some lees deposited on the bottom of the bottles, so the cider must be poured very carefully from the bottle. The advantage is that it doesn't require any special equipment and thus is well adapted for the hobbyist cider maker. Farm ciders are still sometimes made in this way, but these ciders are becoming less acceptable for marketing. In France ciders produced with this method may be called *cidre bouché* or *cidre fermier*, sometimes with the added designation *traditionel*. If the temperature is high enough and yeast is added, the conditioning may be completed in about a month. But better quality will be obtained if the cider is left longer at lower temperature. I personally think six months is a minimum and that a year of aging the cider in bottles is preferable.

Figure 15.8. Riddle rack, as used in Champagne. Photo courtesy of Wikimedia Commons

TRADITIONAL, OR CLASSICAL, METHOD

The traditional method is similar to the simple bottle-conditioning method, with the exception that the lees are removed at the end of the process. This is in fact the Champagne or *champenoise* method, but this name can no longer be used for anything other than a true Champagne wine. Hence, for cider we use one of the two above-mentioned descriptions if a method is to be included on the label. The removal of the lees is done by *riddling* and *disgorging*: the cider is first bottled as described above and capped with a temporary stopper, usually a crown cap, as these facilitate the disgorging operation that will be done later. Many producers use bentonite clay as a fining (clarifying) agent before bottling, as this improves the compaction of the lees. The bottles are then left for the bottle fermentation and aging on their lees for at least six months, though this can be longer. For true Champagne, this period needs to be at least fifteen months.

Once the aging is completed, the bottles are placed in an adjustable riddle rack (see figure 15.8 on page 269). At the beginning of the process, the bottles rest at an angle of 45°. Each day, the bottles are given a slight shake and turn, and their angle is slightly increased, until at the end the bottles are in a vertical position and all the lees are compacted in the neck. Riddling may have a duration of two to four weeks for cider (up to ten weeks for Champagne). Disgorging is the procedure by which the lees are removed: the neck of the bottle is placed in a brine bath (ice, water, and salt) that is colder than the freezing point. The contents of the neck, including the lees and a small amount of cider, freeze. The bottle is still upside down at this moment. It is given a slow rotation to bring it into an upright position, and while this movement is going on, the bottle is uncapped. The pressure then expels the slug of frozen slush from the neck. The bottles are topped up with some cider or a sweet syrup, depending on the type of cider wanted, and the final stopper is installed. This stopper may be a mushroom-type cork, as for Champagne, or a plastic stopper. A wire is installed to hold the stopper securely in place. The operation is somewhat delicate and requires an operator who has the knack, which may be acquired with practice. When successful, it produces a perfectly clear cider without any deposit, which in French is called *cidre mousseux*. In most large cideries, this operation is entirely automated, as the manual procedure is very expensive to apply to a great number of bottles.

THE CHARMAT, OR CLOSED TANK, METHOD

The Charmat method, although created in France, was mostly developed in Italy and has become quite popular for making good-quality sparkling wines and ciders. Its principle is similar to bottle conditioning except that this conditioning is done in large tanks instead of bottles. The tanks have a hermetic closure and are usually made of stainless steel. Fermentable sugar and, optionally, yeast are added to the cider and the closure is sealed. The fermentation produces CO_2, which remains in solution. Once the *prise de mousse* process is completed, the cider is pumped from above the lees, filtered, and bottled using a special apparatus called a *counterpressure filler head*, which allows the bottles to be filled without losing the CO_2 in solution, thus avoiding any foaming (see the sidebar on use of a CO_2 tank on pages 276–278). Alternatively, the cider may be poured from the pressurized keg as a draft cider. The Charmat method is used mainly by commercial cideries because it requires some special equipment for the filtration and bottling. Hobbyists may, however, use Cornelius kegs, which also work fine for this method.

ADDING YEAST

As I mentioned above, we may or may not add yeast to promote re-fermentation. There are many factors that will influence this decision. But first it should be said that it is very unlikely that there would be absolutely no viable yeasts in the cider at the moment re-fermentation is initiated, so re-fermentation would occur in any case. It is mainly a question of how fast and complete we

Altitude Effect on Carbonation Level

My friend Dick Dunn, who makes his cider at high altitude in the Rocky Mountains region, has noticed that a bottle of his cider will have less carbonation if opened and drunk at sea level, and, conversely, a cider made at sea level and served at high altitude will have more sparkle. This effect may be explained by the lower atmospheric pressure at high altitude. According to Dick, the altitude effect may be of a full class: a fully sparkling cider at high altitude may become *pétillant* at sea level, and vice versa.

want this re-fermentation to go. With added yeast, the fermentation will be stronger and will likely proceed to complete dryness in a rather short period of time. Additionally, champagne-type yeast will have better flocculation and form a compact deposit of lees that will be easier to eliminate with the disgorging procedure. If no yeast is added and the initial yeast number is small, there could be an important time lag before the re-fermentation starts, it will proceed much more slowly, and it may not be finished for more than six months—and even then may not go all the way to dryness. For my part, when I started making cider, I always used a partial dosage of champagne-type yeast at bottling. This means I would use one-half or one-third of a yeast pack to prime a 5-gallon cider batch. However, in recent years I have made many batches without yeast inoculation, and although it takes more time for the cider to be ready, I think the quality is improved. I particularly like the fact that in many unyeasted batches, the cider didn't reach complete dryness, leaving a very nice fruitiness. If you use the Champagne method, with riddling and disgorging, then a yeast inoculation of the right type is recommended.

SUGAR DOSAGE

When preparing a natural carbonation, it is important, to give the correct dosage of priming sugar. This quantity of sugar will determine the quantity of CO_2 produced and the amount of sparkle the cider will have. With just a little sugar, the cider might be *perlant* or slightly *pétillant*. And with too much sugar, there will be excessive carbonation: the cider may be violently expelled from the bottle upon opening or make excessive foam when served in the glass. More serious yet, the bottles may explode under the pressure, which is potentially dangerous. Normally, it doesn't matter much if the cider is not quite as sparkling as expected, but if it is more sparkling, that can mean trouble. It is better, then, to err on the safe side and not to force the dosage. For my part, I don't exceed 4 volumes of CO_2, which requires 15 g/L of priming sugar. In comparison, true Champagne normally has around 5 to 5.5 volumes of CO_2.

In chapter 3 I have already given some basic recommendations for a successful natural carbonation. Table 15.3 on page 272 is more complete

TABLE 15.3:
Sugar dosage for bottle conditioning

Volumes of CO$_2$	Type	CO$_2$ in solution (g/L)	Fermented sugar (g/L)	SG drop	Pressure at 25°C (atm)	Type of bottle
1	Perlant	2	2	0.001	0.9	All
1.5–2.5	Pétillant	3–5	4–8.5	0.002–0.004	1.5–2.8	Beer, mineral water
3.5–5.5	Sparkling	7–11	12–20	0.006–0.009	4–6	Champagne

and gives the quantity of fermentable sugar required for different levels of effervescence. I have also added the type of recommended bottle and the drop of SG that will result for each case. Note that 5.5 volumes of CO$_2$ represents a limit that shouldn't be exceeded for cider, and even at this level, excessive foaming is likely to occur upon pouring the cider.

If the malolactic fermentation hasn't happened and you have reason to believe it could happen in the bottles, you should take it into account while dosing the sugar and reduce the quantity a bit. Depending on the acidity of the cider and the extent of the transformation of the malic acid, the MLF may produce 2 g/L of CO$_2$ and sometimes even more. In the article on malolactic fermentation, Section 14.4, there are tips to estimate the amount of CO$_2$ produced.

Another factor that may influence the quantity of priming sugar required is the quantity of CO$_2$ already in solution at the moment of bottling. For example, if the cider is rather young and releases a lot of gas bubbles as it is being racked, you may assume its concentration of CO$_2$ is close to saturation, which is 2 g/L at 59°F (15°C) under atmospheric pressure. In these circumstances you may

reduce slightly the quantity of priming sugar. On the other hand, if the cider has had a long maturation and is very quiet while being racked, you may suppose it contains little CO$_2$ in solution and the priming sugar dosage may be slightly increased. Table 15.3 was built on the assumption that the cider contains sixty percent of the saturation concentration at 59°F (15°C), that is, that it already contains 1.2 g/L of dissolved CO$_2$.

Bottling Procedures

BASIC METHOD FOR A DRY SPARKLING CIDER

This basic procedure applies when the cider has undergone complete fermentation and contains no or very little residual sugar. The SG should be at 1.000 or lower and the cider should be well cleared. The timing would ideally be six months to a year after start of fermentation.

I already described the basic sequence of operations for bottling in chapter 3, and there is nothing really to add here but a few clarifying details. For one, if the cider is well cleared but its

SG is higher than 1.000, this indicates that there might still be some unfermented sugar in the cider. In that case the quantity of priming sugar to add should be reduced. For example, let's assume you want a *pétillant* cider that would be carbonated to 2.5 vols of CO_2. According to table 15.3 you would need to add about 8.5 grams of sugar per liter of cider, which would raise the SG by 0.004. However, if the cider SG is 1.003, this means that the better part of the required sugar could already be there, still unfermented. You could then add only 25 percent of the amount of priming sugar plus a bit of yeast nutrients, because if the fermentation has stopped at 1.003, it probably means that the natural nutrients are exhausted. This would work fine if the cider's SG at complete dryness is 1.000, which is not always the case as we have seen in section 14.5. Some ciders ferment to a SG lower than 1.000, while perries are often perfectly dry at a SG around 1.003. When it is suspected that the dryness SG may be different from 1.000, it is a good idea to prepare a test bottle with a sample of the cider, some yeast, and yeast nutrients. Leave the bottle to ferment a few weeks at room temperature, and when the fermentation has stopped, the SG may be measured. You can then assume this is the complete dryness SG and use that value to evaluate the priming sugar required.

FIRST METHOD FOR A SPARKLING CIDER WITH RESIDUAL SUGAR

The two following methods apply to ciders that have kept a good amount of residual sugar, with an SG higher than 1.010 at the end of fermentation. These methods will enable us to produce high-quality medium-dry to sweet sparkling ciders. The ciders in question should have been obtained by the techniques described in section 15.1 on sweet ciders: they should either have been keeved or have retained some residual sugar after multiple stabilization rackings starting from a nutrient-poor juice.

In the first method, we try to anticipate the SG at which the fermentation will stop naturally, and we bottle the cider when the SG is about 0.005 higher than that value. No addition whatsoever is done at bottling: we simply rack the cider to eliminate the lees and bottle it. As there is a bit of active yeast, there should be no yeast addition. This method is quite standard in France for making sweet sparkling ciders in low-tech installations (i.e., farm ciders). To successfully use this method, it is important to monitor the fermentation as described in section 14.3 on fermentation monitoring and control, and to calculate the speed of fermentation. The ciders for which the method may be suitable are those where the fermentation speed is between 4 to 7 FSU while the SG is between 1.015 and 1.025. Further, the cider should be fairly well cleared in order to avoid excessive lees in the bottles.

With this method it is almost impossible to predict the amount of sparkle with as much precision as with the basic method, so you should always use heavyweight champagne-type bottles even if you expect a *pétillant* cider. As a first approximation, we may assume that the speed of fermentation at the moment of bottling will maintain itself for a period of two to four months after bottling. For example, let's say we have a cider whose SG is 1.018 and speed of fermentation is 5 FSU at bottling time. We can estimate that the drop of density after bottling will be between 0.003 (two months: 60 days × 5 FSU / 100) and 0.006 (four months), which would give a *pétillant* or sparkling cider from table 15.3. It is wise to open a test bottle about two months after bottling, measure the SG, and estimate the speed of fermentation since bottling. If the drop of SG is more than was anticipated, the cider will have to be drunk before the carbonation becomes excessive. Note that because this cider will be carbonated, it will be necessary to degas it before taking the SG measurement, either by shaking or heating it.

Caution: If the temperature in the cider room is very cold during winter, the fermentation may stop almost completely, to pick up again in the spring when the temperature becomes milder. This could lead one to think, wrongly, that the conditions are good to use this first method for sparkling cider. The cider temperature should always be at least 50°F (10°C) when the speed of fermentation is evaluated.

SECOND METHOD FOR A SPARKLING CIDER WITH RESIDUAL SUGAR (CONTROLLED DOSAGE OF NUTRIENTS)

It may happen that the conditions will not permit us to use the first method. The most common reasons are that the cider hasn't cleared at the moment when it would have to be bottled or the speed of fermentation was too slow to insure a good natural carbonation. Then it's better to let it go until the fermentation stops completely and proceed according to the following method.

With this method, we use a very small dosage of yeast nutrients in order to reactivate some in-bottle fermentation, thus insuring carbonation. We should work with a well-stabilized and cleared cider that went through a slow fermentation and whose SG is above 1.010. The procedure is simple, really: rack the cider, add a controlled amount of yeast nutrients, and bottle. I tested this procedure for the first time with a cider from the 2006 harvest. After a year of slow fermentation on natural yeast, the fermentation was stuck at an SG of 1.013. First I considered restarting it, but on second thought I decided to bottle the cider with nutrients, and in effect the fermentation retook in the bottles and continued slowly until the SG reached 1.007, giving an SG drop of 0.006 for a nice sparkling cider. The residual sugar at an SG of 1.007 was 15 g/L for a medium-dry cider. This cider was so good that I decided to present it to the Great Lakes International Cider and Perry Competition (GLINTCAP) of 2008: it earned a gold medal and the Best of Show award.

What is more difficult is to use just the correct dosage of yeast nutrients to obtain the desired carbonation. In effect, we want to add the amount that will permit the yeast to ferment a part of the sugar still in solution in the cider but no more, as we also want the yeast to stop working when the desired carbonation is attained. If too much nutrient is added, then all the residual sugar will be fermented, resulting in excessive carbonation, with all the associated risks.

We have already seen in the articles on nitrogenous substances (chapter 11) and yeast and yeast nutrients (section 14.2) that in addition to sugar, yeast needs some nitrogenous substances to thrive and develop a strong population and that such nutrients may be added by the cider maker in the form of diammonium phosphate (DAP). Tests that I have done (section 14.2) show that a dosage of 15 ppm of DAP added to a nutrient-depleted cider will permit an SG drop of 0.005 to 0.007, which is what we need for a sparkling cider. This corresponds to about ⅓ teaspoon of DAP for 25 gallons (100 liters) of cider. As you can see, for one 5-gallon carboy, this makes a very small amount to measure, something like 1/16 of a teaspoon, or 0.3 gram. Before dosing your own cider, however, I would recommend that you do a test, since not all the yeast nutrient products we find in the trade will have the same strength. Take three or four bottles of this cider, put a different dose of DAP in each (for example 8, 15, and 25 ppm), leave them with an airlock at room temperature for a good while, and monitor the drop of SG. From these results, you should be able to determine the exact dosage you need for your cider. And if you really want to try the method without doing the test, please don't overdo it and stay on the safe side: try it first with a dosage of about 10 ppm of DAP and see what you get. In subsequent batches you may increase the dosage as required.

OTHER METHODS FOR SWEET AND SPARKLING CIDERS

You can easily understand that the two above-mentioned methods are not used in commercial cideries because of the variability of the carbonation thus obtained: one batch may be fully sparkling, while the next one may be just lightly *pétillant*. For the hobbyist, this is not a problem, as we can easily live with this variability as long as the quality of the cider is great. But commercial cider has to be more controlled, and all batches are required to be carbonated to the same level.

In large-scale operations, one of the most common methods to obtain a sweet and sparkling cider is by adding sugar to a dry sparkling cider by the Charmat method. This is usually referred to as *back-sweetening*. At bottling time, the cider goes through a sterile filtration to eliminate the remaining yeast cells, and counterpressure fillers are used. A controlled dosage of sugar is added, as well as sorbate and sulfite to prevent further fermentation.

The traditional Champagne method also makes it possible to obtain a sweet and sparkling cider. In this case, at the moment of disgorgement, a dose of sugar syrup is added to each bottle to give the desired sweetness. Sorbate and sulfite will also be added in this syrup. The riddling and disgorgement process of this method eliminates the yeast just as surely as the sterile filtration mentioned above. The main thing is that much more time is required, which renders this method more costly.

Actually, many of the methods mentioned in the previous section, "Sweetness in Cider," may also be used for a sparkling cider. For example, artificial sweeteners may be used with just about any method without risk of excessive carbonation. Also, pasteurization may be used with the Charmat method mentioned above and could replace the sterile filtration. You could also use the basic method for a dry cider but pasteurize the bottles when only part of the sugar has fermented, thus leaving a *pétillant* cider with residual sweetness. Remember to be cautious with pasteurization of sparkling ciders. Since the pressure may get very high as we have seen, don't carbonate too much and use only the best quality heavyweight *champenoise* bottles.

Working with a CO₂ Tank

Figure 15.9. Carbon dioxide tank with regulator.

A small tank of carbon dioxide like the one shown in figure 15.9 may have many uses in a cidery. We may think this is for professionals only, and in fact no commercial cidery would go without it. But many serious hobbyists are also equipped for working with a CO_2 tank. The investment is not negligible: a complete kit does cost from \$200 to \$400. The tank itself consists of a high-strength steel or aluminum reservoir equipped with a main shut-off valve (black, on top of the tank) and a pressure regulator (on the left). The regulator normally includes two pressure indicators: one for the pressure of the CO_2 in the tank and the other for the pressure at which the gas is delivered. It also includes a valve to adjust the delivery pressure (the knob in the middle of the regulator), an overpressure relief valve, and a shut-off valve at the exit.

PURGING AND BLANKETING

The most simple use for such a tank is for purging the air from a container and establishing a CO_2 blanket on top of the cider to protect it from contact with oxygen. For example, we may inject carbon dioxide into the receiving carboy just before proceeding with the racking. This then minimizes the contact of cider with oxygen. Another application is with a carboy that isn't completely full of cider: an injection of carbon dioxide will force the air out and leave a protective blanket. An important feature of CO_2 is that it is heavier than air and so tends to sink under the air.

FORCED CARBONATION

To do some forced or artificial carbonation, you will need, in addition to the tank and regulator, a keg that may be pressurized: either a Cornelius (or Corny) keg of the type used for soft drinks or a beer keg. These kegs are equipped with two ports: the in port to connect to a source of pressurized gas (i.e., our CO_2 tank) and the out port for dispensing the contents. It then suffices to connect a line from the regulator to the in port of the keg and to adjust the pressure to obtain the desired carbonation level in relation to the temperature. The setting of the pressure will be done according to a carbonation chart, easily found on the Internet, or calculated from Henry's law, which we discussed earlier. For example, if the temperature is 50°F (10°C), Henry's law states that you need to have a partial pressure of 2.59 atm of CO_2 in order to obtain 3 vols of carbonation. Now, in this case the air will have been purged from the keg, hence the relative pressure inside the keg will be this value minus 1 atm, which is the pressure outside the keg. You then need to set the pressure on the regulator to 1.59 atm, which is 23 psi. Actually, you would set the pressure a few psi higher and leave it on for a couple of days. To check if the carbonation is high enough, shut off the main valve from the tank, open the relief valve a second to let the pressure drop, and wait awhile until the pressure is stabilized. If this pressure is 23 psi, the desired level of carbonation is there. If not, it is necessary to leave it under pressure longer. Note that the colder the cider, the easier and faster the desired carbonation will be attained.

SERVING DRAFT CIDER

To serve the carbonated cider (forced or naturally carbonated) on tap, we need to connect the out port of the keg to a simple dispenser tap (as shown in figure 15.10) while the in port is still fed by the CO_2 tank. The keg would, however, have to be kept in a refrigerator. If you like serving the cider this way, you might consider acquiring a special refrigerator just for kegs.

FILTERING

The pressure from a CO_2 tank may be used as a driving force for filtering. Filter pads are then required. Often a series of pads are used, starting with a coarser pad first to remove the larger particles and using a finer pad to finish the filtration. If you are doing what is called *sterile filtration*, then the last pad will need to be 0.5 micron or less to insure the yeast cells are removed. Further, steam will be pushed through the line to sterilize it prior to filtering the cider, thus insuring no microorganism will contaminate the cider after the filter. Filtering may be

Figure 15.10. Setup for serving draft cider.

done from one keg to another one, or the output from the filter may be sent directly to the bottle filler. Note that pumps are also often used to drive the cider through filters. See figure 16.2 of a hobbyist filter setup in the article on cider troubles in chapter 16, page 299.

BOTTLING FROM A PRESSURIZED KEG

In order to be able to bottle the carbonated cider that is in a keg, another piece of equipment is required: a filler head. Without it, the foaming of the cider as it arrived in the bottle would make a mess. The filler head may be either a counterpressure filler or a simpler atmospheric filler. The main difference is that the counterpressure filler has a stopper, which permits a pressure buildup in the bottle as it fills, further reducing the foaming. The model shown in figure 15.11 is an atmospheric filler. In any case, the filling is done in two operations: first some CO_2 is injected into the bottle to purge the air, and then the bottle is filled with cider. We can see in figure 15.11 how this is installed. The tube arriving on the left of the filler head is the CO_2 gas. This is connected to the regulator of the tank through a tee, as some CO_2 also has to be delivered to the keg. The tube arriving on the top of the filler is connected to

the out port of the keg and carries the cider. The filling head itself is a stainless steel tube that goes to the bottom of the bottle and is equipped with two valves. When filling the bottle, the operator first opens the CO_2 valve for a few seconds to fill the bottle with CO_2, then opens the liquid valve to let the cider flow into the bottle. The fact that the bottle is initially filled with carbon dioxide decreases greatly the amount of foaming produced. The bottle closure should be installed quickly after filling.

The author would like to thank Chantal Poissant of Fabrique du vin in Quebec City for generously lending the equipment shown in these photos.

Figure 15.11. Setup for bottling carbonated cider.

◀ 15.3 ▶
Ice Cider

Let the frost come to freeze them first, solid as stones, and then the rain or a warm winter day to thaw them, and they will seem to have borrowed a flavor from heaven through the medium of the air in which they hang.

HENRY DAVID THOREAU, *Wild Apples*, 1862

Ice cider (or *cidre de glace* in French) is a special type of very sweet or syrupy cider that was developed in Quebec during the 1990s. It bears some similarities with the ice wine from Ontario and the *Eiswein* from Germany. Actually, the virtues of frozen and thawed apples have been known for a long time, as we can see by reading Thoreau, and the principle of using the cold to concentrate the sugars or the alcohol of a beverage is also ancient: in 1887, Georges Lechartier reported on some experiments he did, freezing ciders in a brine solution at −20°C, and he mentioned that the operation increased the color, taste, and alcoholic strength of the cider. In a certain sense, we could consider the applejack of the old days a form of ice cider. Applejack was made by letting a finished cider freeze outside on a cold winter night, and in the morning the crust of ice, which contained essentially water, was removed, thus concentrating the residual sugar and the alcohol of the cider. However, ice cider is quite different from applejack, and it's the way of producing it that makes the difference.

Most of the credit for the development of modern ice cider may be attributed to two men who worked independently during the 1990s: Pierre Lafond of Cidrerie Saint-Nicolas near Quebec City and Christian Barthomeuf of Clos Saragnat in Frelighsburg. The ciders they made in the beginning weren't called ice cider but had other names, such as strong sweet cider (*cidre fort doux* or *licoreux*). Starting in 1996, Barthomeuf worked with the cidery La Face Cachée de la Pomme and a few years later with Domaine Pinnacle to develop large-scale production of modern ice ciders using the knowledge he had acquired with the early experiments he did by the turn of the decade. These two cideries are now the largest producers of ice cider and export their products all over the world. During that same period, Lafond did some experimental work in collaboration with Laval University, which led to the creation, in 1999, of the official designation *cidre de glace* for his product. The original concept Lafond developed to obtain the label was to use only frozen apples for the preparation of ice cider, but this was soon widened to permit the use of frozen juice as well. After that, Quebec ice ciders quickly gained international recognition as high-quality products, and they sell at premium prices. Many cideries in colder northern parts of the United States have now also started to produce ice cider.

Making ice cider at home as an amateur is a fairly challenging task, but when all goes well it is very rewarding. Before you try it, I would, however, recommend that you gain some experience making naturally sweet ciders using the keeving or the multiple racking method, and it would also help if you have some familiarity with the monitoring and control of the fermentation speed with the methods that I have described elsewhere.

Ice-cider making differs from normal cider making in two essential ways: the first is that we start with a concentrated juice, which is obtained by freeze concentration. And the second is that we need to stop the fermentation and stabilize the cider while there is still a high sugar content in it. This second point is probably the one that is the most difficult to tackle for a hobbyist.

The Quebec Regulations and Your Own Ice Cider

As Quebec is the world leader in the development, production, and marketing of ice cider, the government has published regulations to protect the name and the product from lower-quality imitations—a bit as the French have done for the name "Champagne": even if one makes a sparkling wine similar to a Champagne, it cannot be named Champagne because of such regulations. This work is not yet complete, but an important first step was achieved in December 2008, when the following definitions and standards were adopted:

"Ice cider": cider obtained by the fermentation of juice of apples that has a pre-fermentation sugar content of not less than 30° Brix achieved solely by natural cold, producing a finished product with a residual sugar content of not less than 130 g per liter and an actual alcoholic strength of more than 7% by volume but not more than 13% by volume.

("Regulation respecting cider and other apple-based alcoholic beverages," *Loi sur la Société des alcools du Québec*, March 2013 revision)

Furthermore, some additional requirements must be met: it is forbidden to add sugar, alcohol, artificial color, or flavor, for example.

This regulation is quite stringent. The pre-fermentation sugar content requirement of 30°Bx corresponds to a starting SG of 1.130 and is more than double the sugar concentration obtained from most sugar-rich apples. The residual sugar requirement of 130 g/L corresponds to a final SG of approximately 1.060. And while it is compulsory to follow this regulation for commercial ice-cider makers who sell their products under the restricted name *cidre de glace* in Quebec, it is also perfectly legitimate for a hobbyist not to follow it. The choice is yours.

DEFINING TARGETS

Before you start however, it would be preferable to have an idea of your target goals as to what sort of ice cider you want to make. These targets should be expressed in terms of the amount of residual sugar and alcoholic strength of the cider. For example, some ice ciders like Domaine Pinnacle are started with a juice that is concentrated to a higher degree than the minimum requirement of 30°Bx. This permits them to obtain an amount of residual sugar higher than 130 g/L (closer to 180 g/L in the case of Domaine Pinnacle) while maintaining an alcoholic strength around 10% ABV. You may choose to start with a lower sugar concentration than 30°Bx. For example, Cidrerie Saint-Nicolas has an ice cider that has less alcohol than the 7% ABV requirement and thus can't bear the *cidre de glace* name. It is nevertheless an excellent product. You may also prefer a finished product that is not as sweet as the requirement of 130 g/L residual sugar. Table 15.4 gives an idea of

TABLE 15.4:
Ice cider combinations

CONCENTRATED JUICE		FINISHED CIDER maximizing residual sugar			FINISHED CIDER maximizing alcohol		
SG	BRIX	g/L RS	FINAL SG	% ABV	g/L RS	FINAL SG	% ABV
1.100	24	120	1.056	5.7	75	1.036	8.5
1.130	30	160	1.075	7	100	1.048	11
1.160	36	200	1.094	8.6	130	1.062	13

the different combinations of residual sugar (g/L RS) and alcohol that can be obtained as a function of the SG of the concentrated juice. The values of SG given for the finished cider indicate at which level the fermentation needs to be stopped to attain the target numbers.

The values of table 15.4 are not absolutely exact, as the true amount of sugar may vary for a given SG or Brix, as we have seen in the article on the real amount of sugar in the juice (section 8.3). They should, however, be close enough for most needs.

Obtaining the Concentrated Apple Juice

The principle of freeze concentration relies upon the fact that a solution that contains sugar will freeze at a lower temperature than pure water. So freezing actually provokes a separation of the sugars because ice crystals that form first contain almost pure water; later, as the temperature drops further, the sugar also starts to freeze. And upon thawing, the first ice that melt contains lots of sugar, while the last ice crystals to melt will contain practically pure water. In summary, when the two phases (liquid and ice) are simultaneously present in the same medium, then the liquid will have a higher sugar concentration than the ice. There are two methods that are used in the production of ice cider:

- The first method is called *cryo-extraction*. This process involves freezing apples, which are pressed when partially melted, so water remains trapped as ice crystals in the apples while they are pressed, and the extracted juice thus has a larger concentration of sugar. Freezing the apples may be done in either of two ways: the apples may remain on the trees and picked once they are fully frozen, but more often the apples are harvested during the fall and kept in cold storage until the temperature is cold enough so they can be brought outside to freeze.
- The second method is *cryo-concentration*. In this case the juice is extracted in the usual manner from the apples that have been kept in storage until the outside temperature is cold enough. After pressing, the juice is brought outside to freeze, and upon melting, the first juice that will flow will have a higher concentration of sugar and will be collected separately.

With this process, it is good practice to treat the juice with a pectinase to clear it before it is put out to freeze: this will help greatly in the clearing of the finished cider (see debourbage in chapter 12).

In commercial operations the cryo-concentration method is by far the most widely used. Its implementation is not difficult, and the guide by Eleanor Leger (2010), *Making and Marketing Vermont Ice Cider* (downloadable from the Internet), gives an excellent description of how it can be done for larger-scale production. It may be noted that although the Quebec regulation requires that the juice used for cryo-concentration has to be frozen by natural cold, this will have no great effect on the quality of the cider, and a good freezer might just as well be used if the freezer in question is large enough for the quantity of juice to be frozen.

Cryo-extraction is also used by some commercial cideries. The normal procedure is to let the apples freeze outside (figure 15.12) and, then, to grind them prior to pressing, while they are still at a subfreezing temperature (a robust mill is required). The image of an orchard in midwinter, its

trees loaded with frozen apples, and a sign to the effect that these apples are reserved for ice cider and should not be picked is more for folkloric and marketing purposes than for actually producing large quantities of ice cider. Just imagine the work involved in harvesting apples when the pickers have to wear snowshoes! (Have you ever tried to climb a ladder with snowshoes?) Then you'd need to carry these apples to the cider house in the snow (snowmobiles can be used, however). And this is assuming that the apples actually stay attached to the tree: there are sprays that are used to help prevent the apples from falling, but the natural process is for apples to fall when they are ripe. Maybe one out of ten remains on the branch. But in some years the freezes arrive before the apples have had time to ripen completely, and then a larger fraction of the apples will remain in the trees through part of the winter. All this is to say that yes, some cryo-extraction is done from apples that are left to freeze on the trees, but mostly on a small scale, as the costs are much higher. Christian Barthomeuf, whom I mentioned at the beginning of this article, makes all his ice ciders of Clos Saragnat with apples that are picked frozen in the trees, but some years there is simply no crop. And some cideries will maintain a block of trees for this purpose and produce a small batch of premium ice cider from these, but the bulk of their production would be from apples that have been harvested in fall.

A few concluding remarks about cryo-extraction: with this process, it is not possible to control the sugar

Figure 15.12. Bins of apples left to freeze at Cidrerie Saint-Nicolas.

concentration of the juice as exactly as in the case of cryo-concentration, and sometimes the juice doesn't conform to the regulations. When this happens, either a second concentration step is done, as I describe below, or the juice is fermented as is, though the name *cidre de glace* can't be used commercially for the final product. Second, I think cryo-extraction gives a better-quality juice for ice cider, in part because the juice obtained from frozen apples is much clearer, and this makes it easier at the end of the process to obtain a nice, clear ice cider. And also, unlike with cryo-concentration, natural cold works differently on the apples than a freezer would, and I believe naturally frozen apples give a better product.

For my part, I like to do a combination of the two methods. For quite a while now, I have used freezing as a way to salvage overripe apples that would not press easily. After melting, apples can be pressed easily without need for grinding (see section 6.1 on apple mills). So I figured I could try to press the apples when they were only partially melted, and it works. I bring the frozen apples inside and let them thaw for three to four hours (this for a box that contains about 30 lb. (15 kg) of apples; more time would be required for a larger bin). It is necessary to mix them once in a while so it is not just the ones on top of the box that thaw. The more time the apples are left to thaw, the more juice they will yield but also the less concentration of sugars there will be. I wait until the apples yield under the thumb, as shown in figure 15.13 on page 284, and it is then time to press them. I prefer to use my basket press for this, but rack-and-cloth presses can also be used. I simply put the whole apples into the basket and apply the pressure. The pressing is slow: it takes two hours under the press to extract this wonderful nectar. In figure

15.14 on page 284, we can see the results of the pressing of partially frozen apples. It is interesting to see the apples simply flatten while giving their juice. And yet this juice is usually still not concentrated enough for ice cider. Typically, I obtain juice at an SG between 1.085 and 1.090 from apples that would have naturally given a juice at an SG of approximately 1.055. So as a second step I freeze this juice to further concentrate it. For this, I use lidded plastic pails with a capacity of about 3 gal (10 liters), filled approximately two-thirds. When it is very cold outside, −5°F (−20°C) or lower, these will freeze overnight. Once frozen, I bring the pails inside and leave them to thaw for a couple of hours before starting to drain the concentrated juice. Draining is quite simple, as can be seen in figure 15.15 on page 284: I open the lid slightly, such that the liquid may pass through, but not the ice, and place the pail on top of a receiving bucket. The flowing juice will be more concentrated at the beginning, and this concentration will decrease as the ice melts. The density or the Brix should be checked regularly, and once the juice is at the target concentration, it should be put aside. However, there will still be some juice and sugar in the remaining ice. If you have some time and would like to get a bit more concentrated juice, you may then let some more juice drain into another bucket. The density will be lower, but this juice may be refrozen to concentrate another time.

To give you a better idea, here are figures from the pressing of my 2011 harvest. For this batch, I had put four boxes of apples in an unheated shed (so the apples would be protected from animals) in November. The apples froze slowly and went through a few freeze-thaw cycles before they became deeply frozen. In mid-January I had 140 lb. (64 kg) of frozen apples, from which I obtained 7.3

Figure 15.13. Partially thawed apples ready to press

Figure 15.14. Flattened apples after pressing

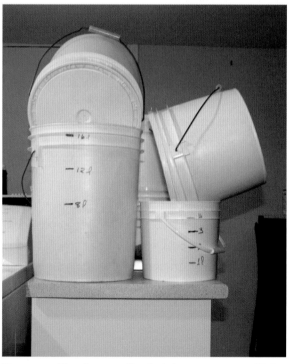

Figure 15.15. Simple setup for draining concentrated juice

gal. (27.5 L) at an SG of 1.086 by pressing the partially thawed apples. I put this juice into four buckets and placed them outside during a very cold night; the following day I took them in to thaw and drain. I got 4 gal. (15 L) at an SG of 1.125, plus 1 gal (4 L) at an SG of 1.070, which I then refroze to give another half-gallon at a high SG the following day. So this procedure is pretty efficient: the yield as weight of juice obtained in relation to the weight of the apples used turns out to be around 30 percent. But a better index is to compare the amount of sugar extracted, and in this case, assuming the unconcentrated apples would have yielded a juice at an SG of 1.055, this process had the same efficiency as a conventional press at an efficiency of 65 percent. It may be noted that the concentrated juice I obtained was at an SG of 1.125 (equivalent to 29°Bx), which is a bit lower than the requirement of the Quebec regulation (30°Bx). I wouldn't have been able to sell this ice cider under the restricted name *cidre de glace*. However, for home production, this starting SG is perfectly acceptable.

Sugar table

Table 15.5 is an extension of the sugar table (table 8.7 on page 175) I gave in the article on sugar in section 8.3. It covers the range likely to be of use for ice cider. I have assumed here that the freeze concentration process has the same effect of concentration on all the solids contained in the juice. Note the line in bold face, which represents the minimum concentration requirement as stated by the Quebec regulation. Table 15.5 gives as a function of the SG:

- ρ, the volumic mass of the juice at 20°C
- Brix, in % (i.e., g per 100 g of juice)

- TS, total solids or dry extract per liter
- S_{avg}, the average sugar concentration
- ΔS, the bounds of the 95 percent confidence interval on S
- $A_{P\text{-}avg}$, the average potential alcohol in %ABV at 20°C

Please refer to section 8.3 for details and limitations.

Fermenting the Concentrated Juice

The preparation for fermentation is no different with ice cider than it is for a normal cider. I take the density and acidity measurements and prepare a yeast culture. The acidity is typically very high because the freeze concentration process also concentrates the acids in approximately the same proportion as the sugars, thus the total acidity (TA) is typically of the order of 12 to 18 g/L of malic acid, a little over twice the acidity the apples would have given without concentration. The pH is low, usually in the 3.0 to 3.2 range. At such a high acidity, adding sulfite for protection of the cider is generally considered unnecessary. One point, however, needs some attention: the freshly extracted juice will be very cold, often around freezing. This is too cold for a yeast culture to develop, and it will be necessary to bring the temperature up before yeast inoculation, to around 60°F (15°C). This can be done while the yeast culture is being prepared.

For yeast, I like to use the Lalvin 71B for an ice cider for the following reasons: in the different comparative tests I have done, the 71B has always been a slower fermenter and has also left a greater amount of residual sugar than a champagne yeast

TABLE 15.5:
Sugar table for freeze-concentrated apple juice

SG	ρ (g/L)	Brix (%)	TS (g/L)	S_AVG (g/L)	ΔS (±g/L)	A_P-AVG (%)
1.090	1088.0	21.57	234.7	191.7	21.6	11.50
1.095	1093.0	22.68	247.9	202.4	22.8	12.14
1.100	1098.0	23.77	261.0	213.0	24.0	12.78
1.105	1103.0	24.86	274.2	223.6	25.2	13.42
1.110	1108.0	25.94	287.5	234.3	26.4	14.06
1.115	1113.0	27.01	300.7	244.9	27.6	14.70
1.120	1118.0	28.08	313.9	255.6	28.8	15.34
1.125	1123.0	29.13	327.2	266.2	30.0	15.97
1.130	**1128.0**	**30.18**	**340.4**	**276.9**	**31.2**	**16.61**
1.135	1133.0	31.22	353.7	287.5	32.4	17.25
1.140	1138.0	32.25	367.0	298.2	33.6	17.89
1.145	1142.9	33.28	380.3	308.8	34.8	18.53
1.150	1147.9	34.29	393.7	319.5	36.0	19.17
1.155	1152.9	35.30	407.0	330.1	37.2	19.81
1.160	1157.9	36.31	420.4	340.8	38.4	20.45
1.165	1162.9	37.30	433.8	351.4	39.6	21.09
1.170	1167.9	38.29	447.2	362.1	40.8	21.73
1.175	1172.9	39.27	460.6	372.7	42.0	22.36
1.180	1177.9	40.25	474.0	383.4	43.2	23.00

Table for concentrated apple juice only; not valid for cider or for chaptalized juice. Properties in g/L are at 20°C (68°F).

like the Lalvin EC-1118. This makes things easier to control and to stop the fermentation. Also, the 71B tends to reduce the acidity, which may be a good thing when a must has such a high TA. I do my yeast culture exactly the same way as for a normal cider. I have never had a successful wild yeast colony on ice cider, possibly because freezing weakens the wild yeasts too much. I have,

however, seen reports claiming it has been done. Maybe the trick is to use as a starter another cider batch that has not been frozen and is fermenting on natural yeasts.

I have tried on a couple of occasions to do a keeve (see section 15.1 on sweetness in cider) with a freeze-concentrated must, but never successfully. The gel never formed. This is unfortunate, as keeving would help control the speed of fermentation and stop it at the right moment. Again, I suspect that freezing does something to the pectins and renders the keeving process impossible, though I don't know if there is any scientific evidence for this. Another possibility would be to keeve a juice obtained by normal pressing of the apples and then to freeze-concentrate this keeved juice. I have not yet tried this procedure, but I think it would have a good chance of working.

One of the most important issues for a successful ice-cider maker is to keep the fermentation under control. If it starts to go too fast, it will be much more difficult to stop. For this, there are two golden rules: cool temperature and low nutrients. As I said earlier, the cider has to be at least warmish for the yeast culture to develop after inoculation, but soon after that it should be cooled down to about 50°F (10°C) or lower so the fermentation doesn't accelerate too much. Thus, close monitoring of the evolution of the fermentation, by measurement of the SG and calculation of the speed of fermentation, is important. On the question of the quantity of nitrogenous nutrients initially present in the juice, this is mostly dependent on how the apples were grown. During the fermentation, stabilization rackings may be used to decrease the nutrient level and the speed of fermentation.

In summary, the actions of the cider maker during the fermentation are:

- Inoculate the must with a yeast culture while the temperature is around 60°F (15°C), and cool it down after a day or two when there are signs that the yeasts have multiplied.
- Monitor the SG and the speed of fermentation regularly, making sure the speed doesn't exceed 200 to 300 FSU.

- If the speed is too fast, bring the cider to a lower temperature and/or rack it to reduce the nutrient level.
- When the SG approaches about 0.010 of the target SG for the finished ice cider, it is time to start the procedure that will stop the fermentation.

Stopping the Fermentation and Stabilizing the Cider

Most professionals will say that this operation is impossible to do for a hobbyist who doesn't have some special equipment. I disagree, but I must admit I didn't succeed on my first trial.

In commercial cideries cold is normally used for stopping the fermentation. Larger cideries will often have a refrigeration coil on their fermentation tanks, which permits a precise control of the temperature and a rapid chilling when required. The other possibility is to bring the fermentation tank outside or to pump the cider to an outdoor tank. This is assuming exterior temperatures are cold enough, ideally around freezing. At this point, some SO_2 would be added, typically around 50 ppm, and after a few days in the cold, the cider would be stabilized by sterile filtration, a process that removes the yeast cells. Then the cider may be left to age, or it may be bottled. Sorbate is generally used with SO_2 at bottling to insure no fermentation restarts in the bottles, since with the quantity of residual sugar in ice cider, in-bottle fermentation would be catastrophic. Some cideries will also pasteurize the bottles to make sure the fermentation doesn't restart. The guide by Eleanor Leger, which I mentioned above, provides good information for a larger-scale operation.

However, in some of the commercially produced ice ciders I have sampled, I have been able to detect the taste of SO_2, which I thoroughly dislike. Also, operations like sterile filtration or pasteurization may affect the taste of the product. So, when I started making my ice cider, and since I didn't have costly equipment like refrigerated fermentation tanks, sterile filtration, and pasteurization gear, I had to find other ways to do it. My tools are cold and racking. I much prefer to avoid the use of chemicals. What helps is that my apples are unfertilized and come from old, standard trees, and thus the juice is quite poor in nitrogenous nutrients to start with. In general, I have found that three or four rackings, combined with cold temperature, is sufficient to stop the fermentation and stabilize the cider.

As an illustration, I have plotted in figure 15.16 the fermentation curve of my 2009 ice cider, where the SG in blue should be read on the scale on the left and the speed of fermentation, in brown, should be read on the scale on the right. On the SG curve, we can see the lag phase was quite long, as the value dropped from 1.120 initially to only 1.110 after twenty days. After that, it started going much faster, and actually, between day 20 and day 29, the average speed was over 400 FSU, which was far too fast. When I measured the SG on day 29, I realized then that the fermentation had been going much more quickly than I had anticipated. So I immediately racked the cider and placed it in a colder location. This operation was successful, as the speed decreased to 55 FSU on average between day 29 and 40. But

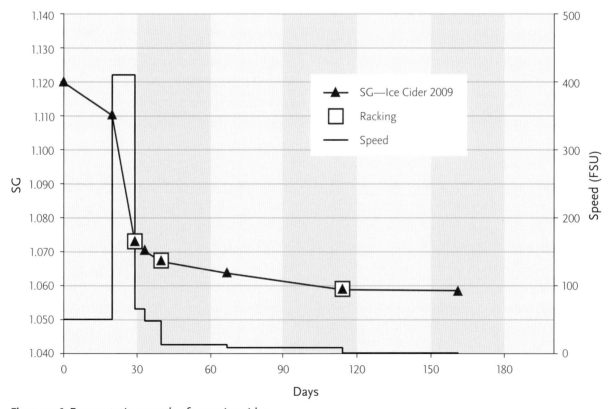

Figure 15.16. Fermentation graph of 2009 ice cider.

in retrospect, I should have taken an SG measurement around day 25 or 26. I would have then been able to take action sooner. In that particular case, however, I was a bit lucky, since the racking done on day 29 was successful. Then on day 40, SG was 1.067 and was approaching the target final SG, which was 1.060. I did a second racking, but I wasn't able to reduce the temperature further, as I had already reduced it as much as I could, and it was then at 41°F (5°C). After this second racking, the fermentation slowed to 13 FSU. Everything was under control, and I could let the cider mature for a couple of months before making the third racking. This last racking really exhausted the tiny bit of fermentation that was still active: an SG check done a month and a half after this third racking showed no change in SG; thus, the cider could then be bottled safely. This was on day 160, a little over five months after the beginning of fermentation. The final SG was 1.059, giving an ice cider with a little under 130 g/L of residual sugar and an alcoholic strength of 8% ABV.

Bottling

Once the cider is well stabilized, it may be bottled. Caution is essential, as these bottles will contain more than 100 g/L of unfermented sugar. To make sure the cider is perfectly stable before bottling, it may be brought into a warmer temperature for a few weeks and if no fermentatinon occurs, it is good sign. For the bottles, I like to use beer bottles with a ceramic closure (e.g., Grolsch bottles), as these will let excess pressure exit and thus avoid bursting. It is also prudent to leave one or two bottles at room temperature while the bulk are kept cool. These warmer bottles may be tested a month or so after bottling to check that there is

no pressure, which would indicate that some refermentation had occurred.

Concluding remarks

The experiments I have done so far show that ice cider can be made successfully in small scale and without costly equipment or use of heavy doses of chemicals. In order to maximize the chances of success, I propose the following guidelines:

- Use apples that are low in nitrogenous nutrients, ideally late-maturing varieties from old, unfertilized, standard trees. Let the apples ripen to the point at which they are almost overripe before freezing them.
- Cryo-extraction of apples that have been frozen and partially melted seems to be the best method for a first concentration, followed if necessary by a second step of cryo-concentration if the sugar concentration isn't high enough.
- Some temperature control during fermentation is absolutely necessary. Ideally, we would want to be able to reduce the temperature to near the freezing point.
- Close monitoring of the fermentation is essential, with precise calculation of the speed of fermentation. This will enable us to make the rackings at the most appropriate moments.

Having said all this, however, I still think more experimentation is required to insure a foolproof method for hobbyists. In particular, I have had some ice ciders that were reluctant to clear, although they were well stabilized. This didn't affect the taste, but the look wasn't as pleasant as it could have been. I think cryo-extraction is better on this issue, but I need to do more tests to be sure. On the question of using a keeved juice, some experiments would be required to find the right way to do it, as this would certainly help the clearing issue and also reduce the amount of nitrogenous nutrients in the juice, thus facilitating the stopping of the fermentation. Finally, as I haven't succeeded yet in obtaining a wild yeast fermentation on ice cider, I would like to do further work on this and find a way.

After Ice Cider, Fire Cider!

Yes, now we have *cidre de feu* in addition to *cidre de glace!* The principle is the same, but instead of using the cold to concentrate the juice, it is fire that is used to evaporate the water from the juice. Fire cider was first trialed in Quebec in 1994 by Normand Lamontagne, who used a maple syrup evaporator to boil apple juice and concentrate it.

After that, the juice could be fermented pretty much in the same manner as for ice cider. As of the beginning of 2013, there were two cideries in Quebec that produced fire cider. And they still do it on a maple syrup evaporator. These products have a high alcoholic strength, around 15% ABV, with a good amount of residual sugar, in the vicinity of 80 g/L, as well. They are thus like an aperitif wine (similar to a vermouth or a Pommeau). To obtain this, the juice would have had to be concentrated to at least 36°Bx or SG 1.160 on the fire. The Quebec regulations on cider seen above were revised in 2013 to define the designation *Fire Cider* as follows: *cider obtained by the fermentation of juice of apples that has a pre-fermentation sugar content of not less than 28° Brix achieved solely by heat, producing a finished product with a residual sugar content of not less than 80 g per liter and an actual alcoholic strength of more than 9% by volume but not more than 15% by volume.*

CHAPTER 16

CIDER TROUBLES AND HOW TO AVOID THEM

Some time ago a friend called me and said that a few months earlier, in October, he had started many primary fermentation pails of cider, which he had left to ferment in a room of his house. The pails were not hermetically closed, just covered with a towel to prevent dust from falling into them. The room was normally heated and was also used to store cases of apples that he hadn't had time to process. He hadn't taken time to care for the cider, and he didn't rack it into carboys equipped with airlocks. By mid-December he went to inspect it and found masses of fruit flies drowned in the cider, which was completely fermented and had started its transformation into vinegar—40 gallons of vinegar! And as a matter of fact, if he had wanted to produce vinegar, he couldn't have done better. All the elements were there: contact with air, high temperature, fruit flies. . . .

I tell this story to illustrate the fact that in the vast majority of cases cider troubles are caused by errors or negligence on the cider maker's part. Naturally, when we read old books dating back to a time when stainless steel was unknown and wooden barrels were used, and it was difficult to sanitize them adequately, cider troubles were much more frequent and varied than they are today.

First, I think it is important here to repeat some recommendations that I gave in the first part of this book and that are your best insurance to avoid problems with your cider:

1. At all times:
   - Sanitize the equipment with a sulfite solution or with a sanitizer.
   - Keep the cider room clean.
   - Do not forget that air is the worst enemy of cider.
   - Avoid all contact between the cider and a material such as iron, nonstainless steel, or copper. In fact, the only materials that should be

permitted to come into contact with the juice or the cider are glass, stainless steel, food-safe plastic, or certain types of wood.

2. After pressing and before fermentation:
   - Add pectinase to the juice or make a debourbage, as this facilitates the clearing of the cider at the end of fermentation.
   - Sulfite the juice. See the article on sulfite, section 14.1, to determine the correct dosage. Do not overdose.
   - Blend the juices in such a way so the pH is low enough to insure protection of the cider.

3. Use a primary fermentation vessel with a good closure. Recently, as he racked his cider, a correspondent on an Internet discussion forum found a drowned mouse in the bottom of his fermenter!

4. Do not wait too long to make the first racking. Leaving the cider in the primary fermenter when the active fermentation is completed is very risky because the air then comes into contact with the cider and may cause the sort of disorder related above.

5. Maintain a cool temperature in the cider room, 60°F (15°C) or less, because spoilage microorganisms will generally proliferate at higher temperatures, from 68°F (20°C) on up.

6. Keep your carboys well filled to minimize the headspace volume: don't leave more than 1 in. (2.5 cm) of space between the cider top level and the bottom of the airlock rubber closure. Alternatively, use some CO_2 as a protective blanket.

7. During and after the secondary fermentation, and all the time the cider is in the carboy, check the airlock regularly and make sure it never gets dry. This is especially important during the winter, as the cider temperature may become lower and thus by thermal contraction may suck the sanitary liquid out of the airlock, leaving it dry and permitting the entrance of air.

This last point is most important. This is the most critical period for the cider, because the yeast population decreases as the fermentation ends, and it can't insure its dominance anymore. Furthermore, no more carbon dioxide is being produced at this stage, and thus it can no longer protect the cider. Often also, during the fermentation the cider level decreases slightly, and if there was half an inch (1 cm) of headspace at the beginning of the fermentation, for example, we may find that this headspace has increased to 2 in. (5 cm) by the end of the fermentation. It is then necessary to raise the level to minimize the volume of ullage (headspace); see section 14.3. As discussed there, different methods are possible (listed here by order of preference):

- Add a bit of cider from the current batch that you have put aside for this purpose.
- Put some sanitized glass marbles or other filling objects into the carboy.
- Add a bit of finished cider from a previous year's batch, fresh apple juice, or water.

Some cider makers also apply a thin layer of vegetable oil, which will float on the surface of the cider, thus isolating it from the ambient air. Keep in mind that a cider that has been sulfited will better tolerate the presence of air because of the antioxidant property of SO_2. Hence, even more vigilance is required if you have chosen not to use sulfite.

The most common cider troubles, and those I discuss here, are film yeast or flower sickness, acetification, mousiness, Brett, hazy ciders that don't clear, and sulfuric or rotten-egg smells. There are other troubles or sicknesses described in older books on cider (see the bibliography). I mention them here only for reference, as these troubles have now practically disappeared, thanks to modern materials and sanitizers:

- **Framboisé,** which affects sweet ciders that contain very little alcohol and have a high pH, is a bacterial problem essentially seen in French ciders and described in the French literature on cider.
- **Oiliness** (or ropiness) and **geranium taint** (see also page 217) are rare disorders caused by lactic acid bacteria of the same type as those involved in malolactic fermentation.
- **Black** and **green ciders** are caused by contact with iron or copper. When there is such a metallic contamination, the cider may look fine until the bottle is opened. At this point some oxidation occurs, and the cider changes color (a bit like apple flesh turns brown when exposed to air). This comes along with an unpleasant harsh-bitter-metallic taste. The most common cause for this is old milling-pressing equipment, pumps, or plumbing fittings that contain iron or copper parts.

Film Yeast or Flower Sickness

Film yeast proliferation is probably the most common problem in cider making. In the discussion forums cider makers regularly ask for information on this, and I have had to deal with this problem a couple of times myself. This sickness is generally caused by a spoilage yeast called *Mycoderma vini* or *Candida mycoderma*, which is an aerobic microorganism that needs air to develop and reproduce

itself. A few other microorganisms of the genera *Pichia* or *Hansenula* may also cause it.

Flower sickness appears as a thin whitish or grayish film on the surface of the cider. If we touch this film, it breaks easily, and some parts may sink to the bottom of the vessel. It generally appears once the fermentation is completed and the cider is left in its carboy, for example, in waiting for it to clear, when air may come into contact with the cider. Every time I have seen this, there was either a dry (empty) airlock, a nonhermetic stopper, or too large a contact surface between the cider and air. Without air contact, the sickness can't develop. If we let the flower develop without intervention, some of the alcohol is broken down, the cider becomes lifeless and insipid, and an unpleasant smell may appear.

Fortunately, this sickness is not too serious, and if taken care of early in its development, it won't affect the quality of the cider. My strategy to eliminate it is simple:

1. With a clean, absorbent paper towel, pick up the film itself and clean the neck of the carboy.
2. Eliminate the air in the carboy, usually by one of the methods mentioned above, and bring the level of cider as close as possible to the bottom of the airlock.
3. Sulfite the cider. The first time I used a dosage of 100 ppm, but the cider still tasted sulfurous even after two years. Clearly, I had added too much. In subsequent occurrences, I used a 30 ppm dosage, which seems sufficient to prevent a reappearance of the sickness.
4. Use a small sprayer, of the sort sold for humidifying houseplants, to vaporize a 0.5 percent sulfite solution inside the neck of the carboy and on the surface of the cider. The quantity of

sulfite effectively used is very small but will be very efficient, as it is concentrated on the most vulnerable areas.

It may be more annoying when the flower develops in the bottles, as the above treatment can't be done on all the bottles. But since the closures should be hermetic, it is usually so slight as to be almost unnoticeable. Adequate levels of free SO₂ at the moment of bottling would prevent flower sickness.

Acetification

Acetification is a serious problem that may completely ruin a cider batch. It is caused by bacteria of the genus *Acetobacter,* which are naturally present in the air and on the skin and flesh of the apples. These bacteria are resistant to sulfite, so unless the juice is pasteurized, there will always be a small population of these bacteria that will survive all the steps of the fermentation. However, and fortunately for us, they need a lot of air and oxygen as well as relatively high temperatures to develop into a proliferating colony.

Acetobacters are aerobic bacteria that transform alcohol into acetic acid; in other words, they transform the cider into vinegar. It is important to understand that this is the natural end of the fermentation process. Our job as cider makers is to promote the early steps that transform the juice into cider, while preventing this final step toward vinegar. And the method is extremely easy: simply keep the air out and maintain a cool temperature—just the opposite of what my friend did, as I related in the beginning of this article.

The first symptoms of acetification may seem similar to those of flower sickness, with the appearance of a surface film. However, in this case the film will not break easily and is rather of gelatinous consistency: this is the vinegar mother that starts to establish itself. If you measure the total acidity by titration at this moment, you should see an increase of the TA because of the acetic acid that forms. If your cider is at this stage, it is quite difficult to cure, and it might be better to accept that you are making vinegar. Bring your carboy into a warmer area, separated from the other cider batches, put some oak chips in it, let the air in, and let it age for one or two years: you will then have an excellent vinegar! You may monitor the extent of the transformation by acidity titration: a fully made vinegar should have a TA of approximately 50 g/L expressed as malic acid (see section 9.2 on acidity measurement). Note that to measure such a high acidity, it is preferable to dilute the vinegar. For example, if you mix one part vinegar with four parts water, you have a one-fifth dilution; then if you get a TA of 10 g/L by titration of this mixture, it indicates the vinegar is at 50 g/L.

As a final note, a very slight acetification is not necessarily a catastrophe. For example, in Spain the *sidra de Asturias*, from the principal cider production area of that country, generally presents a slight acetification that gives the characteristic acidic taste of these ciders.

VOLATILE ACIDITY

The acetic acid features a property that makes it different from other acids in the cider: it is volatile. This means that it readily forms a vapor or fumes, easily noticed by sniffing an open bottle of vinegar. The malic and lactic acids in solution do not have a smell and are not (or only very slightly, in the case of lactic acid) volatile. If there is a lot of volatile acidity, then, it means that acetification has started. It is important to understand that there will always be a small quantity of acetic acid in the cider, and this quantity increases with time. It may take months, years, or decades, but eventually, if the cider isn't drunk, it will turn into vinegar.

We may evaluate the degree of acetification of a cider by measurement of the volatile acidity. This is more important in commercial operations as there is a legal limit, which may vary depending on the state or country of production. Each producer should check local regulations. The volatile acidity (VA) is normally expressed as grams per liter (g/L) of acetic acid equivalent. Important values are:

- VA < 0.7 g/L: excellent and practically undetectable by taste; however, at this level the acetic acid may pleasantly enhance the flavor of the cider.
- VA approximately equal to 1 g/L: still drinkable but should be watched closely and may not keep long.
- VA > 1.3 g/L: problematic, becoming unpleasant.

There are many ways to measure the volatile acidity. The first is a very rough estimation that may be done by a hobbyist on a kitchen stove and doesn't require any special equipment other than a titratable acidity kit. The principle is very simple: the TA of the cider is measured. Then a sample of the cider is boiled such that all the volatile acidity evaporates, and a new value of TA is measured (see the article on measurement of acidity by titration in section 9.2). The difference between the two values of TA corresponds to the volatile acids that have been boiled off. In practice, this boiling process needs to be done with care. The procedure and material required are very similar to the simple residue method for the

measurement of the alcoholic strength described in the article on alcohol (section 14.5), except that the TA is measured instead of the SG. Additionally, to make sure all the volatile acids are evaporated, once about two-thirds of the cider has been boiled off, it is recommended to refill the boiling flask with distilled water up to the original level and to boil it once more until about two-thirds has again been boiled off. This may even be repeated a third time. Finally, the boiled sample is adjusted to the original volume (250 mL, measured at the starting temperature) with distilled water and the second value of TA is measured. Now, if the values of TA are expressed as malic acid equivalent as recommended in section 9.2, then VA would also be expressed in the same units. A correction is required. For this, we know that acetic acid is a monoprotic acid with a molar mass of 60 g/mol and so 60 grams per acid equivalent. We have seen that malic acid is 67 grams per acid equivalent. We then obtain VA:

VA (g/L, acetic acid) =
$$60 (TA_1 - TA_2) / 67 = 0.9 (TA_1 - TA_2)$$

More precise measurement of the volatile acidity is done by distillation and calls for special equipment. Note that a distillation kit intended for measurement of alcoholic strength could be used with minor modification for VA testing. There are two distillation methods that are commonly used:

- The **Garcia-Tena method** is mainly used in Spain. It involves distilling a precise quantity of cider (11 mL) in a small still. The first 5.1 mL of distillate are discarded, then the following 3.2 mL are kept and used for acidity titration with NaOH. The volatile acidity is given by:

VA (g/L, acetic acid) = 18 *N K*,

where *N* is the normality of the NaOH (usually a normality of 1/49 or 1/50 is used for this test; hence, if you have standard *N*/5 normality NaOH, you would dilute it ten times in distilled water to obtain *N*/50) and *K* is the number of mL of NaOH used for the titration.

- The official and most precise method is by **steam distillation** of the volatile acids. In this case, steam from boiling distilled water is pushed through a tube in the sample to be tested. This produces bubbles of steam within the sample, which vaporize the volatile acids. The steam is then condensed to give a distillate, which contains the volatile acids. Titration is finally done to determine the total steam-distillable acidity. Corrections would have to be done to account for the lactic acid, SO_2, and CO_2 that could also have distilled, as these should not be included in the volatile acidity.

Microbiological Faults: Brett, Mousiness

There are many microorganisms that may give taints and off-tastes to a cider. Among these troubles, *mousiness* is a disorder that introduces an odor and taste to the cider that recalls an overpopulated mouse cage that hasn't been cleaned for a long time. *Brett*, which is the short, affectionate name for *Brettanomyces,* is related to horse, barnyard, or stable odors. These taints are generally attributed to the *Brettanomyces* spoilage yeast that may be present in small quantity in the juice because it lives on the skin of the fruit. Mousiness may additionally originate from lactic acid bacteria (LAB), in particular some species of *Lactobacillus,* which are also involved in malolactic fermentation (MLF). The distinction between these two faults is not easy, and a badly infected cider could have some of both. Even a very light contamination of either is, strictly speaking, considered a fault. However it is not necessarily a disaster and you might even think it makes the cider more complex and interesting. Sometimes similar taints originating from MLF are even sought after, like the "old horse" character, a feature of certain ciders from old cideries in Europe that ferment their ciders in old wooden barrels that host the responsible microorganisms. However, as the proportion of the compounds produced increases, the tainted cider becomes really unappealing. Personally, I never had one of my ciders affected, but I did have the displeasure of tasting a few badly infected samples.

There is no solution to cure these troubles. The recommendations given in the beginning of this article are normally sufficient to prevent them. Sulfite is efficient to control the growth of the Brett yeast and LAB, as they are sensitive to SO_2. Hence, these disorders are entirely avoidable. However, if by accident this type of disorder would appear a first time, it may then be difficult to eradicate it. All the material will need to be perfectly sterilized, otherwise it may reappear the following year. I met a cider maker a few years ago at the Cider Days festival whose ciders were all mousy year after year. But he had got used to the taste and actually enjoyed it! The cider drinker's tolerance to these taints is highly variable.

Cider That Doesn't Clear

When everything goes well, the cider clears naturally at the end of fermentation. It may take some time and require patience from the cider maker, but generally within a month after the fermentation has stopped the cider has at least started to clear. But once in a while, it will obstinately refuse to clear and will remain hazy. This may not be a disaster, as the haze doesn't affect the taste or bouquet of the cider and for some may even be a sign of a natural farm cider. But if you like to serve a crystal-clear cider, a cloudy cider is not what you are looking for.

Determining what causes a haze is not easy. Pectin is one of the most common causes, but there are also protein, microbial, and tannin hazes. Testing for a pectin haze may be done with the alcohol test described in the article on pectins in chapter 12: if the test is positive for the presence of pectin, that is, a gel forms or you can see pectin strands, then there is a good chance this pectin is the cause of the haze. As for the other possible causes of non-clarification of the cider, this is not easily determined without analysis.

The best way to avoid a haze in general is by prevention. A pectic enzyme (pectinase) treatment before the start of the fermentation will generally (but not always) prevent the formation of pectin hazes. These enzymes will break the pectin molecules, which will then deposit themselves with the lees. Microbial or bacterial hazes can usually be prevented by good sanitation and the use of sulfite.

However, even with the best prevention practices, the cider sometimes remains hazy. And in particular, perries are known to be more difficult to clear. One perry maker was mentioning on a forum that his perries usually need 6 to 9 months after the fermentation is finished to clear. If you have a pectin haze and didn't add the pectinase to the fresh juice, you can still try a pectinase treatment on the fermented cider. Because the action

Figure 16.1. Fining tests

of these enzymes is reduced in the presence of alcohol, though, you will need to at least double the recommended dosage, and even this doesn't insure the treatment will be effective. You might have better luck with fining. Some of the fining agents I have used with success with ciders and perries include the *Hot Mix Sparkolloid*, the *Kieselsol-Chitosan* tandem, and gelatin followed by a silica solution. These are sold at wine-making supply stores with instructions on how to use them. The best strategy is to take samples from the hazy cider and fill some test bottles. It is then possible to try different fining agents at different dosages on these bottles. And normally, within a day or two, we can see if one or many of the test bottles is working. Figure 16.1 illustrates such a test I have done on a very hazy perry. The two bottles on the left had different dosages of gelatin with silica solution, while the two on the right had Chitosan. Only one of the bottles cleared perfectly, and it had a dosage of twice the normal maximum recommended dosage of gelatin and silica. I was then able to apply this dosage to the whole batch. In the case of very hazy ciders and perries, it is often necessary to use dosages that exceed the recommendations, whereas when there is only a slight haze, smaller dosages are adequate.

Filtration may also be used to render a cider sparkling clear. However, don't attempt to filter a cider that is very hazy, as the filter pad will clog very rapidly. Hence, successful fining is required before filtration (see the sidebar on filtration, "A Hobbyist Filter Unit"). And a final word of caution: both filtering and fining will strip some flavor and tannins from the cider. It then becomes up to the cider maker to take the final decision as to whether he or she prefers a full-flavored cloudy cider or a cleared cider that may not have the same flavor.

An extreme form of pectic haze is a pectic gel. This may happen to ciders that contain a lot of pectin. When the fermentation is fully or almost completed, the pectin coagulates into a gel that, at the beginning of the process, may occupy half or two-thirds of the carboy, as shown in figure 16.2. Alcohol is required for this gel to form, and this is why it happens at the end of fermentation. There isn't much to do: with time the gel will compact itself in the bottom and may finally occupy only 20 to 25 percent of the volume, thus leaving the rest as a perfectly clear cider that

Figure 16.2. Pectic gel.

can be racked and bottled. The gel itself can be used in the kitchen for cooking, so it won't be entirely lost. The pectic gel is then a minor problem, since you still recover the better part of the cider.

Sulfur and Rotten-Egg Taints

These odors are extremely unpleasant, and it may be difficult to identify the exact origin and find a remedy. They are caused by *hydrogen sulfide* (chemical formula H_2S), which may be produced by the fermentation under certain conditions. I've never had sulfur odors in my ciders, but some cider makers on the discussion forums report the problem. It seems that in general the taint is related either to the type of yeast or to the nutrients used. Another possible culprit could be if sulfur was applied in the orchard as a fungicide: some of this sulfur may stick to the skin of the apples and find its way into the must, causing excessive sulfur concentration in the cider and eventually these taints. Sometimes the odor may appear during a very active fermentation and disappear thereafter without a trace. But other times the odor persists, and a recommended remedy is to treat the cider with copper, which eliminates the hydrogen sulfide. As I have never had to take such steps, I prefer to refer you to a good wine-making book or suggest an Internet search for details on this treatment.

A Hobbyist Filter Unit

A small filter unit such as the one shown in figure 16.3 may be used on some ciders that have a very slight haze to render them perfectly clear. There are two filter pads contained in the red, disk-shaped housing. A small air pump pushes air into the carboy and provides the force to drive the cider through the filter pads. The exit of the filter may be sent directly to the bottles or to a receiving vessel, as shown here.

Pads for these units are sold with different ratings indicating the size of the particles they will intercept. A coarse pad is normally rated at 5 or 6 microns (1 micron is a thousandth of a millimeter), a medium pad would be between 1 and 2 microns, and a fine or sterile pad is 0.5 micron, which is fine enough to intercept the yeast cells. Before using fine pads, however, passes with coarse and medium pads should first

Figure 16.3. A hobbyist filter unit

be done to prevent clogging the pads. For making what is called sterile filtration (see section 15.1 on sweetness in cider), all the line after the filter must be perfectly sterilized (for example, by pushing some steam through).

Such a filter unit will, however, be useless in the case of a very troubled cider such as the one

shown in figure 16.3, which had a heavy pectic haze. In this particular case, I didn't really think filtering would be successful, but I still wanted to do the test to convince myself. As I suspected, the pads became completely clogged almost immediately after starting to filter, even though I used pads of the coarser size.

If you often have hydrogen sulfide odors in your ciders, you should try to change the type of yeast you use and/or the regime of yeast nutrients. Some yeast strains are known to produce H$_2$S more easily than others. This is normally indicated on the technical data sheet of the yeast, sheets that we can find in the Internet site of the manufacturer or distributor. For example, the technical sheet for the Lalvin EC-1118 yeast may be found at: http://www.lallemandwine.com/catalog/products/view/581, where it says that this yeast strain has a very low rate of production of H$_2$S. It also seems that this problem occurs mainly when the fermentation is very active with juice from early apples and when the temperature is relatively high: if under those circumstances the nutrients would come to be lacking, then the yeasts might produce H$_2$S in greater quantity. On the other hand, slow fermentations at low temperature of musts that are poor in nutrients are almost never affected, as the fermentation is never very active under such conditions.

Caution: Novice cider makers might not make the distinction between sulfite and sulfide. There is only one letter difference between the two words, but they represent entirely different things. Sulfite, or SO$_2$, is added by the cider maker, and when overdosed has the character of a burning match. Sulfide is hydrogen sulfide (H$_2$S), as discussed above, and produces an odor of rotten eggs.

UNITS AND MEASURES

Liters and Gallons

The liter (L) is the unit of volume most often used in cider making, and the hectoliter (hL) is also widely used in Europe, even though neither is an official unit in the International System of Units (SI). The official unit of volume in the SI system, the cubic meter (which contains 1,000 L), is not really used in cider making.

In the United States the most common unit of volume is the US gallon, while in the UK and Canada the larger imperial gallon is sometimes seen, although these two countries now use metric units and hence the liter. All mentions of gallons in this book are for US gallons unless otherwise noted. Following are conversion formulae for these volume units:

1 L = 0.26 US gal. = 0.21 imp. gal.

1 US gal = 3.8 L = 0.83 imp. gal.

1 imp. gal. = 4.5 L = 1.2 US gal.

   (i.e., 6 US gal. = 5 imp. gal.)

1 hL = 100 L = 26 US gal. = 21 imp. gal.

For the measurement of small volumes, the milliliter (mL) is used, which is a thousandth of a liter, equal to a cubic centimeter. Such small volumes in mL are normally measured with a graduated cylinder, a burette, or a syringe, depending on the quantity and the precision required. For maximum precision, a volumetric flask is used.

Other US units used for volumes include the fluid ounce (see a little further), the pint, and the quart, but these are not used in the present book.

Kilograms and Pounds

A mass is a certain quantity of a substance. In SI units these are grams (g) and kilograms (kg), with 1 kg = 1,000 g. For very small quantities, we use milligrams (mg), with 1,000 mg = 1 g. Weight is a force that is given by the gravitation to a mass. Hence, a mass of 1 kg will weigh 9.8 newtons (N) under the earth's gravity (this is from the well-known Newton's law, $F = m\,a$), but we often round this to 10 N when we don't need precision. By extension and when the discussion is informal, the kilogram may be used as a force or as a weight. We then call it a kilogram-force.

In US customary units, the unit of force and of weight is the pound (lb.). The official but little-used unit of mass in the imperial system is the slug; in informal discussions the pound is often also used as mass and is then called pound-mass (lbm.). The smaller unit of weight is the ounce (oz.) with 16 ounces to a pound. The following conversions may be used:

1 kg = 2.2 lb.
1 oz. = 28 g

For cider-making operations, it is generally more practical to use the SI units (i.e., grams and kilograms). A digital scale with a resolution of 0.1 g and a capacity of 1 kg is highly recommended for measuring small quantities of different substances. Note that strictly speaking a scale is for measuring a force (or a weight), while a balance is for measuring a mass. But in practice, digital scales of the trade are calibrated to give the mass in grams. They would give a false result if you went to the moon to make your measurements (as the gravity is different there), but this is quite unlikely.

Measuring Spoons and Cups

For rough measure of some dry matters and liquids, measuring spoons and cups may be used. Of course, the measure will not be as precise as with a scale or a graduated cylinder (in the case of liquids), but sometimes precision is not that important, as when you prepare a sanitizing solution or add

sugar for priming. One level teaspoon contains a little less than 5 mL. The important word here is "level": it means that you should run a spatula or another edge on the top of the spoon and scrape off any excess matter. Note that measuring cups and spoons are slightly larger in the United States than in Canada and the UK because their dimension is based on the definition of the fluid ounce, which is 4 percent larger in the United States.

1 teaspoon = 4.9 mL (US) ;
   1 teaspoon = 4.7 mL (UK, Can)
1 tablespoon = 3 teaspoons, or
   approximately 14.5 mL
1 fluid ounce = 2 tablespoons, or
   approximately 29 mL
1 cup = 8 fluid ounces, or approximately 230 mL

When using measuring cups and spoons for dry substances like sugar or potassium metabisulfite, we also need to know the relation between volume and mass of the substance, that is, its volumic mass. I have tested substances that may be of interest to a cider maker, with the following results:

White sugar:
   0.75 to 0.87 g/mL
   (170 to 200 g to a cup)
Dextrose:
   0.55 to 0.7 g/mL
   (125 to 150 g to a cup)
Diammonium phosphate (DAP)
   and potassium metabisulfite:
   both approximately 1 g/mL
   (4.5 to 5 g to a teaspoon)
Citric acid:
   approximately 0.85 g/mL
   (4 g to a teaspoon)

Pectinase:

    approximately 0.5 g/mL

    (2.5 g to a teaspoon)

Since the density of a dry matter varies with its compaction and with the size of the crystals, other tests may give different results from the ones I show above. It is always preferable to measure with a scale when precision is required.

Concentrations: g/L and ppm

Most concentrations of a substance in cider or juice are expressed as grams per liter at a certain reference temperature, which is most often 20°C (68°F). For example, the concentrations of sugar, acid, or tannin are always in g/L in this book. We may also see concentrations in percentage, that is, in mass per 100 units of mass of the solution, as in Brix units. When this solution has a volumic mass close to 1,000 g/L, as in cider or apple juice, then the relation between the two is simple, although there might be a difference of the order of 5 percent:

$$1\% \approx 10 \text{ g/L}$$

The equivalent US unit for a concentration would be in ounces per gallon, which is a bit awkward to use and not recommended. For reference, the following relation may be used for conversion:

$$1 \text{ oz/gal} = 7.5 \text{ g/L}$$

Ppm stands for *parts per million*. It is a useful unit for small concentrations. In cider making, we use

TABLE 16.1:

Mass in grams for a given concentration

CONCENTRATION	AMOUNT OF SUBSTANCE FOR COMMON SIZES OF CIDER BATCHES (GRAMS)			
	3 GAL (11 L)	**5 GAL** (19 L)	**6 GAL** (23 L)	**1 hL** (26 gal)
10 ppm	0.1	0.2	0.2	1
40 ppm	0.4	0.8	0.9	4
70 ppm	0.8	1.3	1.6	7
100 ppm	1.1	1.9	2.3	10
150 ppm	1.7	2.9	3.5	15
300 ppm	3.3	5.7	6.9	30
500 ppm	5.5	9.5	11.5	50
1 g/L	11	19	23	100
4 g/L	44	76	92	400
10 g/L	110	190	230	1,000
30 g/L	330	570	690	3,000

it, for example, in the dosage of sulfite, DAP, or enzymes. Thus, 1 ppm is 1 gram of product mixed in 1 million grams of solution, or approximately 1,000 liters of apple juice or cider. One ppm is also approximately equivalent to 1 milligram per liter (1 mg/L) and 10 ppm to 1 gram per hectoliter. We may compute the quantity of a substance to add in grams to obtain a certain concentration in ppm with the following relation:

$$\text{(Mass in grams of substance)} \approx \text{ppm} \times \text{(volume in liters)} / 1{,}000$$

Table 16.1 on page 303 gives the amount of a substance for different concentrations in some sizes of cider batches, including common carboy sizes.

Bushels, Bins, and Tons

When dealing with quantities of apples, the bushel (bu) is a useful unit of measure because it corresponds to a container easily manageable by a single person. The bushel is a unit of volume, and its definition is different in the United States as opposed to Canada and the UK, being 3 percent smaller in the United States:

1 bu (US) = 35.2 L
1 bu (UK, Can) = 36.5 L

For rough calculations, we generally count approximately 40 lb. (18 kg) of apples to a well-filled bushel. This would be less for a level bushel, more like 33 to 35 lb. (15–16 kg).

Bins are used mainly in commercial operations. They are large wood boxes designed to be moved by forklifts. Standard bins usually contain 15 to 18 bushels, or approximately 600 lb. of apples. Half bins and other sizes also exist.

For even larger quantities of apples, as for the production of an orchard, we use tons, which in US units are defined as 2,000 lb., while the metric ton is 1,000 kg: this is 2,200 lb., or 10 percent more than the US ton, a difference that may be neglected most of the time. Hence, we will have 50 to 55 well-filled bushels to a ton of apples. The ton is also used for the loading force unit in a press. In this case, in the metric system, 1 ton is 9,800 N, which is usually rounded to 10,000 N.

COMPANION MATERIALS

The companion materials for this book consist of five spreadsheet programs that may be run on MS Excel or similar programs such as Open Office or Libre Office that can open .xls files. All have been developed as aids on certain aspects of cider making.

Readers may download these programs free of charge. To do so, you need to access the website indicated at the end of the respective descriptions. All files are relatively small (under 100 KB) and may be downloaded even with a slow Internet connection.

Hydrometer Correction and Calibration

This program is designed to facilitate the calibration procedure of a hydrometer, as discussed in section 8.2, "The Hydrometer." Before using it,

you should prepare three reference solutions, two at the extremes of the range of the instrument and one approximately in the middle of this range. These solutions may be prepared with distilled water and either sugar or salt. See the article for details on their preparation.

When the solutions are prepared and their temperature well stabilized at the hydrometer calibration temperature, open the spreadsheet under the "Calibration" tab, take two hydrometer readings in each of the reference solutions, and enter the SG values in the fields with a light brown background on the table of entries. Enter the SG of the reference solutions in the fields with a light green background. You may also enter the date and temperature for future reference, but this isn't used by the program. Once you have finished, the calibration factors—the slope and offset of the calibration line—will be displayed in the two yellow fields. Additionally, the graph displayed may be used to make the correction: the blue line is the calibration line of the hydrometer, which may be compared with the thin black line of a perfect hydrometer.

Once the calibration is done, the "Correction" tab is used to obtain the true SG from the value read on the hydrometer and the measured temperature. Make sure the correct calibration temperature for the hydrometer (60F, 15C, or 20C) is entered in the "Data" area. The true SG value is displayed in the yellow field.

www.chelseagreen.com/hydrometer

The Blending Wizard

This spreadsheet is an aid for blending. It will allow you to predict the SG and acidity of a blend when you know these numbers for the individual components of the blend, as discussed in chapter 13. It is based on a very simple, weighted average routine to compute the SG and acidity of the blend. Please refer to the text in the above-mentioned article for instructions on how to use the wizard.

www.chelseagreen.com/blending

Fermentation Monitoring

The fermentation monitor was discussed in section 14.3, "Monitoring and Control of Fermentation." It provides a framework in which to record the evolution of the fermentation and plot a graph of SG as a function of the time elapsed since the beginning of the fermentation. It also automatically displays the fermentation speed in FSU.

The complete spreadsheet contains an introductory tab that gives basic instructions for how to use the program. Additionally, at the bottom of this sheet you may enter hydrometer data, which will allow you to perform automatically the required corrections as a function of the temperature and calibration. The calibration data for the hydrometer may be imported from the file Hydromtr.xls above.

The following tabs are for two sheets that contain implementations of the monitor, in English and in French, respectively. If you are an English-language user, you may simply delete the French tab, and you may make many copies of the English tab, keeping one copy for each batch of a year, for example. You could thus keep one such file on record for all the cider batches you have made in a given year.

In the monitor table, each line represents one measurement of the cider SG: the inputs are the date, temperature of the cider, SG read from the hydrometer, and (optionally) the acidity. If you made some action or intervention, you may note this in the last column on the right. Temperatures may be entered in either Fahrenheit or Celsius, and the conversion will be automatically made to Celsius when the letter "F" is entered in the green field below the table. From this data, the program calculates the number of days elapsed, the corrected SG, and the speed of fermentation. These are displayed in the columns with a yellow background.

The graph on the right shows a plot of the SG evolution as a function of the date and temperature. A second graph shows the evolution of the speed of fermentation. These graphs may be modified as required.

www.chelseagreen.com/monitoring

Fermentation Model

This is an implementation of the fermentation model that is described in section 14.5, "The Alcohol." From simple data on the must that is to be fermented, it will let you predict the alcoholic strength and final SG of the cider. It will also take into account the sugar that may be added for chaptalization, as described in the article on sugar concentration in chapter 8. Additionally, and this may be one of the most useful features, it may be used for the dosage of priming sugar when a sparkling cider is being prepared and will determine the class of carbonation as seen in section 15.2 on sparkling ciders. The main part of the sheet is within a frame, and on the exterior of this frame, on the right, are some constants and factors used by the program; below, there are some calculation routines. Normal usage of the sheet will, however, be inside the frame, which includes eight sections that correspond to different steps of the transformation of the fresh juice into a finished cider:

1. **Properties and quantity of fresh juice.** In this section the user is asked to enter basic data about the juice: SG, acidity, and quantity of juice. From this, we obtain the Brix, volumic mass, and total mass of the juice.

2. **Adjustment of the sugar content.** If we want to predict the alcoholic strength of a cider, we need to know how much sugar the must contains. However, as discussed in the article on sugar concentration in chapter 8, the exact amount of sugar cannot be known from the value of SG. Only the average value from a large number of samples taken worldwide may be determined, and a given sample may contain more or less sugar than this average value. The user may enter here an adjustment factor that will increase or decrease the quantity of sugar that the program will use for the calculations. Note that the value entered should be between −11.3 and +11.3 percent, as these numbers represent the bounds of the 95 percent confidence interval on sugar content (see chapter 8). The program displays the amount of sugar and the potential alcohol of the must thus adjusted.

3. **Additions to the must and conditions prior to main fermentation.** In this section the user may enter additions of sugar and water to the must for chaptalization or dilution. These are entered as a certain amount per liter, and the program displays the total amount required considering the quantity of juice entered in section 1. The updated potential alcohol and SG after these additions are also displayed.

4. **Condition of the must after the main fermentation.** Here the SG and alcoholic strength of the cider after the main fermentation are computed and displayed. The user may enter a value for residual sugar if this fermentation did not proceed all the way to dryness.

5. **Priming sugar and natural carbonation.** This section is similar to section 3 above, where the user may enter some sugar and water additions. Note that you may specify a quantity of cider different from that entered in the first section, as we are considering the quantity that is being bottled at this stage. The SG of the cider after those additions is displayed.

6. **Finished cider (assuming no MLF).** The program will use the values entered just above, plus the amount of residual sugar entered in section 4, to compute the quantity of carbon dioxide produced for natural carbonation of the

cider. Again, an amount of residual sweetness may be entered for the finished cider. From this information, the following will be displayed: final SG and alcoholic strength, class of carbonation, and sweetness.

7. **Analysis of cider.** In this section we try to predict the results that would be obtained from a chemical analysis of the cider. Values are displayed for the dry extract and sugar-free dry extract (these will be identical if the amount of residual sugar entered is 0). From the amount of dry extract, it is possible to obtain the SG the cider would have if the alcohol was boiled off. From this, a value of alcoholic strength is obtained using regression coefficients based on the Honneyman table. Actually, this simulates the Honneyman method for measurement of the alcoholic strength, and the result obtained is generally very close to the one displayed in section 6 above (to within 0.1% ABV). (See the discussion "A Simple Method for Measurement of Alcoholic Strength" in section 14.5.)

8. **Malolactic fermentation.** This last section computes an approximate variation of the SG caused by malolactic fermentation. The value of total acidity entered in section 1 is used, with the percentage of transformation specified by the user.

In the lower left corner, the calculated ratio of alcohol by volume (ABV) to total SG drop is displayed. Its value is generally between 125 and 130, depending on different adjustments to the model and on whether MLF has been specified or not. (See the discussion on "Estimation of Alcoholic Strength by Gravity Drop" in section 14.5.)

Below the frame is where the calculations are done, their results displayed in their relevant

section in the framed part. First, there is a table where the constituents of the cider are followed along the process. All the true constituents of the cider are considered as being in one of these categories, although this is a gross approximation: water, solids, alcohol, carbon dioxide, or other products of fermentation. Below, there is a line for the fermentable sugar, which is part of the solids. Along the process, the quantity (in grams) of each of these components may increase or decrease in value: for example, during fermentation the amounts of fermentable sugar and solids decrease, while the amount of alcohol, carbon dioxide, and other products of fermentation increase. These amounts are computed from the Pasteur relation, whose coefficients are displayed on the right. Finally, there is a line for the volume of the cider, considering an initial volume (1 liter by default) of fresh juice indicated in the field in green above the table. This volume fluctuates along the process, increasing when sugar is added and usually decreasing slightly during fermentation.

Below this, there is a subroutine that permits the calculation of the approximate volume of a mixture of water, alcohol, and sugar, taking into account the volumic contraction as discussed in section 14.5. The inputs for this routine are the amount of water, sugar, and alcohol in grams, taken from the table described above. Note that an approximation that is done in this model is that the products of fermentation other than alcohol and carbon dioxide are assumed to behave as water in this mixture, hence the entry "Water (+ water equivalent)." This routine is used four times, to obtain the results displayed in sections 3, 4, 5, and 6, respectively.

Finally, below this, there are some calculations that are done to evaluate the variation of mass and volume that may occur during a complete or partial malolactic fermentation.

This model may be tweaked so that the results displayed have a better correspondence with the actual situation of the cider being modeled. In particular, if the final SG displayed doesn't correspond to the measured SG of the finished cider, this may be caused (and be corrected) by one or more of the following factors:

- A biased hydrometer. Check your hydrometer in distilled water, and make sure you have done the adequate compensation if the temperature is different from the calibration temperature of the instrument. Ideally, a complete calibration should be done (see file Hydromtr.xls above).
- An actual sugar content in the juice different from the worldwide average. This may happen for some terroirs and apple varieties. Use the adjustment factor in section 2. The factor that is used to obtain the sugar content (2130 by default) is a worldwide average, and a different value may be more representative of your situation. See the article on the amount of sugar in apple juice, section 8.3.
- Finally, as a last resort, the tweaking factor for volumic contraction may be used to change the final SG of the cider.

Other tweaks that may be done are on the coefficients of the Pasteur relation that determine how much alcohol is produced from a certain quantity of sugar. Some yeast types are known to be more or less efficient for alcohol production. In particular, with a natural yeast fermentation, the coefficient for the rate of production of alcohol could be reduced (for example, to 47 percent). The last tweak is on the amount of carbon dioxide in

solution in the cider prior to bottling for a natural carbonation. This amount is added to the amount produced by the in-bottle fermentation to determine the carbonation of the finished cider. The default value is that there is sixty percent of the saturation concentration already present (i.e., 1.2 g/L), but if at the moment of bottling the cider is quite lively and bubbles freely, it probably means it is fully saturated, and this number could then be increased to 2 g/L. On the other hand, some ciders may have stayed on their lees for a long time, and most of the CO_2 has escaped: the quantity of gas in solution could then be lower.

www.chelseagreen.com/model

Cider Notebook

In this program I have combined the functions described above to obtain a multitab spreadsheet, with the object of keeping one such file for each batch of cider. The first tab is an introductory tab where the batch name may be entered with notes of interest for this cider batch. Tasting notes may also be added there. The second tab includes the blending wizard, where a permanent record of the blend may be kept. Additionally, on this tab I have included a few extra routines. One is for calculation of sulfite addition to the must: from the pH of the juice, the recommended concentration of SO_2 is displayed in ppm, along with the quantity of potassium metabisulfite that should be added to obtain this concentration in the must. A second routine is there to help determine the amount of a substance for a given concentration: this is an implementation of the table in Appendix 1. A hydrometer correction routine is also implemented, as this should prove practical when entering the data in the Wizard. The required data for this correction are in the bottom of the sheet, and the regression coefficients for the hydrometer calibration should be imported from the file Hydromtr.xls.

The third tab of this program is the fermentation model described above, which may be used to model the different additions that may be done to this cider and record these additions. The fourth tab is the fermentation monitor, where the evolution of the fermentation is recorded. Note that the monitor also uses the hydrometer correction data that is on the "Blend" tab.

www.chelseagreen.com/notebook

BIBLIOGRAPHY

Books are important for me, and one of the first things I do when I have a new book in my hands is to look at the bibliography to see if there is a reference I don't know about. I have carefully chosen the books below. They are all, in my opinion, significant books on pomology, orcharding, or cider making; they may have historical value, or they may have influenced me (or this book) in one way or another. Many are written in French: this is in great part because most of the early scientific work that was done on cider was by French scientists. Some I have already cited in the text; others are there mainly for the pleasure they may give to the reader. I have also included a personal comment after each entry.

Nowadays, thanks to the Internet, a number of older books are available for download as PDFs or other formats. These represent an extraordinary source of information that was extremely difficult to obtain just ten years ago. Following are a few good places where interesting books may be found in a digital format:

- Internet Archive (http://www.archive.org) is a US-based site whose objective is to build an Internet library. Most of the titles available are from large university libraries in the United States.
- Google (http://books.google.com) has digitized a great number of books from all countries and in numerous languages. Many may be downloaded integrally, but unfortunately, for many important titles only extracts are available.
- Gallica (http://gallica.bnf.fr) is the digital library of the Bibliothèque nationale de France (BNF, the National Library of France). These are mostly French titles.

When I am aware that one of the books listed below is available in a digital format and easily downloadable, I indicate it.

◆ ◆ ◆ ◆ ◆

Alwood, William Bradford (1903), *A Study of Cider Making in France, Germany and England with Comments and Comparisons on American Work*. Washington: US Department of Agriculture, 114 pages (digital document: Internet Archive).

This is a report Alwood made after a trip to Europe, where he studied the methods used in different countries, with the aim of importing some of these methods to improve the quality of cider made in the United States.

Baltet, Charles (1884), *Traité de la culture fruitière commerciale et bourgeoise*. Paris: G. Masson, 640 pages (digital document: Google).

Baltet was a renowned French horticulturist who introduced many varieties of apples and pears that are still grown today. This is certainly one of the best treatises on fruit horticulture of that period. It includes descriptions and good-quality plates of many varieties of fruits, including a section on cider apples.

Bauduin, Rémi (2006), *Guide pratique de la fabrication du cidre*. Sées, France: CTPC, 68 pages.

This small book is an excellent guide for the preparation of French-style cider and includes a good description of the keeving method as it is nowadays practiced in France to produce sweet ciders.

Beach, S. A. (1905), *The Apples of New York*. Albany: New York Department of Agriculture, vol. 1, 409 pages; vol. 2, 360 pages (digital document: Internet Archive).

The Apples of New York is probably the most important reference for the identification of older apples varieties. Beach describes approximately 5,000 North American varieties, with emphasis on those grown in New York State, at the beginning of the twentieth century. A leading fruit horticulturist of that era, Beach was among the first to do controlled crosses, taking the pollen from the flower of one variety to pollinate another variety. He thus created the Cortland apple, which became a very successful variety.

Boré, J. M., and J. Fleckinger (1997), *Pommiers à cidre, variétés de France*. Paris: INRA, 774 pages.

The most complete modern reference on French cider-apple varieties, this work includes complete technical descriptions of 342 cider apples, with numerous color photographs.

Buell, J. S. (1869), *The Cider Maker's Manual—A Practical Handbook*. Buffalo: Haas & Kelley, 174 pages. Reprinted by Silver Street Media in 2011.

Buell & Brother were manufacturers of mills and presses for cider. This little book is interesting mostly for the descriptions of such equipment that was in use in the United States by the mid-nineteenth century.

Bultitude, John (1983), *Apples—A Guide to the Identification of International Varieties*. Seattle: University of Washington Press, 323 pages.

A modern English pomology treatise, this includes complete descriptions of 252 varieties of apples, mostly English but also many North American, all with color pictures and photos in black and white of apple sections. Unfortunately, this great book is very difficult to find.

Copas, Liz (2001), *A Somerset Pomona: The Cider Apples of Somerset*. Stanbridge, UK: Dovecote Press, 80 pages.

This beautiful book includes the complete descriptions with very nice photographs of eighty of the most important cider apples grown in England.

Coxe, William (1817), *A View of the Cultivation of Fruit Trees, and the Management of Orchards and Cider*. Philadelphia: Carey and Son, 253 pages, plus numerous plates (digital document: Internet Archive).

This is the first important fruit book published in the United States, and it has become a classic. Coxe was also a cider maker, and the book contains some good information on how cider was made at the time.

Crowden, James (2008), *Ciderland*. Edinburgh: Birlinn, 256 pages.

This book is mostly for the pleasure of meeting some great English craft cider makers in their farms or cider houses. A wonderful book for anyone planning a cider trip to England.

Dapena, E., and M. D. Blazquez Noguero (2009), *Description de las variedades de manzana de la DOP Sidra de Asturias*. SERIDA, 69 pages (digital document: www.serida.org).

This booklet gives a complete description with pictures and analysis results for the twenty-two Spanish cider-apple varieties that are accepted for the *sidra de Asturias* controlled designation.

de Boutteville, L., and A. Hauchecorne (1875), *Le Cidre*. Rouen: Léon Deshays, 364 pages (digital document: Gallica).

This work marks a milestone in the history of cider because it is regarded as the first real scientific book on cider, offering laboratory analysis results of juice samples from cider apples and perry pears. In addition to complete descriptions, the authors give volumic mass, sugar concentration, tannin, acids, and pectin for fifty-one varieties. Although it was later shown that their method of sugar dosage didn't account accurately for reducing and nonreducing sugars, making their results erroneous, this book is nonetheless very important.

Dujardin, J. (1928), *Notice sur les instruments de précision appliqués à l'oenologie à la pomologie et à la brasserie*, 6th ed. Paris: Imp. de la Maison Dujardin, 1096 pages (digital document: http://cnum.cnam.fr/redir?M9872).

Jules Dujardin succeeded Jules Salleron as head of the Dujardin-Salleron laboratories, a company dedicated to manufacturing equipment for precision oenology analysis. The company still exists, and some of the instruments they make today are very similar to those described in this book, which is an enhanced instruction manual.

Établissements Simon Frères (four editions between 1897 and 1909), *Guide pratique de la production et la fabrication des cidres et poirés*. Niort, France (digital document, http://www .normannia.info/).

The Établissements Simon Frères was a manufacturer of mills and presses in the beginning of the twentieth century, so this book was as much for marketing purposes as to describe cider-making practices of the time. Three editions are available for download at the above URL.

Garner, R. J. (2013), *The Grafter's Handbook,* 6th edition. White River Junction, Vt.: Chelsea Green.

The first edition of this classic English reference on grafting dates back to 1947. This book has been continuously updated and revised since its first publication (I have the fifth edition, from 1988), and it is still considered the standard reference for all types of grafting, both commonplace and esoteric.

Hall-Beyer, Bart, and Jean Richard (1983), *Ecological Fruit Production in the North.* Trois-Rivières: Richard, 270 pages.

This book is an English translation and adaptation of Jean Richard and Céline Caron, *Guide pratique de production—fruits et petits fruits* (Trois-Rivières, 1981). It has been re-edited a few times, the last (as far as I know) in 1997. This is the first fruit book I acquired shortly after I started caring for the apple trees on my property. And while this book doesn't discuss questions relative to cider, it contains a lot of useful information for growing apples. It is with this book that I learned to prune apple trees and graft new varieties.

Hogg, Robert, and Henry Graves Bull (1878–1885), *The Herefordshire Pomona* (CD version, Marcher Apple Network, 2005).

This book is doubtless the most important work of nineteenth-century English pomology. Just 600 copies were printed, and originals are now extremely rare and expensive. Fortunately, Marcher Apple Network has come out with a version on CD at a reasonable price.

Hogg, Robert, and Henry Graves Bull (1886), *The Apple & Pear as Vintage Fruits.* Hereford, UK: Jakeman and Carver, 247 pages (digital document: Internet Archive).

After completion of their classic *Herefordshire Pomona,* the authors took a deeper look into cider apples and perry pears, their cultivation, and the preparation of cider.

International Organization of Legal Metrology (1973), *International Alcoholometric Tables.* Paris: OIML, 71 pages (digital document: http:// www.oiml.org/publications/R/R022-e75.pdf).

These tables published by OIML enable us to relate the volumic mass to the alcoholic strength and the temperature of alcohol-water mixtures.

Jacquemin, G., and H. Alliot (1902), *La Cidrerie moderne ou l'art de faire le bon cidre.* Nancy: Imprimerie E. Thomas, 735 pages (digital document: Internet Archive).

Georges Jacquemin's main contribution is in yeast. He succeeded in isolating selected pure strains of yeasts to inoculate a must and hence obtain more predictable results. His work wasn't limited to cider but included wine, beer, mead, and distilled alcohols.

Khanizadeh, S., and J. Cousineau (1998), *Our Apples / Les pommiers de chez nous.* Saint-Jean-sur-Richelieu: Agriculture and Agri-Food Canada, 258 pages.

In this bilingual book, we find descriptions (and color photographs for many) of the 254 apple varieties that have been tested at the experimental orchard of the Saint-Jean-sur-Richelieu Station of Agriculture Canada in southwestern Quebec. Many cider varieties imported from England were tested during this program and are described in the book.

Lea, Andrew (2008), *Craft Cider Making*. Preston, UK: Good Life Press, 160 pages.

Andrew Lea is a leading scientist in the field of cider. As an agro-food biochemist, he worked for thirteen years at the Long Ashton Research Center in England. He is the author of numerous scientific publications on the biochemistry of cider and more particularly on tannin. I met him only once at the Cider Days festival, but we regularly exchange correspondence, and he readily shares his knowledge on the discussion forums. His book is one of the best guides for cider making, in particular for the English style. Lea also maintains an Internet site on cider making, *The Wittenham Hill Cider Pages* (http://www.cider.org.uk/).

Lea, A., and J. R. Piggott, eds. (2003), *Fermented Beverage Production*, 2nd edition, New York: Kluwer Academic / Plenum Publishers, 423 pages.

A high-level scientific book that is not easy reading, this is a collection of review articles on the different beverages obtained by fermentation. Of greatest interest for cider makers are an article on fermentation and yeast by D. R. Berry and J. C. Slaughter, another on cider making by Andrew Lea and Jean-François Drilleu, and many articles on wine that pertain to cider, including one on sparkling wines by Patricia Howe.

Leger, Eleanor (2010), Making and Marketing Vermont Ice Cider. West Charleston, VT: Eden Ice Cider (digital document: Making_Vermont_Ice_Cider.pdf.)

An excellent guide for the commercial production of ice cider.

Lloyd, F. J. (1903), *Report on the Results of Investigations into Cidermaking, Carried Out on Behalf of the Bath and West and Southern Counties Society in the Years 1893–1902*. London: Darling and Son, 145 pages (digital document: Internet Archive).

A very interesting English book that relates a series of experimentations on cider making. A true pioneer's work, part of an effort that eventually led to the foundation of the Long Ashton Research Station.

Luckwill, L. C., and A. Pollard (1963), *Perry Pears*. Bristol, UK: University of Bristol, 216 pages.

This book is undoubtedly the most important reference on English perry pears to have been published during the twentieth century. It contains complete descriptions and color photos of over fifty varieties, with some notes on their use for perry. It is still available as a reprint and is highly recommended for anyone wishing to grow these pears and make perry.

Macoun, W. T. (1916), *Apple in Canada, Its Cultivation and Improvement*. Ottawa: Canada Department of Agriculture, bulletin no. 86 (digital document: Internet Archive).

Macoun was horticulturist at the Ottawa Experimental Farm at the beginning of the twentieth century. A prominent personality in the field of Canadian pomology, he participated in the development of many hardy Canadian apple varieties that are still grown, like Melba, Lobo, and Sandow. The Macoun apple was named after him. In addition to this one, his bulletin no. 37, from 1901, and the annual reports of the Ottawa Experimental Farm are also worth reading.

Merwin, I., S. Valois, and O. I. Padilla-Zakour (2008), "Cider Apples and Cider-Making Techniques in Europe and North America," *Horticultural Reviews*, vol. 34, pp. 365–415.

This is a major review article that covers the history and current situation of cider apples and cider production in Europe and North America. It is worth having this article just for its list of references, which includes most of the significant books and articles to have been published on cider. This is a relatively hard-to-find publication, and the likeliest place to look for it is in a university library.

Mohr, W. P. (1988), *Apple Cultivars for Juice and Cider Production*. Smithfield: Agriculture Canada, technical bulletin 1988-6E, 40 pages (digital document: Internet Archive).

This bulletin reports on tests that were done on about one hundred apple varieties, including unnamed selections, English cider apples, and recently released scab-resistant apples. The juice was tested for specific gravity, tannin and acidity content, and general quality. There are also notes on how the different varieties have done in some test orchards in Ontario and Quebec.

Moinet, F. (2009), *Le Cidre—Produire et vendre*. Paris: Éditions France Agricole, 253 pages.

This is a modern French book on the production and marketing of cider.

Morgan, Joan, and Alison Richards (2002), *The New Book of Apples*. London: Ebury Press, 320 pages.

First published in 1993 as *The Book of Apples*, this is a huge reference with short descriptions of over two thousand varieties of apples grown at the Brogdale conservation orchard in England. It includes a well-documented history of the apple and cider, plus a large section on cider apples. A highly recommended book.

Neal, Charles (2011), *Calvados, the Spirit of Normandy*. San Francisco: Flame Grape Press, 768 pages.

Although mostly about Calvados, cider is everywhere in this book. After a first part that describes the preparation of traditional French cider and Calvados, this book introduces us to over two hundred producers of cider and Calvados in Normandy. If you plan to travel to northern France, make sure you bring this book with you! One of the few books written in English about French cider.

Pereda Rodriguez, Miguel Angel (2011), *Elaboracion de sidra natural ecologica*. Madrid: Ediciones Mundi-Prensa, 191 pages.

This book, well grounded in sound science, is on the making of natural Spanish cider without any chemical additions such as sulfite and without a cultured yeast inoculation.

Phillips, Michael (2006), *The Apple Grower*, 2nd edition. White River Junction, Vt.: Chelsea Green, 320 pages.

This is a solid reference on organic orcharding. I met Michael Phillips at a NAFEX meeting in 2003, and we have become good friends. He is always in search of better ways to grow apple trees, minimizing the use of pesticides. His more recent book, *The Holistic Orchard* (2012), which covers other species of fruit trees as well, is also great reading and inspiring. Michael maintains a web site and a discussion forum on organic orcharding (http://groworganicapples.com).

Power, G. (1890–91), *Traité de la culture du pommier et de la fabrication du cidre*. Paris: Lecène, Oudin et Cie, part 1, 1890, on cider-apple tree growing, 166 pages; part 2, 1891, on cider making, 250 pages (digital document: Google).

This is one of the important works from the early French cider scientists.

Proulx, A., and L. Nichols (2003), *Cider: Making, Using & Enjoying Sweet & Hard Cider*, 3rd edition. North Adams, Mass.: Storey Publishing, 224 pages.

When I bought my first cider press in 1989, I also got the original edition of this book, *Sweet and Hard Cider,* published in 1980. It has been my companion book during my learning years in cider making. It is now a bit outdated but is nevertheless a good guide for basic cider-making practices and still sells more than thirty years after its first publication. It certainly holds the record for longevity among cider-making books.

Ribereau-Gayon, Pascal, et al. (2006), *Handbook of Enology*: New York: John Wiley and Sons.

A serious classical reference in enology such as the one above is a complement to a good collection of cider books. And although enology is primarily for wine, there is a large part of this science that also applies to cider: sulfite action, tests for alcohol or acidity, the biochemistry of fermentation, and many other topics. Note there are many other books that could serve this purpose of having a good reference on this topic. You could choose one by M. A. Amerine, for example.

Simmonds, C. (1919), *Alcohol, Its Production, Properties, Chemistry, and Industrial Applications.* London: Macmillan (http://chestofbooks.com/food /beverages/Alcohol-Properties/index.html).

Although this book can't be downloaded, it may be consulted at the above URL. It is a fairly old reference, but the principles exposed are still valid.

Smock, R. M., and A. M. Neubert (1950), *Apples and Apple Products.* New York: Interscience Publishers, 486 pages.

Despite its age, this book remains a solid, relevant reference for everything related to the transformation of the apple and includes a section on cider.

Thacher, James (1822), *The American Orchardist; or, A practical treatise on the culture and management of apple and other fruit trees, with observations on the diseases to which they are liable, and their remedies. To which is added the most approved method of manufacturing and preserving cider. Compiled from the latest and most approved authorities, and adapted to the use of American farmers.* Boston: J. W. Ingraham (digital document: Internet Archive).

The title says it all! Thacher's is a very interesting book from America's early days.

Trowbridge, J. M. (1917), *The Cider Makers' Hand Book—A Complete Guide for Making and Keeping Pure Cider.* Kindle edition, 2012, 120 pages.

First published in 1890, this is the "old" cider maker's handbook, promoting the preparation of high-quality cider, and it is still surprisingly modern in many aspects. I was astounded in particular to find in Trowbridge's book a method for blending after measuring the density and acidity of the juices, which is almost identical with what I present here. This was quite progressive for the time.

Truelle, A. (1896), *Atlas des meilleures variétés de fruits à cidre,* Paris: Octave Doin, 88 pages (digital document: Gallica).

Auguste Truelle was a proeminent French scientist and a prolific writer on cider beween the mid-1870s and until the end of the 1920s. In this book, he describes forty apple varieties considered as the best for cider making. He includes chemical analysis results and good quality color plates of each.

Warcollier, G. (1926 and 1928), *Le Pommier à cidre* and *La Cidrerie.* Paris: J. B. Baillière et fils, 436 pages and 484 pages; adapted and translated by Vernon L. S. Charley as *The Principles and Practice of Cider-Making* (1949), London: Leonard Hill.

In these two books Georges Warcollier sums up the important work done by the early French cider scientists. He was an ardent promoter of modernism and good hygiene in the preparation of the cider and was among the first to describe the keeving process as a distinct operation before the start of fermentation. This is a very important book of that period but is unfortunately not easy to find, either in the original French edition or in English translation.

Watson, Ben (2009), *Cider, Hard and Sweet*, 2nd edition. Woodstock, Vt.: Countryman Press, 183 pages.

In addition to being editor for this book, Ben Watson is an author, and he is currently working on a third edition of his *Cider, Hard and Sweet*. In this book he introduces the reader to the pleasures of cider and gives good guidance on the preparation of our favorite drink. Watson is an ardent promoter of cider and a member of the organizing committee of the Cider Days annual festival. Additionally, he is involved in the Slow Food movement and is very interested in the pairing of cider with different foods.

Williams, R. R., ed. (1988), *Cider and Juice Apples: Growing and Processing*. Bristol, UK: University of Bristol, 123 pages.

Here is an important little book that sums up some of the research that has been done at the Long Ashton Research Center (LARS) in Bristol, England, which is now unfortunately closed. This center was long one of the most important worldwide for research and development of knowledge on cider.

Worlidge, John (1676), *Vinetum Britannicum: or a Treatise of Cider*. London.

Unfortunately, I have never been able to find a copy or a digital version of this ancient book. Some of its illustrations are well known, however, as they are among the most often reproduced of all ancient cider-related plates.

INDEX

</body>

ABOUT THE
AUTHOR

Kamilla Jolicoeur

A mechanical engineer by profession, Claude Joli-coeur first developed his passion for apples and cider after acquiring a piece of land on which there were four rows of old abandoned apple trees. He started making cider in 1988 using a "no-compromise" approach, stubbornly searching for the highest possible quality. Since then, his ciders have earned many awards and medals at competitions, including Best of Show at the prestigious Great Lakes Cider and Perry Competition (GLINTCAP).

Claude actively participates in discussions on forums like the Cider Digest, and is regularly invited as a guest speaker to festivals and events such as Cider Days in Massachusetts and the Common Ground Country Fair in Maine. He lives in Quebec City.

the politics and practice of sustainable living

CHELSEA GREEN PUBLISHING

Chelsea Green Publishing sees books as tools for effecting cultural change and seeks to empower citizens to participate in reclaiming our global commons and become its impassioned stewards. If you enjoyed *The New Cider Maker's Handbook*, please consider these other great books related to food and agriculture.

THE HOLISTIC ORCHARD
Tree Fruits and Berries the Biological Way
MICHAEL PHILLIPS
9781933392134
Paperback • $39.95

THE APPLE GROWER, Revised and Expanded Edition
A Guide for the Organic Orchardist
MICHAEL PHILLIPS
9781931498913
Paperback • $40.00

OLD SOUTHERN APPLES, Revised and Expanded Edition
A Comprehensive History and Description of Varieties for Collectors, Growers, and Fruit Enthusiasts
CREIGHTON LEE CALHOUN, JR.
9781603582940
Hardcover • $75.00

THE SUGARMAKER'S COMPANION
An Integrated Approach to Producing Syrup from Maple, Birch, and Walnut Trees
MICHAEL FARRELL
9781603583978
Paperback • $39.95

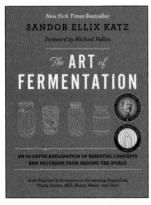

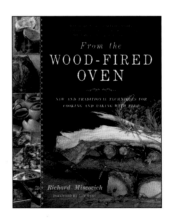